T0305149

Crisis and Continuity

University of Pennsylvania Press
MIDDLE AGES SERIES
Edited by
Edward Peters
Henry Charles Lea Professor
of Medieval History
University of Pennsylvania

A listing of the available books
in the series appears at the
back of this volume

Crisis and Continuity

Land and Town in Late Medieval Castile

Teofilo F. Ruiz

University of Pennsylvania Press

Philadelphia

Publication of this volume was assisted by a subvention from the Program for Cultural Cooperation Between Spain's Ministry of Culture and United States Universities.

Library of Congress Cataloging-in-Publication Data
Ruiz, Teofilo F., 1943–
    Crisis and continuity: land and town in late medieval Castile / Teofilo F. Ruiz.
        p.   cm.—(Middle Ages series)
    Includes bibliographical references and index.
    ISBN 0-8122-3228-3
    1. Agriculture—Economic aspects—Spain—Castile—History.   2. Cities and towns,
Medieval—Spain—Castile.   3. Castile (Spain)—Economic conditions.   4. Castile
(Spain)—Social conditions.   I. Title.   II. Series.
HD2025.C325R85   1993
330.946'3—dc20   93–35573
                                                                        CIP

To Scarlett

En estos campos de la tierra mía,
y extranjero en los campos de mi tierra
—yo tuve patria donde corre el Duero
por entre grises peñas,
y fantasmas de viejos encinares,
allá en Castilla, mística y guerrera,
Castilla la gentil, humilde y brava,
Castilla del desdén y de la fuerza—

Antonio Machado, *Campos de Castilla*

Contents

Abbreviations

ACB	Archivo de la catedral de Burgos
AHDE	*Anuario de historia del derecho español*
AHN	Archivo histórico nacional
Albelda y Logroño	*Colección diplomática de las colegiatas de Albelda y Logroño* (Tomo I: 924–1399), Eliseo Saínz Ripa, ed. (Logroño: Instituto de estudios riojanos, 1981).
Alfonso XI	*Colección documental de Alfonso XI*, Esther González Crespo, ed. (Madrid: Universidad Complutense, 1985).
AMB	Archivo municipal de Burgos
AMS	Archivo municipal de Segovia
Becerro	*Libro Becerro de las Behetrías. Estudio y texto crítico*, Gonzalo Martínez Díez, ed. 3 vols. (León: Centro de estudios e investigaciones "San Isidoro," 1981).
CHE	*Cuadernos de historia de España*
C.C.R.	*Calendars of the Close, Patent, and Fine Rolls*
C.P.R.	(London: Public Record Office, 1901–).
C.F.R.	
Los códigos españoles	*Los códigos españoles concordados y anotados*, 12 vols. (Madrid: Imprenta de la Publicidad, 1847–51).
Colección diplomática calceatense	*Colección diplomática calceatense: Archivo catedral, 1125–1397*, C. López de Silanos and E. Saínz Ripa, eds. (Logroño: Instituto de estudios riojanos, 1985).
Cortes	*Cortes de los antiguos reinos de León y Castilla*, 5 vols. Vols. 1 and 2 (Madrid: Imprenta y Estereotipia de M. Rivadeneyra, 1861–63).

Crónica de Alfonso X   *Crónicas de los reyes de Castilla*, I (Madrid:
Crónica de Sancho IV   Biblioteca de autores españoles, vol. 66,
Crónica de Fernando IV   1953).
Crónica de Alfonso XI

Cuéllar   *Colección diplomática de Cuéllar*, Antonio
Ubieta Arteta, ed. (Segovia: Diputación
Provincial de Segovia, 1961).

Cuentas   Mercedes Gaibrois de Ballesteros, *Historia
del reinado de Sancho IV de Castilla*, 3 vols.
(Madrid: Tipografía de la Revista de archivos, bibliotecas y museos, 1922–28).

Curso de historia   Luis García de Valdeavellano, *Curso de historia de las instituciones españolas. De los orígenes
al final de la edad media* (Madrid: Revista de
Occidente, 1968).

Desde Estella a Sevilla   *Desde Estella a Sevilla. Cuentas de un viaje
(1352)*, María D. Sánchez Villar, ed. (Valen-
cia: Instituto de estudios medievales, 1974).

DMA   *Documentación medieval de la catedral de
Ávila*, Angel Barrios García, ed. (Salamanca:
Universidad de Salamanca, 1981).

Fernando IV   Antonio Benavides, *Memorias de Fernando
IV de Castilla*, 2 vols. (Madrid: Imprenta de
J. Rodríguez, 1960).

FMCL   *Fuentes medievales castellano-leonesas*, J. José
García, F. Javier Peña, et al., eds. Twenty volumes published of a projected one hundred
and three (Burgos, Palencia: Ediciones J. M.
Garrido Garrido, 1983–   ).

Fuentes   *Fuentes para la historia de Castilla*, Luciano
Serrano, ed. 3 vols. (Valladolid: G. del Amo,
1906–10).

IGR, *Texto*   Ismael García Rámila, *Texto cronológico de las
tres "Reglas," por las que sucesivamente, rigió su
vida corporativa esta Real Hermandad fundada
por el ry Alfonso XI en la era de 1376 (año de
Cristo de 1338)* (Burgos: Imprenta Provincial,
1970).

Las Huelgas	Antonio Rodríguez López, *El real monasterio de Las Huelgas y el Hospital del Rey*, 2 vols. (Burgos: Imprenta y Librería del Centro Católico, 1907).
Liébana	*Cartulario de Santo Toribio de Liébana*, Luis Sánchez Belda, ed. (Madrid: Archivo histórico nacional, 1948).
MHE	*Memorial histórico español*, 49 vols. (Madrid: Real Academia de la Historia, 1851–1948).
Oña	*Colección diplomática de San Salvador de Oña*, Juan del Alamo, ed. 2 vols. (Madrid: Consejo Superior de Investigaciones Científicas., 1950–51).
Osma	Juan Loperráez Corvalán, *Descripción histórica del obispado de Osma*, 3 vols. Vol. 3, Colección diplomática (Madrid: Imprenta Real, 1788).
Poema de Alfonso XI	*Poetas castellanos anteriores al siglo XV* (Madrid: Biblioteca de autores españoles, vol. 57, 1966).
"Primitiva regla"	Julián García y Sáinz de Baranda, "Primitiva regla escrita de la Cofradía de Nuestra Señora de Gamonal," *Boletín de la Comisión de monumentos artísticos de la Provincia de Burgos*, 65 (1938), 158–64.
Propiedades del cabildo segoviano	Ángel García Sanz et al., *Propiedades del cabildo segoviano: Sistemas de cultivo y modos de explotación de la tierra a fines del siglo XIII* (Salamanca: Universidad de Salamanca, 1981).
Repartimiento de Jerez	*El libro del repartimiento de Jerez de la Frontera: Estudio y edición*. Manuel González Jiménez y Antonio González Gómez, eds. (Cádiz: Instituto de Estudios Gaditanos, 1980).
Salamanca	*Documentos de los archivos catedralicio y diocesano de Salamanca, siglos XII–XIII*, José L. Martín et al., eds. (Salamanca: Universidad de Salamanca, 1977).

Sancho IV	Gaibrois de Ballesteros, *Historia del reinado de Sancho IV de Castilla* (documentary appendix).
Sepúlveda	*Colección diplomática de Sepúlveda (1076–1454)*, Emilio Sáez, ed. (Segovia: Diputación Provincial de Segovia, 1956).
Siguenza	Toribio Minguella, *Historia de la diócesis de Siguenza y de sus obispos*, 3 vols. (Madrid: Imprenta de la Revista de archivos, bibliótecas y museos, 1910–13).
Silos	*Recueil des chartes de l'abbaye de Silos*, Marius Férotin, ed. (Paris: Imprimerie nationale, 1897).
Viajes de extranjeros	*Viajes de extranjeros por España y Portugal*, José García Mercadal, ed. 3 vols. (Madrid: Aguilar, 1952).
Vida económica	J. José García González, *Vida económica de los monasterios benedictinos en el siglo XIV* (Valladolid: Universidad de Valladolid, 1972).

A Note on Spelling

The spelling of names and places varies from document to document, at times even in those written by the same scribe. For example, the name *Juan* in modern Spanish is rendered in medieval Castilian as *John, Johan, Johanus*, and other variants but seldom as *Juan*. Whenever possible, names have been spelled in their most frequent and accessible usage.

Preface and Acknowledgments

My father's parents left their small village in Gallejones de Zamanzas in the mountains north of Burgos and settled in Cuba at the onset of the twentieth century. Through the years my family traveled back and forth between Castile and Cuba, keeping strong links to their ancestral home. Many of my relatives (on my father's side) still live in Gallejones and in other villages in the valley of Zamanzas, their lives deeply rooted in settlements dating to the very early phases of the Reconquest, a millenium ago. It is a green and beautiful valley, watered by the Ebro River, encircled by rugged mountains and forbidden wastelands.

Having been born and raised in Cuba, and having spent most of my adult life in the United States, I am at home in many places, yet fully at home nowhere. But one of my homes is in that isolated village in the heart of Old Castile (*Castilla la Vieja*). To its history, that of the village and the region, I bring, I hope, a great deal of skepticism and a critical attitude toward the frequent historical idealization of the Reconquest, the Castilian past, and its legacy. The angel of history, as Walter Benjamin wrote, "his face turned towards the past . . . sees one single catastrophe which keeps piling wreckage upon wreckage . . . in front of his feet." But my critical and somewhat pessimistic perception of the wreckages of the past does not diminish my passion, pride, and love for my family, Gallejones, and Castile, nor the joy of telling stories about a place that is also home.

*　*　*

The telling of this story, the completion of this book, has been far too long in the making. I began to research this project in earnest during the academic year 1979–80 when, thanks to an ACLS Fellowship, I was able to undertake extensive research at the Archivo histórico nacional, the Biblioteca nacional, and municipal and ecclesiastical archives in northern Castile. Thanks to the generous support of the Research Foundation of the City University of New York, I was able to return in successive summers to continue my archival research and to follow the itineraries of medieval and early modern travelers along the roads and byways of Old Castile. An NEH Fellowship, together with an appointment to the sylvan and intellectually fertile setting of the Institute for Advanced Study in 1983–84, allowed for the completion of a rough and much longer first draft of this book.

After 1984, however, my own research interests shifted to other areas: the nature of Castilian kingship, the role of festivals in Castilian society. The book was put aside and sorely neglected. A sabbatical year in 1990, half of it spent most rewardingly as a visiting professor at the University of Michigan, together with major changes in my personal life, provided me with the impetus to revise the manuscript and to submit it to the consideration of readers. The publication of this book has been most generously subsidized by a grant from the Program for Cultural Cooperation Between Spain's Ministry of Culture and United States Universities. I am most grateful for their support.

Throughout this long journey, I have had the support of family and friends, above all, from my sons, Daniel and David. For a long time they have been more than good sons; they have been very good and close friends as well. In Spain, New York, Paris, at Princeton and Ann Arbor, I have benefited from the kindness and generous help of the staff of archives, libraries, and universities. At Brooklyn College, where I have taught for twenty years, my colleagues and students have made my life as a teacher a particularly rewarding one. I have learned a great deal and derived much satisfaction from my students, especially from Toba Friedman, our first Marshall scholar at Brooklyn College, student, friend, and most welcomed surrogate daughter. Carol Green, formerly a secretary in the history department, most generously typed large segments of the initial manuscript. Eliza McClennen prepared with great care and patience—considering my many revisions—the maps included in the book. At the University of Pennsylvania Press, Jerry Singerman, Mindy Brown, and Jennifer Shenk offered me a great deal of support and encouragement. The editors saved me from untold inconsistencies and embarrassments, and I am most grateful for their courtesy and careful treatment of my work.

The book, however, never would have been completed without John H. Elliott's encouragement and prodding. My natural inclination has always been to publish my work as articles. John H. Elliott's insistence that I write it as a book, and my own wish to acknowledge, however modestly, my immense personal and scholarly debt to him, were central to the completion of this project. All of us who study the history of Spain here and abroad know well of his kindness and generosity. John Elliott is not only a gifted and inspiring historian, but both he and Mrs. Elliott are kind and generous people indeed. Thanks John and Oonah.

For suggestions, bibliographical leads, sharp and honest criticisms, I am most indebted to Charles M. Radding, who read the manuscript several times—a deed beyond the call of friendship and duty—and helped me, more than I can express, to sharpen and define my arguments. Paul Freedman's insightful comments, careful reading, suggestions, and, most of all, friendship have been most important for my work and personal life for the last decade. I must also thank an anonymous reader for the care and honesty with which she/he read and commented on the manuscript. I hope my revisions show that I did take her/his comments very seriously indeed. Peter Linehan (to whom I owe a great debt in this and many other projects), Adeline Rucquoi, Elizabeth A. R. Brown, Hilario Casado Alonso, Remie Constable, Francisco Hernández, Ruth Behar, David Frye, and Xavier Gil Pujol have all made important contributions to this manuscript. Finally, my late and much missed teacher, Joseph R. Strayer, read and commented most generously on earlier versions of the first two chapters.

Throughout the last two decades, I have incurred a debt of gratitude to many other scholars and friends. Their work and friendship have contributed a great deal to the formulation of my ideas in this book and elsewhere, to my growth as a scholar, and to my sanity. I would like to thank Joseph F. O'Callaghan, William and Carla Phillips (who have done so much for Spanish history in this country), Angus MacKay, Denis Menjot, Inga Clendinnen, James V. Hatch, James F. Powers, Thomas Glick, Heath Dillard, Julio Valdeón Baruque, Manuel González Jiménez, the late Luis García de Valdeavellano, Miguel Angel Ladero Quesada, J. A. García de Cortázar, Jordi Nadal, Felipe Ruiz Martín, Jean Pierre Molenat, María Asenjo, and Miguel Santamaría Lancho. Jacques Le Goff's generous friendship and inspiring insights, Jacques Revel's long and sustaining friendship, Jean Claude Schmitt, and Bernard Vincent have always made my stays at the École des Hautes Études enjoyable and valuable learning experiences.

At Princeton, my long-time friend William C. Jordan, Lawrence Stone (through his combative erudition and the unparalleled experience of the Davis Center), Judith Herrin, Carl Schorske, Giles Constable, Natalie Z. Davis, Peter Brown, David Nirenberg, and many others have given me a nurturing intellectual community for the last twenty years.

Finally, if without John H. Elliott I would not have completed this book, without Scarlett Freund I would not have had the joy of doing it.

Friend, companion, colleague, sister soul, she has commented, revised, and fiercely contested many aspects of this book and recent articles. Beyond "the middle of the road of my life," I found in her and with her a "new life," a true home. To Scarlett, then, I dedicate this book, a very small token indeed of feelings that are ineffable.

Teofilo F. Ruiz

Princeton and New York

Part I

The Land and Climate of Northern Castile

Map 1. The region of Old Castile in the Late Middle Ages.

Today the high peaks of the Cantabrian mountain range separate the autonomous regions of Cantabria and the Basque country from Old Castile proper, although until recently the area north of the mountains formed part of a single political and economic whole. The common history of both Castile and the areas north of the Cantabrian range dates back to the twelfth century, when the ports on the Bay of Biscay connected Castile to the sea by a network of already well-traversed roads. These ancient paths of migration, laid out to circumvent the high peaks of the Cantabrian Mountains, carried Basques and Cantabrians from their steep habitats to their settlement in Castile in the eighth and ninth centuries. Many years later merchants portaged the wool northward to the sea and beyond to the textile centers of Flanders along the same routes.

The medieval byways, built to be traveled by humans and animals rather than by machines, cut through areas in which the transitions between mountain and plain, between green forests, meadows and the rust-colored starkness of the meseta, between wet and dry climates occurred gradually. The contrasts offered by the more recent links between north and south are swifter and more dramatic. Built in the twentieth century over ancient footpaths and dirt roads, National Road 623 reflects the rigid rationality of the modern mind and its deep-rooted assurance in the supremacy over nature of science and technology, which posits the straight line as the shortest distance between two points. But anyone who drives the mere 152 kilometers from Santander to Burgos learns, after vexing hours on this tortuous and narrow motorway (which is, at present, being rebuilt and improved), that in this case the topography of northern Castile got the better of technology. One departs Santander across green hills and lush grazing meadows, a rich dairy region blessed by abundant rain and mild temperatures all year around. Southward the Cantabrian Mountains stand as a barrier, breached in this particular road only by one mountain pass: El Escudo ("the Shield," height 1,054 meters). As automobiles and trucks crawl up the steep and winding road, Cantabria provides a green and beautiful backdrop. Once the pass of El Escudo is reached, clouds, humidity, and green are left behind. Against the deep blue sky of Old Castile, a bare and desolate plain faces the traveler.

I have often crossed this mountain pass, and yet every time I do so I am still taken aback by the swift change and contrast between these two distinct landscapes, between these two different ecological systems.[1] And it is not just on this particular road that such rapid transitions are to be found. Farther west, as one travels from Oviedo to León on the mountain pass of Pajares, in a matter of minutes the traveler moves from the rainy and luxurious valleys of Asturias to the dry and desert-like plain leading to the city of León. Upon their first visit to Spain, many late medieval and early modern voyagers did not fail to register their reactions to these *páramos* (wildernesses) lying along the boundaries between mountain and plain. "A horrible mountain ridge, where one could not see any signs of humanity, any water, only naked and cold rocks without grass or trees," wrote Tetzel, one of the companions of Leon of Rosmithal, during their visit to Spain and Portugal in 1465. As he descended from rainy Cantabria into Castile almost half a century later, Lorenzo Vital, a member of Charles V's entourage, described it as a barren and dry land, where trees could not grow. In 1525 Gaspar Contarini drew a comparison between northern and southern Spain. "All the lands of Spain," he wrote, "are very arid with the exception of Andalucía which is known for its fertility."[2] More fitting and personal perhaps was the spontaneous reaction I witnessed of an old and poor Galician peasant. We shared a compartment in a train going from Santiago de Compostela to Madrid in what was his first trip out of Galicia. In the morning, as the train sped on to Madrid, he looked out of the window, and seeing for the first time the empty and endless plain, he muttered in Galician, "no people, no corn, nothing to eat."

Many staples grew in Castile in the Middle Ages, as they do today, and not everyone sees its vistas as stark and forbidding. For the poets and essayist of the Generation of 1898, and later on for Antonio Machado and his followers, the melancholy fields of Castile offered a beauty and meaning not to be found elsewhere in the peninsula.[3] In antiquity, in the Middle Ages, and into the early modern period, Romans, Visigoths, Christians, Muslims, and Jews praised the richness of Spain, its horses, its wines, its minerals, its men and women. They spoke, of course, not of Old Castile in particular, but of al-Andalus, of Sefarad, of the creation in Iberia of an earthly paradise, of the planting and tending of gardens of pleasure and beauty along the shores of the Mediterranean.[4] But Castile, Old Castile, also received the encomiastic platitudes of its native sons. In the thirteenth century *Poema de Fernán González*, its anonymous author, a monk of San Pedro of Arlanza near Burgos, described Castile as the best part of Spain.

Above all the mountain, the original birthplace of Castile, was a land without comparison, rich in grazing fields, flax, and wool, with plenty of game, fish, wax, gold, and wine. Its knights were the best in the world, and the land had raised more martyrs, saints, and virgins than any other realm.[5]

There were precedents for this exalted view in Isidore of Seville's (c. 560–636) praise of Spain, a panegyric reaffirmed and repeated almost verbatim in the thirteenth century *Primera crónica general o Estoria de España*. Like the chroniclers of France, England, and other medieval kingdoms, those in Castile advanced a vision of homeland as Holy Land, a country of milk and honey, of unparalleled richness and virtue. Little wonder, therefore, that the author of the *Primera crónica general* insisted that the Goths roamed throughout Asia and most of Europe in search of a home and finally chose Spain "for they found it to be the best land."[6] Their praise, moreover, was not just the biased and sentimental judgment of natives. The pilgrimage guide attributed to Aymeric Picaud described the land around Burgos as "full of richness, with gold and silver . . . cloth and strong mares, fertile in bread, wine, meat, fish, milk and honey, though"—and here is the caveat—"empty of trees [and] filled with evil and vicious men." For Andrea Navagero, the Venetian ambassador and a sharp observer of Spanish life, the valley around Aranda de Duero "was fertile and well cultivated."[7]

Where does the truth lie? Picaud, or whoever composed the guide, prompted by his wish to promote the pilgrimage to Compostela, described a land which was certainly most unreal. Nowhere in the region of Burgos in the twelfth century was there gold or silver to be found, unless it was in the garments of a few proud magnates and prelates. The gold and silver of Castile was often mined in Africa, brought to al-Andalus by trade, and extorted or taken by force of arms from the Muslims by Christian warriors. As to cloth, Castile produced mostly coarse fabrics. Luxury woolens and silks came from Flanders or Moorish lands, again to adorn only the very few at the top.[8] Bread, wine, meat, fish, milk, and honey were gained by endless toil from a land not always willing to yield its fruits, and from meager rivers. Strong mares, yes, these abounded but were jealously kept, seldom sold abroad and then only at very high prices.

Old Castile was not as poor and desolate, at least not all of it, as some descriptions by foreign travelers may lead us to believe, nor was it as rich as its apologists were wont to affirm or may have wished it to have been. Nor was Old Castile a uniform plain with one topography, one climate, one ecological system. In the Middle Ages green Cantabria and the Basque region, with a topography and climate quite distinct from that of the northern meseta, were an integral part of the Castilian commercial network centered in Burgos, and were under the lordship of the kings of Castile and León. Both the Cantabrian and Basque coastland served as the shores of the *mar de Castilla* (sea of Castile) and from them, the Castilians looked outward to the north, to markets for their agricultural goods, to suppliers for their insatiable demand for luxury cloth.

There are diverse ways of looking at Old Castile and its history: One can see it as a region defined by geography, climate, and natural resources, or as a region shaped by historical events, bound by commercial interests and political goals. The second of these two perceptions of Castilian reality, the one I favor, requires a recognition, however, of Old Castile's geographical and climatic diversity, and of the way in which Castilians adapted, or sometimes failed to adapt, to these diverse environments. That they did adapt and, to a large extent, still do, was nothing short of remarkable. The land yielded and still yields its fruits reluctantly. It demands a great deal of work which all too often comes to little. The climate of most of the region can best be described as hostile. And although geography and climate are not the sole determinants of the destiny of a people, one must not ignore the burdens that poor soil, inclement weather, and abrupt terrain imposed on the Castilians.[9] What they accomplished—from the humblest farmer harvesting a meager crop of barley, wheat, and rye in a remote corner of the land to the proud Spanish captains building empires in every corner of the world in the sixteenth century—was often gained in spite of the obstacles of nature.

This life of endless struggle against unfavorable natural conditions and the ceaseless battles on the frontier with Islam shaped Castilian and Spanish society for centuries afterward. Castile's institutions, its social, economic, and political structures, were imposed on Andalucía after the collapse of Moorish power in the mid-thirteenth century; they were also carried to the New World by Castilian conquistadors at the onset of the early modern period. The Atlantic enterprise, Columbus's momentous voyage, the hegemony of imperial Spain cannot be fully understood—nor, for that matter, can we explain the weakness and eventual demise of imperial dreams— without the Castilian background.

*   *   *

My purpose in this book, however, is not to tell the deeds of great men and women or the evolution of political and ecclesiastical institutions.

Neither is it to provide an idealized portrait of warring, reconquering Castilians. Rather, it is to show that the Reconquest also had a pernicious impact on Castilian society. Politics and Reconquest are important subjects indeed and worthy of detailed study. Yet, since these themes—the indispensable context for the issues I wish to discuss in the following chapters—have already benefited from the labor of distinguished historians, there is no need to discuss them here. Instead, my aims in the pages below are twofold: First, I wish to examine the structures of rural and urban life in medieval northern Castile, that is, how peasants, artisans, and merchants did their work, lived from day to day, succeeded and failed in the small but meaningful struggles of everyday life. Although in recent years scholars of late medieval Castile have published a plethora of excellent local studies, no one, to my knowledge, has attempted to study the region as a whole.

This unveiling of the structures of northern Castilian society and economy must also include an analysis of the uneasy and, at times, antagonistic ties between the different social groups in urban and rural Castile, that is, between those above and those below, between lords and peasants, between patrician elites and the urban poor. I hope, therefore, to provide a view of the social and economic foundations of Castile as background to its hegemony within the peninsula in the late Middle Ages and to Spain's ascendancy in the early modern period.

Second, I wish to chart the impact of the late medieval crisis on the social and economic structures of northern Castile. What was the nature of the economic, political, and social upheavals plaguing Castile from the mid-thirteenth century on? How are we to explain that, notwithstanding adverse geographical and climatic conditions and endemic political chaos, Castile rose to a hegemonic position within Spain and, by the early modern period, within Europe? In many respects, what I wish to do is to restate and explain in greater detail my interpretation of Castilian and Spanish history, already advanced in my article "Expansion et changement" (*Annales E.S.C.* [1979]). At the same time, I wish to argue against the Malthusian explanation often given in the past as the main reason for the crisis of the late Middle Ages. As I will show, there was no demographic pressure on most of the Castilian countryside. Yet the Castilian realm did not profit from this absence of population pressure before the Black Death; it suffered, rather, from depression and disorganization much earlier than the rest of Europe.

In the past, I have emphasized the swift course of economic, social, and political change. Having reflected over the last ten years and examined the documentation with greater care, I wish to modify my views on the nature of the crisis. Radical changes in late medieval society were more than balanced by the continuity of social and economic structures and by the ability of the mighty and the weak to adapt to existing conditions.

Before attempting to study these issues, we must briefly examine two distinct but interconnected topics. In Part I, I provide a summary of the geographical characteristics and climate of the region, showing the extent to which the topography of the plain and of peripheral regions provided a sense of geographical unity to Old Castile.

Part II explores, in four interrelated chapters, the nature of rural life. The first chapter of Part II outlines the evolution of northern Castilian rural life into the late Middle Ages, seeking to provide a typology of peasant obligations and conditions. The next chapter seeks to answer questions pertaining to how the peasants lived and how they worked the land. What did they plant, and how? How successful were their efforts? The next chapter in this section focuses on the domain of the monastery of Santa María la Real de Aguilar de Campóo; based upon its rich and unusual (for Castile) documentation, I have sought to provide a case study of the social and economic structures, and of their change over time, in a specific region in northern Castile. Part II closes with an overview of the market for land in northern Castile, as well as a study of the patterns of land leasing in the region.

An examination of the market for land serves as a transition to the next section of the book (Part III), an exploration of northern Castilian urban society. In four chapters, I review the institutional and political organization of urban life, the nature of the international and regional trade which linked the different urban centers of Old Castile, and the characteristics of the different social groups inhabiting Castilian cities.

The final section attempts to explain the transformations that Castile underwent in the thirteenth and fourteenth centuries, why they took place, and, finally, what the impact of these changes was on the society at large. The locus of this study is the historical area of Old Castile, a region corresponding roughly to the northern plain but including also the coastal lands of Cantabria and the Basque homeland, as well as the transitional area of the Central Sierras north of Madrid. The chronological boundaries are the end of the twelfth century, when Castile was already poised for its dramatic march into Andalucía, and the mid-fourteenth century, when the Black Death and the civil war between Peter I and the Trastámaras signaled the closing of an age in Castilian society. In this century and a half, new ways of organizing geographical space, of structuring the political, economic, and social life of the realm, came into existence. They shaped the life of Castile and of Spain for centuries to come; they were the very foundations for the enterprises of the Age of Discovery and for the flowering of Spanish culture and political hegemony during the Golden Age.

Notes

1. See Thomas F. Glick, *Islamic and Christian Spain in the Early Middle Ages: Comparative Perspectives on Social and Cultural Formation* (Princeton, N.J.: Princeton University Press, 1979), 51–65; also see my review of Glick's book in *Technology and Culture* (July 1980): 479–81.

2. *Viajes de extranjeros*, 1: 295, 695, 898, et passim. Here and in the next chapter I make liberal use of early modern accounts of travel in Spain. Although chronologically their descriptions come later than the period discussed in this book, their impressions of the topography, methods of cultivation, and climate of Castile can be used with profit for the thirteenth and fourteenth centuries. Ecological and technological change was not that dramatic in the intervening years.

3. See, for example, Azorín's *Castilla*, 7th ed. (Buenos Aires: Espasa-Calpe, 1969); José Ortega y Gasset, *España invertebrada*, 12th ed. (Madrid: Espasa Calpe, 1962), 55–59; Antonio Machado, *Campos de Castilla* (Salamanca: Biblioteca Anaya, 1967). For the attitude of the so-called Generation of '98, see Luis S. Granjel, *La generación literaria del noventa y ocho* (Salamanca: Anaya, 1971), 189–219; Pedro Laín Entralgo, *La generación del noventa y ocho* (Madrid: Diana, 1945).

4. José Antonio Maravall, *El concepto de España en la edad media*, 2d ed. (Madrid: Instituto de estudios políticos, 1964), 17–28; Glick, 53–58 and below: citing al-Razi, Glick quotes Muslim authors who described Spain as resembling "God's paradise."

5. *Poema de Fernán González*, ed. C. Carroll Marden (Baltimore: The Johns Hopkins Press, 1904), 21–23, 156–57: "Pero de toda Spanna Casty[e]lla es mejor / Por qué fue de los otrros [el] comienço mayor / Guardando e temiendo syenpre a su sen[n]or / Quiso acrecentar[la] assy el Cryador."

6. Such exalted views were common elsewhere in the Middle Ages. See Joseph R. Strayer, "The Holy Land, the Chosen people, and the Most Christian King," in *Medieval Statecraft and the Perspectives of History: Essays by Joseph R. Strayer*, ed. John F. Benton and Thomas N. Bisson (Princeton, N.J.: Princeton University Press, 1971), 300–314; Ernst H. Kantorowicz, *The King's Two Bodies: A Study in Medieval Political Theology* (Princeton, N.J.: Princeton University Press, 1981), 249–58 et passim; for Castile, *Primera crónica general*, ed. Ramón Menéndez Pidal (Madrid: Nueva Biblioteca de Autores Españoles, V, 1906), 310–12. See note 3.

7. *Viajes de extranjeros*, 1: 172, 702, 843, et passim.

8. On the movement of gold and other precious metals paid as tribute (*parias*) or obtained as booty from al-Andalus see Angus MacKay, *Spain in the Middle Ages:*

From Frontier to Empire 1000–1500 (London: Macmillan Ltd., 1977), 15–19. For the import of textiles see below, Part III, Chapter 7.

9. See, for example, María de Bolos y Capdevila, Antonio Paluzie, and Angela Guerrero, *Geografía de España* (Barcelona: de Gasso Hermanos, editores, 1969), 70; Ruth Way, *A Geography of Spain and Portugal* (London: Methuen, 1962), 55 et passim.

1. The Limitations of Geography and Climate

"El mal de España," wrote Joaquín Costa, "es el mal de piedra." (The evil of Spain is the evil of stone.) For Costa, a nineteenth-century reformer and a man deeply committed to the revitalization of Spanish rural life, the administrative failures and structural deficiencies plaguing Spanish agriculture were an additional burden to that created by the stones and rocks strewn on the fields of Old Castile and León.[1] Or, as Machado put it with characteristic poetic insight:

> El Duero cruza el corazón de roble
> de Iberia y de Castilla.
>   Oh tierra triste y noble,
> la de los altos campos sin arados, regatos ni arboledas . . .

(The Duero [river] crosses the heart of oak of Iberia and Castile.
  Oh sad and noble land,
of the high plains, of wilderness, of rocky places
of fields without plows, without small rivulets,
without groves . . .[2])

What Old Castile was like in the Middle Ages does not conform either to Costa's pessimistic view or to Machado's poetic vision. Characteristically, the political reformers and writers of late nineteenth- and early twentieth-century Spain thought of the Castilian plain as representing the whole region, ignoring the geographical diversity of what was historically Old Castile. They were correct, however, on the importance of the plain in the history and economy of the entire region. It is with the plain therefore that we must begin.

Geography

With average heights of 2,700 feet above sea level, this vast tableland is cut across by the Sierras, which divide the meseta into Old and New Castile. The upper portion, Old Castile, is the most extensive of the two, running for roughly 150 miles from north to south and around 100 miles east to west. Most of the northern plateau lies at a high altitude above sea level: 66.5 percent of the surface of Old Castile and León lies at altitudes of between 1,800 and 3,000 feet; 31.4 percent between 3,000 and 6,000 feet, with the present provinces of Ávila and León (the latter not in Old Castile proper) with more than 50 percent of their territories located at an altitude of over 3,000 feet. In Soria the lands over 3,000 feet constitute more than 70 percent of the entire province. Only a meager 1.9 percent of the entire region is below 1,800 feet in altitude. Considering that these areas under 1,800 feet are mostly located in León, specifically around Zamora, where the meseta begins to slope toward the sea, the altitude of Old Castile itself is far more impressive. This, therefore, is one of the most important factors in the physical geography of the region.[3]

The northern meseta, which in the Middle Ages constituted the largest portion of the historical kingdom of Castile, is encircled by four mountain ranges. Only in some sections in the west does the plain run unimpeded toward the Portuguese border. Often devoid of vegetation, with naked and rugged peaks, the mountains stand guard around the plain of northern Castile. On the meseta the soil is often mixed with pebbles and large stones, and the arable is, as often, strewn with large boulders. On both sides of the roads crisscrossing the plain, fences of field stones extend endlessly, leading one to despair about the human labor expended in such efforts. There they stand, these fences, boundaries to lands often untilled, unused, yet protected. The fences were and still are symbols of rights of property with little economic purpose. Poor, and now almost desolate, villages along the main national highway leading from Burgos to Madrid had been built of stones and mud. They are dominated by large and arrogant churches, built in an era when Castilians were masters of the world. But Castile, of course, is not all stones.

West of the area of Medina del Campo, the absence of stones forced Castilians to build castles with bricks, such as that of La Mota, as formidable a strongplace as those built of stone. But it is not a coincidence that the fences which defined the right of landholders, the churches erected to the greater glory of God, the castles of powerful lords and kings, and even the houses of the poor were almost always built of stone. Indeed, beyond the

Figure 1. Segovia and surrounding countryside. (Photo by Scarlett Freund)

horizon, wherever northern Castilians looked across the plain, they saw high walls of stone. These mountain ranges were barriers but also points of contact with other ways of life, with peculiar types of agriculture, village life, and political organization.[4]

From the two most important medieval urban centers on the northern plain—Burgos and Valladolid—originated the (north–south) directions along which the course of Castilian history developed, leading to these walls of stone, to these mountain ranges that defined the plain. A few miles north of Burgos, the plain yields to a series of hills and rough terrain. This area, known as the Mountains of Burgos, was the "little corner" where historical Castile was born, a region encompassed by the triangle formed by Espinosa de los Monteros, Villarcayo, and Medina de Pomar: small towns that played an important role as the intermediate links between Burgos and the ports on the Bay of Biscay in the development of medieval commerce. In the same manner, the Mountains of Burgos in the north, like the ridges of the Central Sierras in the south, served as important economic and historical transitional areas between plain and coast, between plain and mountain range.[5]

In the Mountains of Burgos one finds deep valleys and canyons carved by the Ebro River. To descend into these valleys, even today, is to enter into a different habitat and ecology. Above lay the forbidding *páramos*; below, protected by high ridges, with abundant water and isolated somewhat from the violence that plagued the plain in the late Middle Ages, were the valleys. They supported a stable population spread throughout a large number of small villages. Such differences in patterns of settlement—scattered but large villages on the meseta and numerous but small villages in the mountains—can be seen by comparing the number of villages in *merindades* (administrative divisions roughly equivalent to shires or bailliages) in either plain or mountain as listed in the *Libro becerro de las behetrías*, a census of royal and seignorial rights undertaken in the mid-fourteenth century. In the *merindad* of Castilla la Vieja, to offer some examples, there were 534 villages listed; in that of Monzón, in the meseta, there were 97 villages.⁶

In the Middle Ages these hamlets and villages engaged in a fairly diversified subsistence agriculture. The documentation of the monastery of San Salvador de Oña, which had extensive holdings throughout the area of the Mountains of Burgos, shows a mix of cereal-growing, fruit tree (mostly apple) cultivation, and some dairy farming. Any population growth, however, meant disaster or forced migration, as was the case in the medieval period and in the early twentieth century, for these narrow valleys could only support a limited population.⁷

Farther north, beyond the Mountains of Burgos, loom the Cantabrian Mountains. This steep range, a westward extension of the Pyrenees, runs east–west for about 120 miles in the northern region of Spain. With average heights of between 5,000 and 6,000 feet and with peaks in its western portion (the Picos de Europa) reaching over 8,000 feet, the system was— and still is—an effective barrier to communication between the northern meseta and the coastal towns.⁸

Directly north of Burgos over the Cantabrian Mountains lies the modern province of Santander. Politically and economically (as was the case with the Basque provinces to the east), in the Middle Ages Santander was an integral part of Old Castile. Here we find, however, an environment completely different from that of the plain. Its coast, indented with the estuaries of small rivers and well-protected bays, supported a profitable fishing industry and was the setting for important commercial centers, settled after the repopulation of the area in the late twelfth and early thirteenth centuries. First among these Cantabrian coastal towns were San Vicente de la Barquera, Santander, Laredo, and Castro Urdiales, the so-called *Cuatro Puertos* (four ports), though a good number of other protected harbors, especially along the Basque coast—Bermeo, San Sebastián, Fuenterrabía, Plencia, and, above all, Bilbao after 1300—more than held their own in competition with those more westerly ports. Besides its privileged geographical location, which faced the maritime trade routes to England and Flanders, abundant rain and a mild climate allowed sometimes for two annual crops, a luxury not always available a mere fifty miles inland.

Though verdant, and despite what we today consider to be its natural advantages, this region was not looked upon favorably by medieval and early modern travelers. With bread as the main staple of their diet, medieval men and women could not always see other economic possibilities or the usefulness of any crops apart from grains. In the guide attributed to Aymeric Picaud, the land of the Basques was "well wooded and hilly, [but] characterized by a barbaric language, devoid of bread and wine and every other food for the body, only apples, cider and milk, and of course with far too many toll-takers." Almost three hundred years later, the companions of Leon of Rosmithal expressed the same negative reaction to a land without bread and wine and to its ubiquitous toll-takers.[9]

Turning northeastward from Burgos and following along the modern road to the French frontier, one reaches the valley carved by the Ebro River. Across the Oberones Mountains through the Gap of Pancorbo lies the region of the Rioja. Irrigated by the Ebro River and with an average altitude below 1,500 feet, the Rioja enjoys a milder climate than the rest of the northern plain, and it is today, as it was in the Middle Ages, a productive agricultural region. Its wines, now exported throughout the world, were already held in esteem in the thirteenth and fourteenth centuries, and its wheat, barley, and rye were consumed locally and throughout the Basque region. Andrea Navagero, who crossed the Rioja in 1528, thought it was a fertile and well-populated country when compared to what he had seen in other parts of Spain. Almost a century and a half later Antoine de Brunel, after decrying the barrenness of Castile, praised the area around Vitoria as a beautiful and well-tended region.[10] Continuing to move in a northeasterly direction, the traveler runs into the extensive foothills of the Pyrenees, which, then and now, served as a well-defined physical and political frontier for Castile and Spain. Mountain passes—most notably Roncesvalles—however, allowed for easy communication with the outside world.

Directly east of Burgos, Old Castile is separated from Aragon by the Iberian Mountains. Although they have never been an imposing barrier, certainly not as difficult to cross as other natural obstacles around Castile, they helped to shape the political divisions of the peninsula. Of less economic importance than other transitional areas around the northern plain, the Iberian Mountains played no significant historical role in the development of the realm, except perhaps to confirm the direction of Castilian expansion. In many respects, with the exception of the east–west pilgrimage road to Santiago de Compostela, the movement of Castilian history, the slow evolution of its history, has always been along a north–south axis: northward toward the sea and the rest of Europe, southward toward al-Andalus and territorial conquest. In that sense, the Iberian Mountains defined the eastern limits of Castile and prevented, in the Middle Ages and into the present, the different historical regions from forming a nation.

In the south, however, the story is different. Along its meridional border, Old Castile faced another important natural barrier which also served as a point of contact with other regions. In the east, the centers of Aragonese history pointed toward the Mediterranean or toward the south, but in the center of the peninsula, Old Castile had first to contend with the Central Sierras, beyond which lay Toledo and, further south, al-Andalus. To all the attractions that lay beyond, the Central Sierras remained an imposing obstacle. Rising to heights of as much as 9,000 feet (2,750 meters), they effectively divided the meseta into two distinctive historical regions: Old and New Castile. The elevation of the mountain passes (Somosierra, 5,800 feet [1,760 meters]; La Cañada, 4,484 feet [1,367 meters]; Navacerrada, 6,104 feet [1,860 meters]) forced medieval travelers to seek ways around the Sierras or to brave the often adverse conditions found there. Finally, to the west, completing the circle of stone around the plain of Old Castile, rose the mountains of León. They stood, however, somewhat far from the centers of power and commerce on the plain and did not restrict Castilian access to the capital of the ancient Leonese realm.

The coastal regions of Cantabria and the Basque country, the alluvial valleys of the Ebro in the region of the Rioja, the Mountains of Burgos, and the Central Sierras provided alternative habitats, contrasting topographical settings, complementary economic resources to those of the plain. Further, the encircling mountains provided the human capital for the taming and settling of the plain.[11] The history of Castile is not just that of the plain but of the interaction of plain, sea, and mountain. And the dusty roads which crisscrossed the meseta, from Burgos to Valladolid and beyond to al-Andalus, would have carried little traffic without the interdependence of the different geographical settings mentioned above. Yet, when all is said

and done, the northern meseta was and remains "the dominant geographical structural element in Spain."[12] There was also a time not long ago when
it was the dominant historical component of all of the Spains.[13]

THE FLUVIAL SYSTEM OF THE NORTHERN CASTILIAN PLAIN

The high plateau north of the Central Sierras is traversed by two main rivers
and their tributaries. These river networks, in effect, comprise almost all of
the hydrographic features of the northern plain. Once again Antonio Machado describes it:

Castilla, España de los largos ríos
que la mar no ha visto y corre hacia los mares.

(Castile, Spain of long rivers
which has not seen the sea and [yet]
runs to the seas.)

Indeed, both rivers, the Ebro and the Duero, run to the sea, the first to the
Mediterranean, the latter to the Atlantic Ocean. Yet neither of the two
brings Castile to the sea. The northernmost of the two great northern Castilian rivers, the Ebro, does not even run through the plain proper but rather
flows on an easterly course through rocky gorges and deep valleys in the
mountains north of Burgos. Carrying still a small volume of water, the Ebro
contributes little to the economic well-being of the region. A few deep and
narrow valleys are spared by the protection of the mountains and the water
of the river from the desolation of the nearby *páramos*. Even there the Ebro
had, in the past, its own treacherous whims. In the Middle Ages and in
recent memory, before the building of a reservoir to trap the water from
melting snow, the river was unpredictable and dangerous. My own grandfather's mill on the Ebro in the village of Tubilleja in the valley of Zamanzas
was swept away twice in the annual flooding of the river, until he gave up
the struggle and migrated to the New World at the beginning of the century.
    The northern plain is not drained by the Ebro but by the river Duero
and its network of tributaries. Drawing an area of around 38,281 square
miles (99,105 square kilometers), the Duero flows from its sources around
Soria westward to Portugal, reaching the Atlantic at Oporto. Because
evaporation is high and a great deal of water is lost in the porous, thirsty soil
of the plain, little water would ever reach the Atlantic or be left to irrigate
the plain were it not for its tributaries, above all the Pisuerga and its own

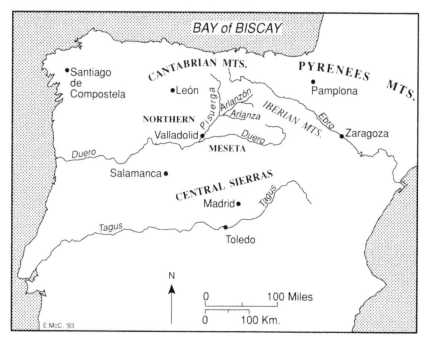

Map 2. Topography of the region of Old Castile and Central Spain.

network of affluents, the Carrión and the Arlanzón, flowing from the rain-rich Cantabrian Mountains. Along these fluvial networks rose the important northern Castilian cities and towns, as well as the most productive agricultural lands. In fact, a casual glance at a map of Castile will show that its scattered towns and hamlets lie almost exclusively on the banks of rivers and rivulets which carried the plain's most vital commodity: water. Yet, the water of the Duero and its tributaries did not extend their benefits very far beyond their banks. The innumerable disputes over water rights, over the excessive building of mills, give an indication of the limits of Castile's fluvial system.[14]

Climate

If the illness of Castile is an illness of stone, then the absence of rainfall and severe cold are often its terminal diseases. In spite of Professor Henry Higgins's aids to correct pronunciation, the rain in Spain does not fall mainly on the plain. The average annual rainfall in the northern meseta

ranges "from twenty to twenty-five inches on the ridges of the Central
Sierras to fifteen to twenty inches in most of the plateau, with as little as
eleven inches in some districts." To compound the problem, rainfall is not
only sparse but irregularly distributed throughout the year.[15]

In some years, as has been the case for the last few years, it may rain
even less, as little as six to eight inches. Heavy rain may fall on specific
localities, but it is rapidly absorbed by the parched soil. Areas nearby may
remain completely dry. On the other hand, in exceptional years, as in the
spring of 1984, rain falls in abundance throughout most of the meseta. Then
Old Castile becomes almost unrecognizable, its fields dressed in green, its
wheat and barley crops growing tall, its harvests plentiful. Rainfalls like
those of 1984 are, unfortunately, few and far between; but when they come,
they transform the face of the arid plain, showing what the true potential of
Castilian agriculture could be in the presence of sufficient water.

In normal years—and it must be pointed out that the spring of 1984
was preceded by several years of extreme drought—rainfall is concentrated
in the spring and fall, while summers tend to be dry and cloudless. Dry
summers following a wet spring are not just a blessing for the millions of
tourists crossing the land, but they also allow the grain to grow to maturity
and the grass to dry easily into hay. What is often a curse, lack of rain, can at
times be a blessing. In 1314, 1315, and 1317, when wet conditions brought
havoc and widespread famine to most European agriculture from the
Pyrenees to the Urals, Castile seems to have been spared and was even
capable of exporting some of its wheat to other countries.[16] Regardless of
the manner in which Castile escaped the disasters of the early fourteenth
century, geography manuals again and again emphasize how these conditions of aridity, a combination of poor soils and adverse climate, have
served to reduce the returns of agriculture, so that to work the land is a hard
and often unrewarding affair. Ruth Way puts it best: "Agriculture is a
somewhat hazardous undertaking for all the natural elements seem to
conspire against man."[17] There is in truth no place to hide from the
weather, or few places in the northern meseta where agriculture, and life
itself, is not affected adversely by climate and topography.

Altitude, lack of rain, rapid evaporation are only some of the problems.
Because of the average height of Old Castile, the region suffers from its own
peculiar weather conditions. Castile experiences sharp contrasts in tem-
perature between winter and summer and even between day and night in
the same season. Winters are cold, and the average number of frost days
annually is large: 121 in Valladolid, 80 in Ávila.[18]

Snow covers the mountain peaks throughout the winter season and, in most cases, for most of the year. To this day, mountain passes are often closed by snowfalls, isolating entire regions for days. Such is the case in the valley of Zamanzas, where my family lives, cut off from the main road almost every year. Snow falls also at the most unexpected times. In late May 1984, as I drove from Madrid to Segovia, there were almost two feet of snow in the mountain pass of Navacerrada.

Foreign travelers in the early modern period recount with obvious surprise and unmasked bitterness the inclemency of the weather at times when good atmospheric conditions were to be expected. In early fall, around mid-October 1517, as Charles I led his court from San Vicente de la Barquera on the Bay of Biscay to Reinosa, the royal caravan met rain, snow, and strong winds on the mountain passes leading into the northern meseta. Because of the bad roads, the roughness of the land, and the mud, the king and his entourage advanced only two leagues a day, their horses in peril of losing their shoes. Similar weather conditions were reported by the Polish ambassador in 1524–25. Traveling from Granada to Valladolid in December and January, he found continuous rain and snow, lost two horses, and took a month to complete his trip. Andrea Navagero met a similar fate as he crossed the mountain pass of La Tablada from New to Old Castile in early January 1529. In 1665 Antoine de Brunel found ice on the road to Burgos in early April, and throughout his trip across Old Castile he complained of the cold, wind, and rain. In late April, as he reached the pass at Somosierra, de Brunel could not help showing his surprise at the hail, snow, and wind he found there "so late in the season." On 28 October 1786, while crossing from Segovia to New Castile, Joseph Towsend found the mountain pass on the Central Sierras covered with snow while the road behind him had also been closed by a raging storm.[19]

The complaints about the weather are far too numerous and widespread throughout the centuries to dismiss them as exceptional events, or as hostile reports by foreign visitors. In the *Libro de buen amor*, Juan Ruiz, the archpriest of Hita, tells of his adventures and wanderings back and forth through the mountain passes of the Central Sierras. Although his escapades occurred in March, in the company of the amorous female he met on the mountain passes, in every one of his crossings he also had to face snow, ice, and cold.[20] Medieval peasants knew, as did the fabled archpriest, of the perils of these unpredictable hail- and snowstorms. In either early fall or late spring, storms came to disrupt their work, to ruin their crops. In the extant documents of San Salvador de Oña, close to the Mountains of Burgos, and elsewhere in northern Castile, special clauses were included in the leasing agreements of peasants with their monastic lords to protect renters from the arbitrary onslaught of the weather. If the crop suffered from hailstorms, snow, or drought, the obligations set by the contract were waived. Whatever was harvested after one of these disasters was divided between tenant and lords in proportions of two-thirds and one-third, respectively, though these proportions varied depending on location and crop (grapes were divided in half).[21]

The impact of unpredictable and often adverse weather conditions are frequently illustrated in contemporary accounts. In 1252 a bitter return of winter, after a false start of spring, destroyed most of the crops in the area of Burgos, leaving great scarcity in its wake. In 1255, the Vena River, a mere brook most of the time, flooded, damaging houses and bridges in the city of Burgos. Three years later, an unexpected late frost destroyed vineyards throughout northern Castile with the accompanying rise in the price of wine. The chroniclers also reported a bad year for bread. In February 1286 flooding of the Vena and Arlanzón once more swept Burgos's bridges, hospitals, and houses located near the rivers, and some of the city inhabitants lost their lives. Similar occurrences were reported later in 1334 when the snow-swollen Arlanzón, a rather puny river during most of the year, caused great havoc in the city. Because of late hailstorms in 1338, the monks of Silos did not have enough wine of their own and had to acquire it at a higher price. Six years earlier, bad weather also led to high prices for bread, and forced the monks of Santo Domingo de Silos to pawn their property in Castañares to cover the cost. Likewise, bad weather in 1337 forced the monks of Santo Toribio de Liébana to borrow money because of poor crops.[22]

Farther south in the region of Ávila, an area high on the plain, where low precipitation and frost are common from November to April, the contemporary reports are equally bleak. A late frost in March of 1234 "burned the trees and the vineyards." In 1301 a severe drought afflicted the lands of Ávila; yet three years later the king could not hunt in the fields of Olmedo (in the countryside of Ávila) because of incessant rain. The river Tormes flooded in 1227 and 1256; the Duero in 1258 and 1264. Years of too much rain alternated with periods of implacable drought. In 1355 the chronicler lamented "the driest [conditions] which men ever saw."[23]

Throughout the realm, the story was more or less the same. The ordinances of the Cortes include numerous references to harsh weather conditions and to its corollary: food shortages and human need. In the first half of the fourteenth century, but especially in 1314–15, 1338, 1345, and 1348, the urban procurators pleaded with the king for remission of taxes because of drought or other weather problems.[24] Popular concern with inclement conditions or the tendency to exaggerate existing difficulties was, of course, not peculiar to Castile, and we know that local chroniclers often paid more attention to unusual weather conditions than to the great issues of the day. But we also know that the late thirteenth and early fourteenth centuries marked a change for the worse in weather patterns for most parts of Europe. Wetter summers and overall cooler temperatures soon led to widespread crop failures and famines. In Castile even a small variation in the climate, especially when it was for the worse, aggravated the already less than benign conditions of its climate and topography. At the same time, cold winters and short summers not only affected agriculture but also determined how Castilians dressed (with what seemed an endless need for woolens), what they ate, and how they built their houses.

The unpredictability of the climate in the northern meseta and in the mountains which encircled the plain made agriculture a hazardous and risky business. The cycle of plowing, seeding, and harvesting followed timetables that were shorter than those in existence in most parts of western Europe. Yet, short as they were, these timetables still left periods—both at the beginning and at the end of the planting and harvesting season—in which killing frosts could do their damage.

How much this preoccupation with the weather was part of the Castilian consciousness can be seen not only in the frequent references to its ravages, but in the almost jocular yet, at times, also plaintive descriptions of the climate by natives and foreigners. Jokesters describe Burgos, the quintessential northern Castilian city, as having two seasons (*estaciones*, meaning seasons, but also stations), winter and the train station. On a more poignant note, Andrea Navagero quoted Don Francisco de Zuñiga to the effect "that Burgos was in mourning for all of Castile and that the sun comes to Burgos, as does everything else, '*de acarreo*' [on the back of mules]. . . . It was too cold, snows and frosts many days, and then the summers, which are short, are usually very hot." "There is a saying in Castile," de Zuñiga added, "that in Burgos there are ten months of winter and two of hell."[25] Reality was not of course as stark as de Zuñiga's description, but at times it was certainly not far from the truth. And if winters' temperatures were, and still are, at times extreme, summers do not show a great improvement either.

We should not think of climate, any more than geography, as the only shapers of Castile's destiny. The unceasing travel of Castilian kings to and fro on the plain in the midst of winter, the same accounts of travelers and literary references, show that snow, wind, and rain could be conquered. Jeromino Munzer tells the story of an elephant, kept at the zoo in Benavente, which died of cold in early January of 1494; but that did not deter kings and magnates from trying to keep elephants and other tropical animals. Navagero quoted the emperor as saying that summers should be spent in Seville and winters in Burgos, since both were best prepared for each respective season—Seville with fountains and water, Burgos with well-protected houses and warm fireplaces.[26]

Human Effects on the Environment

Numerous descriptions by ancient geographers and early modern travelers decried not only Castile's aridity, its lack of trees, the poverty of its agriculture, but also, with a bit of xenophobic excess, the shortcomings in the skills, dedication, character, and physical attributes of its people.[27] Unconsciously, Alfonso X implied as much at the end of his life when, half-crazed by hostility toward his son Sancho, he willed the realm to the king of France (if his grandsons, the Infantes de la Cerda, did not survive him) in the hope of bringing together the business acumen and industry of the French with the warlike nature of the Castilians. Even Olivares offered, as an explanation for his growing political difficulties, the observation that "the soil of France is so rich and ours so dry and rugged."[28]

In truth, northern Castile was not always well-suited or receptive to the agricultural technology of southern Spain, with its emphasis on irrigation. Likewise, the heavy plow, the three-field system, and other innovations which revolutionized northern European agriculture were appropriate neither for the thin soil of Old Castile nor for its agricultural cycle. The barriers to agricultural innovation were, however, far more complex than natural conditions, adverse climate, or relative altitude. Many of the deterrents were also cultural and structural. The same impediments to change are present to this day in many parts of the world. If it is difficult to transform one's culture, diet, and agricultural techniques once, think how much more difficult it is to do so again and again, when for almost a millennium the inhabitants of Castile were constantly challenged by the requirements of new frontiers. When in the eighth and ninth centuries the mountain people from Asturias, the Galaic-Leonese mountains, the region of Cantabria, and the Bay of Biscay descended into the plain and settled it, they had to adapt to new diets, to new forms of cultivation, and to a pattern of life radically different from that which they and their ancestors had known for centuries.

Yet, old customs, culinary traditions, attitudes toward new habitats persist far longer than most historians are willing to admit. Such resistance to change is not difficult to understand; here I have in mind the diet of Spanish immigrants to Cuba and that of their descendants, who after decades still adhered faithfully to a diet of heavy stews, meat, and wine, well-suited for the cold climate of Castile but utterly irrational and most probably fatal in the long run on a tropical island. Having half-adapted and tamed the plain over five centuries, Castilians were not always capable of altering their agricultural techniques or meeting fully the demands of a different way of life. They borrowed heavily from both north and south. Above all, they borrowed heavily from the aesthetic and material culture of al-Andalus, from which there was much to learn; but they did this without changing their fundamental perception of their own habitat, a land of livestock grazing and dry-cereal growing, without accepting or undertaking the almost revolutionary reordering of the land (through irrigation and reforestation) necessary to make the Castilian soil more productive within its geographical constraints, less vulnerable to its inclement weather. Even the Moors, for all their agricultural skill and adaptability, never showed any interest in settling or working the soil of the plain, preferring al-Andalus, a land of orange trees in bloom and running water, which reminded them of their own idealized vision of Paradise. New changes were necessary after 1212, when Andalucía was opened to Christian settlement, and once again Castilians were forced to learn new ways, to eat differently, to think differently. At these new tasks they often failed.

One should not be too hard on the inhabitants of northern Castile, nor should one judge the land only by the desolate *páramos* or its dry plains. There the medieval traveler or the present-day tourist finds no sign of life or, at best, a lonely shepherd at his lonely task. But nearby there was—and there is—life. Life in the mountains or in the northern meseta itself prospered in green valleys with enough water, or along the Duero River network. In the alluvial fans of the Arlanzón and the Pisuerga rivers, along smaller rivers and creeks, rose cities, hamlets, monasteries, castles, and mills, all of them symbols of human toil and ambition. Harsh and poor as the environment of northern Castile was and is, we should not write off the entire region too hastily. Rather, we must visualize Old Castile as a collection of small and distinct localities, each with its own range of possibilities and problems, each with its own peculiar history. Certainly geographic features and climate throughout most of Old Castile were not as favorable as those we find in other medieval realms; yet, in many instances, specific areas were almost gardens when contrasted with the surrounding dry and parched plain of the *páramos*.

Obviously, the Castilians' perception of their habitat was not nearly as negative as the simple examination of climate, geography, and soil conditions might lead us to believe. Those who settled the plain in the eighth and ninth centuries did so in what they probably thought were the most advantageous conditions. Inhospitable areas were left mostly for sheep grazing, as still occurs to this day, or as is done in Dartmoor and similar places in England. This pattern of settlement agreed well with a population always too sparse for the size of the realm. Throughout the late Middle Ages, with few and rare exceptions in favored locations, there is no evidence of demographic pressure on the land as was the case in France and England in the late thirteenth century.[29]

Even if the land required a great deal of work, even if agricultural yields were often not as bountiful as in other parts of Europe, or even Andalucía itself, the Castilians could often do or had to do with what they had, with what they scratched out of the soil. Castilians had long learned to be frugal out of necessity, and empty stomachs, as Braudel has pointed out, were a common theme in Golden Age Spain. One had to make a virtue of an empty stomach, as the knight in *Lazarillo de Tormes* or Don Quixote often did.[30]

There is another factor which may have prevented most Castilians in the Middle Ages from seeing their habitat as it was. Historians, in their attempt to quantify data or to grasp underlying social and economic forces, fail to notice such common traits as feelings, prejudices, and the often irrational reactions of people. Most of us often come to terms with our living conditions, with our daily existence, regardless of its unpleasantness. We embellish them, rationalize them, and insist, often against all logic, how superior they are to the conditions of others. There is an undeniable psychological defense mechanism which allows most humans to come to terms with difficult circumstances, with what we are, with what we have, and, more importantly, with what we do not and cannot have. Why, then, should it surprise us that in spite of all the adversities, Castilians chose to love and praise their land?

Early modern observers of Spain often noted the extreme—and what they felt to be unjustified—pride of its people. Contarini, after praising the prowess and sense of honor of the Spaniards, accused them of being "proud, of little charity to other people and envious." Guicciardini affirmed that they "were proud, believing that no other nation could compare to theirs, always trying to pretend to be more than they were." And thus even in the Middle Ages, as others also did, Castilians pronounced themselves to be the most courageous men in Europe, the best warriors, the truest Christians; their land was the only one that had kept intact the teachings of Saint Peter and Saint Paul.[31] Castile's sky was the bluest, its products the best, and so most Castilians remained there, struggling day after day on a hard land, going on from year to year, as billions of humans do elsewhere, with the often unpleasant tasks of daily life. Thus in the chapters that follow, not just geography and climate but the way in which Castilians conceived of their homeland must remain a constant backdrop to the slow, and at times erratic, unfolding of their history.

Notes

1. Joaquín Costa y Martínez, *Colectivismo agrario en España* (Madrid: Biblioteca Costa, 1915), parts 1 and 2; *La fórmula de la agricultura española*, 2 vols. (Madrid: Biblioteca Costa, 1911–12), 1: 68ff. On Costa's thought see Maurice Jacques and Carlos Serrano, *Joaquín Costa: Crisis de la restauración y populismo (1875–1911)* (Madrid: Siglo XXI, 1977), 113–89.
2. Antonio Machado, *Poesías completas* (Madrid: Espasa-Calpe, 1979), 137–39.
3. Valentín Cabero, *El espacio geográfico castellano-leonés* (Valladolid: Ambito, 1982), 22–23; see also table on p. 24.
4. Fernand Braudel, *The Mediterranean and the Mediterranean World in the Age of Philip II*, 2 vols. (New York: Harper-Torchbooks, 1975), 1: 55, 161, et passim; David Ringrose, *Transportation and Economic Stagnation in Spain, 1750–1850* (Durham, N.C.: Duke University Press, 1970), 17 et passim.
5. José Ortega Varcárcel, *La transformación de un espacio rural: Las montañas de Burgos, estudio de geografía regional* (Valladolid: Universidad de Valladolid, 1974), 30, 132–36, 140–46, et passim.
6. *Becerro*, 1: 78–83.
7. See below, Part II, for agriculture in the region of Oña. Also, Marta Bonoudo de Magnani, "El monasterio de San Salvador de Oña: economía agraria y sociedad rural," *Cuadernos de historia de España* 51–52 (1970), 59–61. As I made final revisions to this manuscript, an excellent new book on Oña appeared: Francisco Ruiz Gómez, *Las aldeas castellanas en la Edad Media. Oña en los siglos XIV y XV* (Madrid: Consejo superior de investigaciones científicas, 1990).
8. Ruth Way, *A Geography of Spain and Portugal* (London: Methuen, 1962), 6–7; W. B. Fisher and H. Bowen-Jones, *Spain: A Geographical Background* (London: Chatto and Windus, 1958), 19–20.

9. *Viajes de extranjeros*, 1: 169, 262.

10. Ibid., 1: 872; 2: 406, 556.

11. On the differences of house types according to location, see de Bolos Capdevila et al., *Geografía de España*, 57–58, 69–75; Fisher and Bowen-Jones, *Spain: A Geographical Background*, 48–52. See also below for differences in how and what was grown in the region.

12. Fisher and Bowen-Jones, *Spain: A Geographical Background*, 16.

13. Cabero, *El espacio geográfico castellano-leonés*, 15, has compared the region to a castle: the plain is the interior courtyard, where the castellan resides; the mountains are the walls of the castle.

14. Fisher and Bowen-Jones, *Spain: A Geographical Background*, 25–29, 135–38; de Bolos Capdevila et al., *Geografía de España*, 154; Way, *A Geography of Spain and Portugal*, 24–29.

15. Fisher and Bowen-Jones, *Spain: A Geographical Background*, 30–40; Cabero, *El espacio geográfico castellano-leonés*, 54–81.

16. On the famines see H. S. Lucas, "The Great European Famine of 1315–17," *Speculum* 5 (1930): 343–77, which does not mention the Iberian peninsula. Castile exported some modest amount of wheat to England in 1317. See T. F. Ruiz, "Mercaderes castellanos en Inglaterra, 1248–1350," in Teofilo F. Ruiz, *Sociedad y poder real en Castilla (Burgos en la edad media)* (Barcelona: Ariel, 1981), 220.

17. Way, *A Geography of Spain and Portugal*, 275.

18. Ibid., 56–58; Ortega Varcárcel, *La transformación de un espacio rural*, 99–103; Fisher and Bowen-Jones, *Spain: A Geographical Background*, 37–38; See tables in Cabero, *El espacio geográfico castellano-leonés*, 58–60. Professor Adeline Rucquoi, commenting on an early draft of this chapter, pointed out correctly that a comparison between Old Castile and the regions around Paris and London are misleading. Geographically and climatically Castile should be compared to Italy. Although this is true, historically Castile defined itself internationally in this period by its relations to France and/or England.

19. *Viajes de extranjeros*, 1: 693, 695, 818–19; 2: 406, 409; 3: 1477.

20. Juan Ruiz, *Libro de buen amor* (Valencia: Castalia, 1960), stanzas 950, 955, 964, 982.

21. See above and AHN, Clero, carp. 298, no. 7 (2-March-1287); no. 12 (22-March-1287); carp. 300, no. 5 (13-July-1290) et passim.

22. *Chronicón de Cardeña* in *España sagrada: texto geográfico-histórico de la iglesia de España*, ed. E. Flórez, vol. 23 (Madrid: D. Antonio de Sancha, 1767), 373–75; Juan Albarellos, *Efemeridades burgalesas (Apuntes históricos)*, 2d ed. (Burgos: Diario de Burgos, 1964), 61: describes a great flood in 1296 as reported in the *Memorias antiguas de Cardeña*; *Vida económica*, 58, 133, 157; *Liébana*, 325–26 (7-April-1337); Peter Linehan, *The Spanish Church and the Papacy in the Thirteenth Century* (Cambridge: Cambridge University Press, 1971), 162–63.

23. Ángel Barrios García, *Estructuras agrarias y de poder en Castilla: El ejemplo de Ávila (1085–1320)*, 2 vols. (Salamanca: Universidad de Salamanca, 1983–84), 1: 87–89.

24. *Cortes*, 1: 484 (1345): "este anno en questamos fue muy grant mortandad en los ganados, e otrosi la simienca muy tardia por el muy fuerte temporal que ha fecho

de muy grandes nieves et de grandes yelos . . ."; also, p. 598 (1345). For further references to adverse weather see Julio Valdeón Baruque, "Aspectos de la crisis castellana en la primera mitad del siglo XIV," *Hispania* III (1969): 5–24; and his "La crisis del siglo XIV en Castilla: revisión del problema," *Revista de la Universidad de Madrid*, 79 (1971): 161–84.

25. *Viajes de extranjeros*, I: 869.

26. Ibid., I: 390, 869.

27. The critical statements of late medieval and early modern travelers about natural conditions and Castilian national characteristics are almost a literary *topos*. Although reflecting real conditions, they also show the growth of anti-Spanish attitudes in the imperial age, and, as such, are worth further study. For general poverty of the land see Strabo in *Viajes de extranjeros*, I: 97, 117–18, 128; Leon of Rosmithal, I: 266, 270; Tetzel, I: 295–97; Antoine de Lalainy, I: 456. On pejorative remarks about behavior or working habits of Castilians: Guide of pilgrims, I: 171; Leon of Rosmithal, I: 265, 268–69; Tetzel, I: 297. See also I: 424: "I have not seen a beautiful face in this region [Vizcaya]"; also, I: 606: "Brutish and proud, full of jealousy"; above all, the perceptive Guicciardini, I: 613–21; and in addition, Linehan, *The Spanish Church*, 104–7.

28. For the wills of Alfonso X see *MHE*, 2: 110–33; John H. Elliott, *Richelieu and Olivares*, (Cambridge: Cambridge University Press, 1984), 160.

29. For demographic change and a full discussion of the impact of the Reconquest on the population of the northern plain, see Linehan, *The Spanish Church*, 107–27, 162, 178–79; Teofilo F. Ruiz, "Expansion et changement: la conquête de Séville et la société castillane (1248–1350)," *Annales E.S.C.*, 3 (mai–juin 1979), 548–65 and below, Part IV, Chapter 10.

30. Braudel, *The Mediterranean*, I: 242.

31. See above and also *Viajes de extranjeros*, I: 606, 613, 900.

Part II

Rural Society in
Late Medieval Castile

The roads that crisscrossed northern medieval Castile pulsated with life, thanks to the anonymous industry of humble men and women. Pilgrims and soldiers had important economic and social functions, but their impact was either sudden or only transitory. And, thus, it was not those dedicated to the glamorous and often cruel pursuit of salvation or booty but rather those dedicated to the daily tasks necessary for the feeding and preservation of humans who were the real and permanent basis of Castilian society. We must begin with them, with those who seldom traveled the road, with those who remained close to the land. Although not as exciting as the dynamics of urban life, nor as stimulating as the study of medieval intellectuals or warring nobility, the world of the peasants, obscure, faceless, often brutal, was the very foundation upon which society in medieval Castile and elsewhere rested.

In this section I will examine how the peasants lived, how they worked their lands, what agricultural tools they used, what they produced, for whom and under what terms. Narrowing the focus, one of the chapters will present specific case studies of rural conditions in northern Castile, seeking to contrast and compare different localities within the region. At the same time, I hope to provide some statistical evidence on the much debated issue of the market for land, as well as to advance some opinions on this historiographical issue. Fortunately, there are a growing number of studies of rural conditions in Castile, and these works provide a vision, albeit still somewhat fragmented, of the basic pattern of peasant life in the region.[1] In spite of this pioneering research, the rural history of Castile has been and still is very often dictated by the works of French and English scholars, and by the models they have constructed in their studies of rural life in northern Europe. The works of Abel, Bloch, Bois, Slicher van Bath, Duby, Hilton, Homans, Kosminsky, Raftis, and others are indeed superb accounts of rural life in specific areas of northern medieval Europe. Most of them are also excellent models of how to do rural history. Yet, what these historians have to say about English, French, or Dutch agriculture does not always apply to northern Castile or does so only in part. In fact, their studies rarely deal with southern Europe in general or Castile, and, when they do so, it is only perfunctorily.

At the beginning of this inquiry into the life and economic activities of the Castilian peasantry, one must take a brief glance at the economic resources and potential of the different ecological subregions which comprised Old Castile. Topographical diversity, mountain, plain, and intermediate regions, created mutually dependent economic zones. In the Middle Ages, each locality attempted, though not always successfully, to grow as much of their most basic needs as was humanly possible. In reality, however, soil conditions, altitude, and climate imposed severe limitations on such desires for self-sufficiency. In very general terms—for it would be more clearly shown in the next section dealing with urban life and commerce—one could say that the main staples of the mountain, that is, the area of Cantabria and the Basque region, were fish, livestock, dairy goods, and fruits, above all, apples. In addition, the great iron mines around Bilbao and elsewhere in the region provided ore for export abroad, to the Castilian plain and to Andalucía. The northern meseta specialized in cereal and wine, though clearly the region of the Tierra de Campos, already shading toward León, and the valley of the Pisuerga River were better suited for growing grain than the region of Burgos. Within the northern plain itself, there were further subtle economic specializations. Valladolid was the "land of bread"; Zamora, further west, the "land of wine"; and, as the extensive references to vineyards show, the area of the Rioja was almost completely given to viticulture.

Finally, the hills north of Burgos, the Central Sierras and other transition areas within the plain served as intermediary links between complementary economic subregions. They did more than that, however. The mountains north of Burgos, as has been brilliantly shown by Ortega Varcárcel, served as a market for oxen, mules, and other carting animals; some of its urban centers—Frías, Medina de Pomar and Villarcayo—functioned as secondary distribution centers and as stages in the trading routes between the coastal towns on the Bay of Biscay and Burgos, the great commercial distribution center on the plain. To a similar extent, Segovia, on the skirts of the Guadarrama and the mountain range which separated Old and New Castile, served also as an intermediate economic zone between contrasting regions. In addition, although some of the monastic and secular lords of northern Castile owned large flocks of livestock, the northern plain was essentially a transit area for the annual transhumance. Nevertheless, most of northern Castile and the regions of Soria, Ávila, and in particular Sepúlveda benefited from the profits of ranching.[2]

We do not yet understand fully the circulation of agricultural goods within Old Castile but have a rough model of the economic interdependence of the different economic subunits in the region, and the links between the rural economy of northern Castile and other areas in the peninsula and abroad. Braudel's description of economic exchanges, quoted in the previous chapters, probably followed to the letter models of economic interdependence already present in the late Middle Ages. Obviously, the active markets for dried fish, salt, cereals, wine, and spices within and outside northern Castile point to complex patterns of trade and complementary rural production.

Rural life in northern Castile was intimately tied to urban centers; often farms operated in the shadows of city walls or within the extensive hinterland or *contado* (*alfoz*) of northern Castilian municipalities. As often, agricultural activity took place under the aegis of monastic establishments, themselves presiding over small towns. On the banks of rivers or, if not, on dry lands (*tierras de secano*), the work of peasants never took place far away from an urban center or from roads which connected their activities to the towns. Thus, these settlements were islands on the plain, joined together by roads, linked inexorably to the cycles of urban life or the routines of monastic establishments. In Castile the boundaries between rural and urban were often vague, at times nonexistent. This is a point to which I will come back again and again in succeeding chapters and which belies my ordering of topics, for the sake of expediency and clarity, under the headings of rural and urban.[3] Such distinctions are, at the end, arbitrary and misleading. In the late Middle Ages most of the cities of the northern plateau, with some notable exceptions, were in reality rural centers. Most often they lived not by the ingenuity of their merchants, but by the toil of their farmers. They lived and prospered as agricultural markets for the exchange and circulation of the products of their respective hinterlands.

This intertwining of town and country was most evident in the landscape. The countryside of northern Castile, with its wide open and uninhabited spaces, struck a responsive chord among geographers and travelers. Guicciardini, another one of those peripatetic Italian ambassadors, commented on how few cities there were in Castile for such a large realm. In the same vein, other foreign visitors described with amazement the barrenness and emptiness of the land. For them, the poverty of Castilian agriculture was unquestionably real. Antoine de Brunel, on seeing the fields of Old Castile for the first time, depicted the land as "all sand with small hills of little fertility, often cut by mountains covered with rocks. From time to time, one finds good plains and valleys which produce the foodstuffs necessary for substance, but nowhere have we seen a land less diversified with fruit trees or gardens." "I do not know," he added, "if the land is not suitable or that the people are not hardworking enough to give it the necessary care."[4]

There is no need to belabor the point anymore. In truth, Old Castile's ecology, topography, and climate were neither those of northern Europe nor, in spite of Braudel, those of the Mediterranean. It straddled both, with the advantages and disadvantages of a diversity of ecological systems. The peculiar nature of the terrain and its climate shaped the patterns of settlement and farming in northern Castile, and these patterns of agricultural activity varied at times from those one would have found in other parts of the medieval West. For foreigners, these distinctions were obvious, and, by the early modern period, the contrasts had become a *topos*, a renewed theme of Castile's poverty and Castilian lack of industry, undermining Spain's dreams of empire and glory. Yet, these structures of Castilian rural life had long been laid and transformed in the crucible of the crises of the Middle Ages.

Notes

1. The studies of monastic domains and even of rural history have blossomed in the last decade. Most of the important works are listed in the bibliography, and here I shall limit my mentions to the most relevant ones. The pioneer and still foremost scholar in the field is José Ángel García de Cortázar, whose *El dominio del monasterio de San Millán de la Cogolla (siglos X a XIII): Introducción a la historia rural de Castilla altomedieval* (Salamanca: Universidad de Salamanca, 1969) remains a landmark, while his *La historia rural medieval: Un esquema de análisis estructural de sus contenidos a través del ejemplo hispanocristiano* (Santander: Universidad de Santander, 1978) and, more recently, *La sociedad rural en la España medieval* (Madrid: Siglo XXI, 1988), see bibliography 277–97, are excellent general treatments of the topic. The next two chapters follow closely García de Cortázar's work. Although I do not agree with some of his assessments, specifically on the issue of demographic decline, I must acknowledge again my intellectual debt to his work. In addition, see Salustiano Moreta Velayos, *El monasterio de San Pedro de Cardeña: Historia de un dominio monástico castellano (902–1338)* (Salamanca: Universidad de Salamanca, 1971). For the later period, see Hilario Casado Alonso's superb *Señores, mercaderes y campesinos: La comarca de Burgos a fines de la edad media* (Valladolid: Junta de Castilla y León, 1987).

2. Geographical manuals emphasize this type of economic specialization. See Way, *A Geography of Spain and Portugal*, chs. 6, 7, 9, and 13; Ortega Varcárcel, *La transformación de un espacio rural*, 102–10, 130–56, et passim.

3. On the question of the relations between city and country see Angus MacKay, "Ciudad y campo en la Europa medieval," *Studia historica* 2, no. 2 (1984): 27–53; Carlos Estepa Díez, "El alfoz y las relaciones campo-ciudad en Castilla y León durante los siglos XII y XIII," *Studia historica* 2, no. 2 (1984): 7–26; J. Langton and G. Hopfse, *Town and Country in the Development of Early Modern Western Europe* (Historical Geography Research Series, no. 3, Nov. 1983). See also Casado Alonso, *Señores, mercaderes y campesinos*, 451–510; José Ángel García de Cortázar et al., *Organización social del espacio en la España medieval: La corona de Castilla en los siglos VIII a XV* (Barcelona: Ariel, 1985), 11–83.

4. *Viajes de extranjeros*, 1: 128, 613; 2: 406, 633, et passim.

2. Peasants and Their Masters

Long before the late Middle Ages, the lands of northern Castile had been transformed by the labor of farmers, dotted by villages where the life of peasants went on according to long-held traditions. We know the rough outline of these original patterns of settlement, dating back to the ninth and tenth centuries. And, in ways which are often peculiar to the region, we can still see, in the villages of Castile, almost unbroken links to this distant past. In the same manner, there is a broad consensus as to the juridical conditions of the Castilian peasantry from the ninth century into the early modern period and of the varied and complex ties which bound most of them to ecclesiastical and lay lords and, sometimes, to the land. Agriculture in Castile had different models from which to choose. Each of them resulted from particular geographical and climatic conditions and were shaped further by political and institutional structures. In each of the subregions comprising northern Castile, one may observe those patterns of cultivation which best suited specific local conditions, as well as ties of dependence between lords and peasants that were, often, most beneficial to those in power.

Before Castile

ROMAN SPAIN

Agriculture in Roman Spain followed the same lines of development that it did in the rest of the Roman Empire. From small and medium range settlements, often colonies of discharged legionnaires, these units of agricultural production changed over the centuries to latifundia, large expanses of land worked by countless slaves. By the first and second centuries A.D. the rural life of most of southern and eastern Spain revolved around the latifundia. Owned by the emperor, members of the imperial family, or by important patricians and senators, the land was worked first by slaves and later on, as the slave population declined, by *coloni*. When the Empire faced severe crises in the third century and central authority ebbed, many of these large estates in Hispania and elsewhere became, for all practical purposes, autonomous. Throughout the third century, but officially sanctioned by law in 332, the *coloni*, the peasants who worked the land, paid rent (*census*) or gave a share of their crop to the owner, as well as performing a series of duties under the terms of their ties to their lord. Often they were bound to the soil, their bondage to be their legacy to their children and their children's children for all time to come.

There is no need, of course, to begin telling the story in so remote a past, but my aim in doing so here is to draw the contrast between northern Castile and Mediterranean Spain. What has been briefly described applies only to specific areas of Iberia, mostly to the southern and eastern portions of the peninsula, but in a few centuries, long by the measure of men's lives but short in terms of historical development, Castilians reached the south, where they discovered rural practices and an agrarian culture that still retained strong ties to Roman rural life.[1] In the age of the Caesars, what later became Old Castile was considered far too poor, its climate too hostile to warrant large-scale cultivation of the soil. Unfortunately, we know too little about agricultural practices in the northern plain to advance any valid conclusions. It is, perhaps, not too presumptuous to suppose that in the few and scattered Roman settlements of the north, small holdings escaped being swallowed up by huge latifundia, the meager returns of these settlements constituting the best defense against the enserfment of the *coloni* which occurred throughout most of the Roman world.

Roman Iberia, that is, the areas on the southern and eastern coast, produced cereal grain, olives, and grapes. As elsewhere in the Mediterranean basin, olive groves marked the northern limit of a distinct agricultural technology and of specific patterns of cultivation. In the later Middle Ages, olive trees could be found far beyond their present habitat, but not even then did they play a role in the economy of the northern plain. From the Roman province of Baetica and other parts of the south, olive oil, wine, and grain were exported to other parts of the Empire. Irrigation, as Glick has shown, was developed and practiced with great success in areas such as Valencia and other southern regions, yet most of the cash crops were raised through dry-farming. There is no evidence that either irrigation techniques or large-scale agriculture were adopted in northern Castile in Roman times. Obviously, with the exception of a few valleys and specific climatic subregions, olive trees did not grow either on the dry plain or in the humid highlands of Cantabria or the Basque regions, nor were the vineyards, with the exception of the Rioja and areas around present-day Valladolid, as productive as those in Andalucía. Furthermore, although the northern plain is well-suited for cereal growing, its lack of outlets to the sea and of navigable rivers—the main avenues of Roman transport—made it unable to compete with the traditional breadbaskets of Rome: Sicily, North Africa, Egypt, and even the Crimea. It comes as no surprise, therefore, that Strabo judged the region to be unproductive.[2]

VISIGOTHIC SPAIN

When the Visigoths entered Spain, they inherited existing Roman agricultural models. They also brought along their own innovative agricultural techniques. Less capable, however, of maintaining the complex mechanisms of long-distance economic exchanges, the Visigoths expanded cereal production and cattle herding to the detriment of olive and wine exports. Large estates survived, now in the hands of the Visigothic royal family, nobility, the church, and those from the Hispano-Roman aristocracy who had been able to integrate into Visigothic circles. Paralleling the survival of the latifundia, however, small holdings, sometimes worked by the Visigoths themselves, also prospered. Serfs and slaves worked most of the large holdings alongside other men and women who, although not tied to the soil, were bound to the owner or lord of the land by a series of contractual and reciprocal obligations: payments of annual rent (*census*), personal services, oaths of fidelity, and similar other bonds.[3]

After the loss of the trans-Pyrenean lands to the Franks in the late fifth century, Visigothic power was centered around Toledo, south of the mountain range which today divides Old and New Castile. Visigothic jurisdiction certainly extended into the northern plain, with important settlements in the region of the Tierra de Campos, but on the whole the occupation of most of the northern meseta remained sparse and unimportant. Moreover, in the same manner in which the Romans had failed to expand their influence or control beyond a few military outposts or settlements in the north, the Visigoths also failed to tame the mountainous regions beyond the plain. In an ironic sense, Old Castile was, for most of its history, a frontier, a buffer zone, a land between a fairly civilized and agricultural south and a primitive and pastoral north. Under Romans, Visigoths, and Arabs, the frontier looked up, northward, while later on, after the rise of Christian power, it looked southward.

ISLAM AND AGRICULTURE

The Muslim invasion in 711 brought to an end Visigothic rule on the peninsula. The Arabs found in southern Spain ancient Roman models of agriculture altered only superficially by the Visigoths. With their uncanny talent for adapting to and improving on new habitats and techniques, the Arabs had a lasting impact on the rural life of southern Spain and of the whole Mediterranean basin. More than adept, however, they were the harbingers of the so-called green revolution, and their introduction of new crops—rice, sorghum and hard wheat—and of a more sophisticated level of husbandry prompted important changes in the agricultural life of all of Spain.[4]

Thomas F. Glick has magisterially summarized these changes and explained them not only in terms of economics but also as "a result of complex processes of acculturation and cultural diffusion." Different patterns of agriculture emerged slowly in al-Andalus over a period of more than four centuries. Glick summarizes them as follows:

1. the steadily increasing predominance of irrigation agriculture and consequently of crops dependent upon artificial water supply;
2. the initial association of this kind of agriculture with foci of Arab settlement in lowland river basins;
3. the relegation of other agricultural sectors (dry-farming, arboriculture, herding) mainly to non-Arab peoples;
4. an increase, over Roman times, in the economic significance of sheepherding; and
5. a corollary of all these—a progressive and general retreat of wheat cultivation, a movement to which many signs point but for which proof is inferential.

Moreover, according to Glick, the "Arabs reserved for themselves and their Neo-Muslim or Christian tenants the fertile lowlands as area for the development of hydraulic agriculture; the Berbers maintained a pastoral and arboricultural economy in the mountain; and cereal dry-farming was continued by the indigenous population whether Christian or Islamized."[5]

Clearly, many of these techniques or new crops were not easily transferable to northern Castile. For one, irrigation was seldom practiced or available in the dry meseta. Without water, rice could not be grown, nor could a good number of other crops or fruits, oranges for one, or olives, withstand the coldness and aridity of the northern plain. But hard wheat and techniques of dry farming taken north by the Mozarabic migration (Mozarabs were Christians who had accepted Muslim customs and dress) in the eighth and ninth centuries became eventually the basic foundation of northern Castilian agriculture and spearheaded its slow transformation from a grazing to a cereal-growing culture.

I have quoted Glick here to such an extent because, even though he is describing an area both chronologically and spatially outside the boundaries of this book, in later chapters we shall see the problems that Christian peasants and landlords faced when confronted with different agricultural patterns. Moreover, while in some respects the Arabs influenced the practices of northern farmers, in many others, Christian and Muslim, northern and southern models of cultivation stood in sharp contrast on the issues of what was produced and how. Nowhere is the gap more evident than in the rich variety of husbandry books we find in Muslim Spain, where Arab agronomists developed a scientific approach to land cultivation, and in the total absence of such a scientific approach to agriculture in medieval Castile, an omission which is painful even when compared with northern Europe. No wonder, therefore, that later Spanish treatises of agriculture often drew a plaintive comparison between the two agricultural models, Arab and Christian, in which the latter was compared unfavorably with the former.[6]

THE RISE OF THE CHRISTIAN KINGDOMS

With the victory of Islam in Spain, a small number of the Visigothic nobility fled into the mountains of the north, where slowly a series of small kingdoms emerged in the eighth century, first in the northern region of Asturias and later spreading to Cantabria and south into the plain of León and the Mountains of Burgos. The rural history of Asturias-León, from the eighth to the tenth centuries, remains to be written. Roughly, early Asturian-Leonese society reflected social and economic structures present in the northern mountains of Iberia from time immemorial. With emphasis on clans or specific family groups, collective ownership of the land, and strong matrilineal and kinship components, these early settlers of the plain practiced a pastoral and seminomadic type of agriculture and rather primitive forms of economic organization.[7]

Both the Visigoths (fleeing north from the Muslim invasion) and the Mozarabs (brought back to the north during the Christian raids of the eighth century or migrating voluntarily during the religious persecutions of the ninth century) introduced into mountain society more advanced agricultural techniques, as well as novel social and political patterns. Both property and work were reorganized along different lines. In ways which can only be outlined vaguely, northern mountain society turned from a collective to a mixed system of private holdings and communal ownership, the latter vested no longer on the clan but often on the village. Moreover, seminomadic grazing gave way slowly or shared a place in the economic life of early Asturian-Leonese society with a cereal-bound agriculture and the establishment of permanent settlements.

Whether this all resulted from Visigothic and Mozarabic examples or was the outcome of adaptation to plain life by mountain people, the result in Asturias-León and later in Castile was one and the same. What we see in these early centuries is "the slow process of cerealization" which took place not only on the northern meseta but throughout northern Europe, and the beginnings of that uneasy relationship between grain and livestock production. As to the lives of the peasants, according to A. Barbero and M. Vigil, the peasant revolt of 774, an event about which we know next to nothing, reveals the resistance of the free local population to their enserfment. The uprising was perhaps the response to the triumph of a small Visigothic elite and their administrative and land-tenure patterns over the indigenous pastoral-oriented population and, as such, part of the larger struggle between mountain and plain people in Spain and elsewhere—a struggle which was not resolved until the onset of the modern age. Almost everywhere else in northern Europe, agriculture and cereal production emerged victorious by the early modern period, but in the northern plain of Old Castile, the issue was not decided until the present. And in the sixteenth and seventeenth centuries the great transhumance interests almost seemed to have had the upper hand.[8]

The Asturian and Leonese kingdom, as well as the newborn county of Castile, were predominantly rural societies. Their urban centers, León, Sahagún, and others, were mostly administrative, episcopal, or military outposts. In an earlier period, cattle ranching and subsistence agriculture dominated the economic life of these fledgling political units. As Bishko and others have repeatedly pointed out, in a land opened to frequent Muslim razzias, movable goods, that is, livestock which could be moved to safety in time of trouble, was a far wiser investment than permanent farming, which could be easily destroyed. In many respects, political determinants—the constant flux and reflux of frontier warfare—had as much to do with economic structures as geography and climate.[9] With the settling of the plain and the pushing southward of the frontier, highlighted by the conquest of Toledo in 1085, the northern meseta was spared to a large extent the uncertainty of border warfare and could settle down to the development of new political, economic, and social structures. Here, with the rise of Castile as an independent kingdom, our story really begins.

Castilian Agriculture in the Late Middle Ages

EARLY DEVELOPMENTS AND THE OCCUPATION OF THE SOIL[10]

As elsewhere in the medieval West, in Old Castile the process of clearing the land, placing it under cultivation, and laying down the patterns of rural life was a long and arduous one. Unlike the general expansion of agriculture in France and England, however, Castilian peasants faced two serious problems. First, they had to deal with the proximity and immediacy of the enemy: Muslims, Aragonese, Navarrese, or Leonese, ready to strike on an ever-changing frontier. Expansion of the arable in any direction of the compass except north meant coming into contact with competing economic and political units. Second, agricultural expansion almost always dictated—because of the peculiarities of northern Castilian topography— an adaptation to new habitats, new crops, and new forms of organizing the cultivation of the soil. Thus, the social and economic structures, the tenor of peasant life which we see already formed in the late Middle Ages, resulted from a long process of trial and error, of continuous uncertainty, of successful and, at times, not so successful adaptation to new necessities and conditions. In a quiet and subdued way the peasants' taming of the vast plain was a far more heroic and lasting enterprise than all the military expeditions or conquests. It was, after all, the first form of conquest. It was also the last.

The broad details of that early occupation of the land can be summarized here in a few words. Northern Castilian society began as an offshoot of the Asturian-Leonese expansion. At its inception, Castile was a small corner in the mountains, or as the thirteenth-century *Poema de Fernán González* proudly attests:

> Estonces era Casty[e]lla un pequenno rryncón,
> Era de castellanos Montes d'Oca Mojón
> E de la otra parte. Fitero el fondón
> Moros tenian [a] Caraco en aquella sazón[11]

In spite, however, of the combative vision of the anonymous author of the *Poema*, during the early ninth century, as Cantabrians and Basques looked southward into the area of the Mountains of Burgos and beyond to the valleys of the Arlanzón, Arlanza, and Duero rivers, they saw an almost empty and untilled plain. The frequent raids of Asturian and Leonese kings in the lands of the Duero River basin during the ninth century and the punitive counterattacks by Muslim armies (we must remember that as late as the early eleventh century, as shown by the successful campaigns of al-Manṣūr [d. 1002], the Moors could strike with impunity deep into Christian territory) had turned the area of the Duero River into a half-deserted area. Whatever population lived there, and most of our evidence on these matters is inconclusive, had either been carried back to the north or had migrated on their own.

Whether the northern plain on both sides of the Duero was completely deserted or not—an issue which has led to a long debate—is essentially unimportant. What is significant, however, is that the repopulation—a better term may be settlement—of most of the northern plateau could proceed apace, disturbed only by Muslim raids but without the need to take the land by force from the powerful caliphate of Córdoba. By the time the Christians reached the Duero and moved beyond this boundary in the early part of the tenth century, they had behind them almost a century of southward movement and settlement in the region north of the Arlanza River. In the tenth century the first Christian enclaves beyond the Duero were swept by al-Manṣūr campaigns, but the Muslims did not occupy the area. Once the power of Córdoba waned, to be replaced by the factional disputes of the kingdoms of *taifas*, the Christians were well poised for the resettlement of towns north of the Central Sierras and the eventual conquest of Toledo in 1085.[12]

As Glick has pointed out, crossing the mountain passes southward meant also the crossing of an important ecological barrier. With the swift transformation of the landscape, these early settlers of northern Castile had to adapt to Mediterranean agricultural techniques and diet, to a civilization of cereal and wine. Left behind, though certainly not always completely, was a life dependent on livestock, dairy farming, and the growing and tending of fruit trees. While the early inhabitants of northern Castile and their descendants in the late Middle Ages understood and adapted to the dry farming of cereals and the tending of vineyards, they could not always forget the economic and cultural patterns of their ancestral mountain habitats. Moreover, the uncertainty of the first centuries of settlement had made livestock an attractive form of investment.

This combination of agricultural pursuits and livestock ranching remained a constant of Castilian medieval economy, but it was most evident in those transitional zones between mountain and plain, between one ecology and another, between two cultures, two different types of rural life. The village in northern Castile where my father's cousins still till the soil in ways not unlike those of his ancestors a millennium ago—their plows, fashioned after the ancient Roman model, are still pulled by cows, and they still adhere to a biannual rotation of fields—is a good example of that uneasy compromise between two different models of agriculture. There, as it usually happens in northern portions of Old Castile, the economic patterns of Atlantic Europe mix with those of the Mediterranean in an uneasy compromise dictated by necessity.

The Status of the Peasants and the Occupation of the Soil Until 1200

The great period of reconquest that ended in the mid-thirteenth century, the settlement of the land, and the occupation or foundation of towns also had important consequences for the juridical status of peasants.[13] Beginning with the early ninth-century mountain people from Cantabria, the Basque region as well as smaller migrations from the south (Mozarab) began to occupy the region north of Burgos and later on to settle on the plain. In these first stages of the occupation of the soil, the opening of new lands for cultivation was often carried out by private individuals or, to be more accurate, by a family or groups of families joined by ties of kinship. This cultivation of lands that were not only empty but that also were not claimed by either Muslim or Christian lords is the process known in Spanish history as *pressura* (also *scalio-ruptura*).[14] Although modern concepts of personal liberty and individual freedom have little or nothing to do with medieval ones, the first settlers of mountain and plain in northern Castile were free men, in that peculiar sense in which such terms can be used in the Middle Ages.

Although the inception of rural life on the northern plains differed from the expansion of the arable in France or England, this unofficial appropriation of the land without lordly sanction was soon followed by the sponsored—both by ecclesiastical and lay lords—repopulation and settlement of rural villages and towns. Most noticeable in this expansion from the north to all other points of the compass but mostly southward was the church. Monastic foundations in the ninth and tenth centuries were the vanguard of rural settlements, and they are the telling signs of how monasteries followed but, more often than not, led in the slow taming of the plain.[15] To private and monastic efforts to populate the land, moreover, one must add those of counts and other lords. Castles and strongholds rose in the mountains of Burgos and on the plain, and indeed many Castilian towns could trace their origins to these early fortifications. These castles stood as protection against Muslim raids or to overlook ancient highways. Not only did they provide the name for the region, but they also tell us about the ways in which the powerful made their presence felt. The activities of private and monastic settlers were at times enhanced, but, more often than not, were increasingly regulated and/or thwarted by lordly ambitions. Either as promoters of repopulation or as beneficiaries of it, the early counts and magnates of Old Castile were able to impose on the land and on the peasants who tilled the soil social, economic, political, and juridical structures that were beneficial to their interests. In crude terms, they accomplished this because of their military functions and naked force, but the legal expressions of their powers were the numerous charters of foundations (*cartas de población, fueros*.) These legal instruments often promoted repopulation of the countryside and towns under terms that were more favorable than lordly settlements elsewhere in the West; but whether generous or not, these early *fueros* attested to the legality of existing social and political hierarchies, to the authority of the lords.[16]

At this stage of the repopulation (late ninth and early tenth century), the nature of the Castilian topography, the movement from mountain to plain, also altered the patterns of settlement and repopulation and the role that lords played in them. While the mountain economy could support only a small number of inhabitants, and thus we find a large number of small hamlets spread through the northern valleys, the immensity and emptiness of the plain required spatial distance. Human settlement was restricted to places with water, always easily available in the northern mountains but not so on the plain. The *Becerro de behetrías* again shows this pattern quite vividly. For while on the one hand the *merindades* (fiscal and administrative units) of Castilla la Vieja, Asturias de Santillana, and most parts of Aguilar de Campóo counted with many localities, those on the plain did not. Though the *Becerro* was compiled shortly after the mid-fourteenth century as a census of royal, monastic, and seignorial rights, most of the places listed in it dated their foundations to a much earlier period. If at all, the *Becerro* reflected the partial demise of that world rather than new conditions.

The so-called Reconquest did not stop, of course, with the occupation of Castile north of the Duero. Partly because of military and political necessity, partly because of the dearth of human resources—a constant problem throughout the history of Castile—by the late eleventh and early twelfth centuries, the settlement of newly conquered lands came more and more to be under the aegis of large *concejos* (municipal councils). Ávila and Segovia on the edge of the northern plain, their respective jurisdictions reaching south of the Central Sierras, are the best examples of the new ways to occupy the land. Granted large *alfoces* (hinterlands) and extensive jurisdictions in the surrounding countryside, these large municipal councils south of the Duero could put on the field formidable military contingents, both mounted as well as infantry (*caballeros* and *peones*), to defend and, as the years went by, to advance the expansionist policies of Castilian kings. They also marked the slow and inexorable progression from private and humble to monastic, to lordly, and finally to royal control, which marked the centralizing tendencies of the Castilian monarchy.[17]

Although already beyond the geographical boundaries of this book, one final stage in the Christian occupation of the soil still lay south of the Central Sierras and was of crucial importance for the subsequent course of northern agriculture. When, after the decisive Christian victory at Las Navas de Tolosa (1212), the Christian armies swept south, they conquered the great urban centers of al-Andalus (Córdoba, 1236; Jaén, 1246; Seville, 1248; Jerez, 1253). The Moors were expelled, first from the cities, and, after the Mudejar rebellion (1264–66), also from the land. Ferdinand III (1217–52) and, above all, his son Alfonso X (1252–84) divided the newly conquered territories among their subjects. These partitions or *repartimientos* took two forms. First, the king bestowed large estates on himself, members of his household, magnates, military orders, bishops, cathedral chapters, and monasteries. These large grants continued in the south the long-standing tradition of the Roman latifundia and served partly as the foundation for Andalusi agrarian structures to this day. The other *repartimiento* was more limited in scope. The king granted urban dwellings and small landed estates, olive groves, and so on to Christians from the north (also to Jews and foreigners) as a way of promoting the repopulation of the now deserted southern cities and their surrounding countryside.[18] Later I will look closely into the problems created, in both Old and New Castile, by this sudden need to adapt to a different climate and topography, to different and more sophisticated ways of working the land.

Castilian Agriculture in the Thirteenth and Fourteenth Centuries

LEGAL STATUS AND OBLIGATIONS OF THE PEASANTRY

As we reach the late Middle Ages, the typology of the juridical status of the Castilian peasantry somewhat comes apart. García de Valdeavellano has already summarized brilliantly this range of social categories and their evolution over time in medieval Castile and in the rest of the peninsula. Along the spectrum we find small freeholders, those whose "liberty" was somewhat restricted, as well as peasants living under that peculiar Castilian institution known as the *behetría* (see below). There is no need to go over this maze of legal definitions which often, I fear, tell us very little about the real and diverse conditions that existed, and under which men and women lived in the villages and hamlets of northern medieval Castile. If they are to this date a focus for discussion among Castilian historians, it is because the freedom or lack of freedom of the Castilian peasantry is part of the present debate on the feudal or nonfeudal nature of Castilian society, a debate that has been most wonderfully deflated by Peter Linehan.[19] More useful, perhaps, is the effort to place the discussion of the juridical conditions of Castilian peasants, their freedom or lack of it, in a comparative context. Fortunately, Paul Freedman's extraordinary book *The Origins of Peasant Servitude in Medieval Catalonia* provides an excellent case study of the development and imposition of serfdom on Catalonian peasants. Geographically closer than France and England, lords and peasants in Old Catalonia also had the lure of the frontier to contend with. In both Castile and Catalonia lords attempted to impose their power and bind peasants to the soil. They failed to do so fully in the former but succeeded quite well in the latter. The explanations of why this was so are to be found in Freedman's book and in the following chapters. They are complex indeed. But throughout this discussion, one must keep Freedman's findings as a reminder that somewhat similar conditions in both Castile and Catalonia eventually led to quite different outcomes.[20]

This is even more critical since the terminology used to describe conditions north of the Pyrenees or in Catalonia itself does not always help us understand the Castilian peculiarities. For example, the word *vasallo* (vassal), so clearly identified with the private agreements that bound free men-at-arms, came to be used in late medieval Castile indiscriminately. Thus, a great and powerful magnate was a *vasallo* but so was a humble peasant burdened by a myriad of manorial dues. More useful to us than antiquated typologies or terms borrowed from English or French social history are the definitions found in thirteenth- and fourteenth-century fiscal documents. They already provide us with glimpses into the conditions of the peasants. Here one must, at the risk of redundancy, emphasize how much peasants' rights and obligations differed from region to region, from village to village within each particular area, and finally within each individual locality. The villages of the valley of Zamanzas, one of which I have mentioned before—Gallejones, Bascones, Tudanca, and others—date back to the beginnings of Castile. Their names rarely appeared in the extant documentation of the late Middle Ages. We know from the *Becerro de behetrías* (1352) that the men and women in the valley of Zamanzas and elsewhere in northern Castile lived and toiled under a wide ranging set of obligations to their kings and to their secular and ecclesiastical lords. Those who inhabited the hamlets and villages of Zamanzas were either *solariegos* or men of *behetrías*.[21]

It was not only, however, where the peasants lived that was significant, but more importantly, whose lands they worked. In the *Becerro* such categories are already provided, and though it dates from 1351–52, this fiscal census reflected centuries of peasant lives. In medieval Castile, the peasants lived and toiled in lands that were broadly classified as *realengo* (royal), *abadengo* (ecclesiastic), *señorio* (seignorial), and *behetría* (also seignorial but with different obligations).[22] Joining these categories of peasants, as a continuous link between Castilian past and present, was the village.

THE VILLAGE COMMUNITY

In the next chapter we will look more closely at how the land was cultivated, by whom, and under what conditions. For now, however, before attempting to present a typology of peasant life, I wish to present some account of village life and organization.[23] We can see only glimpses of this life emerging unexpectedly in the documentation and then, as suddenly, disappearing from view.

In times of trouble or litigation with their ecclesiastical and secular lords, the inhabitants of villages and rural hamlets can be seen standing as one. At the ringing of the church bells, the pettynoblemen, the curate, and those peasants who "owned" a household and property came to the village church or to the opening in front of the church door to voice their opinions and to vote on the pressing issues of the day. In 1340 the *concejo* (village council) of Matute, "clerics, lay brothers, noblemen and peasants, meeting at the Church of San Román . . . at the ringing of bells as it was the usage and custom" ("clerigos e legos, fijosdalgo e labradores, ayuntados dentro en la iglesia de San Román . . . a campana tañida según el uso y costumbre") came together to complain about the troubles in the region to their lord, the abbess of the monastery of the Asunción in Cañas.[24] Similar examples of the participation of clerics and local noblemen in village life, as well as of its organization as a corporate body, come from every corner of northern Castile.

In litigation after litigation, it is the *concejo*, the rural council, which speaks with one voice in its attempt to protect itself and its members from excessive demands or abuses, or, at times, when it wished to legalize its own encroachment. Often we can see that it must have amounted to the entire male population of the village or, at least of those who mattered in the community, being listed as present, speaking as one in the defense of their privileges. Thus in 1343 when the chapter and the rural council of Albelda (really a small town) agreed on the dues to be paid by all the inhabitants of the village for the right of passage through lands of the chapter, twenty-eight men, clerics, village officials, squires, *fijosdalgo* (lower nobility, in present Spanish, *hidalgo*), blacksmiths, butchers, and peasants gathered together in the chapel of Saint Catherine to ratify the agreement as valid. Similarly, in 1323, the rural council of Santa Coloma, twelve men in all, signed an agreement with the prior of the monastery of Santa María de Nájera, which bound the entire village to build a wall around Santa Coloma and to acknowledge themselves as "vassals" of the monastery. Sometimes, as was the case in 1316, almost the entire village had to consent to the selling of communal property. The rural council of Frontada, "good men, clerics, and lay brothers" (three clerics, four lay brothers, eighteen good men [one of them an *escudero*, or squire]), sold a mill to the monastery of Santa María la Real de Aguilar de Campóo. But in Frontada there were other peasants who worked and lived on lands belonging to the monastery. In an earlier census of property (c. 1300), fourteen units of taxation or farms were worked by twelve peasants (seven males and five females) with their names listed next to their payments. This evidence provides us with yet another lower level of the peasantry with little say in the affairs of the village community.[25]

In the communal world of the Castilian peasantry, some were more equal than others: women, newcomers, those who lived by hiring themselves to others, were not called by the ringing of bells to make decisions for all. The apparent leveling structure of rural communities was indeed a mirage, and the rigid social hierarchies that we find in northern Castilian cities also existed in the countryside. Within these villages, as was the case elsewhere in the West, social gradations and social distinctions, based essentially on property or easy access to land, led to the hierarchization of political and economic power at the village level. These distinctions, sharpening with the economic downturn of the thirteenth and fourteenth centuries, were made more onerous by the authority of the village council to sell property or to assign work. Moreover, as urban oligarchs began to purchase houses and land in the countryside around the cities, they acquired not only property but also rights to village property. On 9 May 1301, Blasco Blázquez, about whom we will hear a great deal more later, bought *heredamientos*, that is, lands, houses, gardens, meadows, and flax fields, in Cornejuelos (Corneios) from Menga Andrés. Included in the sale were also lands in the pasture and commons of the village. Within the communal structure of the village, some shared more than others, and some not at all.[26]

The village was the link that bound together all of northern Castile. The village institutional and social structures did not differ very much, regardless of types of lordship or geographical location. Surely, mountain villages were smaller than those of the plain; what peasants planted varied somewhat from place to place. Moreover, many villages had within their boundaries men and women who held lands from different lords, from ecclesiastical establishments, from the king, so that even within one single village the range of duties and payments varied considerably. Thus, half of the village of Caorbio paid its dues to a nobleman, one-half to the monastery of Santa María la Real de Aguilar de Campóo, while in the village of Cernera, three-quarters of the inhabitants paid dues to Don Tello, altogether 108 *maravedíes* (*mrs.*), while one-quarter of the villagers paid eight *celemines* of grain (one-half wheat, one-half barley) to the monastery of Santa María la Real de Aguilar de Campóo.[27] (For coins and units of measure and weight, see Appendix 2.) And yet, for all the diversity and the range of their freedoms, almost all the villagers, with some notable exceptions, depended on and paid to (whether more or less) the king, the lords, or the ecclesiastical establishments.

THE LIVES OF PEASANTS

One of the ways in which we can come face to face with some segments of the peasantry is through their economic activities, that is, when they either sold or bought property. In Chapter 5, I examine the market for land in northern Castile in greater detail, but here the records of land transactions allow us to see another level of individual peasants. Such is the case in the purchases made by Blasco Blázquez, a leading citizen of Ávila, for more than a quarter of a century. Since most of his acquisitions of land were circumscribed to two villages near Ávila, Serranos de Avianos, and Cornejuelos (the latter, in fact, within the parish of Serranos de Avianos itself), one can also observe the process by which village lands, originally fragmented into a large number of freeholders, became the property of one man or one family and, through the terms of Blasco's will, of the cathedral chapter.

Altogether more than seventy-five villagers are mentioned in the documents, though on three or four occasions we can be almost certain that some peasants participated in several transactions. Such was the case of Pedro Domingo *el viejo*, who sold two pieces of land in Serranos de Avianos in 1284 for 60 *mrs.* and, a year later, a house with stables, maslin fields, *herrén*, five hours of usufruct in the old mill, a garden, and other properties in the same locality for 120 *mrs.* Blasco Blázquez's purchases for a period of eighteen years, from 1284 to 1302 (twenty-five purchases in Cornejuelos and twenty-four purchases in Serranos de Avianos) reveal a lower level of the social stratum from that of the well-to-do landholders. The prices of most of the transactions were relatively small, pointing to the modest size of the lands exchanged, albeit that land in Ávila, poor as it was, really cost a great deal. The bulk of these agreements (thirty-nine out of forty-nine) amounted to 300 *mrs.* or less (twenty-nine out of forty-nine less than 200 *mrs.*), with the highest reaching only 600 *mrs.* Often several brothers and sisters sold lands which they had inherited from their parents, as Menga Andrés did in 1301 in her name and that of her brothers and sisters. In most cases the documents state that the sellers are relinquishing *todo*, everything they had, in either Serranos de Avianos or Cornejuelos in return for the purchase price, and, as often, they held the lands as *heredades*—that is, they held the land outright. Did these peasants own property elsewhere in the region of Ávila? Did they remain in the land as tenants? We cannot say, for the documents do not provide us with enough information, but in 1308 (Blasco Blázquez died in 1307) Blasco's properties in Serranos de Avianos, Cornejuelos, and El Villar were assessed at 30,000 *mrs.*, indicating land under cultivation and producing a substantial return. And yet the original investment, at least, in the first two of the aforementioned villages had not reached 10,000 *mrs.*[28]

The checkered history of the small village of Madrigal del Monte also allows us to see the economic activities of individual peasants, as well as the complexities of rights and jurisdictions present in rural Castile and the uneasy coexistence of freeholding with a range of seignorial obligations. A village located in the *merindad* of Candemuño, today a few kilometers west of the road between Burgos and Lerma, Madrigal del Monte dates as a recognizable place from the early repopulation of the countryside north of the Arlanza River. The first documentary mention occurs in 1027 when Doña Esta and Doña Cara donated their possessions in Cogollo and Madrigal del Monte to the countess Doña Urraca. Sometime afterward the village passed from seignorial to ecclesiastic jurisdiction, that is, from *señorío* to *abadengo*, probably through a comital donation no longer extant. By 1168 the bishop of Burgos, Don Pedro, granted a charter (*fuero*) to the inhabitants of Madrigal del Monte.

This particular *fuero*, which was not unlike those granted to similar villages in the area, showed the same liberal provisions enjoyed by new settlements in the plain. It indicates, perhaps, that only in the very recent past the village had been settled as a juridical entity. The inhabitants of Madrigal, "clerics, laymen, and women," were exempted from a series of manorial dues, including *manneriam* (*mañería*), *fossaderam* (*fonsado*) (see Appendix I), as well as the traditional annual obligation to agricultural labor (*sernas*). Additional rights and obligations were also granted, including the right of the villagers, with the bishop's approval, to select the *juez* (judge) and *alcalde* (a judicial official) of Madrigal del Monte. In return, the bishop was to receive a payment in *infurción* (see Appendix I) of one *almud* of wheat, two of barley, three *octavillas* of wine, "et singular anetes duorum dentium aut singulos tocinos bonos medianos." By 1264, while the village remained under ecclesiastical jurisdiction, it had passed from the bishop to the chapter most probably because, as was common in late medieval Castile, one of the bishops of Burgos had donated it to the cathedral chapter. That year the chapter and the citizens of Madrigal del Monte, "vassals of the said chapter," settled a litigation over land rights with the inhabitants of the village of Rubiales and their lord, the abbot of Covarrubias.

Sixty-two years later Pedro Pérez, a citizen of Burgos, was involved in a series of modest transactions in Madrigal del Monte. Between 1324 and 1326 Pedro bought six vineyards, six pieces of land (the size of either vineyards or lands cannot be determined), and a house in the village. Altogether we can identify sixteen sellers, ten of them by name. Nine of them are identified in the documents as *vecinos* or citizens of Madrigal, though the others might have also been neighbors of Madrigal. One was a woman, Doña María, *vecina de* Madrigal; another, Martín Sánchez, was a cleric. Of the sixteen sellers, two—Doña María and Don Gil, *vecino de* Madrigal del Monte—are identified by the descriptives *don* and *doña*, as well as by being *vecinos*, an indication perhaps of their social status in the village. Altogether Pedro Pérez paid only 713 *mrs.* for all the property, a very modest sum indeed which either indicates that the vineyards and lands purchased were exceedingly small or that the price of land in Madrigal del Monte was very low. The highest price paid for a vineyard was 90 *mrs.*, and in one case six men sold a vineyard to Pedro for a paltry 38 *mrs.* As to land, the highest price paid was 123 *mrs.*, and 22 *mrs.* was the highest price paid for a house.

Besides providing us with a view of prices and of the economic resources of Madrigal del Monte, these transactions allow us to see, once again, a complex web of conflicting jurisdiction, rights of properties, and dues. Indeed, a few years later (1332), Pedro Pérez, jointly with his children and a certain Juan Sánchez, sold some of his *heredades* (land that he held outright) to Simón González, a citizen of Burgos, for 160 *mrs*. And yet we know that in 1326, the same year that Pedro Pérez was buying property in Madrigal del Monte, the cathedral chapter of Burgos was renting the income of the village to Gonzalo González, former teacher of King Alfonso XI, treasurer of the chapter of Salamanca, and canon of the cathedral of Burgos.

Who, then, owned what and under what terms? In 1352, the village appears in the *Becerro de behetrías* as still belonging to the chapter and paying 180 *mrs*. in *martiniega* to the king. (For tax terms see Appendix I.) To its lord, the chapter, the villagers paid 60 *mrs*. in *martiniega* and in *infurción*, one *fanega* of bread (half wheat, half barley) per team of oxen. (For measures and weights see Appendix II.) Those with only one ox paid half a *fanega* and widows paid a hen.[29] We are still left with a confused picture as to rights of jurisdiction, property, and peasants' duties. We can also see the changes that had taken place in the payments to the titular lord of the village and also in the dues paid for *infurción* in 1352 as compared to those that had been demanded by the bishop in 1168. The sellers of vineyards and lands in Madrigal del Monte in the period 1324–33 reveal to us once again that small group of free landowners. Of them, Martín Sánchez, the cleric mentioned above, lived in Quintanilla Fumiente, where he was the priest, and Pedro Pérez, when he sold property there in 1333, lived in Burgos, but we must assume that most of the other sellers lived in Madrigal.

One can also look briefly at the case of Miguel Pérez (Peres), *vecino* (citizen of the village) and inhabitant of Oter de Herreros, a village in Segovia's countryside. Miguel Santamaría has made a careful study of Miguel Pérez's purchases in the village between 30 October 1341 and 24 November 1358. Between 1341 and 1351, either alone or with his wife, Doña Inés, Miguel purchased lands, vineyards, and flax fields (fourteen transactions in all) for a total of 843 *mrs*. For the next seven years, his name does not appear in the extant documentation until 1358 when together with nine other people, also neighbors of Oter de Herreros, they purchased lands in the village for 1,500 *mrs*. Between buyers and sellers we have the names of fifty-eight men and women, all of them, except one (a citizen of Segovia), inhabitants of Oter de Herreros or of surrounding villages. This provides us with a rough indication of the population of Oter de Herreros, which must have had two hundred people, a large village when compared to the hamlets of the northern mountains. Moreover, the properties bought and sold, with the exception of the 1358 purchase, were small units, reflecting the fragmentation of most of the Castilian countryside.[30]

These repetitive examples provide firm evidence of the existence of a large, although often anonymous, free landholding population, even in villages such as Madrigal del Monte, theoretically under monastic jurisdiction. Those categories which divided northern Castile into royal, seignorial, and ecclesiastic lands were, in the late Middle Ages, often ephemeral and unstable. For while lordship of the land implied that the peasants owed a whole range of payments and sometimes even labor to the lord, in practice, jurisdiction and rights were often wrested or sold outright without the acquiescence of the lord. The hundreds of late thirteenth- and early fourteenth-century rental or sale agreements (mostly monastic), which forbade peasants from selling or subletting the land to anyone who was not also a vassal of the same lord but, especially, to members of the nobility, gives witness to that swift and violent process by which monastic lands and even those within the royal domain itself were acquired by the nobility and the urban patriciate. Indeed, in spite of all the precautions and royal admonitions, land moved—sometimes by force, other times by greed—from one lordly jurisdiction to another.[31]

One must consider something else when addressing this issue of the free movement of land, for here it serves as a further reminder of the fluidity of the Castilian peasantry even in an age of crisis. I refer to the fragmentation of property. To what extent ownership and/or usufruct were fragmented is difficult to discern from the available documentation, but there is ample evidence of men and women who held, bought, or sold very small pieces of property or rights of usage. Thus, in 1303 María Domingo de Gordón sold a small piece in a vineyard to Pascual Sánchez, the beadle of the church of San Salvador of Ávila, for a paltry 10 *mrs.*, while in 1332 a planted row in a garden (*huerto*) sold for a mere 6½ *mrs.* There are hundreds of similar examples which point to the many men and women in northern Castile who, regardless of their often limited resources and uncertain economic status, owned or held some piece of property. This was most important, of course, in a society where to own something was the most secure way to enhance one's social status.[32]

Peasants of *Realengo*, *Abadengo*, and *Señorio*: Men and Women of *Behetrías*

MEN AND WOMEN IN LANDS OF *REALENGO* AND *ABADENGO*

Peasants living in lands of *realengo* (royal lands) were for all practical purposes proprietors of their holdings, with the right to sell, buy, will or dispose of their lands and houses—or perhaps more accurately, of their usufruct over lands and houses—as they saw fit. Some restrictions, also appearing in the exchanges of monastic lands, can be found in the extant documentation. These were bans in the selling of land to magnates or monasteries or, in the case of monastic holdings (*abadengos*), of selling or renting to secular lords, but these prohibitions were often disregarded. Such efforts at limiting transfers of property and, thus, curtailing peasant rights over the lands they worked reflected the rapid alienation of royal and monastic domains in favor of the nobility, and the often failed attempts of both king and church to redress these illegal appropriations.

Those peasants working royal and municipal lands (under the crown's jurisdiction) paid dues to the king. In Appendix I we can see the range of taxes that were, at least in theory, collected by the crown. As pointed out earlier, however, each village had its own peculiar set of payments, the outcome of ancient local customs, and they differed widely from place to place. For example, the inhabitants of Castiel Pedroso (Castillo-Pedroso in the present-day province of Santander) in the *merindad* of Asturias de Santillana (in the northern mountains) was a village of *realengo*. It contributed to the crown thirty-six *heminas* of bread (twenty of *escanda* [spelt wheat] and sixteen of barley) plus 2 *sueldos* (*ss.*) for each *solar* or unit of cultivation and 2 *ss.* and 2 *coronados* (type of coin) for each hearth. In addition, the village as a whole paid 28 *mrs.* each year in *martiniega*, plus *servicios*, *moneda*, and *yantar* to the *adelantado* (a royal official) and to the *merino*. Within the same *merindad*, the village of Llerena paid 18 *mrs.* annually in *martiniega* and forty *heminas* (twenty spelt wheat, twenty barley) plus 2 *coronados* for each hearth. Moreover, they owed *servicios* and *moneda* whenever voted by the Cortes.[33] Although both villages had what seemed heavy burdens to bear, the inhabitants of Llerena bore a lesser load than those of Castillo-Pedroso. We do not know how many inhabitants these villages had in the mid-fourteenth century when this information was collected, but certainly the account of their dues reflected an earlier and more prosperous time and was, most probably, hardly fitting to the depressed conditions of the latter Middle Ages.

Farther south, in the *merindad* of Santo Domingo de Silos, the village of Monte Negro (today Montenegro de Cameros, province of Soria) paid 733⅓ *mrs.* in *martiniega* each year, 86⅓ *mrs.* for *yantar* and, in addition, *moneda, servicio,* and *fonsadera.* The exactions on Montenegro's inhabitants were heavy, though its location near one of the Mesta routes and, thus, part of the profitable transhumance may help explain its high rate of taxation. In the *merindad* of Santo Domingo of Silos, Montenegro and seven other villages were the only ones listed in the *Becerro* which appeared to be exclusively under royal jurisdiction. This is a rather reduced figure, although one must point out that the *Becerro* is incomplete as far as this *merindad* was concerned and did not include the royal town of Santo Domingo of Silos itself and its *alfoz.* Furthermore, although the crown controlled only eight out of the 129 villages listed for the *merindad* of Santo Domingo, it collected dues, mostly *moneda* and *servicios,* in all the villages of the *merindad.* Altogether these eight villages, Montenegro and the seven others, paid around 4,186 *mrs.* in *martiniega,* 595 *mrs.,* 3 *dineros (ds)*. in *yantar,* and 41⅓ *mrs.* in *escribanía* (the right to name the local scribe). Four of the eight villages also contributed *moneda, servicios,* and *fonsadera.*[34]

Unlike most northern locations, that is, villages that dated from the earlier stages of the Reconquest and which, perhaps, reflecting a more ancient economic order, made their payments in kind, those of the plain did so mostly in cash. And here the distinction was not an economic one— transhumance versus agriculture—for indeed westward, in the cereal-growing *merindades* of Valladolid and Carrión, most of the villages also made their payments in specie. Perhaps in those later settlements, dating from the early eleventh century and afterward, the counts and kings of Castile had greater success in insisting that annual taxes, such as the *martiniega,* were to be paid in cash. Whether or not it benefited the peasants is hard to say. The discernible patterns seem to be a mixture of individual (each *solar,* each hearth) and collective payment in the older and smaller mountain villages, and collective money payments by the more recent and larger villages of the meseta. At least, these peasants working the land under royal jurisdiction had to suffer only under the crown's demands—exactions which, it must be added, had been in many cases waived or commuted. These villages, therefore, did not have to pay the dual burden of royal and lordly obligations.

MEN AND WOMEN OF *BEHETRÍAS*

The ties of reciprocity between lord and peasant which existed in medieval northern Castile sometimes led to a peculiar institution known as *behetría* (or, in the plural form, *behetrías*), and to a unique relationship between the men and women of *behetrías* and their lords. In the simplest terms, the men of *behetrías* (*benefactoría*) freely selected their lords. They did this either from sea to sea (*de mar a mar*), that is, from any lord in the land, or more often in the late Middle Ages, from a specific family, the so-called *behetrías de linaje* (of a specific lineage). In theory, according to Claudio Sánchez Albornoz, the men of *behetrías* could change their lords as many as seven times in one day if the relations proved to be unsatisfactory.

I have yet to find any documentary evidence in the late Middle Ages that these men and women could really exercise their theoretical rights to change lords. The origins of these special agreements went back probably to the early centuries of the repopulation, when the dispersion of agricultural settlements and the poverty of demographic resources in the northernmost part of Castile (the result of the occupation of the Duero River valley) allowed free peasants to enter into advantageous pacts of *commendation* (*encomendación*) with the lords of the region.[35] The arrangements were hereditary, and, by the mid-thirteenth century, we find in the *Becerro* a large number of peasants holding on, at least theoretically, to the same privileges gained by their ancestors almost four centuries before. Free men, yet owing certain seignorial dues to their lords, these men and women occupied, according to Moxó, a transitional stage between the free landholding peasants working royal lands and the free peasants who toiled in seignorial or monastic holdings under heavier fiscal and, at times, even semiservile conditions. As we have seen, however, those distinctions often did not make a great deal of difference, nor for that matter did they for the men and women of *behetrías*. In reality, the late thirteenth and fourteenth centuries saw a progressive deterioration of their rights, and by the next century there was little difference between the men of *behetrías* and those peasants, the so-called *solariegos*, holding land from secular lords.[36]

According to Ferrari, one of the first scholars to undertake a study (albeit one almost impossible to comprehend) of the *Libro becerro de behetrías*, there were around 2,600 localities listed in the *Becerro*. Of those, the census provided information on peasant dues for 2,090 villages or hamlets. One-third of the latter number were villages under the jurisdiction of secular lords, and one-fifth or 418 villages were exclusively places of *behetría*. In addition, one-sixth or around 348 locations were under mixed seignorial and *behetría* jurisdiction. Sánchez Albornoz, on the other hand, has calculated the number of *behetrías* in northern Castile to be 628.[37] Regardless of the exact number of *behetrías*, it is clear that this type of arrangement was of considerable importance, at least in a legal if not a practical sense, for

TABLE 2.1.   Types of Lordship in the
Merindad of Liébana-Pernia.

Number of places listed	129
Ecclesiastical lordships	28
Seignorial lordships	62
Behetrías	2
Mixed	
Seignorial/ecclesiastic	32
Royal/seignorial	1
Behetrías/seignorial/eccles.	3
Behetrías/seignorial	1

Source: Becerro, vol. 1: 551–601.

defining relations between lord and peasants and between the peasants and the land.

In Gonzalo Martínez Díez's excellent edition of the *Becerro*, 2,402 villages, hamlets, towns, and cities are accounted for, though again not all the existing villages in each of the *merindades* listed in the *Becerro* are included. In Table 2.1 we can see the breakdown of at least one *merindad*.[38] In the *merindad* of Liébana-Pernia, most of the villages lay under seignorial lordship. In fact, Don Tello, the bastard son of Alfonso XI, held either full or part lordship in 76 of the 129 villages and places in this *merindad*. Most of the other villages were under the lordship of Fernán García Duque and his family. The number of *behetrías* included in this mountainous *merindad* was indeed insignificant. Clearly, in Liébana-Pernia, as the evidence elsewhere also shows, lordship was concentrated in the hands of a few great men, while ecclesiastical and, above all, royal jurisdictions were on the wane.

Not unlike under ecclesiastical or royal lordships, what these men and women of *behetrías* owed the king and/or their lords changed from one place to another. In 1352, the village of the Puebla (today La Puebla de Valdavia in Palencia and formerly of the *merindad* of Saldaña) was a *behetría* under the dual jurisdiction of John (Juan) Rodríguez de Cisneros, a local nobleman, and the powerful Don Nuño, lord of Vizcaya. The inhabitants paid 120 *mrs.* annually to the king in *martiniega*, as well as *moneda* and *servicios*, whenever voted by the Cortes, but they were exempted from *yantar* (purveyance) and *fonsadera*. In addition, each peasant of Puebla paid 6 *mrs.* a year to Don Nuño and to John Rodríguez, "the lord whose vassals they are," as well as 1 *mr.* a year in *infurción*. We can compare these payments to those made by the men of *behetría* of the village of Villa Abasta (in the modern province of Palencia) in the same *merindad* to the same two aforementioned lords. The king received 90 *mrs.* in *martiniega*, and also *moneda* and *servicios*, while Don Nuño received 6 *mrs.* annually from each vassal and John Rodríguez received a chicken in *infurción*.[39]

In Table 2.2, which details the dues collected by John Rodríguez in different *behetrías*, we can see the variations in the dues which peasants paid to their lords. John Rodríguez de Cisneros held seignorial rights in eighty-nine lordships or *behetrías* spread throughout northern Castile. Table 2.2 also shows what he received in villages of three of the *merindades*.

A more striking contrast can be observed in other parts of northern Castile. Northeast of Palencia, in the *merindad* of Castilla la Vieja (in the southern part of the actual province of Santander and northern area of Burgos), the seignorial obligations of the men and women of *behetrías* ranged from almost nothing to stifling dues. The peasants of Anero (Santander), to offer just a few examples, paid *moneda* and *servicio* to the king whenever voted by the Cortes and nothing to their lords, Pero González de Aguero and Ruy Martínez de Solarzén, except to recognize their lordship. Just a few miles from Anero, the men and women of Pontones, a *behetría* under the same lordship as Anero, also paid *moneda* and *servicio* to the king, but to their "natural" lords, the peasants owed in *nuncio* (mortmain) an ox, or a cow, or 24 *mrs.*, and in *mañería* (dues paid when the peasant died without issue) all their belongings went to the lord. Moreover, for Martinmas, whenever there was a *monte* (cutting of wood), each inhabitant of Pontones gave a piece of bacon, thirty loaves of bread, two hens, and one *cuarta* of barley; each of those who used the lords' oxen (animals) paid one *celemín* of barley, plus the obligation to feed the lords' men when they came to take back the oxen.[40] These dues contrast sharply with the relative freedom from dues of the men and women of Anero and others elsewhere in Castile. We witness here a wide range of possibilities, each village following specific local conditions that were well grounded in ancient customs and practices.

MEN AND WOMEN OF *SEÑORÍOS*

Solariegos is the name given in the medieval documentation to those peasants who lived on and worked the lands (*solares*) of others. With rights of mobility, these non-noble vassals (the documents of the period described them as *vasallos*) paid certain seignorial dues to their ecclesiastic or secular lords—for here, once again, the distinction between lands of *abadengo*

TABLE 2.2. Partial Listing of John Rodríguez's Rights.

Village	Dues
Merindad *of Monzón*	
Villa Miedma (*behetría*)	Each peasant paid 6 *mrs.*, 2 *coronados*; and per team of oxen, 2 *celemines* (1 wheat, 1 barley)
Villa Taud (*behetría*)	Each peasant paid 6 *mrs.*; and per team of oxen, 8 *celemines* wheat, 4 *ss.*; one ox, 4 *celemines*, 2 *ss.*; no animals, 2 *celemines*, 1 *s.*
Villa Serrazino (*behetría*)	Each peasant paid 6 *mrs.*; and per team of oxen, 2 *mrs.*; one ox, 1 *mr.*; no animals, 5 *ds.*
Castriello de la Villa Vega (*solariego*)	Per team of oxen, 16 *celemines* wheat, 5 *cántaras* of *mosto*; 5 *mrs.* for meat; a work obligation every 15 days (from which those with a horse were exempted)
Santa Cruz del Monte (*solariego*)	Per team of oxen, 1 *cuarto* of wheat, 1 *cántara* of wine; one ox, one-half of amount per team of oxen; no animals, one-fourth amount per team of oxen
Villa Gonzalo (*behetría*)	Each peasant paid 6 *mrs.*; per team of oxen, 6 *celemines* (half wheat, half barley); one ox, 3 *celemines*; no animals, 1.5 *celemines*
Merindad *of Liébana-Pernia*	
Hesa de Montejo (*behetría*)	Each peasant paid 6 *mrs.*; and per team of oxen, married couples paid 1 *fanega* of barley; single persons, a half of a *fanega*
Colmenares (*behetría*)	Each peasant paid 1 *fanega* of rye
Merindad *of Castrojeriz*	
Espinosa de Ualde Olmos (*behetría*)	Each peasant paid 6.3 *mrs.* for Saint John
Bovadiella del Camino (*behetría*)	Each peasant paid 6.3 *mrs.* for Saint John

Source: *Becerro*, vol. 1.

(ecclesiastical) and *señorío* (secular) lordship in terms of what was due to each is difficult to determine—in return for protection and the use of the land. In the late Middle Ages, their juridical status had improved from the servile and semiservile conditions (*iuniores* or *collazos*) under which they lived in an earlier period.[41]

As the Christian frontier advanced southward and new lands were settled, the conditions of the peasants had improved, both in the new lands and elsewhere. Seignorial dues, in kind or labor, had often been commuted or reduced by fixed payment in species, a development which was, in many respects, beneficial to lords and peasants. In the lands of the monastery of San Salvador de Oña, most *solariegos* owed only two days of *serna* (work in the demesne of the monastery), one day at plowing time and another at harvest time or during the threshing of grain. In some other instances, peasants gave the monastery four days of work annually: at harvest, to plow the fallow (*barbechar*), and to gather the grapes at vintage time. There is no evidence that any other labor was required except for the occasional communal repair or works (*fazendera*) and other duties that benefited the entire village. Many of those obligations still survive in Castilian and Leonese villages, and I remember repairing a country road in 1976 as part of the obligations due to the village community (where my relatives live) from its citizens.[42]

These labor services, however, were often the object of endless litigation between monastic or secular lords seeking to vindicate their ancient rights and peasants eager to ignore or dispense with them. In 1339, Alfonso Fernández de Aguilar, *alcalde* (judicial official) of the king in the *merindades* of Castile, passed judgment on the suit brought by the abbess and nuns of the Cistercian monastery of San Andrés de Arroyo (in the present province of Palencia) against their vassals, the peasants of the village of San Pedro near Maharabes. The abbess claimed that the inhabitants of San Pedro owed the monastery seven *sernas* or days of work annually: to plow cereal lands, to harvest, and to thresh; as well as the four traditional labors in the monastic vineyards: *escavar, podar, cavar, vinar* (to loosen and weed the growth, to trim the vines, to dig, and to gather the grapes). Moreover, the peasants of San Pedro had to pay the monastery those dues set by *fuero*: *infurción* and one *carral* (barrel or vat) of wine transported at the villagers' expense, wherever the abbess indicated, within nine leagues (31.5 miles) of San Andrés de Arroyo. For six years the vassals of San Pedro had refused to give any labor or make any payment. The laborious inquest undertaken before a final decision was reached lasted more than two years, and those called as witnesses testified that indeed for many years they had seen the villagers of San Pedro perform those duties required by the abbess. Confronted with this evidence, the *alcalde* found in favor of the monastery, while the procurators of the rural council of San Pedro refused to make any statement ("no quisieron decir nada") except to request a copy of the sentence. In 1341, when Alfonso XI confirmed the sentence, the peasants of San Pedro did not seem to have yet complied with the original decision.[43]

Here, we witness a confrontation over manorial dues between a rural council, acting as a corporate body on behalf of a group of *solariegos*, and a rather small and powerless female monastery. That the abbess and nuns of San Andrés had to seek royal protection on this matter and, yet, after three years had failed to find redress for their complaints, reveals to us the fluid conditions of the peasantry, especially in the turbulent fourteenth century. Significantly, there is no evidence that by 1352, a mere decade after the litigation, the monastery had any rights in San Pedro. A village by that name, which seems to correspond exactly to the one examined above, was, in 1352, a *behetría* of Don Nuño, lord of Vizcaya, a nobleman strong enough to protect the villagers and to collect what was due to him without any delays or resistance.[44]

In 1340, the clerics, *hijosdalgo* (petty nobility), and *labradores* (peasants) of Matute met at the church of San Román, with the villagers, whether noble or not, gathering at the call of the church bell. Once there, they complained to the abbess of the Cistercian monastery of the Assumption of Cañas against the fiscal extortion of royal officials, and threatened to abandon the village and move elsewhere unless they received protection. We know that they did not leave the village. Eleven years later, the inhabitants of Matute settled their grievances with the monastery. The agreement between the rural council and the procurators of the Assumption of Cañas reveal to us that, in the intervening years, the peasants had not given one single seignorial due to the monastery. In fact, the peasants of Matute, unprotected against noble and royal violence, had taken actions that were not unlike a modern rent strike.[45]

It was not only by illegal or extraordinary actions that the peasants of *señoríos* protected their livelihood. The legal codes and *fueros* offer some guidance as to the rights and obligations of *solariegos*. As early as 1020, the *fuero* of León permitted *solariegos* to leave the land freely, albeit after forfeiting their rights to it as well as half of their goods. This contrasts with the rights of the men of *behetría* who could, in theory, go anywhere they pleased without any loss of property. The *fuero* of Palenzuela refers to the four *sernas* or work obligations owed by peasants to their lords each year, but it also stated that the lords must provide the peasants with food: bread, wine, and meat two days and bread and wine the other two, "et si hoc non dederint non vadit illuc."[46]

Most Spanish historians of late medieval Castile, especially Marxist and neo-Marxist ones, have emphasized the deterioration in the status of the *solariegos* from the late thirteenth century on. The repressive character of the *Fuero viejo de Castilla*, a noble customary code compiled in the mid-fourteenth century, is often quoted as an example of such a development: "Que a todo solariego puede el señor tomarle el cuerpo, e todo quanto en el mundo ovier; e el non puede por esto decir a fuero ante ninguno." ("That to all the *solariego* the lord can 'apprehend' his body and everything that he [the *solariego*] has in the world, and the *solariego* cannot have recourse to *fuero* [to the law] before anyone.")[47] There is almost nothing in the documentation that attests to these conditions in northern Castile precisely at a time when, as Freedman has shown, the lords had established their undisputed power over many peasants in Old Catalonia. The exception comes from a puzzling document from the monastery of Santa María la Real de Aguilar de Campóo extant at the AHN. In 1304, a certain Alvar Royz de Calabaçano sold all the *solariegos* he had in Val Verecoso (Valberzoso) to Gutier García Calderón for 2,000 *mrs*. Alvar sold them with all the rights he had over them and agreed "de fazer sanos los dichos solariegos" (to turn them in healthy). This document is so unusual that it deserves a more careful examination. Was it a scribal error? In truth, the sense of the entire transaction and the use of the term *solariegos* (people) rather than *solares* (lands) twice in the document make it difficult to argue for a mistake in the writing of the document. Were peasants or the rights over peasants sold and bought in northern Castile apart from the land? No other extant document allows for this interpretation. Half a century later, in 1352, all the peasants of Val Verecoso owed duties only to the abbot of Santa María.[48]

Regardless of the ominous implications of this single piece of evidence and of the harsh language of the *Fuero viejo de Castilla* (the latter refers only to those peasants abandoning the land), other contemporary legislation, such as the *Ordenamiento de Alcalá de Henares* (1348) and even succeeding titles in the *Fuero viejo de Castilla* itself, either tempered or even contradicted the hard line against peasants evinced before.[49] As is usually the case for legal codes, the laws did not always reflect the day-to-day reality of peasant life or the complex patterns of mutual obligations existing between peasants and lords. Here again, as has been seen in some examples above, the *Becerro de behetrías* provides vivid evidence of the wide range of seignorial duties which peasants owed to the same lord from village to village, as well as the diversity of rights and obligations that were found in the different *merindades* of northern Castile.

We should not conclude this chapter without a brief glance at two other groups of men and women who were also part of the rural world of northern Castile but who did not easily fit in the categories drawn above. I refer here to renters and journeymen or hired agricultural workers. In some respects, each of these groups often stood at opposite ends of the social scale: on the one hand, the well-to-do peasant or urban dweller who rented or entered into some sharecropping agreement with a destitute monastery and, on the other, the landless peasants picking up work here and there and barely making it through the year. In examining these two categories, one witnesses a whole range of possibilities, none of them exclusive of each other. What is certain, however, is that the numbers of renters and laborers were on the rise in the later Middle Ages, and that, more and more, they became important components in the rural economy of northern Castile.

RENTERS

In Chapter 5, we will examine in detail statistical samples of the numerous rental agreements extant for northern medieval Castile, but here one can look briefly at the terms under which certain men and women held land and property from others. These terms ranged from short leasing agreements with strict conditions and clauses protective of the owners' rights to long-term (often for the lives of the renters or even inheritable) leasing of specific property which did allow the renters to become in fact, if not *de jure*, holders of the land. I describe conditions here which are, of course, familiar to all and known throughout most of Western society. The house where I grew up as a child was built on land belonging to our parish church, and my father paid a small amount of money every year (*a censo*) for the right of usage. In Castile, as elsewhere in the West, these lifelong or inherited rental agreements lasted until the collapse of the *ancien régime*, and in some cases they persist today.

In the thirteenth and fourteenth centuries, such contracts were the common and often preferred means by which monasteries and cathedral chapters could cultivate and/or turn an income from their domains. Each leasing contract had some unique feature, such as amount of payment, terms of service, and length of contract. Most of the extant agreements from this period come from ecclesiastical sources, a monastery, or another religious institution leasing land or other holdings to laymen or laywomen. Thus, the variable is often the lessor and to what extent his or her wealth and social status influenced the conditions of the arrangements. A look at a few of the "*arrendamientos*" (the documents only rarely use the term *censo* in this period) will suffice here to illustrate once again the diversity of options in existence then.

In 1319, Díaz Sánchez rented one *yugada* (equivalent to the land that could be plowed by a pair of oxen or to fifty *fanegas* of grain) plus half of the pasture grounds in the village of Zapardiel from the cathedral chapter of Ávila for a term of six years beginning the day of Saint Cyprian. This is roughly an agricultural unit capable of supporting one family, although the rented property also included a team of oxen (two in Castile), agricultural utensils, and buildings. He agreed, in return, to pay three *cahizes* (twelve *fanegas* per *cahiz*) of wheat bread each year on the same day, a rent far exceeding the average production of small tenants in monastic lands elsewhere in Castile (see Chapter 5).[50] Díaz Sánchez's rent should have been roughly one-third to one-quarter of the grain production of the land. In theory, only fifty *fanegas* of wheat could be sown in a *yugada*, though in practice one and a half *fanegas* were required for each *obrada* (one *yugada* equals fifty *obradas*). Of the entire holding, half or most probably less than half was planted, with the other half allowed to remain fallow. Under optimal conditions, which one can seriously doubt often existed in the lands of Ávila, the yield for wheat would have been 1:4 or 1:5, that is, one *fanega* of wheat or one and a half *fanegas* sown to four or five *fanegas* of wheat reaped, which would have meant between 100 and 125 *fanegas* (only half of the *yugada* would have been under cultivation).

It is doubtful, however, that the arable was all given to wheat, and probably only enough wheat was planted to satisfy the rent to be paid to the chapter. The rest of the land was surely given to barley and perhaps to rye, which had higher yields than wheat. This was often the breakdown of the arable, as shown in the description of a similar property in San Sánchez rented out to Don Yague by the chapter of Ávila in 1287. Here, the grain stored for seeding the following year came to twenty-two *fanegas* of wheat, thirteen of barley, fourteen of rye, and ten of *garrovas* (carob beans for fodder).[51] Under any circumstances the land went mostly to pay the rent and to support Díaz Sánchez and his family, and one must assume that the grazing lands provided him with a profit.

There are many other examples of rental agreements that involved the transfer of substantial holdings. The cathedral chapter of Segovia leased most of its property to its canons at a nominal rent, and they, in turn, subleased the lands at a higher fee and pocketed the substantial difference. Elsewhere in Castile the patterns of land leasing also ranged from the small renter barely holding on for dear life, to important men and women who leased as a way to further their fortunes. We can see an example of the latter in the agreement which Don Díaz Gómez de Sandoval and his wife, Doña Inés Álvarez, undertook with the abbots and monks of Santa María la Real de Aguilar de Campóo. In 1266 the monastery gave a large "*heredad*" to the couple in Castrillo de Río Pisuerga: lands, vineyards, gardens, trees, and mills in exchange for an annual rent of 202 *mrs.* and seven *moyos* of bread (three of wheat, two of rye, and two of barley), with the prohibition to alienate the property and the duty to maintain the mills. Díaz Gómez de Sandoval and his wife belonged to the Sandoval family group, which held important lordships throughout northern Castile in the mid-fourteenth century. We must suppose that they did not operate the land directly, for this would have been one among many other properties, and that they would have, in turn, either subleased it to enterprising peasants or farmed the land through salaried rural workers or on a sharecropping basis. On the one hand, the monastery probably sought to obtain a guaranteed income and, perhaps, to gain the goodwill of a powerful local nobleman; on the other hand, Díaz Gómez and Inés Álvarez gained control over a rather sizable income-producing property. In the troubled times that followed, the final outcome could not be doubted; by 1352 Castrillo de Río Pisuerga had passed from an *abadengo* of the monastery to a *behetría* of Díaz Gómez's descendants. What began as the right to farm the land had become, in less than a century, actual property.[52] Again, one witnesses here complex economic conditions and, as will be seen in succeeding chapters, to this equation we must also add a growing number of urban dwellers who rented or purchased land as a complement to their commercial activities and/or as means of enhancing their social status. We must turn finally to our last category of peasants, those who worked the lands of others for a salary.

Salaried Workers

Increasingly, as we turn into the late medieval period, a variety of agricultural tasks were performed by peasants in return for salaries and meals. The consolidation of rural property into the hands of a few well-to-do peasants, powerful noblemen, and the urban patriciate, together with new economic necessities, marked the transition from ancient forms of labor service and manorial ties to different ways of organizing labor and production. We run the risk of erring by characterizing this type of peasantry as a rising landless proletariat. In truth, we do not know enough about their social status or their ties to the land and to other social groups in society during the thirteenth and fourteenth centuries. Surely, as in previous categories, some of the peasants were better off than others. We must also assume that a good number of them held lands that were too small to provide them with enough to survive, and, thus, that these peasants were forced to seek seasonal employment elsewhere. Likewise, one can suppose with a great deal of certainty that their numbers were greater on the plain than in the mountain areas of northern Castile, where the small property worked by one single family was the norm, and greater in New Castile and Andalucía than in Old Castile.

Some of these farmhands were hired for a short while—during a few critical days of the agricultural year, at the height of the planting or harvesting season—others for longer periods, almost year-round, as was the case in some monastic domains. The *fueros*, legal codes, and ordinances of the Cortes spell out clearly the conditions under which they worked; in doing so, these legal instruments offer implicit testimony to the importance of salaried farm workers in the agricultural life of Castile. In the influential *fuero* of Sepúlveda, the duties of the *yuvero* (the caretaker of the plowing animals, also the man who plows the field and sometimes the owner of the plowing team who hired himself at plowing time) are described in great detail. His work was not limited to caring for the oxen and plowing the fields, but also included other duties, such as carting the grain in winter, building fences, thatching houses, or performing any other task his employer might request. The language of the *fuero* indicates that the *yuvero* himself also hired and paid for additional help, serving as a subcontractor for the working of the land. The *yuvero*'s salary was usually one-fifth of the harvest plus maintenance, but, as with everything else, this varied somewhat from place to place. The *fuero* of Sepúlveda also regulated the relationship between the *yuvero* and an employer who was, in this particular instance, the actual owner of the plow and animals, but in northern Castile one also finds *yuveros* who owned animals and plows. In Andalucía, these plowing-team owners often became the elite of rural villages, jealously keeping and maintaining their oxen and agricultural tools.[53]

The 1338 accounts of several Benedictine monasteries in northern Castile show the importance of hired labor in the cultivation of monastic lands. At San Pedro de Cardeña, a monastery studied in detail by Moreta Velayos, the vineyards were almost exclusively worked by salaried farm workers. In good years, "when God brings the vintage to fruition and protects it from storms," the monastery's vineyards were expected to produce around 2,400 *cántaras* (sixteen or seventeen liters per *cántara*), of which 300 *cántaras* had to be utilized elsewhere. The monks and dependents at Cardeña needed around 2,500 *cántaras* for their own use; and in 1338, when the accounts were written, the vintage did not come to more than 1,000 *cántaras*. And yet, to produce this paltry amount, the abbot and monks had to pay 2,000 *mrs.* in wages and maintenance to the workers tending the vineyards and an additional 1,000 *mrs.* for the vintage and transportation of the wine to the monastery. In years such as 1338, when only about 1,000 *cántaras* were produced, the expenses of salary per unit came very close to the actual cost of a *cántara* of wine in the open market (3 *mrs.*). Workers employed at Cardeña, Oña, Silos, and other monasteries often received clothing, shoes, food, and wine for the year in addition to their annual salaries which, as seen above, could have made the cost of labor onerous for the financially troubled monasteries of northern Castile.[54]

We have two chronological boundaries for the evolution of salaries (rural or otherwise) in late medieval Castile: Alfonso X's imposition of wage and price ceilings at the *ayuntamiento* of Jerez in 1268, and Peter I's careful regulation of the salaries of rural workers in the *Ordenamiento de menestrales* of 1351. These two documents provide important clues to the strong inflationary trends marking the late Middle Ages, as well as to the economic and social transformations of Castilian society which will be examined in later chapters. They also offer vivid evidence as to the importance of hired farmhands in Castilian agricultural production, to regional differences, and to the economic and social gradation among salaried farmhands. Above all, these wage ceilings point to royal and aristocratic wishes to keep labor costs down at a time in which their own incomes were declining rapidly. Table 2.3 compares rural wages in 1268 and 1351. Inflation, of course, must be taken into account. More importantly, this comparison also shows the range of farm occupations and their ranking according to income, and most probably status, within the village.

I must return here to an earlier point. One of the common assumptions about Castilian history—and I confess to having fallen prey to this fallacy—has been that journeymen were found throughout Castile, but that their number increased as one moved southward. This, of course, helps to emphasize the dichotomy between the survival of a fairly large, free, land-owning peasantry in the north and a landless, rural proletariat in the south. The work of González Jiménez and others, as well as the extant documentation, indicate that qualifications are in order (see Part IV). Perhaps the conditions one may observe in northern Castile are those of peasants who, owning or holding from others small or unproductive parcels of land, hired themselves or their children out at the peak periods of the agricultural cycle. This salaried labor was, probably, the only thing that stood between them and a life of deprivation. One must remember that those hired had to be provided, by custom, not only with a salary but also

TABLE 2.3.   Salaries in Castile in 1268 and 1351.

Occupation	Wages in 1268
Mancebos (journeymen, plowboys)	
In Andalucía	12 *mrs.* annually
From Toledo to the Duero	4 *mrs.* annually
From the Duero to the Road to Compostela	6 *mrs.* annually
North of the Road	10 *mrs.* annually
Mancebas (journeywomen)	6 *mrs.* annually
Nannies	10 *mrs.* annually
Peones with "azada e con su foce" in June, July, and August	
In Andalucía	3 *ss.* daily
In the north	7 *ds.* daily
Podadores (tree trimmers)	8 *ds.* daily (no food allowance)
Carpenters and masons	
In Andalucía	4 *ss.* daily
Those helping with vintage	1 *s.* daily

	Wages in 1351		
	From St. John to Martinmas	From Martinmas to St. John	Total
Plowboys working with mules	6 *cargas* of bread	60 *mrs.*	120 *mrs.*
Plowboys working with oxen	4.5 *cargas* of bread	40 *mrs.*	80 *mrs.*
Sheepherders			80 *mrs.* plus food
Harvesters			One-tenth of the harvest
Nannies			80 *mrs.*

Sources: M. del Carmen Carlé, "El precio de la vida en Castilla," and her "Mercaderes en Castilla," appendix; *Cortes*, vols. 1 and 2.

with meals. Such a combination of added income and food must have made farm work, if not attractive, at least a saving alternative in the rural world of late medieval Castile.

My intention in the preceding pages has been to provide a typology for the different categories of peasants in northern Castile and to illustrate, through examples, the nature of the relations between peasants and their lords and the land. While one can argue that such classification, based mostly on juridical and fiscal obligations, is barely useful or valid, the evidence does provide a rough outline of the range of conditions under which men and women lived and toiled in medieval Castile at the end of the Middle Ages. As has been seen, each community had its own peculiar pattern of organization, duties, and rights, and thus generalizations are difficult to make. Slaves and serfs were still found in late eleventh-century Castile but had almost disappeared from the north by the late thirteenth-century. Instead, a whole gamut of small, free landholders, semi-free men and women working the lands of others, renters, and journeymen formed a large and often anonymous mass upon whose shoulders rested the basic structures of Castilian society.

Notes

1. On Roman Spain, see Luis García de Valdeavellano, *Curso de historia*, 131–34; also his *Historia de España: Desde los orígenes a la baja edad media* (Madrid: Revista de Occidente, 1952), 1: 189–214; Glick, *Islamic and Christian Spain*, 65–66 et passim. See also Thomas F. Glick, "Agriculture and Nutrition: The Mediterranean Region," *Dictionary of the Middle Ages* (New York: Scribners, 1982), 1: 79–88.

2. See Thomas F. Glick, *Irrigation and Society in Medieval Valencia* (Cambridge, Mass.: Harvard University Press, 1970).

3. García de Valdeavellano, *Historia de España*, 1: 320–27. On the early medieval rural economy, see Georges Duby, *Rural Economy and Country Life in the Medieval West* (reprint; Columbia, S.C.: University of South Carolina Press, 1990), 5–165.

4. Andrew Watson, "Towards Denser and More Continuous Settlements: New Crops and Farming Techniques in the Early Middle Ages," in *Pathways to Medieval Peasants*, ed. J. Ambrose Raftis (Papers in Medieval Studies, 2, Toronto: Pontifical Institute of Mediaeval Studies, 1981), 67–70.

5. Glick, *Islamic and Christian Spain*, 66.

6. Francisco Luis Laporta, *Historia de la agricultura española* (Madrid, 1798), 32–33 et passim. Also Ángel M. Camacho, *Historia jurídica del cultivo y de la ganadería en España* (Madrid: Establecimiento tipográfico de J. Ratés, 1912).

7. García de Valdeavellano, *Historia de España*, 1: 526–39; *Curso de historia*, 233–56; Abilio Barbero y Marcelo Vigil, *Sobre los orígenes sociales de la Reconquista* (Barcelona: Ariel, 1974), 370–71.

8. Watson, "Towards Denser and More Continuous Settlements," 69–71; Miguel Caja de Leruela, *Restauración de la abundancia de España*, ed. Jean Paul Le Flem (Madrid: Instituto de estudios fiscales, 1975), xv–xxxii et passim..

9. On the ranching character of Castilian society, see C. J. Bishko, "The Castilian as a Plainsman: The Medieval Ranching Frontier in La Mancha and Extremadura," in *The New World Looks at Its History*, ed. A. R. Lewis and T. F. McGann (Austin: University of Texas Press, 1963), 47–69; also, his "The Peninsular

Background of Latin American Cattle Ranching," *Hispanic American Historical Review* 32 (1952): 491–515.

10. In the general discussion below I follow the classical studies on the occupation and working of the soil by Marc Bloch and Georges Duby but, more relevant, García de Cortázar's pioneer works on Castilian agriculture and rural life. Although it deals with a later period and the region of New Castile (with a different ecology and agricultural pattern), see David Vassberg, *Land and Society in Golden Age Castile* (Cambridge: Cambridge University Press, 1984), and for Old Castile, Ángel García Sanz, *Desarrollo y crisis del antiguo régimen en Castilla la Vieja* (Madrid: Akal, 1986).

11. *Poema de Fernán González*, stanza 170a–c. On the origins of Castile see Justo Pérez de Urbel, *El condado de Castilla: Los 300 años en que se hizo Castilla*, 3 vols. (Madrid: Editorial siglo ilustrado, 1969–70), especially vol. 2.

12. See Claudio Sánchez Albornoz, *Despoblación y repoblación del valle del Duero* (Buenos Aires: Instituto de historia, 1966), 121–343. See also Salvador de Moxó, *Repoblación y sociedad en la España cristiana medieval* (Madrid: Rialp, 1979), 27–45, 201–16; Jean Gautier-Dalché, *Historia urbana de León y Castilla en la edad media (siglos IX–XIII)* (Madrid: Siglo XXI, 1979), 99–103. For the conquest of Toledo, see García de Valdeavellano, *Historia de España*, 1: 820–27.

13. For the idea of webs of reciprocity, which I use throughout this section, see Ruth Behar, *Santa María del Monte: The Presence of the Past in a Spanish Village* (Princeton, N.J.: Princeton University Press, 1986), 189–202. For a general discussion of servile ties north of the Pyrenees, see Marc Bloch, *Feudal Society*, 2 vols. (Chicago: University of Chicago Press, 1966), 1: 241–79.

14. *Curso de historia*, 241; Moxó, *Repoblación y sociedad*, 46–78.

15. A long list of monastic foundations marking the southward progress of the repopulation is found in Pérez de Urbel, *El condado de Castilla*, 1: 309–17. For the role of monasteries in the repopulation see 1: 307–46.

16. On *fueros* in general, see Alfonso García Gallo, *Manual de historia del derecho español*, 3d ed., 2 vols. (Madrid, 1967), 1: 378–85; García de Valdeavellano, *Historia de España*, 1: 773–80.

17. On Ávila and Segovia, see Barrios García, *Estructuras agrarias y de poder*, 1: 127–41; Armando Represa Rodríguez, "La tierra medieval de Segovia," *Estudios segovianos* 21 (1969): 5–16; Moxó, *Repoblación y sociedad*, 201–16.

18. García de Cortázar et al., *Organización social del espacio en la España medieval*, 123–94.

19. *Curso de historia*, 330, 333. For the discussion on "feudalism," see Peter Linehan, "The Toledo Forgeries c.1150–c.1300," in *Falschungen im Mittelalter* (Hannover: Hahnsche Buckhandlung, 1988), 1: 643–48. See the latest entry into the debate by Isabel Alfonso with the revealing title, "Cistercians and Feudalism," *Past & Present* 133 (1991): 3–30, and also below.

20. Paul Freedman, *The Origins of Peasant Servitude in Medieval Catalonia* (Cambridge: Cambridge University Press, 1991), 1–153.

21. Located in the *merindad* of Castilla la Vieja, Gallejones was a place of *solariegos*, owing dues to *fijosdalgo* and to the monastery of San Martín. Tudanca and Tubilleja were *behetrías*. Vascones was under the lordship of Doña María, wife of

Diego Pérez. *Becerro*, 2: 440, 448, 492–93. For a description of these terms, see below.

22. See Juan Carlos Martínez Cea, *El campesinado castellano de la cuenca del Duero: Aproximaciones a su estudio durante los siglos XIII al XV* (Valladolid: Concejo general de Castilla y León, 1983), 60–94. For the use of the word *vasallo*, see below.

23. Lacking in Castile are the formidable manorial records that have allowed for vivid reconstruction of rural life in England and France. Studies of the village community in England are numerous, above all, those undertaken by J. Ambrose Raftis and his disciples, and colleagues at Toronto. See, among others: Raftis, *Tenure and Mobility: Studies in the Social History of the Medieval English Village* (Toronto: Pontifical Institute of Mediaeval Studies, 1964); *Warboys: Two Hundred Years in the Life of a Medieval English Village* (Toronto: Pontifical Institute of Mediaeval Studies, 1974). There is a general but evocative treatment of the village community in George C. Homans, *English Villages of the Thirteenth Century* (Cambridge, Mass.: Harvard University Press, 1941), and a corrective to Raftis and the Toronto School in Zvi Razi, *Life, Death and Marriage in a Medieval Parish: Economy, Society and Demography in Halesowen, 1270–1400* (Cambridge: Cambridge University Press, 1980). For Castile, there is the recent and most useful book by Ruiz Gómez, *Las aldeas castellanas en la edad media*.

24. AHN, Clero, carp. 1025, no. 18a (30-March-1340).

25. *Albelda y Logroño*, I, no. 162, pp. 262–65 (25-November-1343); AHN, Clero, carp. 1033, no. 5 (20-December-1323); carp. 1668, no. 1 (20-February-1316), carp. 1665, no. 1 (c. 1300).

26. On Blasco Blázquez, see below. AHN, Clero, carp. 24, no. 18 (9-May-1301).

27. *Becerro*, vol. 1, no. 20, pp. 432–33; no. 45, pp. 444 et passim. For an idea of what a *maravedí* bought, the following information may be of some use. In 1268 a farm worker earned 6 *mrs.* a year plus food and clothing in northern Castile. In 1294 the royal physician earned 10 *mrs.* daily. See María del Carmen Carlé, "El precio de la vida en Castilla del rey sabio al Emplazado," *CHE* 15 (1951): 32–156.

28. On Blasco Blázquez, see Barrios García, *Estructuras agrarias y de poder*, 2: 133–54. Blasco's purchases with the name of sellers are found in *DMA*, nos. 109–17, pp. 97–105; nos. 119–23, pp. 108–11; no. 125, p. 113; no. 128, p. 115; no. 130, p. 116; nos. 131–32, pp. 116–18; no. 139, pp. 123–24; no. 174, pp. 170–71; no. 178, p. 176; AHN, Clero, carp. 24, nos. 5, 6, 8, 9–20; carp. 25, nos. 1–6b, 8–11, 16–17; carp. 26, no. 10. Other transactions in Serranos de Avianos and Cornejuelos, mostly by the chapter, are found in AHN, Clero, carp. 26, no. 4 (22-May-1304); no. 13 (22-June-1308); carp. 28, no. 1 (21-April-1338); carp. 29, no. 6 (22-May-1342), no. 7 (21-January-1343), no. 13 (22-January-1351), no. 14 (22-May-1351), no. 20 (23-January-1356), no. 21 (24-January-1356), no. 22 (30-July-1356); carp. 30, no. 3 (21-June-1358), no. 4 (28-June-1358). Notice the dates of purchase, reflecting perhaps the use of income from an anniversary endowed by Blasco's will. Neither of the two towns is mentioned in Pascual Madoz, *Diccionario geográfico-estadístico-histórico de España* (Madrid, 1845–50; facsimile repr., Valladolid: Ambito, 1984), of the mid-nineteenth century, nor in the early *Censo de población de las provincias y partidos de la corona de Castilla en el siglo XVI* (Madrid: Imprenta Real, 1829). For all the economic activity, the villages might have not survived the disasters of the fourteenth century.

29. This note covers the entire history of Madrigal del Monte as discussed in the previous paragraphs. *Documentación de la catedral de Burgos (804–1183)*, *FMCL*, 13: 33–34 (see 34, n. 1); 282–84; *Fuentes*, 2: 109; Teofilo F. Ruiz, "The Transformation of the Castilian Municipalities: The Case of Burgos, 1248–1350," *Past & Present* 77 (1977): 16, n. 50; ACB, vol. 30, f. 582 (6-May-1326); *Becerro*, 2: 317.

30. Miguel Santamaría Lancho, "La gestión económica del cabildo catedralicio de Segovia, siglos XII–XIV" (Master's thesis, Universidad Complutense de Madrid, 1980). Also AHN, Clero, carp. 1959, no. 9 (30-December-1341), no. 10 (6-June-1342), no. 14 (22-April-1346), no. 15 (4-December-1346), no. 16 (25-January-1347), no. 17 (25-January-1347), no. 18 (8-February-1347), no. 19 (19-April-1347); carp. 1960, no. 1 (19-April-1347), no. 2 (21-March-1348), no. 3 (27-February-1349), no. 4 (17-March-1350), no. 5 (10-March-1351), no. 8 (24-November-1358).

31. Some examples will suffice. See *Documentación del monasterio de San Salvador de Oña (1319–135)*, *FMCL*, 6: 214–17, 219–21, 234–36 et passim. AHN, Clero, carp. 1732, no. 18 (7-November-1344). See also *Cortes*, 1: 274, 277, 330, et passim in which urban procurators protested the alienation of the royal domain to ecclesiastical institutions and magnates.

32. AHN, Clero, carp. 26, no. 2 (30-April-1303); carp. 28, no. 1 (1-April-1305). *Fijodalgo*, the term used in medieval documents to describe the lower nobility, means literally "son of" someone with property. Land was often referred to as *algos*.

33. *Becerro*, 2: no. 151, p. 204; no. 154, p. 205.

34. *Becerro*, 2: 617–20; 1: 76.

35. On *behetrías* see *Curso de historia*, 341–43; Claudio Sánchez Albornoz, "Las behetrías: La encomendación en Asturias, León y Castilla," *AHDE* 1 (1924): 158–336, and his "Muchas páginas más sobre las behetrías," *AHDE* 1 (1928): 5–14.

36. Moxó, *Repoblación y sociedad*, 430–36.

37. Ángel Ferrari Núñez, *Castilla dividida en dominios según el Libro de las Behetrías* (Madrid: Ograma, 1958), 165; see also n. 35.

38. *Becerro*, 1: 74.

39. *Becerro*, 2: 89, 91–92.

40. *Becerro*, 2: 576–78. See *Curso de historia*, 252–53.

41. For *iuniores* and *collazos*, see *Curso de historia*, 349–350; García de Cortázar, *La sociedad rural*, 29–30.

42. Juan José García González, "Rentas de trabajo en San Salvador de Oña: Las sernas (1011–1550)," *Cuadernos burgaleses de historia medieval* 1 (1984): 119–94; see also Behar, *Santa María del Monte*, 181–251; María I. Alfonso, "Las sernas en León y Castilla: Contribución al estudio de las relaciones socio-económicas en el marco del señorío medieval," *Moneda y crédito* 129 (1974): 153–210.

43. AHN, Clero, carp. 1734, no. 17 (1-January-1341).

44. *Becerro*, 1: 248.

45. AHN, Clero, carp, 1025, nos. 18a, 18b, 19, (30-March-1340; 26-November-1351).

46. Camacho, *Historia jurídica del cultivo*, 69, 76–77.

47. Ibid., 81; text in Alfonso García Gallo, *Manual de historia del derecho español*, 4th ed., 2 vols. (Madrid: Artes gráficas y ediciones S.A., 1971), 2: 479. See the sober discussion of this issue in García de Cortázar, *La sociedad rural*, 225–32. For conditions elsewhere in the peninsula, see Paul H. Freedman, "The Enserfment

Process in Medieval Catalonia: The Evidence from Ecclesiastical Sources," *Viator* 13 (1982): 225–44, and his recent book, *Origins of Peasant Servitude*, 154–78.

48. AHN, Clero, carp. 1665, no. 7 (26-July-1304); *Becerro*, 1: 448.

49. Camacho, *Historia jurídica del cultivo*, 81–83; Moxó, *Repoblación y sociedad*, 439.

50. See below for leaseholds. AHN, Clero, carp. 27, no. 6 (24-September-1319).

51. *DMA*, 119–20 (17-August-1266).

52. AHN, Clero, carp. 1658, no. 18 (17-August-1266); *Becerro*, 1: 237.

53. *Fuero de Sepúlveda*, tit. cxxxii. See also AHN, Clero, carp. 1658, no. 2 (?-May-1258); *Cortes*, 1: 77–78.

54. Salustiano Moreta Velayos, *El monasterio de San Pedro de Cardeña*, 236–37, 248–50; also see his *Rentas monásticas en Castilla: Problemas de método* (Salamanca: Universidad de Salamanca, 1974), 34, 90–91.

3. Working the Land: The Village Community

As we know the broad juridical conditions of those who worked the soil, we can also see the outline of how the land was tilled and what it yielded, as well as the general pattern of agricultural techniques in late medieval northern Castile. As everywhere else in the medieval West, the first settlers of the plain—few in number, scattered over an empty land, and armed with meager tools—cleared the woods with fire to make room for cultivation. As late as the thirteenth century, the ordinances of the Cortes imposed on those who burned forests and woods harsh penalties—throwing the guilty individual into the fire. This serves as a vivid reminder that almost half a millennium after the settlement of the plain, scarcity of labor and the lack of tools made fire still one of the preferred techniques for clearing the land.

We should not, however, think that the process of deforestation had succeeded completely. The accounts of early modern travelers reveal to us a very uneven landscape. Thick woods where no one lived alternated with areas where the countryside was so bare of trees as to force its inhabitants to use dried dung and grass as fuel. And some travelers, such as Lorenzo Vital, a member of Charles I's entourage in 1517–18, went so far as to recommend a policy of reforestation. But overall, a recurring lament in the accounts of early modern travelers complained of the high price of firewood in some parts of Castile.[1]

Not surprisingly, in the thirteenth and fourteenth centuries and to this very day, rural councils, monasteries, and secular lords engaged in protracted litigations over their conflicting rights to the use of *montes* (wooded land) and pasture and the indiscriminate cutting of trees. Such were the complaints voiced by the monastery of San Pedro in Gumiel de Izán against the men and municipal council of Roa. In 1301 the *vecinos* of Roa entered the woods of the monastery by force and felled the trees. The monks of San Cristobal in Ibeas de Juarros also complained to the king in 1272 that the men of the council of Arlanzón and other places cut their trees because the royal fine for doing so was too low (5 *ds.*) to deter these illegal activities. The king complied with the men's demands, raising the fine to five *sueldos* (*ss.*), but there is no evidence that this helped very much; the conflict continued.

I do not think, however, that these disputes over wood reflected a shortage of wooded areas throughout northern Castile. Rather, they reveal scarcity in some specific areas, together with the limitations of rural communities and monasteries in best utilizing these resources, for many of these disputes (which we know through the records of arbitrations or when the abuses mounted to the point of requiring royal intervention) occurred at a time of marked demographic decline, when villages were being deserted throughout northern Castile. Yet, one can see in areas such as the region of Dueñas (province of Palencia) that most of the property sold in Frausillas, Sacalahorra, and other rural communities had *montes* (wooded areas or brush) as boundaries.[2]

In the destruction of woods by fire, and in the innumerable disputes which issued from indiscriminate felling of trees, we come face to face once more with the dichotomy between private and communal forms of ownership. In a sense, the history of Castilian agriculture can be seen as the slow privatization of the land, a process which was not fully completed in the late Middle Ages and has not been finalized even today. Woods, pastures, and mills were held by the village and its citizens. The *vecinos* (house owners and landowners in the village jurisdiction) shared *suertes* or *veces*, the usufruct of communal properties. In practice, these rights of usage were sold, inherited, and exchanged with few restrictions, although in theory they remained the communal property of the rural councils. Thus on 19 May 1301, Menga Andrés of Cornejuelos (near Ávila), in her name and that of her brothers, sold for 330 *mrs.* houses, lands, flax fields, gardens, pasture lands, woods, and so forth, as well as rights to the water and commons in the village. A month later Domingo, also of Cornejuelos, sold property as well as rights in the commons for 50 *mrs.*[3]

The Agricultural Cycle

While forests were burned or felled in parts of the plain to make room for cultivation, the mountain regions of Cantabria and the Basque country always retained an adequate supply of wood. This is the case in the valley of Zamanzas, where firewood can be gathered without great effort to this day, but, of course, logs are not easy to transport over difficult mountain passes to the plain in the south. In the plain or in the northern valleys, once the woods were cleared for cultivation, the agricultural cycle began. There is no reason to believe that Castilian rural practices were radically different in the Middle Ages from what they are today in some isolated rural communities of the north, except for a few gas-powered tools, pesticides, and fertilizers.

In northern Castile, the basic patterns of how the land was worked changed slowly. We are, perhaps, less willing today to accept the premise— proposed so often in northern European models of agricultural life—of wide and accelerated rural change fueled by technological innovations. In northern Castile the three-field system, the heavy plow, the use of horses in farm labor had little or no impact in the period before 1350. Throughout the region a biannual crop rotation was practiced. A few vague references in a handful of lease agreements between the monastery of San Salvador de Oña and a number of peasants and town dwellers (in which one of the conditions was to leave, at the end of the lease, one-third of the land plowed fallow and another third seeded) are not enough to presuppose a triennial system of crop rotation.[4] In northern Castile half and, often, more than half of the arable was left fallow (*barbechar*), while the other half was cultivated, with the fields being rotated (at least in theory) the next year. This is the system known as *año y vez* which, in many respects, was best suited for the soil and climatic conditions of northern Castile.[5]

Frequent days of frost in April and even May, as well as in early autumn, served as a deterrent to a long growing season. The *Especulo* (a mid-thirteenth century legal code) set the time to harvest cereals as beginning with the first day of July and extending to the middle of August; gathering the vintage began eight days before Michaelmas (29 September) and ended a month after. In Salamanca, a lease agreement set mid-April as the end of the planting season for spring wheat. Farther north, in the region of Oña, another lease agreement between the monastery of San Salvador and its *vasallos* (peasants holding land from the monastery) at Nuez de Río de Urbel established the time to plow the fields as being between the feasts of *Carnestolendas* and Saint Andrew, that is, from three days before Ash Wednesday to 30 November. This more or less set the boundaries for the farming year, though *Carnestolendas*, being a movable feast, might have been too late for spring plowing. These dates varied in northern Castile from locality to locality, for royal edicts did not always take into consideration regional circumstances. Far more reliable evidence of the agricultural cycle are the dates on which rental payments, whether royal, seignorial, or ecclesiastical, were due. In Oña, north of Burgos, the monastery collected payments in kind as early as the feast of Saint Mary on 15 August, but no later than her feast on 8 September. Monetary payments were due on 11 November for Martinmas, as were the royal dues of the *martiniega* throughout the land.[6]

South of Oña, Saint Michael's Day was far more common as a date for the payment of rents. In 1312 John Rodríguez leased land from the monastery of Santa María la Real de Aguilar de Campóo, agreeing to pay 100 *fanegas* of grain (half wheat, half barley) on Michaelmas. This was one of many examples from a region that had a few more extra days in its agricultural calendar than Oña. Similarly, the nuns of San Andrés de Arroyo, near Aguilar de Campóo, rented lands in San Román to the rural council of Enestar in return for an annual payment of 120 *fanegas* of grain placed in the monastery by the feast of Saint Michael. Since a fine of 10 *mrs.* daily accrued for each day's delay, one could safely assume that the crops were harvested by the end of September at the latest. Further south still, in a village of the lands of Segovia, but already south of the Central Sierras, a certain Don Bartolomé rented lands from the monastery of Santo Domingo in Madrid, also making his annual payments on Michaelmas. Westward, in the area of the Rioja, the collegiate church of Albelda received its monetary payments on Martinmas and its rent in kind on 8 September.[7] By late September, as can be seen from the dates above, the harvest was in throughout northern Castile, and only a few weeks were left to plant winter cereals before frost and snow hardened the soil and brought with them the reduced quota of chores of the winter season. In the late 1960s, before television reached their remote valley, my relatives in Gallejones de Zamanzas gathered firewood, fed and watered their stabled animals, sat close to the fire, played cards, and slept throughout most of the winter.

Agricultural Labors

The arable in northern Castile demanded continuous attention during the growing season. The cycle of rural work so clearly defined in the *sernas* (the work duties of some peasants) covered all the farm activities between the plowing of the fields in early fall and spring to harvest time in late summer: *arar, sembrar, cosechar, trillar, segar, barbechar* and *vendimiar* (plowing, seeding, harvesting, threshing, hay harvesting, plowing the fallow, and gathering of the vintage). Farm work, however, is a great deal more than a series of high points in the moving round of rural life. During the planting season and after, the land required extensive work and care: weeding the field; plowing the fallow twice, thrice, even as much as five times; grazing the livestock; and many other duties. Yet, those high points, the "labors," were very important indeed. In northern Castile ecclesiastic and lay lords sought to secure help at those critical times, even if it meant relinquishing their ancient rights over the peasants' time during other parts of the year.

In 1266 and 1268, the monks of San Salvador de Oña offered improved work terms to their peasants in the villages of Villella, Gornaz, Rebolledillo, and Montenegro as a way of retaining their services at crucial stages in the agricultural year. Instead of one day of labor every fifteen days, and one day every eight days in August, the monks reduced the duties to two days for the men and women of the first three villages and four days for those of Montenegro for the entire year. The monastery's "vassals" of Villella, Gornaz, and Rebolledillo came once a year to plow and another day for the threshing of the grain. Those with a team of oxen and a plow or, at least, an ox or any other plow animal had to help with the plowing. Those without animals were to help in haymaking. Additional divisions of these two *sernas* among the three villages provided for transportation of the grain to wherever the monastery indicated, for harvesting the vintage and so forth. In addition, those holding the usufruct of the three villages from the monasteries had the obligation of providing a specific amount of bread, wine, onions, and cheese to the peasants whenever they came to perform their duties. The peasants of Montenegro, on the other hand, had their work duties reduced to four days annually: to seed the fields, to thresh the grain, to plow the fallow, and to gather the grapes. They also received a similar allotment of food.[8]

A dispute in 1340–41 between the villagers of San Pedro and the monastery of San Andrés de Arroyo also allows us to observe the work duties of the peasants but also, more important in the context in which we examine this information now, the pattern of peasants' work in late medieval Castile. Those of San Pedro (who had refused to recognize the monastery lordship) were required, among other things, to work for the nuns of San Andrés, planting the crops, haymaking, threshing the grain, and performing the four traditional vineyard duties (see below). But it is not only the scattered documentary sources that provide us with the guidelines for the agricultural cycle. In Juan Ruiz's *Libro de buen amor*, one follows the changing pattern of the seasons and of the rural landscape, with the tending of the vine and the growing grain in spring and early summer, the harvesting and haymaking in late summer and early fall, and the manuring and plowing of the fallow before winter.[9]

Here we have the landmarks of the agricultural year in Castile extending from late winter or early spring to mid-fall. These agreements between peasants and their lords and the literary references also provide us with clues as to how the land was worked. The harvesting in large estates was most probably done by hired hands, seasonal workers paid in money, but who also worked for a share of the crop and food allotments. The initial plowing of the fields for planting was probably done by the *yuveros* (the plowmen), the somewhat independent and, oftentimes, prosperous owners of a plow team. They collected one-fifth of the crop in return for their work. We can see them in the villages, almost always identified by the descriptive *don*, such as Don Abril, a *yuvero* near Dueñas, or Don Yague and many others whose plows and oxen were indispensable for working the land of Castile.

By the thirteenth and fourteenth centuries, most monasteries in northern Castile and, probably, lay lords as well could no longer rely on their dependant peasants—their "vassals," in Castilian terminology—to perform the work required. This fact is evident in the 1338 accounts of Benedictine monasteries, which reflect the reduction of work duties (as a means for keeping peasants on the land) and the increased leasing of monastic domains during this period. Similarly, ordinances of the Cortes and royal legislation, which seldom sought to promote agriculture in a positive manner, nevertheless went to great pains to set up a scale of wages for agricultural labor, especially in times of crisis. [10]

While lords made arrangements to retain enough peasants on their lands to perform the essential agricultural tasks—either through work duties or hiring—other activities also required human labor. The livestock had to be taken to pasture, and the gardens (*herrenes*) near the village, often just behind the peasant household, also demanded close attention. The arable and vineyards had to be manured. Often this latter task was accomplished by simply allowing the livestock to graze the stubble left after the field had been harvested, as was done in Salamanca and elsewhere, or by allowing them to graze in the fallow. Pigeon houses, mentioned in the extant documentation, were built in the middle of vineyards or gardens in imitation of Muslim husbandry; the pigeons' droppings were collected regularly and added to human and animal waste to fertilize the fields, and the pigeons themselves served as tasty morsels for the tables of the rich. In 1337, the nuns of San Andrés de Arroyo purchased gardens, houses, bed sheets, blankets, and a pigeon coop located in the garden for 5,000 *mrs*. And in 1284 Juan Martín purchased one garden, four and a half *aranzadas* of vineyard, and one pigeon coop in the village of Calvarosa for 1,700 *mrs*. Whenever we find transactions involving *palomares* (pigeon coops), the prices are considerably higher than those paid for gardens or vineyards alone. These pigeon coops must have been large affairs, and their high price points to the importance and dearth of manure in northern Castile.[11]

As was the case elsewhere in the West before the agricultural revolution of the late eighteenth century, there was never enough manure to go around in northern Castile. This fact, when taken together with the specific climate and geography of Castile, helps explain the extended fallowing needed to replenish the soil. Thus, throughout Old Castile rental agreements insisted that, at the terminus of the contract, the lessee should leave a *buen barbecho*. A good fallow was sometimes plowed as many as five times in the year, but certainly not less than twice (see below).

Vineyards, with their four traditional labors (*escavar*, to loosen a weed growth; *podar*, to trim vines; *cavar*, to dig; and *vendimiar*, to gather grapes), required even closer attention than grain-producing lands, although vineyards were also far more profitable on the whole than were grain-producing fields. Wherever we turn in northern Castile, we see agreements drawn between monasteries and their peasants guaranteeing or at least hoping to secure help in the tending of vineyards. Again, our often-mentioned poor but vocal nuns of San Andrés protested in 1341 that the peasants of San Pedro had failed for the last six years to give them their due: the four traditional vineyard labors plus a barrel of wine placed wherever the nuns wished within nine leagues. Farther north, at Oña, the monastery of San Salvador—far more powerful than San Andrés de Arroyo—secured the help of the peasants of Villella, Gornaz, and Rebolledillo to gather the vintage. Similarly, numerous leasing agreements by which monasteries rented away vineyards, above all in the region of the Rioja, sought to protect the monastic supply of wine; when they were unsuccessful, we find, as in Nájera in 1304, the plaintive protests of a monastery that lacked wine.[12] Since vineyards, once abandoned, were difficult to begin anew, owners were forced to give the land away in troubled times or to make concessions to maintain the vineyards under cultivation. Even small landholders were forced into such grants by what, at first sight, appears to have been a shortage of labor. On 13 December 1357, María, the widow of Adán Pérez, leased her two pieces of vineyard in Navarrete (in the Basque homeland, bordering with the Rioja) to Pedro Martínez. The latter was to perform all the customary labors in the vineyards, to plant and replant "as it was the custom of the town of Navarrete from the 15 of March on for five years." After the term was done, the vineyard was to be divided by lot into two equal parts, one for María and the other for Pedro. Thus his labor was the only payment required.[13]

Besides providing an indication of the cycle of viticulture from the Ides of March onward, the grant cited above and similar extant contracts point to the importance of vineyards within the rural economy of Castile. This statement must be qualified, however, for the importance of wine was closely related to its urban markets. As shall be seen in later chapters, towns jealously kept or tried to keep a monopoly over the production of wine by extending the area around their walls where grapes could be cultivated and gathered for the exclusive use of town dwellers. Such was the case in Santander, which extended its viticultural jurisdiction three leagues around the town.[14] But both in urban and rural communities, liturgical and dietary consideration made a regular supply of wine a necessity. The Benedictine accounts of 1338, and specifically those of San Pedro de Cardeña, show how expensive—indeed unprofitable—it was for the monasteries to keep their own vineyards; yet they all had to have wine regardless of the economic burdens. And thus in northern Castile the village communities tended vineyards wherever the climate and geography allowed it, and wherever their lords' needs made it a requirement.[15]

TOOLS AND ANIMALS

Plowing in Old Castile was done almost exclusively with the so-called Roman plow common to the Mediterranean, although northern Castile was not fully a part of the Mediterranean world. This is not to say that throughout Old Castile there was a uniform type of plow; in fact, there is a somewhat obscure reference that seems to indicate the existence of winter and summer plows. Caro Baroja's erudite study of Spanish plows shows the subtle variations that existed and still exist in the region, but the surviving medieval inventories are too laconic on this issue to permit a full reconstruction of the different types of plows. One is limited, somewhat, to the few extant pictorial representations. Nevertheless, it is clear that the heavy-wheeled plow (the *carruca*) was not to be found in medieval Old Castile; if this plow was used in Castile at all, its usage would have been exceptional. This was to be expected, since the Roman plow, made of wood and iron but also with a fire-hardened wood tip, was best suited for most of the soils of northern Castile and indeed for all of Iberia.

The plowmen's animal of preference was the ox, a team of two oxen being the norm. Yet wherever we turn in the region in the late Middle Ages, we find a disproportion among the land supposedly under cultivation, the number of plows available, and the oxen needed to work the arable. In San Andrés de Arroyo, in Segovia, in the lands of Burgos, in Ávila, and in Oña, there seems never to have been enough animals to cultivate all of the land. Moreover, the different categories of taxes, from Nájera to Oña to Campóo, show that the majority of peasants owned only one ox or other animals or, worse yet, that many owned no plowing stock at all. This lack of sufficient agricultural utensils and animals underscores once again the importance of hired or contracted labor, especially of the *yuvero*, who in many respects was not unlike the owner of expensive farm machinery who rents his tractor to farmers. Plowing with mules and/or horses, which would have quickened the task of working the land, was known in northern Castile, and there are references to their use in the ordinances of the Cortes in 1351 and in literary works. But the use of mules and sometimes horses as plow animals must not have been common until the eighteenth century, and even then the use of such animals would be rare because of their cost. In the Middle Ages teams of cows employed as plow animals—as used by my relatives in Gallejones to this day—were perhaps not unusual, and would have consequently led to decreases in the cows' milk production, fecundity, and weight. In the absence of cows, it is likely that humans would have pulled the plows or worked the fields with harrows and shovels. Thus the *fuero* of Sepúlveda stated that when the *yuvero* had no animals, he had to work the fields by hand.[16]

The agricultural inventories more often than not refer to "*yugos cornales*," that is, yokes that were tied to the horns. As Caro Baroja has shown, other types of yokes, specifically neck yokes, are also found in Spain, but, as is the case for plows, the references are too vague to allow for a clear picture of what they were really like. In a few documents from San Andrés de Arroyo, there are references to *yugos* "*ariscoes*" as well as to the common *yugo* "*cornal*" (horn). It is difficult to say with certainty what "*ariscoes*" means here, but in modern Spanish *arisco* is translated as "wild, untamed," so perhaps these were special horn yokes for difficult animals.[17]

There are only a few elaborate inventories of agricultural tools extant in Castile for the period before 1350. To my knowledge, the best such records are found in a few rental agreements drawn up between the nuns of San Andrés de Arroyo and their tenants. In many respects, these inventories of rural property are not different from what may be found elsewhere in the West. In Castile, however, whenever and wherever we find such inventories, one common theme runs through them—that is, the disproportion between the surface theoretically under cultivation and the often inappropriate number of plows and agricultural tools provided to the tenant. Was there in truth such a dearth of farm equipment, or did hired labor and plowmen play so important a role in the rural economy as to make a full complement of agricultural utensils unnecessary?[18]

In 1321, the abbess and nuns of San Andrés de Arroyo leased their house of El Pozo, near Aguilar de Campóo, to Ferrand Pérez and his wife María Miguélez (familiars of the monastery). They rented the property for ten years or ten harvests beginning at Michaelmas for 180 *moyos* of bread (half wheat, half barley) to be paid the day of Saint Cyprian (16 September). In addition, the monastery was to receive two fat pigs at Martinmas and two new carts for the feast of Saint John (23 June). This was a considerable rent in kind, 180 *moyos* (360 *fanegas*) or around 568.8 bushels. Since this was probably only one-third or one-quarter of El Pozo's total yield, one can assume a figure between 540 and 720 *moyos* or between 1,080 and 1,440 *fanegas* of wheat and barley. (Twelve *fanegas* a year was the normal annual requirement of bread per person.) We also know that rye was raised in El Pozo, since forty-eight *moyos* of rye were given as seed by the monastery. Considering such a large property, we must assume—and there is tangential evidence to confirm this assumption—that the land was subleased and parceled out in smaller units to other peasants. The lease agreement stated that the land should be subleased only to *labradores llanos* (plain peasants) and by implication not let out to exempted clergymen or noblemen.

Yet, even for such an extensive unit of land, the animals and tools available were insufficient. In the list below, we can see a partial inventory of what the couple received upon entering the lands of El Pozo on Michaelmas, 1321.

Partial Inventory of Tools and Animals at El Pozo
  4 pairs of oxen (8) valued at 1,200 *mrs.*
  4 yokes with all the corresponding equipment (ropes and *melenas*—
    cloth or hide placed below the yoke to protect the oxen—and 1 *ssonso*
    [bell?])
  1 ass
  10 plows
    2 *cornal* yokes (see next line)
    2 *cornal* ropes (straps for yoking oxen by the horns)
    3 *cabezales* (forepart of carts or carriages)
    3 pairs of bed sheets, 9 long robes of skin or fur, 11 blankets, and 24
      cloaks
  12 *satos* (12 pieces of sown land?)
    2 barrels for flour
    2 *calderas* (cauldrons)

2 iron-knobbed clubs

1 *caldero* (bucket-like, semispherical cauldron), 2 iron spoons (probably large), 3 sets of iron table settings (spoons, knives)

1 fire shovel, 3 (hair) sieves

2 cups made of wood, 13 *colgadizas* (hooks to hang clothing, etc.?)

10 hens, 2 roosters

6 hoes and/or mattocks, 2 adzes, and 1 sickle

1 large ox

7 threshing harrows

1 *soncejo* (bell?)

20 pigs, 5 suckling pigs

4 *colodras* (wooden can to measure wine, or milk pail)

And enough shovels, drag-hooks and rakes for the labor of the house.[19]

For such a large enterprise the number of oxen, asses, chickens, and pigs is indeed very small, and the couple may have had to bring some livestock with them to add to the existing inventory. Moreover, although the house had an abundant supply of blankets and cloaks, its furnishings were scant. How typical this was of the entire region is difficult to determine. In the few cases for which evidence is available, the amount and types of household goods and livestock are similar to that described above. In the inventory of tools and animals, it is important to note the gap between plows (10) and teams of oxen (4). Does the excess of six plows reflect earlier and more prosperous times, or was this a common proportion throughout Castile and the West? The dearth of inventories of rural tools and animals makes it difficult to provide a definite answer for northern Castile. On the other hand, the evidence available on the rural holdings of the cathedral chapter of Segovia also reveals a period before 1250, when a great deal more of the arable had been under cultivation. By 1300 the imbalance between plows and teams of oxen was similar to those of San Andrés de Arroyo.[20]

Table 3.1 shows the relationships between rent, plows, oxen and other animals, and yokes as well as, in one instance, the seed grain provided by the monastery.

One must again raise the question as to how accurate these inventories or the accounts available for Segovia were, although sporadic references from Liébana and elsewhere, which tell us the amount of livestock these monasteries owned, seem to confirm the evidence from San Andrés de Arroyo. This somewhat belies the common suggestions that monastic institutions owned large flocks of livestock, mostly sheep, which formed

TABLE 3.1.   Rents in San Andrés de Arroyo.

Date	Property	Terms	Rent	Given
19-December-1300	House of San Pelayo	20 years	80 *moyos*, annually and the tenth	5 pairs of oxen, 2 fat pigs, 7 yokes, 6 plows, 9 sheep, 8 pigs, 3 goats, 2 hens, 1 rooster
31-October-1306	House of San Roman	8 years	40 *moyos*, and 2 fat pigs	5 oxen, 3 cows, and other animals
19-October-1315	House of Matalevaniega	11 years	5 *moyos*, 2 fat pigs	24 *moyos* for seed (10 wheat, 7 rye, and 7 barley), 3 oxen, 3 yokes, 2 plows
20-November-1321	House of El Pozo	10 years	180 *moyos*, 2 fat pigs, 2 new carts	8 oxen, 6 yokes, 10 plows, 10 hens, 2 roosters, 25 pigs, 120 *moyos* for seed (40 wheat, 40 rye, and 40 barley)

Source: AHN, Clero, carp. 1732, nos. 5, 7, 14; carp. 1733, no. 2.

the large rivers of animals flowing back and forth through Castile along the roads of the Mesta. Perhaps this was the case after 1350, when the export of wool to Flemish markets made the transhumance a very profitable business; it was perhaps so for a few privileged monasteries in the period before the mid-fourteenth century, but for most ecclesiastical institutions, middling independent farmers, and almost all of the Castilian peasantry, the reality was quite different. And thus the few inventories, or the numerous arbitrations, which determined the dues of peasants by the number of plow animals they owned, reflect vividly a world in which animals and tools were often scarce. We should now turn from these peasants and their farm animals to the world in which they lived and to the manner in which they related to the land and to those above them.

Land and Work in Northern Castile

We have already glimpsed at the Castilian countryside through the eyes of foreign visitors and seen cultivated fields clinging around the walls of cities and the outskirts of villages and, in between, a vast, uncultivated, and seemingly empty place. The center of this world was the village or *lugar* (place). The peasants' dwellings were surrounded by gardens, which were often fenced; extending beyond, in an uneven and irregular patchwork, lay the grain fields and vineyards. Wherever a river, however small, ran, dams and mills rose to catch and transform the power of water into energy.[21] Here and there we find a *monte* (a wooded area or brush) or the remnants of one. This was and remained—in some cases until the present day—the heterogeneous landscape of the plains in the late Middle Ages. Fairly small fields of wheat, barley, and rye—the rye probably far more frequent than what the extant documentation indicates—but rarely oats shared the arable with even smaller vineyards. Fruit trees, scattered throughout the arable and often used as boundary markers, alternated with crops of chickpeas, beans, and legumes.

Pasturelands and *montes*, the indispensable wooded and brush areas on the edge of the village, were held and used by the villagers often with, but sometimes without, the tolerance of lords. Meadows and flax fields by riverbanks bordered each other in illogical sequence. This inferred description, of course, can seldom be backed by a real example, but here and there one finds working farms that resembled this depiction. In Chapter 5, as we examine the buying and selling of land and real estate in northern Castile, we will see that most properties—such as those sold by Juan Pérez and his wife Mari Gómez to Domingo Pérez, choirmaster of the cathedral of Ávila in 1294—included houses, grain lands, vineyards, meadows, woods, pastures, fruit trees, and flax fields.[22]

There are two predominant landscapes in Old Castile: mountain and plain. Each determines to this day what was cultivated and how. They shaped and still shape the structures of village life and, to a lesser extent, the bonds tying Castilian peasants to the land, to nearby towns, and to their lords. North of the plain, a dairy economy and fruit trees predominated over cereal and grape growing; yet, contrary to the reports of foreign travelers, mountain villages also sought to grow grains and grapes even against difficult odds.

The reality of peasant life—whether in the mountains or on the plains, in Castile or in the rest of the West—was that bread and wine were the basic staples of life. They had to be produced from the soil regardless of how suited the region was for their cultivation. Moreover, wheat and barley were still the preferred form of payment (when peasant dues were paid in kind) by monastic and lay lords, and their production was encouraged even in dairy and viticultural lands. In Santander, for example, Alfonso X, Ferdinand IV, and Henry II granted citizens the right to plant vineyards for three leagues around the walls of the town as a way to secure the supply of wine in a region which, because of its soil and climate, was certainly not ideal for viticulture. In Oña, the monastery zealously promoted the planting of fruit trees and the conversion into money of its rents, but it also sought to preserve a more than ample source of grain and wine. Throughout the region, in remote and mountainous Liébana and elsewhere, the almost universal presence of grain and grapes in the arable gives intimations of the typical landscape of the northern plain.[23]

This diversified countryside, wherever the soil allowed for it, was often the norm in northern Castile, although we also sometimes find areas, such as Frausillas near Dueñas or the Rioja region, where one staple predominated. And yet evidence of a few vineyards in the former and scattered reports of cereal growing in the latter point to the heterogeneity of what was cultivated in the Castilian lands.

Fragmentation and Consolidation of the Arable

The diversity of agricultural goods throughout most of Castile was, however, only one aspect of the northern Castilian countryside. Fragmented peasant holdings were also the norm in Castile, as the research of Miguel Santamaría and Vicente Pérez Moreda on the lands of the cathedral chapter of Segovia as well as the evidence from the property census of Ávila (1303) and elsewhere shows. The latter historian of Segovia has studied the size of 213 different units of production. Table 3.2 shows the distribution of these cereal-growing units by surface area in *obradas* (between 1 and 1½ acres).

The surviving documentation from other parts of Castile seldom provides as much information regarding the actual size of the holdings as that which exists for Segovia. Sometimes, however, we can obtain an approximation of the actual size of the peasant's land from the amount of rents paid. For example, at the end of the thirteenth century, the men and women who worked the lands of Santa María la Real de Aguilar de Campóo appear to have had units so small that one wonders how they were able to survive.

Regardless of the size of the holdings, one of the realities of agricultural life was the dispersion of farm property throughout the countryside. Rights to use the mills were also fragmented to the point where one individual could own as little as one-half of one-eighth of a turn, as was the case in the mill of Suso, or Huço, near Aguilar de Campóo. Fragmentation of rights of usufruct can also be found in salt wells and, to a lesser extent, in

TABLE 3.2.   Cereal-Growing Land
Units in Segovia.

Size of Unit (*in* obradas)	Number of Units
Less than 1	28
1–2	68
2	30
3	27
4	15
5	7
6	7
7	5
8	8
9	2
10	3
12	6
14	2
15	1
16	1
20	1
22	1
30	1
Total	213

Source: *Propiedades del cabildo segoviano*, 57,
cuadro 4.

houses. In Ávila in 1301, five *aranzadas* (447 deciares) of vineyard were
divided into seventeen different portions, and this type of fragmentation of
the land was not the exception but the rule.[24]

Sharing the land with the sizable holdings farmed by prosperous
farmers, monasteries, and secular lords were a myriad of peasants working
small pieces of land, or more often several small pieces of land. Some
peasants held a portion of the land outright; others worked as renters and
sublessees of the property, as the Segovian documentation implies; and still
other peasants worked as tenants and day laborers. The wide range of types
of properties and/or usufruct, as well as the forms of cultivation that shaped
the Castilian landscape, began to alter radically in the late thirteenth and
fourteenth centuries. The forces that led to the division of large properties
into smaller units (partible inheritance, perpetual leases, breakdown of
monastic domains) were sometimes effectively balanced and even reversed

by a dynamic process of consolidation of farm property into the hands of a few families and institutions, a process most vividly evident in the seignorialization of water mills, urban property, and the lands surrounding the Castilian towns (see Chapter 5).

We must turn our attention, once again, to the organization of the land. Whether fragmented or consolidated, the land was also a stage for the endless competition between open fields and enclosures. In northern Castile we are no longer in the open-field countryside of northern medieval agriculture, with its long strips dictated by the heavy plow, but in a mixed and heterogeneous landscape. Gardens were almost always enclosed. Vineyards, especially when located near roads, were often fenced or bounded by trees or hedges. Otherwise, vineyards required a guard permanently on the watch for stray animals invading the orchards or for passersby helping themselves to the fruit of the vine. Fences, often of stones but also of growing hedges, frequently were a matter of contention. Thus, in 1336 the cathedral chapter of Burgos and the municipal council of the city went to arbitration over a stone fence which the chapter had built around one of its gardens outside the gates of the city. Bickering over whether anyone had the right to enclose the land also reflected the growing concern with defining boundaries and rights-of-way, for which there is abundant documentary evidence from the late twelfth century on. In the area of Burgos, as Luis Martínez García has clearly shown, most of the transactions of property between 1150 and 1250 included specific provisions for rights-of-way to public roads. Nor should we take the frequent usage of *"entrada"* (entry) and *"salida"* (exit) in land transactions as an empty formula; rather, these terms reflected the growing concern with defining boundaries and property.[25]

By the late thirteenth century, villages throughout northern Castile appealed to royal and regional authorities for a definition and legal recognition of their boundaries. Litigation with nearby villages or monasteries often resulted in surveys and the placing of land markers (*mojones*) to delimit the actual size and ownership of property of individuals and corporations. For all practical purposes, these newly defined limits served the same purpose as fences and were yet another way of reorganizing the landscape along new or more "modern" lines. Parallel to this development, an active market for land served the same trends toward consolidating and defining the actual physical boundaries of the land.[26]

Fields along the path of the transhumance were often permanently enclosed by hedges. And here again, we meet yet another variant on the endless conflict between open and closed fields, for the needs of the trans-humance sometimes ran counter to the peasants' need to protect their fields from wandering livestock. Moreover, hay fields and grazing lands, orig-inally part of the communal holdings of the village, had been in some cases partly privatized. Usufruct rights to the commons were sold, inherited, or exchanged as private property. That was certainly the case in Serranos de Avianos, a village in Ávila's hinterland, and in other areas of northern Castile. According to the *fuero* of Soria, the *dehesas de pasto* (enclosed pastures) were reserved for the collective use of the community's livestock, but each *vecino* (citizen) could also enclose up to two *aranzadas* (approx-imately 2.2 acres) as a *prado de guadaña* (scythe field for fodder) from 1 March to the feast of Saint John when the land reverted to communal use. At Salamanca, the *vecinos* could fence three *aranzadas* from the commons in both summer and winter. There is no need to discuss here the obvious advantage this represented for the *vecinos* (those owning property in the village) over those without property. The commons could be fenced be-tween the end of winter and the beginning of summer when the animals needed new pastures the most.[27]

In 1253 Alfonso X intervened in a dispute between the abbey of Santo Domingo de Silos and the town's council, ordering that fences be put up in the commons between 1 March and the feast of Saint John and for the municipal livestock to graze freely only after 24 June. In 1336 the nuns of San Salvador de El Moral received from the rural council of El Peral permission to graze their livestock (including eight pairs of oxen) in the pasturelands of El Peral "after the *cotos* (fences) were removed." Any dam-ages the animals may have done to the fences, vineyards, and grain fields were to be paid according to a previously agreed upon scale. The *fueros* of Salamanca, Cuenca, Cáceres, Sepúlveda, and others also indicate the pres-ence of fences (some of stone, others just hedges; some of them at least five hands high) around vineyards, gardens, and pastures. What we witness here resembles the present-day villages of León and Castile: a seasonal enclosure of the land under cultivation which, with the exception of gar-dens (which were almost always enclosed) and grain fields (almost always open), varied according to the specific period in the agricultural cycle and the location of the village.[28]

These heterogeneous landscapes were, as pointed out earlier, given mostly to grain. Duby, in a felicitous phrase, wrote that "the demesne, therefore, was cereal-growing by tradition, viticultural by the lord's inclina-tion, and pastoral by financial interest."[29] This description befits Castile as a whole and particularly monastic domains such as Cardeña: its lands were long given over to cereal cultivation, except where the excessive expense of viticulture was borne for the liturgical needs and gift-giving services of wine. One could also say that Castile grew cereal by necessity, but tended its vineyards and kept flocks for financial reasons. One cannot always establish the ratio between lands given to grain production and those given to vineyards for all of Castile. Each region had its own peculiar structure, and the ratio depended on many factors: soil, climate, markets, economic needs. In Segovia, the 1290 census of the property of the cathedral chapter shows an eight to one relationship: that is, grain cultivation occupied eight times the area of vineyards. Since grain growing on the Castilian plain was essentially dry farming, this is a ratio to be expected throughout most of the region, and perhaps with an even higher ratio in favor of grains in other parts of Castile. In the lands of the monastery of Santa María la Real de Aguilar de Campóo or in those of Las Huelgas around Dueñas, vineyards are almost never mentioned either in the frequent extant transactions or in the census of property. These documents show a landscape dominated by cereal cultivation, whereas in the Rioja, an area well suited for viticulture, references to vineyards are so numerous as to reveal to us an area of great specialization. There, it seemed, grain cultivation was at times essentially a subsidiary activity.

Crops

Wheat, barley, rye, and, in very few instances, oats, dominated the arable. The ratio of wheat to barley and to rye followed local customs and variations. In Segovia, with its humid soil, rye seems to have been favored over wheat and barley. In Juan Ruiz's *Libro de buen amor*, the toll-keeper in the mountains south of Segovia offered rye bread to the wandering monk, reflecting the local peasants' dependence on rye for their daily bread.[30] But the example of Segovia was perhaps exceptional only in being well documented. Throughout most of northern Castile, the evidence points to the preeminence of wheat and, above all, barley as the crops of choice, if not for the peasants, certainly for their lords. Again and again from Campóo to Oña, to Burgos, to the Rioja, and elsewhere in the region, the extant sources show that whenever manorial rents were collected in grain, they were paid mostly in wheat and/or barley.

Such is the vision which Salustiano Moreta Velayo conveys to us in his study of San Pedro de Cardeña, a monastic domain in which cereal lands were given almost exclusively to wheat and barley. Similarly, García de

TABLE 3.3.   Payments in Grain in the *Merindad* of Aguilar de Campóo.

Type of Payment	Number of Payments
Half barley/half wheat	73
Barley (by itself or mixed with smaller amounts of wheat)	31
Wheat (by itself or mixed with smaller amounts of barley)	22
Rye (mostly by itself but sometimes combined)	26
Rye, wheat and barley in equal proportions	3
Barley and rye	26
Rye or barley	1
Bread (*pan*)	1

Source: Becerro de behetrías, vol. 1, sect. 7.

Cortázar emphasizes the importance and frequency of the two aforementioned cereals, explaining the scarcity of rye and oats due to the limitations imposed by biannual rotation and climatic conditions.[31] Table 3.3, compiled from the *merindad* of Aguilar de Campóo, shows the breakdown of those payments that were made in cereals. This particular *merindad* spanned mountain and plain; the type of cereal rendered in payment often reflected the geographical location: rye in the water-rich mountains, wheat in the dry lands of the plain.

We would be deceived, however, if in this particular instance we were to take the documentary evidence at face value. There are strong indications that peasants grew rye in the same proportion in which they did barley and wheat and that, in some cases, rye was the preferred crop. One must consider the favorable yields for rye as compared to wheat, and that, on the whole, rye required less investment of seed and work: fallowing lands planted with rye had to be plowed only thrice while fallowing the land after wheat planting required four or more plowings. Thus, regardless of the need for humidity, it is perhaps not unjustified to assume that rye was often cultivated even though the extant documentation does not always allow us to verify this. In fact, leasing agreements more often than not indicate that when seeds were granted to the lessees, fairly equal amounts of rye, barley, and wheat were provided, although rents were collected almost exclusively in barley and/or wheat. In 1321, according to a document examined earlier, the abbess and nuns of San Andrés de Arroyo leased some of their land. The rental payments in grain amounted to 180 *moyos* of bread (half wheat, half barley), but the monastery provided 40 *moyos* of wheat, 48 of rye, and 40 of barley to the renters for planting. Similar examples can be found for other parts of Castile.[32]

Oats, on the other hand, are mentioned with even less frequency than rye, and there is no tangential evidence to disprove the fact that this was indeed a marginal crop. The few mentions in the accounts of the chapter of Burgos, the monasteries of Santo Domingo of Silos, San Millán, and elsewhere do not really amount to much.[33] But then, of course, in the rural world of late medieval Castile, where horses or mules were only rarely used for agricultural tasks, there was not a pressing need for oats. As to the cycle of planting, there is no direct evidence to guide us, but climatic conditions in northern Castile and the availability of manpower may have favored winter crops over spring crops. Once harvest and vintage were completed by late September, there was still time to plow and sow the fields before frost hardened the soil. In late March or early April, however, it was still an uncertain business to begin anew the annual agricultural cycle. In a biannual field-rotation system, as was the case in Castile, there is not always a clear distinction between winter and spring fields as in northern Europe. In September and October, when the harvest was just in, when field hands were available and the farm animals at peak strength (having more grazing, stubble on the fields, and so on), it was advisable perhaps to plant as much of the arable as possible. We do not know how many people were drawn south in late winter and spring by the transhumance and by the seasonal agricultural cycle of Andalucía, and to imply that spring labors may have suffered from a shortage of hands may be sheer speculation. Yet, I think that the evidence from many parts of Castile, as shall be seen in succeeding chapters, points to severe demographic dislocations in the thirteenth and early fourteenth centuries, and these were probably more severe in early spring than in early fall.

We find different types of leguminous plants complementing wheat, barley, and rye in most parts of Castile. Against the overall pattern of farm production, their cultivation appears insignificant. Our best evidence comes again from the area of Segovia, either because, thanks to the work of Angel García Sanz and other historians of Segovia, we know more about agriculture there than anywhere else in northern Castile, or because special climatic and topographical conditions allowed for the cultivation of this type of crop there. Everywhere else, one finds only a few and scattered references.[34] Flax fields, on the other hand, were regular components of the Castilian landscape. The numerous references to small flax fields, from the northern parts of Old Castile to the Central Sierras, next to rivers and creeks, reveal local workings of linen, and in the *Becerro de behetrías* there is at least one mention of dues paid in linen. As for the working of flax into cloth, we have only insignificant direct evidence, but the rural data indicates that such work must have been done.[35]

YIELDS

We come now to a troublesome issue, one for which there is no real answer. I refer to the question of agricultural yields. Historians of medieval Castilian agriculture have agreed that yields were lower in Spain than they were in northern Europe. Of course, even for northern Europe the seed/yield ratios varied from place to place. Slicher von Bath reports normal seed/yield ratios of 1:5 for wheat, 1:8 for barley, 1:4 for oats, and 1:7 for rye. "In practice," he adds, "these figures are well above the average which in general fluctuated at about 1:4 for wheat, 1:3–5 for barley, 1:3 for oats, and 1:5.5 for rye." García de Cortázar reports yields of 1:3.4 and 1:4.2 for wheat and barley in the lands of the monastery of San Millán de la Cogolla (Rioja) in the later Middle Ages, and similar ratios are reported for Silos in 1338.[36] In the seventeenth century, the best lands for dry-farming enjoyed yields of 1:7–8 for wheat and 1:10–14 for barley. For the 1840s, Ringrose reports yields of 14 hectoliters of grain per hectare in the Netherlands, of 13.2 in Great Britain, and of only 6.2 hectoliters per hectare in Spain—one of the lowest in Europe. In the region of Ávila, as late as the nineteenth century, ominous yields of 1:2 were reported.[37]

If we return to the late Middle Ages, the reports from San Millán de la Cogolla and Santo Domingo de Silos, regions which did not have adverse agricultural conditions, seem to be representative for most of northern Castile with, perhaps, just slightly better results in the region around the Pisuerga River and the Tierra de Campos. If such was indeed the case, then the best yields in northern Castile matched the low to middle average of agricultural yields in other parts of western Europe. This is of course not surprising, considering the climatic and geographical conditions discussed in Chapter 1.

There are, however, a series of other factors that may have also contributed to these slightly lower yields. First, unlike the case in England, France, and other parts of northern Europe where Cistercian farm practices served as models for agricultural development, there is no evidence that Castile followed such models. Cistercian monasteries were never very important, or certainly could not compete either in wealth or in importance with the older Cluniac foundations or with the spreading influence of the new

Mendicant orders. Moreover, in his study of Cistercian monasteries in Castile, Vicente A. Alvarez Palenzuela argues that their economic organization did not differ a great deal from existing models, and thus Cistercian innovative agricultural practices were absent from Castile. Second, while the Muslims had a long tradition of husbandry—a tradition reflected in careful manuals and research on the topic—and while there were also very good northern examples of treatises on husbandry (most notably, Walter of Henley's work), medieval Castile lacked examples of such meticulous study or serious approaches to agriculture. True, the *Siete Partidas* gives a perfunctory endorsement to agriculture, but practical royal measures to protect and encourage agriculture were rare. As Glick has shown, there was indeed a strong interaction between al-Andalus, with its advanced farming technology and widespread irrigation practices, and the Christian north. Technology transfers did take place, and much was altered and exchanged in terms of diet, clothing, and culture, but one must recognize the weight of tradition in rural life as a deterrent to new agricultural techniques. The people of the plain, the people of dry cereal-growing lands, did not take very well to southern models. Even when victories in the battlefield opened the richness of al-Andalus to Christian settlement, the northern Castilian peasants continued to farm as they had done in the north, and thus in some cases, as in that of Murcia, they failed miserably in their endeavors to keep the land productive.[38]

The relative scarcity of animals also reduced yields. In earlier pages we have seen the small ratio of farm animals to the extension of the arable, and one must also wonder at the small flocks of such monasteries as Santo Toribio de Liébana—theoretically in the dairy-rich area of the mountains. At Liébana, a livestock inventory of 1316 shows only five oxen, two asses, nineteen pigs, thirteen piglets, fifty-two goats and kids, and one mule. Similar paltry flocks were found elsewhere.[39] Again, in a rural society where fodder crops were subordinated to wheat (the preferred currency of manorial payment) and where the harvesting of hay as winter fodder was often limited by geography and privatization of the commons, the local scarcity of livestock in comparison to the great herds of the Mesta should not surprise us. The scant mention of grazing lands in transactions during the late Middle Ages (see Chapter 6) is telling evidence of their secondary importance. This shortage of animal resources contributed to an endemic shortage of manure—a topic already dealt with earlier but worth reviewing again. In this respect, the Mesta provided benefits only to a few specific areas and far too small to compensate for the damages it inflicted on agriculture. Moreover, the Castilian peasantry did not have easy access to other sources of fertilizer such as marl, which was available, if only in limited amounts, to peasants in England and France. Allowing the livestock to graze in the fallow, opening the arable to the beasts after the harvest was not enough. In most parts of northern Castile, therefore, the peasants were caught in a vicious circle: not enough animals, not enough manure, smaller arable, lower output and yields.

Working against such odds required a great deal of labor. As we have seen, the fallow had to be plowed between two and five times. Grain-producing lands required extensive weeding through the growing season, and the vineyards even more so. Not surprisingly, the cost of cultivating the land was often prohibitively high. Mention has already been made of the high cost of rural labor the Benedictine monasteries faced in 1338. A *hereda-miento* of the monastery of Santo Domingo of Silos located in the same village produced ninety-eight *almudes* of barley in 1338. Eleven *almudes* were reserved for seeding for the following year—which provides a somewhat loose approximation of the yields for barley (1:8.9) in what were the best fertilized and tended lands of the monastery. But this left only eighty-seven *almudes*, which at 3 *mrs.* per *almud* would have brought 261 *mrs.* in the open market. Yet, the cost of sowing and harvesting was 202 *mrs.*, and this sum did not include spoilage, transportation of the grain to the market, its grinding, or other incidental labor during the growing season. In fact, barley cost nearly as much to grow as it brought in.[40]

As has been seen, life and work in the northern Castilian countryside did not depart radically from the general pattern of most of the rest of the West in the late Middle Ages. Rural life differed, however, from those realms north of the Pyrenees in its reliance on the Roman plow and the two-field system. This resulted from the fairly successful adaptation of Castilians to their peculiar soil and ecology rather than from technical backwardness. Yet, the imbalance between tools and land, between available arable and peasants—that is, too few tools for the amount of arable, too much of the arable and too few peasants to cultivate it—points to a turn for the worse in many localities by the first half of the thirteenth century and afterward. This was, to a large extent, the result of distinctive problems of population flow between the north and the south and of demographic shortcomings, at a time when northern Europe was still experiencing general demographic growth. We should now address these issues in greater detail and see how the social and economic structures of rural life changed over time in a specific location.

Notes

1. *Viajes de extranjeros*, 1: 270, 702, 869, 1473, 1502, et passim.
2. AHN, Clero, carp. 233, no. 13 (22-March-1301); carp. 250, no. 7 (17-October-1272); carp. 232, no. 9 (14-August-1347). See Chapter 5.
3. AHN, Clero, carp. 24, no. 18 (9-May-1301); carp. 25, no. 2 (12-June-1301). For use of the commons in twentieth-century Spain, see Behar, *Santa María del Monte*, 203–64.
4. For the emphasis on the widespread acceptance of new agricultural technology in northern medieval Europe, see Lynn White, Jr., *Medieval Technology and Social Change* (Oxford: Clarendon Press, 1962). On the other hand, see Georges Duby's careful assessment in his *Rural Economy and Country Life*, 16–22. For references in the documents that may indicate a triennial rotation, see AHN, Clero, carp. 303, no. 4 (?-February-1292); carp. 306, no. 3 (15-February-1308); no. 14 (10-May-1311); carp. 307, no. 15 (29-January-1315).
5. García de Cortázar, *La historia rural medieval*, 45–46; Marta Bonaudo de Magnani, "El monasterio de San Salvador de Oña: Economía agraria y sociedad rural," *CHE* 51–52 (1970): 65; *Propiedades del cabildo segoviano*, 56–65.
6. *Especulo* in *Leyes de Alfonso X*, 1 (Ávila: Fundación Sánchez Albornoz, 1985), 5, tit. 6, ley vi, 456; *Salamanca*, 479 (1281); *Oña*, 2: 593–95. For England, see Homans, *English Villages of the Thirteenth Century*, 39–103, 354–63.
7. For rental dues throughout Castile, see Chapter 5. Also AHN, Clero, carp. 1667, no. 3 (2-October-1312); carp. 1733, no. 20 (28-March-1332); carp. 1360, no. 1 (31-August-1346); *Albelda y Logroño*, 1: 250–51, 261–62, 274–75.
8. *Oña*, 2: 688–89, 691–92.
9. AHN, Clero, carp. 1734, no. 14 (12-June-1339); no. 15 (8-November-1339); no. 16 (14-February-1340); no. 17 (9-January-1341). The last document describes in detail the *sernas* of the men and women of San Pedro. Juan Ruiz, *Libro de buen amor*, stanzas 1270–1298.
10. For mentions of *yuveros* see *Documentación del monasterio de Las Huelgas de Burgos (1231–1262)*, in *FMLC*, 31: 192, 213, 326–27 (where *yuvero* is not identified by *don*). For laborers, see Moreta Velayos, *El monasterio de San Pedro de Cardeña*, 222–23, 250–57. See below for leasing and salaries.
11. Camacho, *Historia jurídica del cultivo*, 61, for *ordenanzas* of Salamanca. For pigeon coops, see *Salamanca*, 493–94 (27-February-1284); AHN, Clero, carp. 1734, no. 7 (4-May-1337). See also Behar, *Santa María del Monte*, 215–17. For the north, see Homans, *English Villages of the Thirteenth Century*, 40, 60, et passim.
12. *Oña*, 2: 688–89 (1266); AHN, Clero, carp. 1734, no. 17 (7-January-1341); carp. 1032, no. 20 (12-March-1304).
13. *Albelda y Logroño*, 1: 321–23. See Chapter 5.
14. *Colección documental del archivo municipal de Santander: Documentos reales (XIII–XVI)*, ed. Manuel Vaquerizo Gil and Rogelio Pérez Bustamante (Santander: Ayuntamiento de Santander, 1977), 63–64, 74–76.
15. For vineyards in northern Spain, see Alain Huetz de Lemps, *Vignobles et vins du nord-ouest de l'Espagne* (Bordeaux: Bibliothèque de l'école des hautes études hispaniques, 38, 1967); *Vida económica*, 67, 78, 230–31; Moreta Velayos, *El monasterio de San Pedro de Cardeña*, 169, 250.

16. For plows, see Julio Caro Baroja, "Los arados españoles: Sus tipos y repartición. (Aportaciones críticas y bibliográficas)" *Revista de dialectología y tradiciones populares*, 1 (1949): 3–96. See also *Fuero de Sepúlveda*, tit. cxxxii; Pascual Martínez Sopena, *La tierra de Campos occidental: Poblamiento, poder y comunidad del siglo X al XIII* (Valladolid: Institución cultural Simancas, Diputación provincial de Valladolid, 1985), 523–35; Homans, *English Villages of the Thirteenth Century*, 42–46. For plowing with mules, see *Cortes*, 2: 114 (1351) et passim; see also Juan Ruiz, *Libro de buen amor*, stanzas 237–244. See below for inventories in San Andrés de Arroyo.

17. On yokes in general, see Bernard H. Slicher van Bath, *The Agrarian History of Western Europe, AD 500–1850* (London: Arnold, 1963), 63; Caja de Leruela, *Restauración de la abundancia de España*, 162, argued in the seventeenth century that in Naples "oxen carts could travel twenty-two and twenty-four miles each day . . . which are seven or eight leagues. I do not know if this is because they [the oxen] pull from their neck and not from the head as in Spain." See also *Propiedades del cabildo segoviano*, 69–70.

18. For northern Europe, see Homans, *English Villages of the Thirteenth Century*, 79–81; Duby, *Rural Economy and Country Life*, 21. For Castile, see *Propiedades del cabildo segoviano*, 92; Martínez Sopena, *La tierra de Campos occidental*, 533.

19. AHN, Clero, carp. 1733, no. 2 (20-November-1321).

20. *Propiedades del cabildo segoviano*, 65–66.

21. The study of mills in Castile has already attracted a great deal of scholarly attention. See, for example, Glick, *Islamic and Christian Spain*, ch. 7; Teofilo F. Ruiz, "Tecnología y división de propiedad: Los molinos de Burgos en la baja edad media," in *Sociedad y poder real en Castilla*, 73–93; Adeline Rucquoi, "Molinos et aceñas au coeur de la Castille septentrionale (XIe–XVe siècles)," *Les Espagnes médiévales: Aspects économiques et sociaux* (Nice: Faculté des lettres et sciences humaines de Nice, 1983), 107–22; Jean Gautier-Dalché, "Moulin à eau, seigneurie, communauté rurale dans le nord de l'Espagne (IXe–XIIe siècles)," in *Etudes de civilisation médiévales, IXe–XIIe siècles: Mélanges offerts à E. R. Labande* (Poitiers: C.E.S.C.M., 1974).

22. *DMA*, 155–56.

23. AHN, Clero, carp. 307, no. 1 (10-February-1312); carp. 308, no. 1 (5-February-1316); carp. 311, no. 15 (17-January-1339), et passim. See also Bonaudo de Magnani, 52–60; Jean Gautier-Dalché, "Le domaine du monastère de Santo Toribio de Liébana: Formation, structure et modes d'exploitation," *Anuario de estudios medievales* 2 (1965): 65–70.

24. On mills see AHN, Clero, carp. 1663, no. 4 (9-May-1299); carp. 1664, no. 7 (n.d.) et passim. Ruiz, "Tecnología y división de propiedad," 84, 89–93. For salt mills, see *Fuentes*, 3: 302, 304, 311–12, 322, 326, 388. For division of land in Avila, see AHN, Clero, carp. 25, no. 7 (5-September-1303). For fragmentation of vineyards in Segovia, see *Propiedades del cabildo segoviano*, 57. For houses, see below.

25. For vineyards, see Bonaudo de Magnani, 56; AMB, clasif. 750 (16-January-1336); Camacho, *Historia jurídica del cultivo*, 72–74; Luis Martínez García, "La concentración de la propiedad urbana burgalesa mediante la concesión de 'pasadas de tierra,' (1150–1250)," in *La ciudad de Burgos: Actas del congreso de historia de Burgos* (Madrid: Junta de Castilla y León, 1985), 89–90.

26. For litigations over boundaries, see *Oña*, 2: 738–39 (28-January-1275); 778–

79 (26-April-1277); 814 (26-June-1279); AHN, Clero, carp. 232, no. 9 (29-August-1255); carp. 239, no. 17 (2-September-1290) et passim.

27. Julius Klein, *The Mesta: A Study in Spanish Economic History, 1273–1836* (Cambridge, Mass.: Harvard University Press, 1920), 20–22. For the selling of commons in Serranos de Avianos, see above and passim. Camacho, *Historia jurídica del cultivo*, 73. In the documents of the cathedral of Santo Domingo de la Calzada, the chapter leased land to Juan Martínez, a blacksmith, under the condition that he plant a vineyard and fence it with a stone fence: *Colección diplomática calceatense*, 100–101 (7-September-1291).

28. *Silos*, 203 (7-September-1253); *Fuentes*, I: 144–45 (26-April-1336); Camacho, *Historia jurídica del cultivo*, 72–74. For fencing and removal of fences from the arable and common lands in modern Spain, see Behar, *Santa María del Monte*, 197–99.

29. Duby, *Rural Economy and Country Life*, 273.

30. *Propiedades del cabildo segoviano*, 53–56; Juan Ruiz, *Libro de buen amor*, stanza 1030.

31. García de Cortázar, *San Millán de la Cogolla*, 286; Moreta Velayos, *El monasterio de San Pedro de Cardeña*, 219.

32. AHN, Clero, carp. 1733, no. 2 (20-September-1321); another example in carp. 1732, no. 7 (31-October-1306).

33. Moreta Velayos, *El monasterio de San Pedro de Cardeña*, 218. See also Casado Alonso, *Señores, mercaderes y campesinos*, 121, 125–26.

34. *Propiedades del cabildo segoviano*, 54, 56; Casado Alonso, *Señores, mercaderes y campesinos*, 38–40.

35. *Becerro*, I: 443; *Fuentes*, I: 122–23.

36. Slicher von Bath, *The Agrarian History of Western Europe*, 18–19, 172; García de Cortázar, *San Millán de la Cogolla*, 288–89; Glick, *Islamic and Christian Spain*, 93; José Ángel García de Cortázar, *La época medieval: Historia de España Alfaguara*, II (Madrid: Alianza Editorial, 1973), 241; Duby, *Rural Economy and Country Life*, 99–103.

37. Ringrose, *Transportation and Economic Stagnation in Spain*, xx; Nicolás Cabrillana, "Los despoblados en Castilla la Vieja," *Hispania* 119 (1971): 516–17. See also the low yield figures reported by García Sanz, *Desarrollo y crisis*, 156, cuadro 24.

38. Vicente Ángel Álvarez Palenzuela, *Monasterios cistercienses en Castilla (siglos XII–XIII)* (Valladolid: Universidad de Valladolid, 1978), 236–39, 254; Javier Pérez-Embid, *El Cister en Castilla y León: Monacato y dominios rurales (s. XII–XV)* (Valladolid: Junta de Castilla y León, 1986), 420–59; Glick, *Islamic and Christian Spain*, 102–4. On northern husbandry, see Duby, *Rural Economy and Country Life*, 88–90, 387–90 and citations therein. On Muslim husbandry, see Emilio García Gómez, "Sobre agricultura arábigoandaluza: Cuestiones bibliográficas," *Al-Andalus* 10 (1945); Lucie Bolens, *Les méthodes culturales au Moyen Âge d'après les traités d'agronomie andalouse: Tradition et techniques* (Geneva: Droz, 1974), and her *Agronomes andalous du Moyen Âge* (Geneva: Droz, 1981).

39. Gautier-Dalché, "Le domaine du monastère de Santo Toribio de Liébana," 86.

40. *Vida económica*, 209–10.

4. The Lands of Santa María la Real de Aguilar de Campóo in the Late Middle Ages: A Case Study

An overview of northern Castilian agriculture provides the reader with a series of generalizations that may or may not be true of particular regions. We must reexamine the questions raised earlier on the nature of Castilian agriculture and see how they apply to one specific area of northern Castile. Thus this chapter is, among other things, a case study, an exercise in microhistory.

My sample is a case study of rural life in the lands of the monastery of Santa María la Real de Aguilar de Campóo, and my aims here are threefold: First, I wish to examine the patterns of real-estate transactions, as well as leasing agreements between the monastery and its dependant tenants. Second, citing the evidence of an extant census of more than five hundred peasants (c. 1300) and of their obligations to their ecclesiastical lord, I will discuss the patterns of peasants' dues, work, and lives at the beginning of the thirteenth century. Third, whenever possible, I will attempt to compare the rural conditions in the lands of Santa María de Aguilar de Campóo, as depicted by the census, with the evidence provided by the *Becerro de behetrías* in the mid-fourteenth century. The diverse themes that I explore in this chapter must also be placed within the context of the material discussed in the next chapter, in which I examine hundreds of transactions involving the selling and leasing of lands throughout most of northern Castile.

The Domain of Santa María la Real de Aguilar de Campóo

The monastery of Santa María la Real de Aguilar de Campóo, a male monastery of the order of Premôntre, dated its foundation to the twelfth century. Located in the *villa* of Aguilar de Campóo (today in the province of Palencia), the monastery was under the jurisdiction of the bishop of

Burgos during the Middle Ages. Aguilar de Campóo, on the banks of the Pisuerga River, held a privileged position at the crossroads of several major commercial routes. From the Bay of Biscay ports of San Vicente de la Barquera southward—through Cabuerniga and Cabezón de la Sal (with important salt wells) and also southward from Santander—the road headed to Aguilar de Campóo through Reinosa, and from Aguilar further south to Palencia and Valladolid. Even though this way through Aguilar de Campóo did not have, in this period, the importance of the routes further east linking Burgos and the coast, it was nevertheless an option available for the region's trade. More important, however, was the road southeast connecting Aguilar de Campóo with Burgos and a series of small roads connecting the town on the Pisuerga with the fertile Tierra de Campos on the west and part of the Burgalese hinterland in the northeast.

The valley of the Pisuerga was, by Castilian standards, a fairly prosperous agricultural region.[1] The town itself was, throughout most of the period, a royal town, and it was granted to Don Tello, one of Alfonso XI's bastards, only toward the middle of the fourteenth century.[2] Royal jurisdiction in the region provided a modicum of protection for Santa María, even though, from the mid-thirteenth century on, the monastery frequently had to protest against noble excesses and the abuses of royal officials.[3] Moreover, the monastery engaged in numerous litigations with other ecclesiastical entities and, above all, with the *concejo* (city council) of Aguilar de Campóo and the rural *concejos* in its own domain. We will have the opportunity to examine these conflicts later, but one must remember that this endless round of litigations and arbitrations, more often than not decided in favor of the monastery, was an ingenious and useful way of preserving the integrity of the domain.[4]

The life of the monastery, however, was not always fraught with trouble. Donations, royal and/or seignorial, increased the wealth of the monastery. In 1255, Alfonso X granted to the monks one-fourth of the *portazgo* (tolls) collected on Pie de Concha—a *puerto* or internal custom station north of Aguilar—in return for some properties the monastery owned in Aguilar de Campóo. Before the spread of the Black Death throughout Castile in 1350, Pie de Concha collected around 3,000 *mrs.* annually, of which the abbot and monastery of Santa María received some 750 *mrs.*[5] The many privileges and royal exemptions received through the first two hundred years of its foundation, the mills it owned, crowding the banks of the Pisuerga, and its lands and vassals spread through northern Castile speak to us of Santa María's economic power, but the signals of trouble and growing economic difficulties also become more visible as one turns to the fourteenth century.

Society and Economy in the Lands of Santa María

The documentation of Santa María la Real de Aguilar de Campóo extant at the Archivo histórico nacional, *Clero* and *Codices* sections, provides a partial view of economic conditions and activity in the region. Between 1240 and 1359, one finds approximately ninety-eight real-estate transactions. As I have noted elsewhere, these documents probably represent only a fraction of far more numerous exchanges of property in the area, and we must assume that the monastery participated in many more economic transactions than the ones for which documentation has survived. A few of the extant documents are defaced beyond readability; others refer tangentially to transactions for which we have no direct evidence, probably documents now lost or exchanges never recorded. Moreover, I have also included in this sample the evidence from San Andrés de Arroyo and other monasteries nearby. Although they do not provide as many surviving documents as Santa María de Aguilar de Campóo, they help us obtain a wider vision of economic and social conditions in the region.

I have not included pious donations to the monastery or those granted in return for maintenance or burial, nor exchanges of properties in which, at least according to the documents, no money was transferred from buyer to seller among the transactions considered here. There were fifteen such exchanges of property, most of them between the monastery and petty nobles and free peasants in the region. The indications are that these exchanges were undertaken to consolidate property in certain areas or to gain some desirable property, such as mills. In some cases, both ends were accomplished in a single transaction. On 7 April 1290, the monastery made such an arrangement with Díaz Roys; the monastery gave Díaz lands, vineyards, houses, *solares*, gardens, meadows, and pasturelands in Melgar de Yusso in exchange for two mills in Miranda near two other mills owned by Santa María. Thirty-one donations of lands, mill rights, houses, and other types of property complemented exchanges and monetary transactions as means for augmenting or, in some cases, defending the monastic holdings from encroachment by the nobility.[6]

The ninety-eight transactions involved overwhelmingly lands, gardens, mills and/or mill rights, meadows, and pastureland, or included such

TABLE 4.1.   Mills of Miranda and Huço (9 May 1299).

Right Purchased by Monastery	Price Paid (in mrs.)
One share (una *vez*)*	31 *mrs.*
Two shares minus one-third share	52 *mrs.*
One share plus one-third share	47⅓ *mrs.*
One share	31 *mrs.*
Two shares	62 *mrs.*
One-half share	15½ *mrs.*
One-third of a share	10 *mrs.*
One-third of a share	10 *mrs.*

Source: AHN, Clero, carp. 1663, no. 4 (9-V-1299).

*The right to grind once a month.

vague language as *todo lo que tiene* (all that he or she has) or *todo cuanto hay* (everything there is). There are only six mentions of vineyards and two of fruit trees. No mention of flax fields is found in the extant documentation. This was essentially a cereal-growing land, and the banks of the Pisuerga River were far too valuable for flax. As is the case with most extant documents in Castile, those of Santa María do not specify the amount of land being sold, thus it is impossible to make a statement about prices. In 1299 the monastery bought rights in the mills of Miranda, near other mills acquired nine years earlier, at the prices shown in Table 4.1.

Since these transactions involved several mills, one may conclude that 31 *mrs.* was, at least in the area of Campóo and in late thirteenth-century Castile, the price for one turn or one hour(?) of grinding monthly. Yet in the first half of the thirteenth century, probably fifty or sixty years earlier, a completely different set of prices can be found. Some friars bought milling rights in the mill of Suso (Huço) at the rates shown in Table 4.2.

Several comments are in order. First the prices of mill rights had gone up: one-half *vez* cost between 2 *mrs.*, 2 *ss.* and 2 *mrs.*, 3 *ss.* before 1250, and 15½ *mrs.* in 1299, although one must also add that inflation was rampant after the 1260s. Second, property and, in this particular case, rights of grinding were fragmented into almost minuscule proportions: one-half of one-eighth. The series of documents provides other prices. Rights to four and a half *veces* of grinding sold for 147 *mrs.* in 1313, which is very much in line with the prices of 1299. On the other hand, in 1307 the monastery paid 2,600 *mrs.* for one-fourth of the mills and *aceñas* on the Pisuerga River by Aguilar de

TABLE 4.2.   Transactions at the Mill of Huço (before 1250).

Right Purchased	Price Paid
One-half share (*vez*)	2 *mrs.*, 2 *sueldos* (*ss.*)
One-fourth share	4 *ss.*
One-half share	no price
One-sixth share	4 *ss.*
One-half share	2 *mrs.*, 3 *ss.*
One-third share	2 *mrs.*, 3 *ss.*
One-fourth share	2 *mrs.*, 2 *ss.*
One-half and one-half of one-eighth share	3 *mrs.*, 6 *ss.*

Source: AHN, Clero, carp. 1664, no. 7 (n.d.). Written in Castilian; probably mid-thirteenth century.

Campóo. The fact that they were *açeñas* (the term always indicated the more sophisticated vertical mills) and their location in Aguilar certainly influenced price regardless of the period.[7]

Returning to our analysis of the ninety-eight transactions, we can break them down into a series of useful categories; these should be compared with the overview of land transactions throughout northern Castile provided in the next chapter. Table 4.3 provides some preliminary indication of the different trends in prices and in the buying or selling of land found in the documentation of Aguilar.

In the extant documentation of Santa María la Real, almost two-thirds of the buying and selling of land took place before 1300, with a clear drop-off in the first half of the fourteenth century. This pattern is quite consistent with the evidence from other regions of Castile. In fact, throughout northern Castile the number of extant documents (not only those limited to transactions or exchanges of property) for the first half of the fourteenth century is considerably less than for the second half of the thirteenth century.

Forty-three transactions involved exchanges of money of less than 50 *mrs.* (including two transactions in 1305 by which the monastery purchased two pieces of land for two *fanegas* of bread—half wheat, half barley—at around 4 *mrs.* per *fanega*). Fifty-eight of the transactions amounted to less than 100 *mrs.*[8] This is somewhat compensated for by some rather large purchases, especially after 1300. In 1341, Gutier González de Padiella and his wife, Johanna Gutiérrez, sold all they owned of a mill on the Pisuerga

TABLE 4.3.   Land Transactions in the Region of Campóo.

A.   *Number of Transactions by Decade*

	Before 1300		1300–59
Date	No. of Transactions	Date	No. of Transactions
1240–59	10	1300–1309	7
1260–69	4	1310–19	8
1270–79	9	1320–29	10
1280–89	12	1330–39	9
1290–99	13*	1340–49	2
No date**	13	1350–59	1
Total	61		37 TOTAL 98

B.   *Number of Transactions by Price Range*

	Before 1300	1300–59	
Price (in *mrs.*)	No. of Transactions	No. of Transactions	Total
1–50	37	6	43
51–100	9	4	13
101–200	4	4	8
201–300	4	2	6
301–400	3	3	6
401–500	0	2	2
501–999	1	4	5
1,000+	3	10	13
Payment in kind	0	2	2
Total	61	37	98

Source: AHN, Clero, carps. 1657–74.

*Twelve of the thirteen transactions in this decade are found in one document, consisting of purchases of milling rights. See above.
**These are documents from the thirteenth century.

River, including dams, lands, and all the milling rights, to Johanna's sister for 4,000 *mrs*. Mills, as noted earlier, were often expensive property; furthermore, this sale appears to have been undertaken to settle a testament and, as was the case for a good number of land transactions in the period, to consolidate property, in this case, by placing the mill in the hands of one owner.[9]

One should look more closely at these large (more than 1,000 *mrs.*) land transactions for clues to the dynamics of land exchange in the area (see Table 4.4). Of these thirteen transactions, the monastery appears as a buyer four times. Two of its purchases, in 1281 and 1283, were in San Cebrián de Mudá, north of Aguilar de Campóo in the *merindad* of Liébana-Pernia. They represented an important investment in a region in which the monastery already had property and held rights. By 1351, half of the village belonged to Santa María la Real and the other half was the *behetría* of three noblemen. Each of the monastery's vassals paid an annual *infurción* of two *fanegas* of rye and eleven *dineros* (*ds.*)[10] The other two transactions probably involved no exchange of money, since the amount of the sale was to be given back to the monastery for anniversaries. One of them, that of 1307, involved parts in mills and *aceñas* (vertical mills) on the Pisuerga River and thus marked one further step in the consolidation of milling rights and ownership in Campóo itself. One should note in passing that the donor, Gonzalo García de Aguilar, had purchased shares in the mill from Domingo Miguel, who had been *alcalde* of Aguilar on at least five previous occasions—in 1284, 1287, 1291, 1305, and 1310—and who was in all probability an official of the *concejo* of Aguilar de Campóo for at least a quarter of a century.[11]

Santa María la Real appears as a seller in these large transactions only once in 1295; as it happened, the lands could not be alienated and had to be sold back to the monastery. In most of the other transactions, we witness exchanges of property between relatives to settle wills or to consolidate property. Such was the case in 1303, 1319, 1325, 1335, and 1341. Of particular importance for its implications for the social history of the region are the transactions of 1304 and 1338. In the first instance, Gutier García Calderón bought rights over *solariegos* (those owing seignorial dues) from Alvar Royz de Catalabaçano in Val Vercosa. No land or property is mentioned, though it is clear that if *solariegos* or the rights they owed were transferred, then dues from the peasants (at least *infurción*) and perhaps *sernas* or work on arranged dates were included. By the time the *Becerro de behetrías* was compiled forty-seven years later, Val Vercosa was fully in the hands of the abbot of Santa María la Real, and each inhabited *solar* or unit of cultivation paid three *fanegas* of bread (half wheat, half barley) annually in *infurción*. In addition, the peasants of Val Vercosa paid 84 *mrs.* in *martiniega* (one-half for the king, one-quarter for the abbot, one-quarter for the *adelantado*) plus *servicios*, *fonsadera*, and *moneda*.[12]

The transaction in 1338 provides different types of clues. Clearly, as seen

TABLE 4.4. Large Land Transactions in the Area of Campóo (1281–1341).

Year	Buyer	Seller	Price	What Was Sold
1281	Monastery	Doña Toda and daughter	1,200 *mrs.*	Houses, lands, fruit trees, orchards, and rights in the church of San Cebrián
1283	Monastery	Gutierre Royz	3,000 *mrs.*	Houses, lands, pasturelands
1295	Doña Mayor Díaz	Monastery	1,500 *mrs.*	Houses, lands, mills, vineyards
1303*	John Abbat and Domingo Pérez (brothers)	John González	1,100 *mrs.*; cannot alienate	One-third of what he owned (land had been bought from town council of Aguilar) *Solariegos?*
1304	Gutier García	Alvar Royz	2,000 *mrs.*	
1307	Monastery	Gonzalo García	2,600 *mrs.* and payment for anniversary	One-fourth of mills on the Pisuerga
1315	Monastery	Diego Pérez and daughter	4,000 *mrs.* and payment for anniversary	Lands
1319*	Domingo and Doña María	Mari Estévanez, three daughters, and son-in-law	2,600 *mrs.*	Lands, houses, pastures, gardens
1325*	Ferrant Royz	John Royz and wife	3,500 *mrs.*	Everything he owned
1335*	Ferrant Fernández de la Dehesa	García Fernández de la Dehesa	1,500 *mrs.*	Houses, mills, vineyards
1338	John Gutiérrez	Gonzalo Pérez	1,500 *mrs.*	Lands
1339	John Pérez and wife	Ferrant Yánez	1,240 *mrs.*	Houses in Aguilar
1341*	Teresa González	Gutier González and wife	4,000 *mrs.*	Half a mill

Source: AHN, Clero, carps. 1657–1674.

*Buyers and sellers are relatives.

in 1307, 1338, 1339, and 1341, real estate in the town of Aguilar de Campóo was a great deal more expensive than that in the countryside, especially if the properties were mills near the walls of the town. In the 1338 transaction, we see glimpses of the social structure of Aguilar as well as the social mobility of northern Castile. Gonzalo Pérez, son of a cloth merchant of Aguilar, had entered the church and, with his brother, sold lands, inherited from his father, near the town market. This was most probably the means of settling an inheritance. In 1349 Gonzalo was canon of the cathedral of Burgos and archpriest of Aguilar. His will, drawn up that year, reveals to us a man of considerable wealth and property in the area of Aguilar, with important familial and social ties there as well as a sentimental attachment to his hometown. The chaplaincies that he founded in the cathedral of Burgos were reserved for his relatives and, in their absence, for citizens of Aguilar de Campóo.[13]

LEASING THE LAND

We should turn now to the *arriendos* or lands given by the monastery either for life or on a short-term basis, what is known in Castile as *censo* or *census*. Altogether between 1240 and 1359 there are twenty-three such contracts extant in the documentation of Santa María la Real. This number does not include the *prestamos* or outright grants of land made by the monastery as compensation for services rendered, or perhaps as a form of tribute to unruly nobles in the region from whom it sought protection or, at least, an allaying of their ambitions. Donations of the latter type occurred in 1309, 1311, and 1327.[14]

The extant documentation shows the growing difficulties the monastery faced in cultivating its lands. By 1300 most of its domain was worked through sharecropping agreements. A shortage of manpower is evident from a series of disputes between some peasants of Cernera and the monastery. In 1313, Fray Domingo de Cinco Villas, representing the monastery of Santa María, and thirteen men and women from Cernera argued their conflicting positions in the presence of an arbitrator, Yusto Pérez, *alcalde* of Aguilar de Campóo. Originally, the monastery had granted uncultivated land to these peasants in return for their recognition of Santa María la Real's lordship and their obligation to work the land. Eighteen years later, the land remained fallow and the peasants worked for a lay lord elsewhere; yet, they had not relinquished the monastery's property. In a deposition to the Infanta María, Lady of Las Huelgas, the peasants claimed that it was impossible to repopulate the farms granted in 1313 because there were not enough men and women to do so. For a good number of years, perhaps even close to two decades, the monastery held good lands that were going to waste and from which it received no income. This fact and such evidence as royal willingness to reduce the number of peasants on the tax rolls in Cillamayor, Villadiego, and other villages in the region of Aguilar de Campóo—from twenty-five to seventeen taxpayers in Cillamayor to cite just one case—made leasing agreements a preferred solution in the face of labor shortages and growing attacks on the monastic domain.[15] Table 4.5 provides an overview of the evolution of leasing in the lands of the monastery.

Twenty-three leases of land over a period of more than a century is indeed a meager number. Yet, the monastery of Santa María la Real already had most of its demesne farmed out to sharecroppers and lifelong tenants. Nowhere in the documentation is there evidence of direct farming of the demesne, although some must have taken place, especially in gardens and vineyards. Unfortunately, without records comparable to those extant for Benedictine monasteries in 1338, we can only theorize about such activities. Also surprising is the vague nature of these agreements. In many of them, there is little indication of what is being rented, on what terms, or for how long. This is not always unusual in Castile, but the monastery's letting of land or real estate on such imprecise terms compares unfavorably with the very elaborate contracts drawn up by the nuns of San Andrés de Arroyo, a monastery located nearby.

More than two-thirds of the leasing of monastic land took place after 1300, when economic and political pressures on most ecclesiastical institutions in Castile were increasing, and labor shortages, as mentioned earlier, may have influenced the economic policies of the monastery. There is little one can deduce from the time span of the agreements or the terms of payment. Leasing of property for the life of the lessee, for life plus twenty years, or forever were the common terms used for drawing up these types of contracts. In some cases the monastery demanded an acknowledgment of vassalage from the renters (*que sean vasallos*) which here, of course, means something quite different from the lord-vassal relationships of northern Europe. In two particular cases, one in 1261 and the other in 1317, the renters (a couple in the first instance and three brothers and a sister in the other) agreed to pay 1 *mr.* and one pound of wax respectively in *mañería* and *nuncio*, the first, an ancient seignorial right. Its survival into the mid-thirteenth century does not equate with the vision of renters or, at least, those who entered into the 1261 agreement, as free and prosperous farmers.[16]

TABLE 4.5.   Leasing Agreements in the Region of Aguilar de Campóo.

A.   *Rentals by Decade*
Before 1300   *1300–1359*

Date	No.	Date	No.
Before 1250	1	1300–1309	1
1250–1259	0	1310–1319	5
1260–1269	4	1320–1329	0
1270–1279	0	1330–1339	6
1280–1289	0	1340–1349	3
1290–1299	2	1350–1359	1
Total	7		16

B.   *Rentals by Lessee/Lessor*

Lessee	Before 1300	1300–1359	Total
Ecclesiastical institution	1		1
Family and/or couple	5	6	11
Group of men	1	3	4
Single male		5	5
Single female		2	2
Total	7	16	23

Lessor	Before 1300	1300–1359	Total
Monastery	6	15	21
Sublease		1	1
Other ecclesiastical institution	1	—	1
Total	7	16	23

C.   *Length of Contract*

Term	Before 1300	1300–1359	Total
For life or "forever"	5	9	14
Not stated	2	3	5
Four years	0	1	1
Five years	0	1	1
Nine years	0	1	1
Ten years	0	1	1
Total	7	16	23

TABLE 4.5.   *Continued*

D.   *Type of Payment*

Payment	Before 1300	1300–1359	Total
In kind	1	5	6
Work and/or in kind or specie	2	4	6
In specie	3	2	5
Not stated	1	5	6
Total	7	16	23

Source: AHN, Clero, carps. 1656–74.

What one witnesses in most of these rental agreements, however, especially after 1300, is the monastery of Santa María la Real's letting out of mostly uncultivated land on somewhat favorable terms. In the lease agreement of 1317, the abbot and monks rented a *solar* to the aforementioned three brothers and sister who agreed to build houses, to inhabit the said land, and to pay one *fanega* of wheat, one piece of *tocino* (bacon), and one pound of wax. In addition to the land, the monastery also promised burial places in the monastery for its four tenants. Thus, economic necessity, piety, and ancient manorial rights come together at Campóo to reveal the survival of reciprocal noneconomic ties adjoining new economic forms. At the same time, the monks of Santa María la Real feared the permanent loss of their domains and insisted, therefore, on oaths of vassalage and fidelity, or the often-repeated clause that forbade the selling or alienation of the lands to lay lords.[17]

Payments in kind were rendered on the September feast of Santa María and payments in money on the feast of Saint Martin, both of them traditional dates for payment in most of northern Castile. The amounts due in rent fluctuated from as low as 1 *mr.* per year to the 130 *mrs.* paid by Pedro Ruiz and his wife María Gómez for the house of Santa María de Posadorios in 1297, or the 3,000 *mrs.* plus one-tenth of their harvest given by Diego Gómez de Sant Doval and his wife, Elvira Fernández, for vineyards, gardens, fruit trees, mills, and lands in Castrillo de Río Pisuerga. In other instances, payment came in odd combinations: ten pieces of bread, two hens, two *quartos* (*cuartos*) of wine, seven *celemines* of barley, and 6 *mrs.* annually. The largest rental was contracted in 1334, when Marina García and her two sons, Gonzalo González and M(artín?) González took over the monastery house, woods, and lands of San Agustín for the life of Marina plus twenty years. The mother and her two sons agreed to give to the monastery two hundred and fifty *fanegas* "of bread" (half wheat, half barley). Sixty *fanegas* were to be brought to the monastery on the September feast of Santa María and one hundred and ninety delivered to the church of San Agustín (a dependency of Santa María la Real). Furthermore, oxen had to be provided to transport four carts of wood, three *procuraciones*, one good pig, two sheep, three cheeses, one hundred pounds of lard, half a dozen fish, fifty sardines, three pounds of oil, produce from the garden, clothes, one scapular, and many other things far too numerous to include here. This was obviously an extensive property, as measured by the accompanying payment, but within the overall pattern of the granting of monastic land, this transaction was the exception rather than the norm. Overall, the land or properties let out seem to have been small, capable of supporting one family or at the most two or three families and no one else.[18]

Of the twenty-three properties parceled out by the abbot and monks of Santa María la Real, we know the location of seventeen. They were spread over fifteen different villages in the *merindades* of Monzón, Aguilar de Campóo and Liébana-Pernia. Of these fifteen villages, twelve had passed from the hands of Santa María la Real into those of lay lords by 1351, when the monastery is not listed as holding lordships in any of them.[19] In two cases, we have direct evidence of rental agreements in which, despite specific bans on the alienation of the holding, the lands had already passed into secular hands. For example, in 1266 the monastery let a sizable property in Castrillo de Río Pisuerga to Don Diego Díaz Gómez de Sandoval and his wife, Doña Inez Álvarez, in return for 202 *mrs.* and seven *moyos* of bread (three wheat, two rye, two barley). In the *Becerro de behetrías*, almost one hundred years later, the village was a *behetría* of John Fernández de Sant Doval, most probably a descendant of Diego Díaz Gómez de Sandoval. In 1304, the abbot and monks of Santa María rented a large holding in the village of Barzenilla to Doña María, the widow of Fernando Díaz, for the term of her life. The rent amounted to 100 *fanegas* of bread (one-third each of wheat, barley, rye). By the mid-fourteenth century, two parts of the village were in the hands of Fernando Díaz Duque (the son or grandson of María), and only one-third remained in the lordship of the abbot of Santa María.[20]

There are even better examples of how swift the pace of usurpation of the monastic domain was or, indeed, of how fragile was the hold the monastery had over its own land. A few examples will illustrate this. In 1333, the abbot and monks of Santa María rented out a house and twelve *aranzadas* of land in Castrillo de Villa Vega for five years. In the *Becerro de behetrías*, the lands had become part of the lordship of John Rodríguez de Cisneros. The very sizable holding of San Agustín granted in 1334 (discussed above) had also been lost to the monastery by 1351. And, even more surprising, the lands of Santa María in Dehesa de Romanos, rented in 1350 to local residents and paying a rent of fifty *fanegas* of bread (half wheat, half barley), had, one year later, ceased to be part of Santa María's domain. Instead, it had become a *behetría* of Fernán García Duque, probably a relative of the nobleman who had expropriated the monastery's property in Barzenilla.[21]

The extant documentation reveals the leasing of vineyards on only two occasions. In one instance, the monastery carefully excluded vineyards from the extensive property let out in a rental agreement granted in 1334. The area of Campóo, lacking favorable soil or climatic conditions for its cultivation, did not have a strong viticulture tradition. Yet, the monastery sought to preserve its own supply of wine, probably to serve its liturgical needs, but also for its gift and hospitality value. As we saw earlier when the records of land transactions included the right to burial in the monastery, there is not always a strict economic explanation for the behavior of medieval men and women. More than profit or self-interest moved them, and the actions of individuals and ecclesiastical corporations can only be understood in terms of a complex mixture of tradition, routine, and the demands of emerging economic and social structures. Nothing, therefore, is simple or easily grasped and, regardless of the appearance of preciseness that tables and figures provide, we have only an incomplete understanding of how and why medieval men and women acted, especially on economic issues.[22]

A Comparison with the Lands of San Andrés de Arroyo

Before we turn our attention to other aspects of rural life in the lands of Santa María la Real, it may be useful to compare the nature of exchanges of land and rental agreements undertaken by Santa María la Real with those of the nearby monastery of San Andrés de Arroyo. In fact, the nuns of San Andrés shared the lordship of several villages with the monks of Santa María. San Andrés's domain was spread over at least fifty-seven different villages and places in four *merindades* of northern Castile, making the task of collecting rents and administration not an easy one. There are some differences between the documentation of the two monasteries. San Andrés's documents are far more detailed and specific than those of Santa

María, but they are not sufficiently numerous to allow one to draw over-arching conclusions. Table 4.6 shows the buying and selling transactions for San Andrés, listed according to the same criteria applied to the records of Santa María.

San Andrés de Arroyo and Santa María la Real shared a similar geo-graphical space and faced the same problems of noble usurpation and the abusive royal agents' disregard for their long-held privileges. The nuns at San Andrés also engaged in expensive litigation against laymen, other ecclesiastic institutions, and rural councils seeking to protect their rights. Nor was the Cistercian monastery spared the disasters posed by the royal minorities or the endemic violence plaguing most of Castile at the turn of the century. The local market in the village of Santa María de la Vid over which the nuns held jurisdiction ceased to exist, and the village itself became uninhabited and barren by the early fourteenth century. The nuns' plaintive appeals to Alfonso XI or, rather, to his tutors in 1318 reveal their financial losses and increasing impotence over time. Even the small royal grant of 36 mrs. weekly from the tolls of Aguilar, given to the nuns long before the trouble of Alfonso XI's minority, was in arrears for a year.[23]

San Andrés de Arroyo had no more success in retaining the faith and service of its vassals throughout the land than had Santa María la Real. For even if the men of San Pedro recognized the abbess of San Andrés as their lord in 1340 after protracted litigations, they did not pay a penny nor do any work for the monastery for six years, and by 1351 they had abandoned the lordship of the nuns altogether.[24] And yet, in spite of all the similarities between the two monasteries, there are intrinsic differences in the extant documentation, differences that are clear from a quick glance at the respec-tive tables shown below and which become much sharper when examined in detail.

We do not find in the sparse documentation of San Andrés the dis-parity in the number of transactions before and after 1300 that we found for Santa María. More important, the prices paid are significantly different. Unlike our previous sample, eleven acquisitions—more than half of the total—were for amounts greater than 500 mrs., a considerable sum if we consider that the approximate annual salary of a baker was 60 mrs. and that of an advocator (procurador de pleitos) was 200 mrs.[25] One must note also how few extant transactions amount to less than 100 mrs. These nineteen transactions reflect almost exclusively the exchange of property for money between the well-to-do of the region and the monastery. Not surprisingly, vineyards and mills (the former seldom found in the contracts of Santa

TABLE 4.6.   Land Transactions of San Andrés de Arroyo.

A.   Number of Transactions by Decade

Date	Before 1300 No. of Transactions	Date	1300–59 No. of Transactions
1230–39	4	1300–1309	1
1240–49	2	1310–19	2
1250–59	0	1320–29	1
1260–69	1	1330–39	5
1270–79	0	1340–49	0
1280–89	0	1350–59	0
1290–99	3		9
Total	10		TOTAL 19

B.   Number of Transactions by Price Range

Price (in *mrs.*)	Before 1300 No. of Transactions	1300–59 No. of Transactions	Total
1–50	1	1	2
51–100	1	0	1
101–200	2	0	2
201–300	2	0	2
301–400	1	0	1
401–500	0	1	1
501–999	1	1	2
1,000+	2	6	8
Total	10	9	19

C.   Number of Transactions by Category of Buyer

Transactions in Which the Buyer Was:	Before 1300	After 1300	Total
Couple	1		1
Man	1		1
Monastery	8	9	17
Total	10	9	19

TABLE 4.6. *Continued*

D. *Number of Transactions by Category of Seller*

Transactions in Which the Seller Was:	Before 1300	After 1300	Total
Other ecclesiastical institutions	1	0	1
Group of men	3	2	5
Single man	1	4	5
Couple	3	1	4
Single woman	1	2	3
Family	1	0	1
Total	10	9	19

Source: AHN, Clero, carps. 1731–35.

María) are mentioned in almost every transaction. Moreover, the monastery's pattern of acquisition indicates a conscious decision to consolidate its holdings in a few villages. Four of the transactions involved lands, vineyards, gardens, meadows, and mills in Pladanos; another four were in Quintana Tello; two were in Olea (?); and two were in Santa María de la Vid. There is little one can say about the social status of the sellers. They were most probably well-to-do free peasants and petty noblemen. In some cases the sales were intermediate transactions in the settlement of a will. In the only purchase under 100 *mrs.* that is extant for the period after 1300, the nuns of San Andrés bought a *solar* in Quintana Tello from Doña Sancha Pérez, daughter of the monastery's blacksmith, for 50 *mrs.* She had previously purchased it from Roy Díaz de Sant Cebrián. Sancha Pérez and others like her belonged to or were relatives of that middling group of artisans, small merchants, and prosperous farmers, the people most active in the land market during this period.[26]

It is in the *arriendos*, the property let out by the abbess of San Andrés de Arroyo, that we discern patterns quite distinct from those of Santa María la Real. Previously, we had the opportunity to examine some of these rental agreements, for as indicated, they provide careful inventories of agricultural tools. In Table 4.7 we may look in detail at those extant between 1230 and 1360. The number is so small that we have the luxury of examining them in some detail, although no sweeping conclusions can be advanced.

The fact that there were nine rental agreements over a period of almost eighty-one years leads me to assume that here, as elsewhere, the numbers indicate only a small portion of a larger market, the records of which have

TABLE 4-7.   Land Rentals in the Domain of San Andrés de Arroyo.

Date	Lessee	Lessor	Terms	What Was Leased
1251	San Andrés	Twenty-one men from San Pedro de Arroyo	Cultivate vineyard; harvest to be divided in half	*Serna*
1300	San Andrés	Couple (familiars of monastery: Domingo Pérez and María Fernández)	For 20 years, pay 80 *moyos* (half wheat, half barley), 4 carts, the tenth, 4 oxen, plus wine	House, lands, pastures, and a mill
1306	San Andrés	Couple (Juan Lucas and María Martínez)	For 8 years, pay two pigs for St. Martin and 40 *moyos* (half wheat, half barley) for San Cebrián	House, lands, and pasture; five oxen for 300 *mrs.*
1310	San Andrés	Single male (Alvar González)	For 15 years, 500 *mrs.* and 400 *fanegas* (half wheat, half barley)	Gardens, mills
1315	San Andrés	Single male (clergyman: John González)	For 11 years, 500 *mrs.* entry fee and 5 *moyos* (half wheat, half barley), two fat pigs, 24 *moyos* (10 wheat, 7 rye, 7 barley)	Farm and church
1318	San Andrés	*Vecinos* of Padilla	Crop to be shared in halves	*Villas*
1321	San Andrés	Couple (familiars of monastery: Ferrand Pérez and María Miguélez)	For 10 years, 180 *moyos* (half wheat, half barley), two fat pigs, and two carts	House of El Pozo
1332 (March)	San Andrés	Village	For 10 years, 120 *fanegas* (one-third each of wheat, barley, rye), one day of plowing, seeding, or threshing	Pasture, lands
1332 (April)	San Andrés	Single male (Pedro Álvarez)	For 5 years, 48 *fanegas* (half wheat, half barley), and 150 *mrs.* entry fee	Lands

Source: AHN Clero, carps. 1731–34.

been lost or destroyed. On the other hand, the terms dictated in the contracts point to the nuns' reluctance to part with their lands, even after detailed protective measures were in force. Two of them, the rental agreements of 1251 and 1318, were outright concessions of at least half of the property rented. In both cases, a *serna* in San Millán and lands in Padilla, the properties were not under cultivation, and the monastery gave one-half away in return for the work to be done on its own half. Significantly, there were no contracts for life. The longest term, twenty years in 1300, was granted to familiars (*familiares*) of the monastery, who were less likely to expropriate the monastic holdings. The properties were undoubtedly quite large, and five of them drew sizable rents in kind, as compared to the rents of Santa María la Real. Often an entry fee was demanded or some additional payment in issue, such as the tenth that was to be paid by Domingo Pérez and María Fernández in 1300, or the 500 *mrs.* and 150 *mrs.* initial payments respectively made by Alvar González in 1310 and Domingo Simón in 1332. On the other hand, the men of the municipal council of Enestar rented the house of San Román, near Villanueva de Henares, for ten years in return for 120 *fanegas* of bread (one-third each of wheat, barley, rye), plus the obligation to work and to bring their oxen one day every week during the plowing, seeding, and threshing seasons in San Andrés's lands at El Pozo.[27]

In one instance, the rental agreement of 1321, the nuns of San Andrés de Arroyo rented the house of El Pozo near Aguilar de Campóo to a couple, Ferrand Pérez and his wife, María Miguélez (both familiars of the monastery), for 180 *moyos* of bread (half wheat, half barley) payable on the feast day of San Cebrián. Although examined already in the previous chapter, this contract deserves notice again. As was the case for most of the other rental agreements extant in the documentation of San Andrés de Arroyo, payments for this property were spread out through the year. If grain was usually paid each year by the feast of San Cebrián, by Saint Martin the couple had to give two fat pigs to the monastery, and on Saint John's Day, two new carts. In return, besides the property, the couple received eight oxen (four teams of two oxen each), an ass, agricultural tools, clothing, ten hens, two roosters, twenty pigs, and a large inventory of other rural implements and household goods. More important, the agreement includes the seed lent to the renters to plant, forty *moyos* of wheat, forty-eight *moyos* of rye, and forty *moyos* of barley.

The amount of seed provides us with a rough estimate of the cultivated arable. If we turn *moyos* into *fanegas*—and one should emphasize again that these conversions are not always very accurate since each locality had its own set of measures—we end up with about 111.5 *fanegas* of rye and 92.9 *fanegas* each of wheat and barley which, altogether, make six *yugadas*, or six standard units of production. Each of the *yugadas* was to be worked by a team of two oxen. However, from Pérez Moreda's research in the area of Segovia, we know that between 1.25 and 1.5 *fanegas* of wheat were required for each *obrada* or *fanega* (as a unit of area) of land, two for barley, and one or less for rye. Following those calculations, we end up with a cultivated area of around 111.5 *fanegas* (as units of land area) or *obradas* (two *yugadas*, each *yugada* equaling 40 to 50 *fanegas*) of rye, 62 *fanegas* of wheat, and 46.5 *fanegas* of barley, or around four *yugadas* altogether. Thus, the animals given to the renters by the monastery were sufficient, one of the few instances in which arable and working animals matched.

If we use the seed/yield ratios from the accounts of Silos—approximately 1:4 for wheat, 1:6 or 7 for barley, and 1:3.5 or 4 for rye—and we assume that nothing went wrong with the weather, then, converting the results back into *moyos*, we have an approximate total production of 574 to 575 *moyos* of cereal from which the tenant paid roughly one-third. The monastery took more than half of the wheat (90 *moyos* out of roughly 142) and more than one-third of the barley (90 out of approximately 240), while the peasant kept his 190-plus *moyos* of rye. These are, of course, extremely rough calculations, but I believe the general trend of what the monastery took and what the renters kept has not been distorted. Obviously, this was a very large property when compared with the minuscule holdings we are going to examine below, and subletting is already implied in the contract. The agreement also insisted that the land could only be let to *labradores llanos* (non-noble farmers). Undoubtedly this was a profitable operation for both monastery and renter, and the accounts provide a good, if not always precise, glimpse of the diversity of rural exploitation in northern Castile.[28]

The Peasants of Santa María la Real: Work and Dues in the Census and the *Becerro*

Now, after a long digression into San Andrés's domain, we turn once again to the lands of Santa María. We must focus our attention on an extant survey (*apeo*) of lands held by the monastery. This is one of the few detailed inventories of land and peasant dues extant for northern Castile before the Black Death, and as such it deserves particular attention. Although the document is undated—a few pages seem to be missing at the beginning of the text—it can be assigned to the period between the second half of the thirteenth and the early part of the fourteenth century. Therefore, it provides us the opportunity to compare peasant dues at the turn of the century with those recorded in the *Becerro de behetrías* more than fifty years later and to see, once again, the evolution and travails of Santa María's domain over an extended period of time.

Several years ago I undertook and published a preliminary and somewhat flawed analysis of this census. Since then, Carlos Merchán Fernández's edition of the text has provided for an easier examination of the evidence, although his edition is missing entries in several places and contains several errors. A few illegible lines and later additions or corrections to the original document also prevent us from a complete and exact rendering of the evidence. What we have, however, is still one of the best sources for peasant life in medieval Castile.[29]

The survey contains the names of approximately 559 peasants, though there were more people on the land than those directly identified by name. In several instances, more than one individual held land from the monastery, as seen, for example, in entries such as "Mari Pedros, the wife of Fangundo [Facundo] with her sons who paid ten *heminas*" or "the land of Don Martino and his brothers" also paying ten *heminas*.[30] If we accept the average estimate of persons per household to be between 3.5 and 4.5, we are dealing here with a population of around two thousand peasants. This is a rather small figure if we consider the extension of the monastic domain, and the fact that it extended over more than fifty-seven villages. Clearly, the monastery did not hold sole lordship over all these villages, but rather shared it with other ecclesiastical and secular lords. Even so, one can see the limited human capital that already existed before the worsening conditions of the early fourteenth century and even before the onslaught of the Plague.

Of the 559 peasants mentioned as holding land from Santa María, 466 were males and 93 were females. The women who held the land by themselves are often described as widows; their children (recognizable by the matronymics or by explicit references in the text) can be found working monastic lands elsewhere in the same village or in localities nearby. The 93 women represent 16.6 percent of all the peasants listed in the census as holding lands from Santa María, a figure which is a bit higher than those given for women in other parts of Europe. Moreover, at least in this instance, their dues did not differ markedly from those paid by men, and thus their holdings must have been fairly close to the norm.[31]

The survey lists more than 560 units or parcels of land. Among them there is explicit evidence that at least eighteen *solares* had gone to waste (*yermos*) and were therefore no longer under cultivation. There are strong indications that thirty-seven additional units and perhaps even more had been abandoned. If we take the lowest suggested number of eighteen, this amounts to a negligible percentage in terms of the entire domain. The figure of fifty-five units, however, represents close to 10 percent of all the units of production lying uncultivated, a forewarning of the more severe conditions to come in the mid-fourteenth century. Moreover, we do not know how much of the arable in each unit was actually worked. The payments to the monastery are uniformly small, so the amounts indicated here are very close to the average standard unit for one peasant family. In addition, in only a few instances is there evidence of the same individual holding more than one parcel. There is also the possibility that the area under cultivation, as in other parts of Castile, was shrinking.

We know that peasant men and women contributed to the monastery; the question is, how did they make their payments? Overwhelmingly, payments were made in kind, either in a combination of barley and wheat or of grain and a piece of meat or bacon, and in a few instances of grain, bacon, and money. At least one unit, the *solar* of John de la Villella, paid one pound of wax for *infurción*; another unit contributed five *eminas* of garden produce; and another one a *rodezno* (cogwheel), most probably for use in one of the monastery's mills. In the case of Matalevaniega, a place about which we will learn a bit more below, sixteen peasants paid half of *infurción*, but what this corresponded to materially was not spelled out. Four peasants in the village of Menaza paid five *quartos* (two of wheat and three of barley) plus three *obrades de bos* (probably *boj*, or boxwood).[32] Table 4.8 shows an approximate distribution of the types of payments made. The table does not include the several *solares* for which no contribution is given but which may have all paid two *modiis* (*moyos*); nor does it include the few entries that were erased or mutilated. It does, however, include the *solares yermos* (i.e., abandoned), reflecting what was collected there in a not too distant past.

The survey does not always make clear what manorial dues are being paid. Generally, one must assume that these were contributions for *infurción*, that is, the *cens* or rent for the use of the land (often equivalent to one-fourth of the harvest). Sometimes, this is indicated explicitly as, for example, two *mrs.* for *infurción*, five *solidii* for *infurción*, or as in the heading, "These are the *enfurciones* of Cernera." On the other hand, for the villages of Matamorisca and Cillamayor, the *apeo* indicates that the tenth was also

TABLE 4.8.   Types of Payment by
Peasants to the Monastery.

Form of Payment	Number of Peasants
Grain	301
Grain and bacon/meat*	81
Grain, meat, and money	49
One-half *infurción*	16
One-fourth *infurción*	1
One *infurción*	1
Others**	6

Source: AHN, Clero, carp. 1665, no. 1.

*The meat was often expressed in monetary value.
**See above (payments in honey, *rodezno*, etc.). The amount and nature of what was paid for *infurción* is not stated.

being collected. In this case it amounted to two *modiis* of wheat, one *modius* of rye, and ten *quartos* of barley in Matamorisca and four, and a half *modii* of rye, three *modii* of barley, and five *quartos* of wheat in Cillamayor, followed by what must have been the villagers' individual contributions for *infurción*.[33]

The monks of Santa María la Real collected their seignorial dues in amounts of grain, grain and meat, or money which were fairly uniform throughout the monastery's widely scattered domain (see Table 4.9). Altogether there were seventy-two different types of payments or combinations of payments, a fact that seriously complicates any attempts to calculate the total amount of grain paid in rent by the peasants listed in the survey. However, it is clear that a substantial number of peasants paid a standard amount, whether it was ten *eminas* or five *cuartos* or five *cuartos* and a piece of bacon or meat. Still, a note of caution is necessary, for different measures were used throughout the lands of Santa María ("to the measure of Aguilar," "to the measure of Villadiego," "to the measure of Cernera"), and we know from other contemporary documents that a good number of villages had their own measures, usually wooden boxes. In any case, the measures kept at Aguilar de Campóo seem to have been the ones most commonly used, and a *fanega* or a *cuarto* or an *emina* there must have been fairly close to a *fanega* in Frontada or Villadiego. We can, thus, attempt to convert

TABLE 4.9.   Standard Payments Made by Peasants.*

Type of Payment	Number of Peasants
Ten *eminas*	77
Five *quartos* (*cuartos*)	69
Two *quartos* (*cuartos*)	47
Five *quartos* and one piece of bacon	39
Three *quartos* and one piece of bacon	21
One *modius* (*moyo*)	24
One-half *infurción*	16
One *moyo* and eighteen *dineros*	11
Sixteen *dineros*	11

Source: AHN, Clero, carp. 1665, no. 1.

*Includes categories of payment made by a minimum of ten peasants.

eminas, cuartos, and *modii* into some common measure easily understood by the modern reader, such as the *fanega* (1.58 bushels in modern equivalence). If we use García González's estimates for San Zoilo de Carrión in 1338 (Carrión was in the general area of Santa María's lands), we can then calculate that one *carga* was equal to eight *cuartos*; one *cuarto* was equal to six *celemines*; and the *fanega* was twelve *celemines*. Elsewhere in Castile, one *cuarto* was often four *celemines*. We can calculate that five *cuartos* were the equivalent of between 1⅔ *fanegas* and 2½ *fanegas*. In the early modern period, three *eminas* made a *fanega*, but in Guipuzcoa the *emina* was equal to one *celemín*, and in the *Becerro* one *emina* was also equal to one *celemín*. If we use the latter measure as a guide, then ten *eminas* made ten *celemines* or a bit less than a *fanega* (twelve *celemines*). On the other hand, the *modius* was probably around two *fanegas*. If these approximate measures and equivalences are close to accurate, then the average contribution of most peasants in the lands of Santa María la Real was within a narrow range of between 1 and 2½ *fanegas*.[34] These calculations still leave us with a substantial number of peasants who paid less than that. For the moment, however, we should put aside questions as to the total amount of grain produced and the implications of these figures for the lives of peasants.

Payments in money alone are far easier to quantify. They amounted to 30.5 *mrs.*, 35 *ss.*, and 176 *ds.* If we add to this figure those payments in specie that were added to payments in kind (41.5 *ss.*, 260 *ds.*), then the monastery collected a total of 30.5 *mrs.*, 76.5 *ss.*, and 436 *ds.* Any attempts to convert *sueldos* and *dineros* into *maravedíes* are fraught with pitfalls, for this was a period during which coinage fluctuated wildly, and there is no clear evidence as to the rate of conversion. But at 10 *ds.* per *maravedí*—which was the going rate in Ávila in 1299—the monastery did not raise even 100 *mrs.*, a very small figure indeed.[35]

When we compare these figures to those found in the *Becerro de behetrías* a few decades later, there does not seem to have been any radical change in how the *infurción* was collected. The evidence for the lands of Santa María la Real or for the rental agreements discussed earlier does not show any dramatic conversion of seignorial dues into money rents, as has been argued for other parts of the west. Of course, grain was eventually sold and added to the cash flow of the monastery, but, as we have seen earlier in the case of Benedictine monasteries, transportation costs, losses along the way, and other factors did not allow for very much profit.

Let us now turn to a more focused discussion of the text. The largest individual contribution in grain seems to have been that of the men of Cabria. Ten *solares*, or units of taxation, are listed in the survey. That of Juan Pérez paid three *cuartos* (one of wheat, two of barley) and 6 *ds.* At the bottom of the page, there is an entry (missed by Merchán) for Lazarón de Cabria for "6 *qr. trigo e de ordio* 13 *qr.*," that is, six *cuartos* of wheat and thirteen of barley, followed on the next page by the names of eight other men paying the same (*al tanto*). If, indeed, these eight men paid the same as Lazarón—roughly 7.5 to 9 *fanegas* or between 11.8 and 14.2 bushels of grain—this was a very substantial figure. It is a sad commentary on the fate of northern Castilian agriculture in general and Santa María's domain in particular that by the mid-fourteenth century there were no peasants left working the land in Cabria, and only *hijosdalgos* (petty noblemen) lived there.[36]

Equally interesting as a reflection of the changing conditions in Castilian agriculture is the evidence from Lomilla. Located around two and a half miles southwest of Aguilar de Campóo, the thirty peasants or *solares* listed in the survey paid *infurción* to the monastery according to a formula explicitly stated next to the name of the place. Peasants with two teams of oxen (four oxen) paid four *modii* (*moyos*) of bread (half wheat, half barley). Those with one team (2 oxen) paid two *moyos* (half wheat, half barley). Those with one ox contributed one *moyo* (half wheat, half barley), and those without animals but with a hearth (*que fiziera fumo*) paid two *cuartos* (half wheat, half barley). In 1351, the lordship of the village was shared equally between the monastery of Santa María la Real and the powerful monastery of Las Huelgas. If such was also the case in the late thirteenth century,

Lomilla must have been a large and prosperous village with more than two hundred inhabitants. Even if there were no other peasants living there under a different lordship, this would still have been a rather large village. (Its size may be explainable, perhaps, by its proximity to Aguilar de Campóo and to a well-traveled road.)

Of the thirty peasants listed as contributors in Lomilla, twelve, or 40 percent of the total, were women—a significantly high number. It is obvious from the names listed that a good number of the peasants, men and women, were related to each other. Unfortunately, the documents for Lomilla, unlike the rest of the documents—which almost always state the amount of grain paid in *infurción*—identify only four peasants as making payments. For example, María Iváñez is listed as paying "2 qr. a medias" (half wheat, half barley); Don Ague "2 moyos a medias"; and these entries are followed by the names of nineteen peasants with blanks next to their names. The *solar* of Domingo Estévanez paid two *moyos a medias*, and listed next is Juan Gílez, who paid one and a half *moyos*; seven more names are given, but with no indication of their payments.

We know that when the *apeo* was drawn, at least two of the tenants had a team of oxen each and that Juan Gílez owned one ox. As to the other two, several possibilities can be considered. For example, each of the tenants listed may have paid as much in *infurción* as that listed above: that is, twenty-one peasants contributed two *moyos*, eight peasants contributed one *moyo*, and one, María Iváñez, had no plough animals and paid two *qr*. I have serious reservations about this reading on several grounds. First, in the years prior to the *apeo*, the possibility that a peasant could own two plowing teams was still considered when the tax records were drawn up, but by the time the *apeo* was written no one in Lomilla owned four oxen. By the mid-fourteenth century, the possibility of a peasant having two plowing teams was not even considered. Under its "Rights of the Lords" heading, the *Becerro* had indeed rephrased the criterion for the payment of the *infurción* to reflect lower economic expectations:

> [The peasants] give each year to the Lord to whom they are vassals: he who plows with one pair of oxen and for *los préstamo* [temporal or lifelong concession of land] which they give with the *solares*, three *fanegas* and eight *celemines* of bread, half wheat and half barley, and he who plows with one oxen, half of that *infurción*, and he who has no ox or [who is] a widow, each gives eleven *celemines* of bread.[37]

If we apply the standard for *infurción* to the rest of the *apeo*, very few of the more than 550 peasants paid two *moyos*. We know that plowing animals were in short supply almost everywhere in Castile, and to suppose that in one village twenty-nine out of thirty peasants owned either a team or at least one ox seems preposterous.

The other possibility is that they paid nothing, but this explanation is also difficult to accept, and with it one is left with more questions than answers. In Frontada, where Santa María received *infurción* from nine male and six female *vasallos* or tenants (their number was reduced to one by 1351), the monastery received two *moyos* (half wheat, half barley) from two peasants; five *cuartos* (or a bit more than a *moyo*) plus a piece of bacon from six of them; four *cuartos* or one *moyo* from one; three *cuartos* from four; and two *cuartos* from the last two. If one applies the definitions for *infurción* from Lomilla—and there is really no reason to think that such a standard was universal—then two out of the fifteen peasants of Frontada may have had a team of oxen, seven may have had one ox, and the rest none. Still, this was a great deal better than most of the other peasants listed in the document,[38] but it makes the example of Lomilla difficult to accept. If we can draw any conclusion, it is either that Lomilla was a rare exception or that the majority of the peasants working the lands of Santa María la Real depended on the *yuvero* (the plowman) for their annual plowing. Perhaps the village, with its enduring communal organization, maintained the oxen and plows necessary for the survival of the community.

We must again examine the evidence of Lomilla within the context of the entire survey. By the second half of the thirteenth century, none of the inhabitants of Lomilla owned two teams of oxen, though it may have been possible that some in the village had done so in the recent past. By 1352, this was not even a possibility. The impoverishment of Lomilla and probably other villages in northern Castile is vividly reflected in the decline in the number of plow animals and in the falling rate of taxation. As noted earlier, by applying the formula of two *moyos* of *infurción* for a team of two oxen, we see that few of the more than 550 peasants listed in the survey owned even a single ox in the late thirteenth century, and the succeeding century was worse. The most frequent payments for *infurción* found in the survey were ten *eminas* or five *cuartos*. The ten *eminas* (roughly ten *celemines*) correspond to the two *cuartos* or eleven *celemines* paid in Lomilla by peasants who did not own an ox, as listed in the *apeo* and the *Becerro de behetrías*. The five *cuartos* correspond to the payment due from a peasant owning an ox or another plowing animal (probably a cow). Table 4.9 (above) provides a point of reference (if the standard from Lomilla can be applied elsewhere) regarding the availability of animals in the lands of Santa María. In this sense, it is important to note the glaring differences from village to village and within the individual villages themselves. In a place such as Caorbio, the *infurción* was (with the exception of the sons of Juan Pérez, who paid one *moyo*) either two *cuartos* or ten *eminas* plus six *ds.* in meat for the other fourteen peasants, while in Cillamayor everyone contributed either five or ten *cuartos*—from two to four times more than the amount paid by the men and women of Caorbio.[39] We are thus face-to-face here with a population composed mostly of very small holders, so perhaps it would be more useful to examine the evidence from the other end—that is, by asking who the smallest contributors were and determining the means by which they were able to survive on the small harvests indicated by their payments of *infurción*.

The smallest contribution listed in the *apeo*, *sexto e media* (one-sixth and one-half of a sixth?), was paid by the *solar* of Asencio; this entry was followed by that of Pedro Yuánez, a *solariego* of Rebilla who paid three *sextos* (*sextario*). As to the first contribution, there is little one can say. Pedro Yuánez, however, paid around one and a half *celemines*, a very small amount indeed. He is followed in the list by Ladrón Yuánez, perhaps a brother or other relative, who paid two *cuartos*. The survey shows that for some peasants the *infurción* was equal to a fourth (*dan la quarta*), but it cannot be assumed that such was the case for all peasants listed in the *apeo*. In fact, except for one entry which describes the *infurción* as being worth 5 *ss.* and another which states it to be 2 *mrs.* (notice the very wide gap between these two figures), there is no clear statement in this or any other document from Santa María la Real as to how much the *infurción* actually was or what percentage of the total farm production it represented. As we saw above, García de Valdeavellano described the *infurción* as a variable tax which, depending on the locality, "could be one fourth of the produce or the tenth." In 1338, the lands near Carrión were given out at a fourth or a fifth. In any case, whether a fourth, a fifth, or a tenth, *infurción* or *census* was by no means the only due paid by peasants. As we know from the mid-fourteenth century *Becerro*, contributions to the crown sometimes took a larger share of the peasants' income than did *infurción*. To give just one example, the villagers of Valdespino, which belonged to Don Tello (a prince of the blood royal), paid *moneda*, *servicios*, and *fonsadera* to the king. In addition, the village as a whole paid 140 *mrs.* to Don Tello in *martiniega* and 20 *mrs.* for the *yantar* (*gite* or purveyance); for *infurción* couples paid four *celemines* of bread and 4 *ds.*, and single people or widows paid half that amount.[40]

At the rate of a fourth, which seems to be the most frequent rate for *infurción*, it appears that the fairly prosperous farmers listed in the *apeo* could have raised an average annual crop of around sixteen *fanegas*, mostly of wheat and barley. It is likely that as much as half of that amount went to pay royal and seignorial dues, plus the necessary amount saved for seeding. If these calculations are correct, our prosperous farmers in the survey were left with around eight *fanegas* or (at the present rate) 12.6 bushels (758.4 pounds) a year, a figure well below the twelve to fourteen *fanegas* per year assigned to monks as their annual bread allotment in 1338. It also compares unfavorably with Wilhelm Abel's description of the average annual production of some English peasants holding a semi-virgate (one-eighth of an acre).[41] There is, of course, a caveat to these calculations. Although in Castile most of the payments in kind were made in wheat and barley, as indicated in an earlier chapter, it is most probable that rye was also harvested and kept for the peasant's use. There is no way to assess the true importance of rye in the diet of the peasant, although literary evidence, such as Juan Ruiz's *Libro de buen amor*, points to the widespread consumption of rye bread among poor peasants. The same difficulties exist in calculating the importance of garden produce, dairy farming, use of the resources from nearby woods, apiculture, and other agricultural pursuits that would add to the peasants' income.

Yet, even with these reservations, one can safely assume that most areas of northern Castile, and certainly those of Santa María la Real—with its two-field system, sparse agricultural gear, unfavorable climate, and topography—did not always compare favorably with England or France. At the same time, one must also remember that a good number of the peasants listed in the *apeo* paid less than five *cuartos* for *infurción* and probably harvested crops that kept them barely at—and often below—the subsistence level.[42] How can this be explained?

The survey explicitly shows a fair number of brothers, sons, daughters, and other relatives working on different plots throughout the monastic domain. For example, "Marina Gonzálvez, la cabezuda" paid ten *eminas* in *infurción*. She was followed in the list by her sister, who contributed a similar amount of grain. Gonzalvo (Gonzalo) Domingo's entry, for an *infurción* of ten *eminas*, was complemented by an equal payment from his brother-in-law. These and many other examples—and one must assume that the document does not fully reveal more extensive kin relations—lead me to speculate that most families held several small plots individually and pooled their resources for survival. On the other hand, there is evidence that some individuals held more than one plot and, thus, what they paid in *infurción* for one unit did not fully reflect all of their available income. Pedro

Yuánez, already mentioned as paying a very small *infurción*, may also be the same person who held lands from Santa María in Villanueva del Río and who paid six *eminas* of rye as his *census*. In fact, the survey allows for a reconstruction of families. We have the example, mentioned above, as well as another to which I have also referred, that of a certain Fangundo who shared a plot with Paulos, paying ten *eminas*, while his wife Mari Pedros and his sons contributed the same amount in *infurción* elsewhere. In a place such as Piedrafortún, for which the survey lists twenty-seven peasants, there is some evidence that almost half of those listed were closely related. This fragmentation of plots among members of the same family group—a confirmation of partible inheritance—points to a pattern of small parcels scattered throughout the villages' arable in Santa María's domain, as was the case nearly everywhere else in northern Castile.

The survey also shows that a good number of the tenants had other occupations, a fact that may help explain how they were able to survive on what appear to be very small incomes. Their work on the land was supplemented by income obtained elsewhere and vice versa. Eight *solares* were held by small monastic houses from around Campóo; two other solares were in the hands of squires. One can assume that these ten units, and presumably others, were in the hands of absentee tenants and were worked by some of the peasants listed in the *apeo* for a salary or for a share of the crop. The document also shows in some instances evidence of artisanal activity that supplemented farming. A rough breakdown by trade is presented in Table 4.10. There were probably others on the list who are not identified directly, but who may have had other work elsewhere. This factor would help to explain, to a degree, the small plots that were the norm in the survey. Clearly, some of these individuals held the usufruct of the land, but it was probably cultivated by someone else. Extra income from a trade or from agricultural labor may have made the difference between life and death.

TYPES OF GRAIN IN THE *APEO*

We turn now to the question of the types of grain that were and their proportions. A conclusive answer is of course not possible, for we still have the unresolved issue of rye: a crop certainly grown by the peasants but seldom reflected in the dues they paid. One must assume that in each instance where the document does not state explicitly the type of grain collected, it is likely that the grain was barley. For those which can be identified and, allowing for the difficulties of such calculations, we have a

TABLE 4.10. Trades and Artisanal
Occupations in the Lands of Santa
María.

Occupation	No. of Tenants
Blacksmith	7
Shoemaker	4
Tanner	2
Butcher	2
Innkeeper	1
Painter	1
Bell ringer	1
Cleric	1
Minstrel	1
Teacher	1
Municipal official	1
Servant or attendant	1
Petty-merchant	1
Sexton	1
Miller	1
Total	26

Source: AHN, Clero, carp. 1665, no. 1.

rough breakdown of around 35 *moyos*, 272.5 *cuartos*, 15 *eminas*, and 5 *teia*
(*tercia*) of wheat; 33.5 *moyos*, 459.5 *cuartos*, 51 *eminas*, and 3 *sexteros* of barley;
and 13 *moyos*, 12 *cuartos*, 12 *eminas*, and 3 *sexteros* of rye. The largest number of
entries consisted in payments of the *infurción* in proportions that ranged
from half barley, half wheat to ratios of 4:3, 3:2, 2:1, 3⅓:1⅔, 6:4 of barley to
wheat and other combinations in which the amount of each grain was
expressed in different measure. For example, Marí(a) Míquez or Miguéllez
from Barzenilla contributed an *infurción* of one *quarto* of barley and one
sextero of wheat. There are three instances in which the grain collected for
either the "tenth" or the *infurción* is given without a tally of individual
contributions. The mills of Salinas brought in fifteen *moyos* in *infurción* (five
wheat, five barley, five rye), while Matamorisca contributed a tithe of two
moyos of wheat, one *moyo* of rye, and ten *cuartos* of barley, and Cillamayor
gave four and a half *moyos* of wheat, three *moyos* of rye, and five *cuartos* of
barley.[43]

Although more barley was required as seed for a given area than either wheat or rye, and although barley needed greater attention during the growing season, it still appeared to have been the preferred form of payment in the survey. (This is somewhat corroborated by the *Becerro* and by the 1338 monastic accounts.) On the other hand, monastic lords, more often than not, opted for wheat. Thus, in the lands where the monks of Silos cultivated directly in *la era* or land adjacent to the monastery, they harvested 144 *almudes* of wheat, 100 *almudes* of rye, and 85 *almudes* of barley and vetch, while at Arauze de Miel the breakdown was 144 *almudes* of wheat, 54 *almudes* of rye, and 40 *almudes* of barley. Table 4.11 allows us to compare these amounts to those collected on land they did not work directly (Table 4.11). In San Zoilo de Carrión the rents of the prior amounted to 501 *cargas* (1.5 *almud* per *carga*) divided equally between wheat and barley, and similar additional examples can be gathered from the 1338 accounts.[44] The point, of course, not to belabor this further, is that there was always an underlying tension between what monastic and secular lords wished to receive and what ancient customs had set as the form of payment. In this case, *infurción* was probably the least flexible of the manorial dues, and it was paid, more often than not, in barley.

The Crisis of the Fourteenth Century in the Lands of Santa María la Real

We must now contrast the evidence of the survey with that of the *Becerro de behetrías* for different purposes altogether. I would like to examine here changes over time in the lordship of Santa María la Real, and what these changes reveal about the early fourteenth-century crisis and the particular problems faced by monastic institutions in the face of noble and royal usurpation. When we consider that these changes may have taken place within a period of between fifty and seventy-five years, they are nothing short of dramatic.[45]

Shortly after the mid-fourteenth century, the jurisdiction, either whole or partial, of Santa María la Real extended through forty-three villages or places. In the earlier survey, however, the monastery had *vasallos* or dependent peasants in close to sixty different localities. And the records of land transactions and rentals show that the domain extended through rural communities far beyond that number. Merchán calculates that the monastery's jurisdiction extended over 160 villages and places.[46] More striking, however, is the evidence in the *Becerro* that documents the decline in the

TABLE 4.11.   Rents Collected by Santo Domingo de Silos in
1338 (in *Almudes*).

Place	Wheat	Rye	Barley
Castro Cenica	19	16	25
San Martín de Requexo	84	84	84
Tarada	10	0	10
Enebreda	14	14	14
Guimara	60	60	60
Mercadillo (deserted because of war)	0	0	0
Espinosa de Cervera	45.25	40	58
Huerta	91	90	107
Redondiella	12	12	12
Sanoveña	100	10	0
Briongos	20	0	24.5
Vañuelos de Suso	9	9	9
Aruelos	14.5	0	29
Salas	0	0	8
Espinosa de Valdolmos	6	6	6
Sant Coronado	11	11	11
Quintana de Arpideo	50	50	50
Ribicella	3	0	3
Momolar	0	8	0
Tomel and Villavela	10	0	10
Pineda	3	0	3
Valcalomic	3	0	3
Peniella Trasmonte	4.5	0	4.5
Quintana Seca	4.5	0	4.5
Total	573.75	410	535.5

Source: Vida económica, 195–97.

number of peasants paying dues in specific communities. The monastery shared rights and jurisdiction in hamlets and villages throughout northern Castile with powerful ecclesiastical lords or, even more dangerous, with ambitious secular magnates. Of them, none presented a greater threat than Don Tello, one of Alfonso XI's many illegitimate children by Leonor de Guzmán. Don Tello had acquired a large seignorial domain in and around Aguilar de Campóo through his father's lavish settlement and by outright expropriation. Matamorisca, where Santa María la Real had collected a sizable tithe, was by the early 1350s completely in the hands of Don Tello. In Frontada, the monastery had received *infurción* from fourteen or fifteen peasants when the *apeo* was drawn, but by the mid-fourteenth century, there was only a single peasant paying to Santa María—the rest of the villagers were under the lordship of Don Tello. In Brañosera, the *apeo* listed fifteen peasants paying dues to the monastery (thirteen male, two female) around 1300. By the time the *Becerro de behetrías* was compiled, two-thirds of the village was under the jurisdiction of Don Tello, and the remaining third was divided equally among the abbots of Santa María la Real de Aguilar de Campóo and two other monasteries. It is indeed very doubtful that by then the monks of Santa María held jurisdiction over more than two or three households.[47]

Wherever the extant documents permit such comparisons, we see that the number of *vasallos* owing rent to the monastery had declined, in some cases catastrophically. Even if we take into account the effects of the plague (and there is little concrete one can say about its demographic impact), we witness a progressive decline in the number of peasants under the jurisdiction of Santa María, a pattern that was probably common to most of the region. Moreover, one can also observe a radical erosion of Santa María la Real's lordship, which in this case had little to do with the onslaught of the Black Death and much to do with seignorial ambitions and violence in the first half of the fourteenth century. One of the clearest manifestations of this crisis was the decline in rents, not only in the number of peasants paying dues, but also in the lower amount of their individual contributions. Even *infurción*, a rent which frequently reflected ancient customary arrangements between lords and peasants, was reduced and, in some cases, in a noticeable manner. This can be seen in Table 4.12, where most of the localities (in the *apeo* and the *Becerro*) that can be matched are included, but which does not include the many places where the monastery had lost all its jurisdiction or those that had been deserted.[48]

A few general comments can be advanced from a perfunctory examination of Table 4.12. In the *Becerro* we no longer find the range of payments listed in the earlier survey. This is not to say that such a range did not exist, but that perhaps what we see in the later document is the standard payment for *infurción*. Peasants paid less or more depending on the amount of land they cultivated and their social and economic standing in the village. As is to be expected, after half a century of crises there is evidence of a decline in rents and in the number of taxable units. This trend seems to have applied to most of Castile, although local variations and conditions often were far more important than general trends.

TABLE 4.12.   Comparison of Dues (*Infurción*) in the *Apeo* and *Becerro*.

Location	Apeo (*c. 1300*)	Becerro (*1352*)
Cillamayor	Thirty to sixty *celemines*, plus one piece of bacon (eight *vasallos*)	Sixteen *celemines* of wheat, two *fanegas* of barley, and 1 *mr.* (shared jurisdiction)
Barzenilla	Six to thirty-six *celemines* (five *vasallos*)	Thirty-six *celemines* and 8 *ss.* (under Santa María's sole jurisdiction)
Villa Vega	Three *cuartos* (three *vasallos*)	Three cuartos and 5 *ds.* (one *vasallo*)
Santa María la Nava	Twenty-four *celemines* (two *vasallos*)	Sixteen *celemines* (one *vasallo*)
Piedrafortún	Twelve *celemines* (rye) and 15 *ds.* to twenty-four *celemines* and 18 *ds.* (thirty-one *vasallos*)	Sixteen *celemines* of rye
Rebilla	Twelve *celemines* and 18 *ds.* to thirty *celemines* and 2 *ss.* (eleven *vasallos*)	Twenty *celemines* and 16 *ds.*
Rebilleia	Six to twelve *celemines* (two *vasallos*)	One man remaining; he paid nothing
Caorbio	Ten *celemines* and 6 *ds.* in meat to twenty-four *celemines* (fifteen *vasallos*)	Six *celemines*
Quintalla de Bercosa	Thirty *celemines* and one piece of bacon (twenty *vasallos*)	Twenty-four *celemines*
Frontada	Eighteen to forty-eight *celemines* (fourteen *vasallos*)	Six *celemines* (one *vasallo*)
Cenera	Six to twenty-four *celemines* (ten *vasallos*)	Eight *celemines* (three-fourths of the village to Don Tello; one-fourth to Santa María)
Villella	Twelve *celemines* and 6 *ds.* to eighteen *celemines* (two *vasallos*)	Twelve *celemines* (one *vasallo*)
Matamorisca	Eighteen *celemines* (one *vasallo*)	Two *celemines* (all under Don Tello)
Menaza	Thirty *celemines* and three *obradas* of *bos* (four *vasallos*)	Thirty-six *celemines* and 8 *ds.*
Cabria	Eighteen *celemines* (nine *vasallos*)	Deserted, only noblemen
Lomilla	(See text above)	
Matalevaniega	Twelve to thirty *celemines* and 22 *ds.* (twenty *vasallos*)	Sixteen *celemines* (half Santa María, half San Andrés)

TABLE 4.12.   *Continued*

Location	Apeo (*c. 1300*)	Becerro (*1352*)
Brañosera	Two *ss.* to 1 *mr.* (eight *vasallos*)	Five *mrs.* (two-thirds of the village under Don Tello; the other third, divided among the monasteries of Cervatos, Santa Cruz, and Santa María)

Source: AHN, Clero, carp. 1665, no. 1; *Becerro* vols. 1, 2.

A detailed examination of the extant documentation of Santa María la Real de Aguilar de Campóo and that of San Andrés de Arroyo has shown that there was an important transformation in the economic structure of the region and a dramatic change in the demographic resources of the area. The crisis of the late thirteenth and early fourteenth centuries was, most probably, somewhat ameliorated by the tenacious manner in which the monastery and its dependent peasants sought to hold on to the order and continuity of their collective and individual lives. Under the circumstances, their deeds were quietly heroic. But, now, we must turn to the questions of economic exchanges in northern Castile and identify broader patterns of change over time.

Notes

1. On Aguilar de Campóo and on the monastery see Luciano Huidobro y Serna, *Breve historia de la muy noble villa de Aguilar de Campóo* (Palencia: Excelentísima diputación de Palencia, 1980). This is a reedition of the 1954 first edition. Far more important is Carlos Merchán Fernández, *Sobre los orígenes del régimen señorial en Castilla: El abadengo de Aguilar de Campóo (1020–1369)* (Málaga: Universidad de Málaga, 1982), which studies the formation of the monastic domain. Although the book contains many errors—in the transcription of the documents, in its methodological approach, and, simply, in its historical interpretation—it serves, nonetheless, as a useful background for what I wish to discuss here. I had used the manuscript extant in the AHN (a census of peasant dues) for my first venture into this topic; see my "Une note sur la vie rurale dans la région d'Aguilar de Campóo" in *Les Espagnes Médiévales: Aspects économiques et sociaux* (Nice: Faculté des lettres et sciences humaines de Nice, 1983), 13–20. I will refer to both the manuscript and published sources in this chapter. Also, although not dealing directly with the

region of Campóo, see Angel Vaca Lorenzo, "La estructura económica de la Tierra de Campos a mediados del siglo XIV," *Publicaciones de la Institución "Tello Téllez de Meneses"* 39 (1977): 229–399; 42 (1979): 203–387.

2. *Becerro*, 1: 444.

3. Examples of conflicts with either noblemen or municipal councils in the region can be found in AHN, Clero, carp. 1657, no. 8 (14-March-1255), no. 13 (4-July-1257); carp. 1661, no. 11 (10-March-1286); carp. 1662, no. 11 (20-May-1293); carp. 1666, no. 19 (26-March-1312); carp. 1667, no. 9 (13-April-1314); carp. 1670, no. 2 (13-March-1338) et passim.

4. For the use of litigation by an ecclesiastical institution as a means to preserve its domain, see Paul H. Freedman, *The Diocese of Vic: Tradition and Regeneration in Medieval Catalonia* (New Brunswick, N.J.: Rutgers University Press, 1983), 115–40.

5. AHN, Clero, carp. 1657, no. 10 (12-November-1255); Merchán Fernández, *Sobre los orígenes del régimen señorial*, 8off; *Becerro*, 2: 179.

6. AHN, Clero, carp. 1662, no. 3 (7-April-1290). See Merchán Fernández, *Sobre los orígenes del régimen señorial*, 175–222.

7. AHN, Clero, carp. 1665, no. 20 (4-April-1307); carp. 1667, no. 6 (19-October-1313); for *açeñas* see Glick, *Islamic and Christian Spain*, 231–35.

8. For these two transactions, see AHN, Clero, carp. 1665, no. 10 (13-May-1305). For prices, see below.

9. AHN, Clero, carp. 1673, no. 4 (12-December-1341), no. 5 (13-December-1341).

10. *Becerro*, 1: 558.

11. On the transaction see AHN, Clero, carp. 1665, no. 20 (4-April-1307). Domingo Miguel is identified as *alcalde* in the following documents: AHN, Clero, carp. 1661, no. 2 (15-March-1284), no. 17 (23-August-1287); carp. 1662, no. 6 (10-March-1291); carp. 1665, no. 12 (20-October-1305); carp. 1666, no. 7 (4-February-1310).

12. AHN, Clero, carp. 1665, no. 7 (26-July-1304); *Becerro*, 1: 448.

13. AHN, Clero, carp. 1672, no. 11 (21-June-1338); ACB, vol. 46, f. 438 (23-July-1349).

14. AHN, Clero, carp. 1666, no. 5 (22-March-1309), no. 13 (26-March-1311); carp. 1669, no. 15 (12-January-1327).

15. AHN, Clero, carp. 1667, no. 8 (17-December-1313); carp. 1667, no. 9 (13-April-1314); carp. 1670, no. 8 (22-January-1331).

16. AHN, Clero, carp. 1658, no. 6 (22-July-1261); carp. 1668, no. 7 (25-April-1317). On *mañería* and *nuncio* see *Curso de historia*, 252–53.

17. AHN, Clero, carp. 1668, no. 7 (25-April-1317).

18. AHN, Clero, carp. 1658, no. 7 (3-April-1262); carp. 1663, no. 22 (25-August-1297); carp. 1666, no. 14 (8-July-1311); carp. 1667, no. 6 (7-December-1313); carp. 1671, no. 3 (15-February-1334).

19. Some examples of places no longer under the jurisdiction of Santa María are found in the *Becerro de behetrías*: *Becerro*, 1: 237 (Castrillo de Río Pisuerga); 1: 228 (Castrillo de Villa Vega); 1: 260 (Dehesa de Romanos); 1: 524 (Villa Escusa) et passim.

20. AHN, Clero, carp. 1658, no. 18 (17-August-1266); *Becerro*, 1: 237; AHN, Clero, carp. 1665, no. 5 (3-May-1304); *Becerro*, 1: 556–57.

21. AHN, Clero, carp. 1670, no. 18 (4-August-1333); *Becerro*, 1: 228; AHN, Clero, carp. 1671, no. 3 (12-February-1334); carp. 1674, no. 9 (21-November-1350); *Becerro*, 1: 260.

22. AHN, Clero, carp. 1670, no. 18 (4-August-1333). References to vineyards and maintenance of church is found in AHN, Clero, carp. 1671, no. 3 (15-February-1334).

23. AHN, Clero, carp. 1732, no. 16 (25-July-1318): the village of Santa María de la Vid "se yermo e sse despoblo"; carp. 1733, no. 9 (10-February-1327), in which the nuns complained about their payments being in arrears.

24. AHN, Clero, carp. 1734, no. 16 (14-February-1340).

25. *Vida económica*, 105.

26. AHN, Clero, carp. 1733, no. 18 (21-December-1330). For the land market, see Chapter 5.

27. All the transactions are found in AHN, Clero, carp. 1731, no. 8 (19-February-1251); carp. 1732, no. 5 (19-December-1300), no. 7 (31-October-1306), no. 9 (22-July-1310), no. 14 (19-October-1315), no. 15 (12-January-1318); carp. 1733, no. 2 (20-November-1321), no. 20 (28-March-1332); carp. 1734, no. 1 (16-April-1332). The lease agreements include elaborate inventories and obligations not fully reflected in Table 4.7.

28. AHN, Clero, carp. 1733, no. 2 (20-November-1321); *Propiedades del cabildo segoviano*, 53 et passim. See above for yields.

29. The document is reproduced by Merchán Fernández, *Sobre los orígenes del régimen señorial*, 243–62. My article is "Une note sur la vie rurale dans la région d'Aguilar de Campóo." The census to be examined in the following pages is in the AHN, Clero, carp. 1665, no. 1. It is not the only *apeo* of property extant among the records of Santa María. AHN, Clero, carp. 1664, nos. 8, 10, 12, 13, 15, 16, 20, and carp. 1665, no. 2, also contain surveys of Santa María's property, but unlike 1665, no. 1, these other surveys either do not contain an elaborate list of peasant dues, are incomplete, or are almost illegible.

30. AHN, Clero, carp. 1665, no. 1, f. 1; Merchán Fernández, *Sobre los orígenes del régimen señorial*, 242.

31. AHN, Clero, carp. 1665, no. 1. "El de maría pedros la muger de fangundo con sus hyjos," "el de la suegra," "el de domingo hijo de doña Benita," f. 2, "el de la madre de Marcos," "el de la mujer de ferrando de felecha" et passim. Also see Teofilo F. Ruiz, "Notas para el estudio de la mujer en el área del Burgos medieval," in *El pasado histórico de Castilla y León*, 3 vols. (Burgos: Junta de Castilla y León, 1983), 1: 425–28.

32. AHN, Clero, carp. 1665, no. 1.

33. For *infurción*, see *Curso de historia*, 251.

34. *Vida económica*, 71. See also *Becerro*, 3: 123–24; Behar, *Santa María del Monte*, 370–71.

35. *DMA*, 174–75.

36. AHN, Clero, carp. 1665, no. 1; *Becerro*, 1: 515.

37. AHN, Clero, carp. 1665, no. 1; *Becerro*, 1: 425.

38. AHN, Clero, carp. 1665, no. 1; *Becerro*, 1: 427.

39. AHN, Clero, carp. 1665, no. 1; Caorbio is not listed in the *Becerro*, while the lordship of Cillamayor was shared with the abbess of San Andrés de Arroyo and two other lay lords. To Santa María the peasants paid sixteen *celemines* of wheat and two *fanegas* of barley, plus 1 *mr.* (roughly approximate to the dues owed in the earlier *apeo*). *Becerro*, 1: 438.

40. AHN, Clero, carp. 1665, no. 1; *Becerro*, 1: 426–27; Moreta Velayos, *Rentas monásticas en Castilla*, 85.

41. *Vida económica*, 93; Wilhelm Abel, *Agricultural Fluctuations in Europe: From the Thirteenth to the Twentieth Centuries* (London: Methuen, 1980), 32.

42. Not that conditions elsewhere were very promising either. See note 41 and Slicher van Bath, *The Agrarian History of Western Europe*, 21–22, 41–45.

43. AHN, Clero, carp. 1665, no. 1.

44. For Table 4.11 and Carrión, see *Vida económica*, 169–97.

45. Merchán Fernández, *Sobre los orígenes del régimen señorial*, 153.

46. Ibid., 224.

47. *Becerro*, 1: 422, 431, 441.

48. Luis Martínez García, *El Hospital del Rey de Burgos: Un señorío medieval en la expansión y en la crisis (siglos XIII y XIV)* (Burgos: Ediciones J. M. Garrido Garrido, 1986), 306–25, argues for localized demographic pressure in certain lands of the Hospital. While this may be so, his findings do not diminish the evidence for northern Castile which shows the impoverishment of demographic resources. I doubt very much that the problem was, as he affirms, scarcity of land.

5. The Market for Land in Late Medieval Castile: Selling and Leasing the Land

In previous chapters I have sought to offer an overview of the general structures of Castilian agriculture, and, as has been seen, in some respects rural life in Castile was not very different from that of other regions of the medieval West. In the following pages, however, I would like to examine northern Castilian country life from another perspective, that is, from the vantage point of economic exchanges between peasants and between rural and urban dwellers. Specifically, I will examine two types of transactions: (1) buying and selling of land and (2) leasing of rural property or emphyteutic agreements.

The Controversy over the Market for Land

Interspersed among royal charters and the written deeds of the powerful, hundreds of contracts of the purchase and leasing of land survive in the rich documentation of late medieval Castile. Indeed, the bulk of the extant evidence consists of documents evincing the economic activity of people who were relatively powerless. They emerge in history through their transactions—once, twice, but seldom more—buying, selling, or leasing land, soon to disappear from our sight forever. What do these transactions of land and other types of property reveal about the structure of Castilian society? What do they tell us about the economic and social status of those who sold their small holdings and of those who invested in rural property in the Castilian countryside?

The existence of such documentation dating back to the early eleventh century is the more remarkable since what has survived certainly represents only a small portion of a much larger number of transactions undertaken in late medieval northern Castile. In northern Castile, unlike other parts of Europe—as for example, in England, where manorial records provide an invaluable source for the study of transference of property in rural areas, or in Catalonia and Italy, where early notarial activity assured the survival of both secular and ecclesiastical evidence—the extant documentation comes almost exclusively from ecclesiastical archives. These sources, therefore, mainly record the acquisition of property by the church or of lands that over time passed into the hands of monasteries, cathedral chapters, or churches; thus, a whole category of transactions of land and real estate which did not concern either clergymen or ecclesiastical institutions has been lost to history.[1] Moreover, we must assume that a whole subset of transactions among the very poor were never recorded. These probably consisted of an oral agreement, a handshake or kiss, an exchange of oaths and symbolic tokens of what was being transferred in the presence of witnesses. The cost of drawing up the documents and reluctance to enter the world of the written word may have been among the factors that precluded the recording of many small transactions. Such informal agreements remain, of course, a part of economic exchanges to this day, even in developed societies. Thus historians have only an occasional glimpse of these transactions and the people involved in them. One must keep in mind, therefore, that in discussing the peasant market for land we do not always see the whole spectrum of society. It is often only the stories of those who wrote or whose activities were recorded that can be fully told.

Although the surviving documentation is incomplete, it does offer a variegated view of rural and urban economic activity and life in medieval Castile.[2] In the following pages I would like to focus on these transactions for what they were first and foremost: exchanges of property. I refer here to the peasant market for land, a topic which, although studied in detail for medieval England, has yet to be examined for Castile. The difficulties in doing so are twofold: First, as substantial as the pertinent documentation is for Castile, it does not match either the volume or the preciseness of English manorial records. What can be learned about English transference of land is far more than one can hope to know in other parts of the medieval West. The records of land transactions in northern Castile seldom provide us with information as to the size of the property, and they are not always specific as to the nature of what is being purchased. Such expressions as *todo lo que tengo, todo lo que me pertenece* (everything I have), or simply *heredad*, *heredamiento*, which are found in many transactions, do not allow us to calculate the price of land per unit over time, nor can we be certain as to how much land was being sold or bought.[3] Often, price is the only clue to size, but this is a most unreliable indicator of the extent of the property purchased: One must assume that large exchanges of money correspond to similarly large parcels of land and vice versa, but the price of land also depended on where the land was and when it was sold, as well as on inflation, climate, and other factors. One must also take into account the different prices for vineyards, flax fields, or grain-producing lands.

The second difficulty one faces in studying the peasant market for land in northern Castile, or elsewhere for that matter, is conceptual. Was there a real "market for land"—with "market" understood here in its modern economic meaning, that is, as "the buying and selling of land for money on a large enough scale to constitute something like a 'market' in the sense in which the word is used by economists"?[4] What does the existence or lack of such a market mean for our understanding of the structures of medieval society?

Zvi Razi has summarized this debate in a clear and concise manner, albeit one that promotes his own views on the subject. On the one hand, a group of historians led by J. Ambrose Raftis and the Toronto School of Medieval Studies argues that the aftereffects of the plague—demographic decline and economic stagnation—led to a weakening of communal bonds "where private and independent interests took precedence over those of groups."[5] Following this approach, Alan MacFarlane sees the market for land as revealing the presence of "individualistic farmers, pursuing a quasi-capitalist system of production"; and, going far beyond Raftis and his group, he argues that "the village community never existed." Thus one witnesses, at least in England, the breakdown of the "feudal" order and the onset of modernity represented above all by the "selfish" and aggressive transference of land in exchange for money. Razi and others have undertaken to test and challenge these ideas by showing (as Razi does for Halesowen) that many of these market exchanges were in reality inter-familial transactions, or at least transactions between close neighbors, thus undermining the image of freewheeling English medieval peasants engaged in selling and buying land.[6] The type of family reconstruction which Razi undertook is seldom possible for other parts of Europe or even England before 1400, but one can grant the point that if the extant documentation allowed for it, one might discover far more interfamilial exchanges than what the sources indicate.[7]

In the context of northern Castilian economic life, both explanations leave a great deal to be desired. The implication raised by the English debate is that, despite numerous qualifications, the existence of a peasant market for land contradicts a well-defined and long established model for the peasants' relationship to the soil and, more significantly, to their lords.

A "quasi-capitalistic" peasant market for land weakens the ideological un-
derpinnings of "feudal" and manorial structures built over many decades of
historical and ideological elaborations. Likewise, when the "market for
land" is revealed to be not really a "market" but mostly transactions between relatives and neighbors, these findings underscore the permanence of
communal structures beyond the economic changes and transformations of
late medieval society. What is somewhat neglected in this discussion, however, is the possibility that both approaches can be partially correct. Moreover, what one can say about buyers, at least in northern Castile, does not
always apply to sellers, and we cannot ignore the peculiarities found as we
move from one locality to another. Signs of economic independence
among the peasants, greed, the wish to expand one's holdings do not
necessarily mean the complete overthrow of communal tradition. In fact, as
Ruth Behar has shown conclusively, both models of rural life have survived
and still survive in an uneasy relationship in Spanish villages.[8]

Furthermore, what is missing from the English discussion is the interaction between town and country. Clearly, in northern Castile and elsewhere in the West, the so-called peasant market for land cannot be studied
in isolation. The city dwellers who were buyers and lessees of farmland in
the *contados* (or *alfoces*) of northern Castilian towns were of the utmost
importance in the creation of a "market" for land. They were also instru-
mental in lively economic transfers between people unknown to each other,
who were thus outside the interfamilial or close neighborhood patterns of
transactions.[9]

The Peasant Market for Land in Late Medieval Castile

In the following pages, I argue, based on the extant documentation, that we
err in looking at land transactions for the purpose of fitting them into
preconceived models of economic structures and development. In order to
discuss the peasants who sold their land, we must do without the strait-
jacket of "feudal" or quasi-capitalistic constructs.[10] In Castile, the peasants
were economically, politically, and socially oppressed, and their burdens
ranged along a wide spectrum of obligations and dues that were dependent
on many diverse factors. But northern Castilian peasants in the late Middle
Ages were not so rooted to the land that they were inseparable from it. In a
region far less "seignorial" than we may be willing to admit, those peasants
who sold and leased land were not at all powerful. Indeed, some of them

sold small pieces of land that could barely support them, but the documentation shows them as responsible, autonomous economic actors. And in Castile there is no definite boundary, as has been argued for England, between a period when peasants did not buy and sell land and the emergence of a market for land.[11] As far back as evidence exists, peasants sold and bought land. The transition from what one may call traditional or non-economic exchanges to more "modern" or market transactions was far more subtle than indicated by some English scholars, and it did not depend solely on an increase in the number of transactions. Moreover, when peasants bought and, far more often, sold land, they almost always did so as if the land were held as an allod. Purchase of rural property often carried with it some obligations to the crown, in the form of territorial taxes, and sometimes to ecclesiastical lords. Yet the language of the extant sources seldom indicates anything but a market in freehold land. Nor are there any signs that the peasants required their lords' permission to dispose of their property.[12]

Table 5.1 shows the number and pattern of selective land and real estate transactions in northern Castile between 1240 and 1360.

The region examined in Table 5.1 is the same as that studied in previous chapters, that is, an area coinciding roughly with historical Old Castile, although documentation from Salamanca is also included. The terminus of this inquiry should have been the mid-century proper, but I have extended the date to include the years immediately after the plague (1350) to see what, if any, its impact was ten years later. But the documentary evidence on the aftermath of the plague is scant. Only a few transactions are extant for the period, and they do not differ markedly in nature from those dated before 1350. If anything at all can be deduced from the sources, it is that economic transfers of land and real estate suffered a severe slowdown in the 1350s. On the other hand, a downturn in economic activity was already evident in the late 1330s and 1340s.[13]

Table 5.1 requires a bit further explanation. Buyers and sellers have been divided according to whether they belonged to the ecclesiastic or secular estate. Within the former category, I have made a distinction between institutions and individuals. Reflecting the ecclesiastical nature of the documentation, the bulk of the purchases were undertaken by religious institutions first and then by clerics, the immense majority of them canons, the deans of the cathedral chapters of Ávila, Burgos, Salamanca, and Segovia, as well as secular priests. These individual acquisitions, however, were clearly for personal and not institutional gain, undertaken for the economic and

TABLE 5.1.   Land and Real-Estate Transactions in Northern
Castile (1240–1360).

Buyers	No. of Transactions
Ecclesiastical	
Institution	445
Single male	292
Single female	2
Secular	
Single male	256
Single female	45
Couples	69
Families	11
Groups	3
Municipal councils	3
Unknown	7
Total	1,133

Sellers	
Ecclesiastical	
Institution	32
Single male	57
Single female	19
Secular	
Single male	434
Single female	149
Couples	268
Families	126
Groups	27
Municipal councils	6
Unknown	15
Total	1,133
Transactions undertaken to settle a will	37
Transactions between relatives	16

Location	
Rural	799
Urban	334
Total	1,133

Table 5.1.   *Continued*

Type of Property	No. of Transactions
Farmland*	217
Land**	416
Vineyards	154
Mills/milling rights	68
Gardens	58
Meadows/grazing lands	25
Others (flax fields, fish ponds, barns, rivers, pigeon coops, orchards, beehives, etc.)	32
Houses (includes stores, warehouses, etc.)***	229

Price Range (in mrs.†)

0–50	342
51–100	143
101–200	134
201–300	92
301–400	68
401–500	52
501–1,000	64
1,001–5,000	125
5,001+	32
Unknown	81

Source: See documentary sources listed in Abbreviations.

*This includes such general designations as *heredades, algos,* "everything I have," etc. In most cases, the main item is land, but it is accompanied by other diverse holdings usually found in medieval rural holdings.

**Includes land alone as well as land together with no more than two other types of property, i.e., vineyards, gardens, etc.

***Most of the transactions involving houses did not state the actual number of houses. The documents often use the term *casas* (houses). Most of the houses were urban, but the figures include village houses.
†The value of the *maravedí* fluctuated wildly throughout the late thirteenth and fourteenth centuries.

social benefit of the buyers and their families, although, at times, part of the property passed on to the church through donations and wills.

Such categories as families or groups were not always uniform and were almost always found as sellers. Families were, more often than not, widowed mothers and their children selling property. In 1329, to cite one example, Doña Juana and her sons and daughters sold the Algos of Castellanillo for 300 *mrs.* to Master Sancho, the prebendary of the cathedral of Ávila. But a widower and children as buyers were not rare either. In 1305 a man and his three adult sons sold land to the monastery of San Salvador de Oña for 700 *mrs.* In these and other, similar cases, including those involving groups of people who at first glance appear to be unrelated, we are probably witnessing the settlement of an inheritance, even if this is not explicitly stated in the documents.[14] Inheritances were partible throughout Castile, and many of the sales undoubtedly reflected the conversion of property into money as the easiest and fairest way of dividing an inheritance. The direct references to sales that were undertaken to settle inheritances are relatively few, but the disposition of the property of those who died intestate, especially in rural areas, must have been an important motive for selling. We have many examples of whole sets of transactions that were undertaken either to settle an inheritance or to reassemble property dispersed by the terms of a will. In a single day, 9 May 1299, fourteen different people sold milling rights to the monastery of Santa María la Real de Aguilar de Campóo in ten different transactions. The records of the purchases indicate that a good number of the sellers were related by blood (brothers, sisters, nieces, nephews, and so on) and most probably all fourteen belonged to the same family group. They all sold milling rights in the same mill (near the *huço*) in what was clearly the settlement of an inheritance. On the other hand, Pedro Sarracín III's purchases in 1292 and similar later purchases were the means by which he consolidated the former property of his uncle Gonzalo Pérez which had been dispersed upon his uncle's death.[15]

Laymen, alone or in groups, bought land more often than laywomen did by a ratio of almost six to one. Yet, although the overall number of males selling land remained higher than that of females, the ratio was roughly only three to one. Of course, when clerics are included, the proportions are much higher among buyers, at a ratio of twelve to one, while for sellers it remains three to one. Couples are included in the table as such only when the language of the document makes explicit that both husband and wife shared economic responsibility over what was sold or bought. Thus, if we add the number of married women to those selling by themselves, without male participation, we have evidence for an important female presence in land and real estate transactions. We must also assume that if numerous small transactions were never recorded or are not extant, the actual number of women appearing as economic actors would be larger. Applying the patterns of distribution of property between males and females in late medieval Castile, we may expect to find most women at the level of small landholding and tenure. (Such is the case in Table 5.3, as will be seen below.) In those instances where Jews and Moors surface in the documentation (overwhelmingly in transactions of urban property), their purchases were basically similar to those of Christians.[16]

There is one further issue that requires some elaboration here. Razi argues that many of the land transactions at Halesowen in England took place between relatives or close neighbors. The extant evidence for Castile shows the contrary. Most of the buyers were either ecclesiastical institutions, clerics, or outsiders to the community, mostly from nearby cities or towns. Even in the cases in which the buyers were locals, there is evidence that their purchases were often more than just exchanges between relatives or friends. In fact, the evidence suggests that they sought to consolidate holdings by buying contiguous lands. Such is the example of Miguel Pérez studied in detail by Miguel Santamaría Lancho. Miguel Pérez was a *vecino* and *morador* (a citizen as well as an inhabitant) of Oter de Herreros, a village in the diocese of Segovia. Between 30 October 1341 and 24 November 1358, there are fourteen different transactions involving Miguel Pérez. Miguel bought lands, vineyards, flax fields, a house, and other rural properties either by himself or in conjunction with his wife, Doña Inés, or nine other men, as was the case in the last extant transaction. The fourteen transactions included numerous pieces of land scattered around the village of Oter de Herreros. For example, on 19 April 1347, in a single transaction he purchased a flax field, a pasture lot, and twelve pieces of land, most of them small and dispersed throughout the area. As could be expected in a small village, some of the sellers were related to each other and probably even to Miguel.[17] The point, of course, is not so much whether buyers and sellers were related, but the intent of the transactions. In this particular case, it was certainly for reasons other than providing extra land for an heir, settling an inheritance, or helping out a relative in need. It was clearly an investment which likely enhanced Miguel Pérez's social standing within the village and most certainly also advanced his economic well-being.

Land was the item most often bought and sold. By land, we mean grain-producing land already under cultivation, but also, as the documents sometimes tell us, land suitable for cultivation. Agriculture in medieval northern Castile was seldom a specialized or exclusive activity concentrated in one commodity. Often, when land was sold, the transaction included pasturelands, flax fields (where geography and climate allowed for them), meadows, and so forth. What we see here is the tendency and often necessity of medieval peasants to produce as much of a variety of products as they could. In spite of growing trade and economic interdependence in the region, Castilian peasants seldom would have dared to depend on one staple. There are innumerable examples of transactions in which, although land was certainly the most important item transacted, other types of agricultural property were also included. Most commonly we find transactions in which *heredamientos* (literally "inheritance" or land held as an allod, but in the Castilian context also *tierras de pan llevar* or "grain-producing lands") or *todo lo que tengo* ("everything I have") are the expressions used to describe a whole range of agricultural property.

For example, on 28 August 1284, Blasco Martín, together with his two daughters and their respective husbands, sold *todo quanto heredamiento* they had in Serranos de Avianos to Blasco Blázquez. In this particular case, the property was not described in detail, although we can extrapolate what it was from similar transactions in the same village. In May 1242 Fernando Díaz de Cerezo and his wife, Doña Endolza, sold their *heredad*, cereal-growing lands, vineyards, village houses, *solares* (property held as an allod) inhabited and uninhabited, gardens, mills, meadows, grazing lands, waters, trees, woods, and fountains, with rights and all that was enclosed therein. They sold these properties for 500 *mrs.* and a cape to the monastery of Las Huelgas of Burgos. In a large number of the transactions included in Table 5.1, the word *heredad* is used without further elaboration. At times, however, the amounts paid seem far out of proportion to the description of what was being sold. In 1249 five Burgalese brothers made three separate purchases in the village of Villamorica. In all three they acquired lordship over the lands, vassals, vineyards, houses, *solares*, gardens, mills, meadows, and so on, but the price of the first two transactions, respectively 15 *mrs.* and a cape and 40 *mrs.* and a cape, does not really equate with what was being bought.[18] Was the land so inexpensive? Was there a hidden charge in the purchase which we cannot see? Or was the language of most transactions just an empty formula?

When we turn to other types of property transactions in northern Castile, we see that vineyards, mills (or, to be precise, mill rights), and, to a lesser extent, gardens followed land as the items most frequently bought and sold. Clearly, vineyards and mills, far more often than land, were bought and exchanged for their financial return. Though vineyards were bought and sold almost everywhere in Castile, in those regions which were best suited for viticulture, as for example the Rioja, the concentration on vineyards as the preferred item of exchange reveals an active submarket in wine. Moreover, whenever boundaries were given, vineyards were always located adjacent to roads, a fact that points to their market-oriented production. The investment of Pedro Pérez, a citizen of Burgos, is revealing in this respect. Between 1324 and 1326 Pedro bought six vineyards, six pieces of land (sizes are not stated), and a house in the village of Madrigal del Monte. Altogether his total investment amounted to the modest sum of 713 *mrs.* The most expensive vineyard sold for 90 *mrs.*, and in one of the transactions six men sold a vineyard to Pedro for a paltry 38 *mrs.* The top price paid for land was 123 *mrs.*, and 22 *mrs.* was paid for the house. Here we find an urban dweller investing in a village that was not very close to the city, and, as we know from the documentation, he also later sold some of his property there at a profit. As I have shown elsewhere, Pedro Pérez's purchases of vineyards and lands also served him as the means for social promotion to the rank of non-noble knight of Burgos. The documents seldom allow us to see the movement of property through several transactions, but surely Pedro Pérez was not the only person who bought land and later sold it at a profit.[19]

The evidence shows an active market in mill rights or usufruct with a tendency toward the progressive seignorialization of mills by their passing into the hands of powerful local corporations, mostly chapters, from the late twelfth century on. Mill rentals also show wide fluctuations, reflecting changing economic conditions and belying the old-fashioned view of un-yielding and conservative economic policies. Indeed, as shown in an earlier chapter, in thirteenth- and fourteenth-century Castile cathedral chapters were either willing or forced to lower rental prices when economic conditions dictated it. This appears to have been the case in 1314, when both bad weather and civil war led to an economic downturn; again in 1344, a time of great difficulties in northern Castile; and far more drastically in 1350, after the plague.[20]

I have left the subject of houses (mostly urban) for last because this chapter's emphasis is on land transactions. In a later chapter we will have the opportunity to examine urban transactions in greater detail. Here it suffices to say that in northern Castile there was an active market in urban real estate, gardens, barns, and so forth within the city walls. Such properties often commanded prices that were four or more times higher than the

TABLE 5.2.   Purchases by the Cathedrals
of Burgos and Salamanca.

Date	Burgos	Salamanca
1200–1249	134	30
1250–1299	4	3

Source: Documents from ACB. Also in FMCL,
vols. 13, 14, 16, and 17. AHN, Clero, carps.
1886–88, Salamanca.

prices paid for similar properties in the countryside. In the twelfth and early
thirteenth centuries cathedral chapters in northern Castile gained, either
through purchases or donations, the lion's share of urban properties. These
acquisitions remained an integral part of the chapters' economic well-being
into the early modern period. After the mid-thirteenth century, however,
purchases by the northern Castilian chapters declined radically, as Table 5.2
shows for Burgos and Salamanca. At mid-century, the chapters' purchases
were emulated and eventually surpassed by urban dwellers who sought to
purchase houses within the city walls and to establish their rights to citizenship (vecinaje).[21]

Urban Buyers: Individuals and Ecclesiastical Corporations

Here we must proceed from a general discussion of land exchanges to
specific examples. The latter may provide better insights into the nature of
the market for land in medieval Castile and, far more important, the reasons
medieval peasants and urban dwellers bought and sold land. Our best
source for information comes from buyers who over a period of time made
a sizable number of purchases in one given locality and who, as far as the
documents allow us to see, did so to further their economic interests. In this
sense, the economic relationship between town and country is most crucial.
If we set aside ecclesiastical corporations for a moment, we see that most of
the purchases listed in Table 5.1 were made by a handful of individuals. They
were either laymen or clerics, and their acquisitions were clearly aimed at
advancing their own fortunes, building a family estate (in some cases a
patrimony or entailment), enhancing their social status in town and city, or
in a few instances, providing a charitable endowment worthy of the donor.

With one notable exception, all those who appeared often as buyers in the so-called peasant market for land were city dwellers. Even the exception, Miguel Pérez, may have been either an agent for Segovian interests or himself a "citizen" (*vecino*) of both Segovia and Oter de Herreros. This is indeed a point worth reemphasizing. In Castilian villages, we witness a few well-to-do peasants purchasing land and rural property. These were the people Moxó has aptly described as *campesinos hacendados* (landed peasants). But with the exception noted above, we seldom have more than a few references to transactions that show their role in the land market as buyers. What we have for late medieval northern Castile, however, is the undeniable evidence of acquisitions made by city inhabitants. This, however, promotes a false impression of a sharp dichotomy between town and country. As pointed out earlier, in northern Castile the distinction between the two was virtually nonexistent. Urban oligarchs, canons, even urban middling groups, almost without exception, owned property in the countryside around the Castilian towns, derived part or most of their income from rural rents, and lived on their farms at least part of the year, often from the feast of Saint John (in June) to that of Saint Michael (in September) at the height of the agricultural cycle. Investment in rural property was, after all, an important aspect of the economic and social life of the Burgalese patriciate and that of other Castilian towns. In Burgos, this was the case not only for the city's two dominant families, but also for lesser men. In Ávila, where the ruling elite was not engaged in commerce (unlike the case in Burgos), land purchases and the building of rural estates were even more important.[22]

In this respect the example of Blasco Blázquez is revealing and worthy of reexamination. Here we see one man's efforts to acquire as much land as possible in one specific area of Ávila's countryside. A member of the *linaje* of Blasco Jimeno, one of the ruling families of Ávila, Blasco Blázquez had been a royal judge in Ávila from at least 1283 to 1289; he served as archdeacon of the cathedral of Ávila from 1297 to 1303 and as dean of the chapter between 1303 and 1307. We have fifty extant transactions in which Blasco or his agents appeared as buyers between 1284 and 1302. Of these transactions, twenty-five concerned the purchase of rural property in the village of Serranos de Avianos and twenty-five involved acquisitions in its dependent locality of Cornejuelos. According to Barrios García, both locations bordered on Blasco Blázquez's own lordship of San Adrián. Clearly, the fifty transactions signify only a part of what must have been Blasco's much larger role as a buyer in these two villages and elsewhere in the region of Ávila.

One should also note that most of the land acquired in Serranos de Avianos and Cornejuelos was willed, donated, or sold to the chapter, but not without what seems like a very profitable return to Blasco's sister.[23]

Table 5.3 shows the range of prices and types of property bought by Blasco. Above all, the table reveals a whole spectrum of sellers who were not powerful landholders. The sellers in these transactions were average peasants who were often selling the little land they held. Significantly, all of them exchanged land or other types of rural property for money in ways which reveal them to be independent and responsible economic actors. Some of the sellers seemed to have sold all they had in order to settle an inheritance. This fact may account in part for the twelve families or groups (probably also comprising relatives) that appear as sellers. In two cases this is made explicit: Menga Andrés, the widow of Gil Blázquez, sold to Blasco everything she and her brothers had inherited from her mother in Cornejuelos (maslin fields, gardens, mills, pastures, and pasture rights in the village commons) for 33 *mrs.* in 1301. Also in 1301 Doña Juana, on behalf of her brothers and sisters, sold property in the same village to Blasco for 600 *mrs.* Twenty-six of the sellers appear to have disposed of all the property they owned in one or the other of the two villages. Did they own property elsewhere? Did they buy within the same locality with the money they obtained in the transaction? Were the formulaic phrases *todo heredamiento* or *todo lo que tengo* misleading? Indeed, in 1299 Domingo Sancho and his wife, Andariezo, sold "everything they had" in Serranos de Avianos for 100 *mrs.*; yet two years later the couple sold a pair of houses with a barnyard in the same village to Blasco Blázquez for 60 *mrs.*[24] The records of transactions also give us a vague understanding of who these sellers were. The use of *don* and *doña* to describe some of the sellers or their relatives points to people with some social standing within the villages. The use of such words as *heredad* as well as the selling of rights to the commons indicate that the land was held, at least in practice, as an allod with little or none of the so-called feudal or seignorial obligations. Moreover, a good number of the sellers were *vecinos* (citizens of the villages) with all the rights to the commons which derived from citizenship in the village.[25]

When we turn to institutional buyers, the pattern of acquisitions is quite similar. Thanks to the recently published documentation of the monastery of Las Huelgas of Burgos, we can reconstruct the process by which the nuns built what must have been a large and contiguous state in and around Dueñas between 1229 and the early 1260s.[26] Dueñas, located on the west bank of the Pisuerga River on the road that led from Palencia to

TABLE 5.3.   Purchases by Blasco Blázquez, 1284–1302.

	No. of Transactions
A. Type of Property Purchased	
Farmland (see Table 5.1)	40
Land (see Table 5.1)	6
Mills/milling rights	1
Gardens	3
Grazing land	1
Team of oxen	1
Rights to village commons	2
B. Price Range of Transactions (*in* mrs.)	
0–50	7
51–100	11
101–200	12
201–300	10
301–400	7
401–500	0
501–600	2
Unknown	1
Total	50
C. Sellers *	
Single male or group of males	20
Single female	3
Couples	15
Families/groups	12
Total	50

Source: DMA, AHN, Clero, carps. 23–30.

*Ninety-six individuals were named among the sellers, including fifty-six males and forty females (two transactions refer to brothers and sisters but do not specify their numbers). The descriptive *don* or *doña* is used to identify only nine of the sellers; however, many of their parents are also described as *don* or *doña*.

Valladolid, was a large and strategically placed town. Although quite distant from Burgos, it secured for the monastery a key holding on a much-traveled commercial route. Between 1229 and 1262, Las Huelgas made fifty-three purchases of land in Frausillas (where the bulk of the transactions took place) and in a number of small hamlets around Dueñas and close to Frausillas (see Table 5.4).

TABLE 5.4.   Purchases by the Monastery of Las Huelgas of
Burgos in and around Frausillas (Dueñas), 1229–62.

	No. of Transactions
A. *Type of Property Purchased*	
Land (exclusively)	53
B. *Price Range** (*in* mrs.)	
0–5	43
6–10	10
Total	53
C. *Sellers***	
Single male	19
Single female	4
Couples	20
Families/groups	14
Total .	57***

D. *Type of Boundary to Land Bought by Las Huelgas*	No. of Boundaries
Land owned by peasants	71†
Monte (wooded, uncultivated rough)	100
Carrera (roads, byways)	22
Land owned by Las Huelgas	13
Land owned by another ecclesiastical institution	5
Vineyard	1

Source: FMCL, vols. 30, 31.

*The highest amount paid by the monastery was 9 *mrs.*; the lowest
was 4 *ss.*; and the average was 3 *mrs.*
**One hundred and eight peasants were mentioned as sellers, includ-
ing sixty-five males and forty-three females. The descriptive *don* was
used thirty times; *doña*, thirty-four times.
***Four peasants sold their land twice; one peasant sold land three
times.
†Of this amount, nine boundaries were on land owned by John
Adrián.

Clearly what distinguishes these transactions from others examined elsewhere in this chapter is the uniformly low prices paid for land. Moreover, by comparing other purchases in the area, we see that they were mostly restricted to cereal lands. With the exception of two purchases of vineyards for 54 *mrs.* and 47 *mrs.*, respectively, in Vega de San Miguel, the exchanges in Frausillas and in other localities around Dueñas rarely surpassed 5 *mrs.* We are here perhaps finally face-to-face with the lowest level of landholders in the social and economic hierarchy of the peasantry. And yet, a close examination of those mentioned as owning contiguous lands or listed as witnesses reveals clear signs of social stratification. John Adrián in Frausillas, the family of Martin Castrillo, Don Elo's family in Vega de San Miguel, Don Elo once again, Don Lobón, and the Tis family in Sacalahorra appear as owners of numerous, if small, plots. We can follow the passing of property from one generation to another and observe how certain families maintained their presence and independence in spite of Las Huelgas's growing economic sway. There is, of course, another side to the coin, for by reconstructing boundaries we can also see how, in a period of just three decades, the monastery of Las Huelgas became the principal landholder around Dueñas.

We should turn here from the fairly well-to-do peasants who managed to resist Las Huelgas's purchasing onslaught to those who often sold everything they had. In the case of Frausillas, our largest sample, very few peasants appear selling land more than once. Their names are seldom listed as owners of bordering property or as witnesses. If we extrapolate data from the few documents in Frausillas where the size of the land sold is stated, we can see the unequal relationship between buyers and sellers. I have calculated the average price of the *obrada* (the area of land which could be plowed in one day, or between forty-six and fifty-three *áreas*) of land at two *sueldos*. If this price applies to other transactions, the majority of the lots sold did not have, on the average, more than twelve *obradas*. This simply was not enough to support a family.

The question, of course, is why did the nuns buy—and, relatedly, why did the peasants sell? Las Huelgas's economic activity is easily comprehended. From the twelfth century to around the mid-thirteenth century, monasteries and cathedral chapters in northern Castile engaged in an aggressive policy of acquiring urban and rural property, both for the obvious purpose of creating consolidated/contiguous holdings and of securing sizable rents. This pattern of acquisitions, demonstrated not only by Las Huelgas but by other ecclesiastical institutions throughout northern Castile, was not very different from that of an earlier age. Although better records are available for the later period, the actual number of purchases did not increase dramatically, and, in fact, as we have seen above (Table 5.2), the number of properties bought by monasteries and cathedral chapters declined sharply.[27] The difference was in many respects qualitative, having to do with where and for what reason the property was purchased and, above all, who the purchaser was.

Before 1200, in Burgos and in other parts of Castile as well, we find many different buyers, but few of them acquired more than a handful of properties. Moreover, we do not find the distinctly urban character of later transactions. Before the late twelfth century, ecclesiastical institutions were still benefiting from generous donations by nobility and the crown. These donations began to disappear at the turn of the century. After that date and after the 1240s, the urban patriciate's decisive participation in the market for land marks that not so subtle transition which Jacques Le Goff, in a different context, has aptly described as moving "from heaven to earth."[28] What we witness in this period is a twofold process: First, from the 1200s on, the urban oligarchies of Castile began to monopolize important benefices in cathedral and collegiate chapters. Once this was accomplished, they turned ecclesiastical income to their own benefit. This development can be seen clearly in the changing pattern of acquisitions throughout northern Castile from purchases by chapters to personal acquisitions by members of the chapter. Second, town dwellers, often possessing money gained in long-distance trade or from ranching income, turned to the task of building estates in the surrounding countryside. The rise of a new urban mentality and its concomitant mercantile practices—which in northern Castile dated to the late eleventh century—now confronted the more traditional patterns of rural economic organization and mentality.

Creating a Market for Land

While we may assume with some degree of certainty the reasons monasteries and/or individuals bought property, the question remains as to why the peasants sold their lands. Moreover, what did they do after they sold their lands? Unfortunately, the evidence is not always available nor is a single explanation entirely satisfactory to answer these questions. The easiest answer is that in Castile the peasants who sold their land did so because of the opportunity to migrate south. This theory is most feasible for the period between the Christian victory at Las Navas de Tolosa in 1212 and the years after the final conquest of most of Andalucía in the 1250s when the area was opened to Christian settlement. The *repartimientos* (records of the distribution of Moorish property to new Christian settlers) of Seville, Jerez, Murcia, and Cádiz show the geographical origins of those receiving land and real estate in the region: the bulk of them are from the northern meseta. Moreover, in addition to the south's climatic advantages, land prices were quite low there, while rural salaries were and remained higher than in northern Castile. Yet numerous transactions of land and real estate took place in the north before 1212, a period when the Christian-Muslim frontier was fairly stable, and they continued after the 1260s when the attraction of Andalucía waned or when, in fact, there were cases of reverse migration.[29]

The attraction of the frontier could not be the sole explanation, and there must have been many other reasons that motivated peasants to sell their holdings. Many of these have already been examined by historians in their assessments of the peasant market for land in England. Others have been implied above: they involve the settlement of an inheritance, economic need, or the peasants' inability to resist the predatory purchases of a powerful man such as Blasco Blázquez or of an ecclesiastical institution. In fact, in Castile some of the transactions explicitly stated that they took place to pay debts to Jewish moneylenders. It is clear that in the late thirteenth and early fourteenth centuries many peasants in villages throughout the land were incurring heavy debts, and their lands were sold, often under judicial order, to pay those debts. In many respects, this is another way in which town and country interacted, certainly not to the benefit of the latter.[30] But these were not the only forces at work.

In the late 1250s and throughout the next half-century, other factors came to the fore. In this respect the royal charters to the non-noble knights of Castile (also extended to canons and clerics shortly after 1256) included important economic concessions that may have encouraged land transactions. Those serving or working (as farmhands) for non-noble urban knights and for canons could own tax-exempted land valued up to 100 *mrs*. Are we seeing here some segments of the Castilian peasantry becoming tenant farmers to rising urban and ecclesiastical oligarchies while keeping holdings worth less than 100 *mrs*.? After all, as reflected in the range of prices included in Table 5.1, that amount in the late thirteenth century certainly bought enough land to support a family with ease and more. Moreover, as we move into the fourteenth century, the level of political violence rose to become a serious disruption to agricultural life.[31]

It is not inconceivable, then, that many peasants sold their lands, or at least part of them, to seek not only exemption from taxes but also the protection of a monastery, or of a member of the nearby city's mounted militia. The evidence is often only tangential, but it points very strongly to a process by which peasants sold their land even as they remained on it as tenants. There is really no other explanation. Castile did not enjoy the demographic surplus that obtained in some regions of late thirteenth-century France and England, and this gives a completely different outlook to the peasant market for land in Castile. If we examine carefully the purchases made by the monastery of Las Huelgas in Frausillas, we observe that the arable purchased was most often bounded by *montes*, wooded and uncultivated land. Similar evidence from Segovia shows that Castile might have had abundant land but most probably not enough hands to cultivate all of it. The realm had too few farmhands before 1300 and even fewer after. With some local exceptions, there was no pressure on marginal lands in northern Castile, but rather a scarcity of labor. Moreover, there was also in this period a dearth of agricultural tools and work animals, which may help explain the willingness of peasants to sell and, by remaining on the land as tenants, to gain access to oxen and agricultural tools.[32] Why would monasteries or urban oligarchs have purchased land if there was no one to work it?

The seignorialization of rural and urban property in late medieval Castile somewhat parallels similar developments in other parts of Europe, although that "seignorialization" was not, as far as the documents let us see, the works of seigniors but rather of non-noble urban dwellers. In Castile, however, there is the same reaction to the decline in rental income and the rise of labor costs after 1350 that occurred elsewhere in the medieval West. Yet the mechanisms that led to this process were somewhat different and are not always easy to describe. For example, as pointed out earlier, we do not know much about day laborers and their role in agricultural production except that they performed most of the important agricultural tasks in the Benedictine monasteries of northern Castile. We can assume that these laborers also owned land as freeholders, perhaps not enough to support their families or allow for independence, but something to call their own. Thus in Castile the bonds between peasants and lords and among peasants themselves were underlined by a considerable number of peasants who owned land outright or held it through perpetual leases under conditions that were, theoretically at least, less binding than those in other parts of northern Europe or than those seen in the extreme case of Catalonia. In the latter, peasants were finally placed under servile obligations around this period. This does not mean, of course, that the level of exploitation and outright extortion under which the peasantry suffered was less than in the rest of Europe, but at least they were spared the humiliation of a *remença* payment (manumission fine).[33]

By the first half of the fourteenth century, when land rents began to decline throughout the region—a decline most vividly evident in the crown's acceptance of drastic reductions in the numbers of those inscribed in tax rolls—the king and secular and ecclesiastical lords found themselves with far fewer people to tax or to extort money from than ever before. Moreover, economic conditions as well as long-standing customs hardly permitted an increase in contributions to make up for lost revenues. In these scrambles for income, the crown and the lords exacted money in whatever way they could, from direct appropriation of monastic lands, to forced loans and outright thievery.[34]

In this context, what do the transactions of land and real estate show us? The evidence points to a lively transference of rural and urban property from the hands of the weak and poor into the hands of the rich. In contrast to the English sources, which show perhaps an earlier step in this process at the village level, what we see in medieval northern Castile is the obvious consolidation of land into the hands of a few powerful men or corporations. Unlike the case in other parts of Europe, however, these exchanges of property did not take place within the framework of a rising population, or as a result of so-called Malthusian pressures. The emerging economic and social distinctions within the Castilian rural communities—conflicts that were aggravated by the membership of the rural petty nobility and the clergy in the village council—led to social tensions. This situation was further compounded by the growing economic gulf between urban buyers and rural sellers, and the tensions produced by this distance often led to violence.

Although I do not suscribe *in toto* to Brenner's explanation of economic development in late medieval Europe—that is, that noble violence and power defied and affected the workings of demographic forces and market mechanisms, and that thus the structure of class relations (between lords and their dependent peasants and within the village community itself) had a great deal to do with that economic development—one cannot ignore it altogether as an important factor in the changes that took place in late medieval northern Castile and in the creation of a market for land.[35] In the specific case of northern Castile, the transference of property from those below to those above was more often than not the way in which urban oligarchs and cathedral-chapter canons and deans translated their commercial profits or ecclesiastical income into landed estates (inexpensive landed estates, one might add). But why should this surprise us at all? As far as the documents go back in Castile there is evidence of this movement of property from those "below" to those "above." In some cases, especially in troubled times, the peasantry may have been a willing accomplice. Yet through leases both for life and for a limited number of years (a topic which I examine below), land was redistributed back to the peasants under conditions not unlike those in existence when they owned the land. The progression from fragmentation to consolidation of the land and back again, as noted earlier, was a recurring pattern in Castilian and Leonese villages until the very recent past.

Leasing of Lands

The letting of land under terms that ranged from a few years to a "lifetime" or "forever" served as an economic counterpart to the market for land and real estate. As in the case of land transactions, the evidence for leaseholds in thirteenth- and fourteenth-century Castile is overwhelmingly ecclesiastic. I have no doubts that lay lords, prosperous independent farmers, and urban oligarchs also let their lands in return for an annual rent, work, or both, but we seldom have any direct evidence of these activities. Similarly, there are very strong tangential indications that the subletting of farmlands was common. This was to be expected when the property leased was a large one, but the practice was probably also in force among small landholders, reaching downward into the lowest level of the peasantry. As we have seen above, cathedral chapters in Segovia and probably in other parts of Castile leased part or most of their holdings to their own canons at favorable rents. The canons, in return, often subleased it back at a higher rent, and the difference between the two rents was the benefice or income assigned to each individual member of the chapter.[36]

Because of the ecclesiastic nature of the documentation, our understanding of economic changes in northern Castile remains partial. In the sources extant for the period before 1350, those letting their lands were overwhelmingly monasteries and cathedral chapters. As indicated in an earlier chapter, monastic institutions in late medieval Castile seldom worked their demesne directly. Instead, they let their lands to farmers under various types of arrangements. To put it simply, monasteries and chapters gave lands to peasants, often with work animals, agricultural utensils, seed and/or money, for a few months, for years, for life, or for as long as there were descendants. In return the tenants paid an annual rent. The payments could be in kind, in specie, or in both; sometimes the rent included other obligations, such as maintenance of a church, the offering of masses, duties of purveyance, work on specific dates (*sernas*), recognition of lordship, and a myriad of other responsibilities and restrictions. Some contracts, as was always the case in Oña, included careful provisions to protect the lessee from inclement weather and loss of his or her crops. Other agreements were carelessly drawn or so succinct as to provide little or no information about the terms of the rental or economic conditions at that point. All these instruments are known in Spanish history as *censo* or *census*, a word, again, which is deceiving when directly translated from its northern context. In truth, few documents before 1350 use the word at all, and it was only in a later period that the term *censo* (meaning here the annual rent paid for land and/or real estate often held in perpetuity, although theoretically the real dominium remained with the initial grantor) came into frequent use.

In previous chapters we have had the opportunity to examine some leasehold agreements as well as the social position and gender of those renting lands. Table 5.5 shows the number of rental agreements, to whom the property was leased, and under what terms.

At first glance Table 5.5 is not very revealing. The number of extant leases is greatest for the period between 1280 and 1299 and then again between 1330 and 1349. Both high points coincide with troubled decades: the first with the conflict between the Infante Don Sancho and his father, Alfonso X, and the civil war during Ferdinand IV's minority; and the second reflective perhaps of the widespread noble violence and harsh economic conditions affecting northern Castile during the later decades. This is, of course, only a guess, since it would follow from this that the decade of 1310–20, corresponding to the anarchy of Alfonso XI's minority, should show a similar trend. Moreover, these records reflect only the fragmented remains of a much larger sample, and what survives likely represents a distorted vision of the past. We know from the *Cuadernos de contabilidad* of the cathedral of Burgos, from the 1303 census of property of the cathedral chapter of Ávila, and from other similar sources that the number of urban and rural properties leased was far greater than what the extant records show. Furthermore, more than one-third of our sample comes from the documentation of the monastery of San Salvador de Oña, and thus our sample is skewed to mirror the peculiar characteristics of that particular locality.

TABLE 5.5.   Rental Agreements in Northern Castile and Oña, 1230–1360.

A. *Rentals by Decade*

Dates	Rentals of Northern Castile	Rentals of Oña	Total
1230–1239	5	5	10
1240–1249	7	3	10
1250–1259	7	5	12
1260–1269	16	9	25
1270–1279	16	41	57
1280–1289	19	25	44
1290–1299	29	19	48
1300–1309	15	12	27
1310–1319	16	8	24
1320–1329	10	9	19
1330–1339	18	8	26
1340–1349	26	4	30
1350–1359	18	1	19
1360	2	0	2
Total	204	149	353

B. *Forms of Payment*

Payment	Northern Castile	Oña	Total
Money	90	53	143
Money and kind	21	41	62
Kind	63	52	115
Unstated or other obligations	30	3(42)*	33(42)*
Total	204	149	353

C. *Types of Renters*

Renter	Northern Castile	Oña	Total
Village council	7	4	11
Single male	107	107	214
Couples**	28	15	43
Groups/families	47	19	66
Single female	7	4	11
Ecclesiastical institution	4	0	4
Unstated/unclear	4	0	4
Total	204	149	353

TABLE 5.5.   *Continued*

D. *Length of Lease*

Term	Northern Castile	Oña	Total
Forever	11	18	29
For life of tenant	105	73	178
One year	1	0	1
Two years	2	0	2
Three years	3	0	3
Four years	6	0	6
Five years	5	1	6
Six years	4	3	7
Seven years	2	2	4
Eight years	1	2	3
Nine years	4	2	6
Ten years	6	13	19
Eleven years	3	0	3
Twelve years	3	5	8
Fifteen years	2	6	8
Sixteen years	0	1	1
Nineteen years	1	0	1
Twenty years	4	8	12
Twenty-two years	1	1	2
Twenty-four years	1	1	2
Twenty-five years	0	1	1
Thirty years	1	3	4
Unstated (probably for life)	38	9	47
Total	204	149	353

Source: Documents listed in Abbreviations.

*Obligations to offer mass, plant trees, work, and so on in addition to payments in kind/money or both.
**Some instances include more than one couple.

What then can be said? First, as in the patterns we found among those purchasing and selling lands, males alone leased land in far larger numbers than any other category of lessees. Indeed, in contrast to what we have seen in the data for land transactions, women are seldom found as renters. This is not surprising since monasteries would have been reluctant to rent to women alone. A good number of the males leasing land from monasteries and/or churches were ecclesiastics themselves, and these leases may often reflect those particular arrangements, mentioned above, by which income was assigned to clerics. In the case of groups or families (kinship ties are not easy to establish unless explicitly stated), it is clear that in most cases a group of people or relatives joined together to work lands too large for one single individual or family. In 1316 the monks of Santa María la Real de Aguilar de Campóo gave a *solar* to eleven people (among whom were four couples, and five were related as brothers and sisters) for their lifetimes at a rent of 24 *mrs*. payable annually at Martinmas. In addition this group or extended family had to recognize that they were *vasallos* (vassals) of the monastery. Similarly, the monastery of La Vid rented grain-producing areas to sixteen millers in 1347 for seven years at the substantial rent of 120 *fanegas* of bread (20 of wheat, 50 of barley, and 50 of rye) annually and the promise that the millers would not alienate the lands to noblemen.[37]

In these and other examples, we can witness the mechanisms by which people sought to pool their energies and resources to obtain a desirable lease. Rural councils—for which we have only a handful of examples—also took advantage of the difficulties faced by monasteries in working their lands. In 1336 the monks of San Pedro of Gumiel de Izán leased their pasturelands in Pineda to the rural council of the same location for twenty years. The village would pay six rams and six carts of wine a year in return for the use of the pasture. Most probably, the monastery's flock had been reduced, so by letting its pasture the monastery was able to provide some meat and wine for its depleted table.[38]

When we turn to forms of payment, we find those made in kind and those made in specie fairly balanced. Table 5.5 is somewhat deceiving on this point. Even when rents were paid in kind (usually in grain), there were always some monetary obligations attached to the leasehold. More often than not, the agreement included payment of the tenth, a *procuración*, rights of purveyance, or other monetary obligations. Conversely, when payments were made in money, they were often accompanied by contractual obligations to repair the church, sponsor masses, plant trees, repair property, and so forth. Even the simplest contracts hid complex reciprocal obligations which bound lessor and lessee by far more than just a fixed rent. In 1288 the monastery of San Salvador de Oña leased lands in Santa María de Rivarredonda to Domingo Abad for ten years at a rent of twenty-eight *fanegas* (half wheat, half barley) every other year, payable by the feast of the Virgin in September. The grain was to be carried to Oña at the tenant's expense. In addition, Domingo agreed to pay the tenth for all the property and at the conclusion of the lease to leave half of the arable with a good fallow ready to plant. As in similar leases, Domingo also promised not to alienate the property to any lord.[39]

Similarly, the way in which rents were paid varied from locality to locality. The nuns of San Andrés de Arroyo collected their rent almost exclusively in kind, ranging from small rentals of 5 *moyos* of grain to a very large rent of 400 *moyos* and 500 *mrs.* (the only instance of money being paid among the extant leases of San Andrés for the period before 1350). In this single instance, there is a good possibility that the 500 *mrs.* was entry money.[40] In the area of the Rioja the collegiate churches of Albelda and Logroño preferred to collect their rents in coinage. Overwhelmingly the property leased consisted of vineyards, and rents for them—reflecting the market-oriented nature of the vine—were invariably collected in money or in a share (half) of the vintage. Of the twenty-nine extant vineyard leases, twenty-three required payment in issue, often small amounts ranging from as low as 2 *ss.*, 8 *ds.* to 40 *mrs.* Between 1238 and 1358 the average rent paid was around 13 *mrs.* per unit annually. This points to the leasing of small vineyards for an equally small amount of money. Rents seem to fall off after 1350. In at least one instance, María, the widow of Adán Pérez, gave her lands to Pedro Martínez to plant as a vineyard. At the end of five years, they were to divide the vineyard in half with no other payment required.[41]

In other places, such as Covarrubias, money was also the preferred form of payment for rent, with amounts ranging widely from 2.5 *mrs.* to more than 650 *mrs.* annually.[42] This wide range in the amounts of rents paid reflects the variety of properties leased, from minuscule to quite sizable holdings. Often the amounts paid for rentals reflected market or economic conditions, and some of the contracts included clauses for an increase in rent after a certain time had elapsed or when a new tenant came aboard. Moreover, as has been indicated before, leasehold agreements often included provisions to protect the lessees from inclement weather or unusual adverse conditions.

Elsewhere, as for example in Oña, the monasteries usually preferred lifetime or long-term leases, with payments in kind, almost exclusively in grain. One would think, however, that with the frequent debasing of coinage typical of the period between the late 1260s and the mid-fourteenth century, the monks of Oña and other monasteries would have opted to collect the rents in kind, but this was not always the case. Instead, they adopted a policy of diversifying the sources and types of income they received in order to protect as much as possible the financial life and well-being of their particular institutions. Nowhere, however, was the flexible response to market conditions more obvious than in the leasing of mills. Mills or milling rights could command very high prices, and the cathedral chapter of Burgos, to give just one example, rented its mill of Santo Domingo for 1,000 *mrs.* annually in 1306, half payable at Saint John's Day, the other half at Christmas.[43] In the account books of the chapter of Burgos, we can see the fluctuation of mill rents for a period of almost a century (Table 5.6).

These rental figures are indeed revealing. They tell us that a swift economic change was taking place in northern Castile and in Burgos proper. Within a few years rents increased or decreased depending on demand, crop conditions, and so forth. In 1350, after the onslaught of the plague, rents plummeted by more than 50 percent from the level of 1344, though the chapter hoped for some upturn in the rents they collected.

Length of leaseholds also reveal to us the Castilians' practical outlook when dealing with the demesne. Short-term leases were mostly reserved for mills. Beyond that, leases could be given for any number of years. More often than not, however, rentals were made for the life of the tenant or "for all the generations to come." By renting in this manner, the monasteries and chapters sought to secure a source of income, as well as to keep their lands under cultivation. It was perhaps the only possible response to increasingly difficult conditions. All the clauses that requested that tenants acknowledge the lordship of the institution and that forbade the letting of the land or renters from alienating or selling the lands often came to naught over the course of time, but ecclesiastical institutions had to face the challenge of the day rather than concern themselves with what the future might bring, and this they did fairly successfully. For the peasants, lifelong leases or leaseholds "forever" guaranteed possession of the land, a very desirable possession within the mental boundaries of the medieval world.

One also finds a good number of rental contracts requiring the renters to inhabit the land (*poblar*), to repair what seemed to be half-ruined farms, to plant vineyards and fruit trees. In addition, lands were given *ad laborem*; that is, monastic lords were willing to relinquish half of the land granted in return for placing it under cultivation. This evidence speaks to us across the centuries of a rural world in times of difficulties, plagued by localized demographic shortages, noble violence, bad weather, and often inefficient management. It was a world increasingly dependent on city finances. Often, as one searches through the documents, the eye is struck by the references here and there to monastic debts. Not surprisingly, by 1338 monasteries were selling portions of their domains to pay for loan charges

TABLE 5.6.   Rents in the Mills of the Cathedral Chapter of Burgos (in *mrs./ss./ds.*).

Mill	Rents Listed for Specific Years						
	1277	1279	1282	1314	1325	1344	1350
Sobre Villa Ayuda	100	282/4	187/6	136/3.5	550	440–480	100–120
Villa Ayuda	101/4/4	103/ /4	212/2/9	168/3.5	380	440*	200–230
Trapero (Sotrajero)	153	179/1	155/5	246/6	400–450	450–500	200
Solaz	0	60	60	not listed	200	not listed	300
Santo Domingo	20	105	196/4	not listed	500–600	600	300–350
Hospital de S. Gil	80	100	102	not listed	290–320	280–300	110
Yuánez Arias	78/6	190	218/8	not listed	600–650	600–700	300
Posadillo	5/2/3	146	132/2/7	not listed	600	600–650	280–330
Martín Cardeña	26	26	26	not listed	210 + penalty	200	
Afga	30/5/2	120/5/4	134 + 20	233/6	700	400	400
Malarco	28	42	55/ /9	77	120	200	80–100
Santo Sepulcro	fallen	fallen	fallen	destroyed			
El de la Vega	26	15	not available	70	125	100	100
El de la Puenta	15	15	not available	38	40–60	50	
Santa Gadea	67	109/2	not available	30	210–260	empty	60
Oreiuello (Orejuelo)	26	26	not available	not listed	200	520	300
Tejadillo	26	26		42	130	120	50–55

Source: ACB, *Cuadernos de contabilidad.* Capitular, mayordomía, vols. I–II.

*Rent fluctuated in annual contracts.

or the crushing weight of royal taxation. As discussed above, farms were also being auctioned to meet the debts to Jewish moneylenders.[44]

Was there a peasant market for land? Were peasants selling, leasing, and, from time to time, buying? Yes, and in great numbers if, as I argue, what is extant is only a meager remnant of far more intense systems of exchanges. But this so-called peasant market for land and its parallel leasing of lands in life-term or perpetual contracts tell us very little indeed as to whether capitalism was around the corner, or whether, if one could look deeper into the documents, one could see that the traditional patterns of rural life had changed little. Sitting at the knees of greed and necessity, of familial duty and fear of God, buyers, sellers, lessors, and lessees of land and real estate went on with the very mundane and common requirements of everyday life. These patterns can sometimes be fitted neatly into developmental constructs, but more often than not they resist such categorizations. In northern Castile late medieval land and real-estate transactions reflected the peculiar moment and circumstances of the realm and give us glimpses of the mentalities and the types of social and economic organization which allowed then, as it does today, for the powerful to rule over the weak.

I am of course not saying anything new here. Angus MacKay has already said as much and far better than I could. The intrusion of mercantile capital, of an urban mentality into the rural world—in the specific case of the market for land—did not mark the emergence of capitalism, but only a change in the manner in which urban dwellers, whether secular or ecclesiastic, derived economic benefit from the land.[45] What I have shown in the previous pages is the evidence of a market for land and real estate in northern Castile. This market was defined by the intrusion of urban mentalities and economic practices into the rural world. The slow interaction of both was a long and continuous process, unresolved and undecided in northern Castile even within living memory, and it is still an observable and present reality in most parts of the world. It is, therefore, to that urban world that we must turn now to inquire into the reasons leading to the ascendancy of northern Castilian cities over the countrysides.

Notes

1. The sections of this chapter dealing with the market for land appeared in Teofilo F. Ruiz, "La formazione del mercato della terra nella Castiglia del basso medioevo," *Quaderni storici* 65 (1987): 423–52. Into the fourteenth century, the bulk of the extant documentation for northern Castile survived in cathedral and monastic archives. A large part of those collections are currently kept at the Archivo histórico

nacional. The internal evidence of these sources also shows them again and again to be incomplete. See Ruiz, *Sociedad y poder real*, 84. Important documentary collections for great noble houses also begin in earnest after 1350. See Pascual Martínez Sopena, *El estado señorial de Medina de Rioseco bajo el almirante Alfonso Enríquez (1389–1430)* (Valladolid: Universidad de Valladolid, 1977), 54–83; Salvador de Moxó, "De la nobleza vieja a la nobleza nueva: La transformación nobiliaria castellana en la baja edad media," *Cuadernos de historia: Anexos de Hispania*, 3 (1969).

2. For the use of transactions for family reconstruction, see Ruiz, "The Transformation of the Castilian Municipalities," 3–33; and "Los Sarracín y los Bonifaz: Dos linajes patricios de Burgos, 1248–1350," *Sociedad y poder real*, ch. 5.

3. See, for example, AHN, Clero, carp. 24, no. 16 (9-May-1301), in which Blasco Blázquez (see below) purchased "todo quanto hay salvo tierra con su pan" in Serranos de Avianos (near Ávila) for 400 *mrs*. See also AHN, Clero, carp. 27, no. 3 (29-April-1317): Gómez Gil, archpriest of Ávila, purchased *heredamientos* in San Miguel de Serrazuelos (region of Ávila) for 120 *mrs*. For similar sales of *heredades* in Oña (north of Burgos), see AHN, Clero, carp. 297, no. 12 (18-July-1285); no. 21 (14-February-1286); for *todo lo que tengo*, carp. 301, no. 6 (27-June-1292) et passim. *Heredad* means property owned outright. See *Heredad* in *Diccionario de historia de España*, 2 vols. (Madrid: Revista de Occidente, 1952), 1: 1337. For *heredad* as grain-producing land, see below.

4. One of the most recent contributions to the debate is P. D. A. Harvey, ed., *The Peasant Land Market in Medieval England* (Oxford: Clarendon Press, 1984), above all Harvey's introduction, 1–28. See p. 22 for his argument on transactions which were never recorded. Also Paul R. Hyams, "The Origins of a Peasant Land Market in England," *Economic History Review*, 2d. series, 23 (1970): 19; Zvi Razi, "Family, Land and the Village Community in Later Medieval England," *Past & Present* 93 (1981): 3–36; Edmund King, *Peterborough Abbey, 1086–1360: A Study in the Land Market* (Cambridge: Cambridge University Press, 1973), 55–62, 168ff. Because of the nature of the Castilian documentation, the emphasis in this chapter is not on transactions between peasants of somewhat equal social and economic standing, although a few of these transactions are examined here, but rather on purchases made by the fairly well-to-do from those below them.

5. Razi, "Family, Land and the Village Community," 3–4, 29; see also his *Life, Marriage and Death in a Medieval Parish: Economy, Society and Demography in Halesowen, 1270–1400* (Cambridge: Cambridge University Press, 1980).

6. See note 5. For the contrary view, see Raftis, *Tenure and Mobility*; Alan MacFarlane, *The Origins of English Individualism: The Family, Property and Social Transaction* (Oxford: Blackwell, 1978). Again, I should emphasize that a great deal of these arguments turn on the impact of the Black Death on rural society. Most of the evidence presented in these pages comes from before 1350, and one of my contentions is, in part, that important transformations had already taken place, at least in Castile, in the pre-plague years. I was first attracted to this topic and to the comparative aspects of it by Giovanni Levi's provocative paper, "The Market for Land: England, Colonial America, India and a Village in Piedmont in the XVIIth Century," presented to the Social Science Seminar at the Institute for Advanced Study, Princeton, April, 1984.

7. The Castilian documentation seldom provides indications of kinship. As shall be seen below, however, most of the Castilian transactions were *not* between relatives or close friends.

8. Behar, *Santa María del Monte*, 189–285.

9. For bibliography on the relationship between town and country, see Part II, introduction, note 3, above.

10. In Castilian medieval history the controversy is whether "feudalism" (meant here as one of the required stages of Marxian development) existed in Castile. These issues have already been debunked by Elizabeth A. R. Brown, "The Tyranny of a Construct: Feudalism and Historians of Medieval Europe," *American Historical Review* 79 (October, 1974): 1063–88. For Peter Linehan's ideas on the topic, see below.

11. For the arguments regarding the emergence of a land market in late twelfth- or early thirteenth-century England, corresponding to "an abrupt change in familial attitude towards its property," see King, *Peterborough Abbey*, 61ff., 168ff.; Harvey, *The Peasant Land Market*, 12, 27. This entire discussion cannot be conducted without at least acknowledging the questions raised by Robert Brenner's "Agrarian Class Structure and Economic Development in Pre-Industrial Europe," *Past & Present* 70 (1976): 30–75, and the subsequent debate in *Past & Present*, nos. 78, 79, 80, and 97. See below.

12. The most common restrictions are often found in life-term leases of land. Monastic lords implicitly accepted the possibility that the land or the right to the lease could be sold in the future. They requested that the land not be alienated or that it not be sold or leased to noblemen or those exempted from taxes. See for example AHN, Clero, carp. 1658, no. 15 (27-May-1267); carp. 1733, no. 2 (20-November-1321); carp. 1033, no. 5 (20-December-1323); carp. 1025, no. 15 (24-February-1328).

13. The general slowdown in transactions in the 1330s and 1340s can be seen in the following examples from the cathedral of Burgos and the monastery of Santa María la Real de Aguilar de Campóo.

Decade	No. of transactions in Burgos	No. of transactions in Aguilar de Campóo
1320–29	41	10
1330–39	30	9
1340–49	28	2
1350–59	4	1

Source: ACB; AHN, Clero, carps. 1670–1674.

14. AHN, Clero, carp. 27, no. 16 (24-March-1329); carp. 305, no. 10 (17-July-1305).

15. On partible inheritance, see Lutz K. Berkner and Franklin F. Mendels, "Inheritance Systems, Family Structures, and Demographic Patterns in Western Europe, 1700–1900," in *Historical Studies of Changing Fertility*, ed. Charles Tilly

(Princeton, N.J.: Princeton University Press, 1978), 209–33; Peter Laslett and Richard Wall, eds., *Household and Family in Past Time* (Cambridge: Cambridge University Press, 1972); Ruth Behar and David Frye, "Property, Progeny and Emotion: Family History in a Leonese Village," forthcoming in *Journal of Family History*. See also examples in AHN, Clero, carp. 1663, no. 4 (9-May-1299); ACB, vol. 50, f. 152 (25-January-1292); vol. 49, f. 96 (28-December-1292); vol. 49, f. 98 (4-February-1293), et passim.

16. For women as buyers and renters of land as well as for references to minorities, see Ruiz, "Notas para el estudio de la mujer en el área del Burgos medieval," 419–28; on women in Castile, see Heath Dillard's excellent book, *Daughters of the Reconquest: Women in Castilian Town Society, 1100–1300* (Cambridge: Cambridge University Press, 1984).

17. Although I have transcribed all the records of these transactions at the AHN, Clero, carp. 1959, nos. 9, 10, 14–19 and carp. 1960, nos. 1–5, 8, the analysis of these exchanges comes from Miguel Santamaría Lancho's unpublished thesis on the cathedral chapter of Segovia's economic policies. I would like to thank Professor Santamaría for all his help and kindness.

18. *DMA*, 103–4. For Blasco Blázquez, see below. Also *Documentación del monasterio de Las Huelgas de Burgos (1231–1262)* in *FMCL*, 31: 115–16, 186–90.

19. On Pedro Pérez, see Ruiz, "The Transformation of the Castilian Municipalities," 16, n. 50. For an example of selling at a profit, see AHN, Clero, carp. 1959, no. 5 (20-December-1337). In 1337 Llorente Yuánez and his wife sold part of a house in Segovia to the cathedral chapter for 280 *mrs*. The house had cost them only 130 *mrs*. originally.

20. See above. On mills, see Chapter 3, note 21. One example of the fluctuation of rent income from the mill of Villayuda (owned by the chapter) will suffice here.

Date	Rent
1277	101 *mrs*. 4 *sueldos*, 4 *dineros*
1279	103 *mrs*.
1280	60 *mrs*.
1282	212 *mrs*. 2 *ss*. 9 *ds*.
1314	168 *mrs*. 5½ *ss*.
1325	380 *mrs*.
1344	310 *mrs*.
1350	200 *mrs*. to rise to 230 *mrs*. the following year.

Source: ACB, *Cuadernos de contabilidad*. See also Part IV.

21. For the ownership of urban property by cathedral chapters in Burgos, see ACB, *Cuadernos de contabilidad*, which show the large number of houses owned by the chapter within the city walls and the rents they collected from those houses. Also Hilario Casado Alonso, *La propiedad eclesiástica en la ciudad de Burgos en el siglo XV: El cabildo catedralicio* (Valladolid: Universidad de Valladolid, 1980), 97–137. For

Ávila, *DMA*, 223–32, 416–48. For rights of *vecinaje*, see below and Ruiz, "The Transformation of the Castilian Municipalities," 11–20.

22. See Salvador de Moxó, "Campesinos hacendados leoneses en el siglo XIV," *León medieval: Doce estudios* (León: Instituto de estudios leoneses, 1978), 165–98. For restrictions on urban inhabitants living in the countryside, see the *fuero* of Treviño in *MHE*, 1: xxiii–xxiv et passim. See also Ruiz, "The Transformation of the Castilian Municipalities," and below, Part III.

23. Barrios García, *Estructuras agrarias y de poder*, 2: 135–51, 147, n. 37. See Table 5.3 and *DMA*, 215. In a census of property owned by the chapter of Ávila there is an entry on Blasco Blázquez's property. He had given his lands in Serranos de Avianos, Cornejuelos, and El Villar to the chapter. We know he spent 10,831 *mrs.* in purchasing property in the first of these two locations; yet his sister, María Blázquez, was willing to pay the chapter 30,000 *mrs.* for that property plus El Villar.

24. AHN, Clero, carp. 24, no. 18 (9-May-1301), no. 19 (9-May-1301); *DMA*, no. 178; AHN, Clero, carp. 24, no. 5 (1-March-1301).

25. This is clear from at least two of the transactions in which rights to the use of the village commons were sold outright. AHN, Clero, carp. 24, no. 18 (9-May-1301); carp. 25, no. 2 (12-June-1301).

26. On Las Huelgas, see Antonio Rodríguez López, *Las Huelgas*, 1: 33–319.

27. As to the evolution of purchases over a long historical period, see Pérez-Embid, *El Cister en Castilla y León*, 369–512, which shows the evolution of sales and leasing into the late fifteenth century.

28. The remark "du ciel à la terre" comes from Jacques Le Goff's presentation to the Society of Fellows, Columbia University, in the spring term, 1985. See also below for a more detailed discussion of this transformation.

29. See Julio González, *Repartimiento de Sevilla*, 2 vols. (Madrid: Consejo Superior de Investigaciones Científicas, 1951); *Repartimiento de Jerez*, XLVI–XLIX; Juan Torres Fontes, *Repartimiento de Murcia* (Madrid: Consejo Superior de Investigaciones Científicas, 1968); Ruiz, "Expansion et changement," 550–55; Manuel González Jiménez, *La repoblación de la zona de Sevilla durante el siglo XIV* (Sevilla: Universidad de Sevilla, 1975), 22–25.

30. Some examples of land being sold to pay debts to Jews are found in Aguilar de Campóo: AHN, Clero, carp. 1667, no. 12 (26-February-1315); from the area of Logroño: *Albelda y Logroño*, 138; from Oña: *Oña*, 2: 669–70; from Rioseco, AHN, Clero, carp. 354, no. 5 (2-December-1285), no. 6 (12-January-1290), no. 7 (19-February-1290), no. 9 (7-December-1292); from La Vid, AHN, Clero, carp. 383, no. 10 (14-October-1347), et passim.

31. On political violence, see Ruiz, "Expansion et changement." See also Julio Valdeón Baruque, "Aspectos de la crisis castellana en la primera mitad del siglo XIV," *Hispania* 111 (1969): 5–24, and Part IV. On Alfonso X's charters to the non-noble urban knights and to ecclesiastics, see Ruiz, "The Transformation of the Castilian Municipalities," and *MHE*, 1: nos. 43, 44, 45, 68, 102, et passim.

32. On the boundaries at Frausillas, see above. For Segovia, see *Propiedades del cabildo segoviano*, 65–68, 87–106. The dearth of agricultural tools can be seen in a very carefully drawn and descriptive series of leasing agreements undertaken by the nuns of San Andrés de Arroyo between 1300 and 1332 and already examined above: AHN,

Clero, carp. 1732, no. 5 (19-December-1300), no. 7 (31-October-1306), no. 9 (22-July-1310), no. 14 (19-October-1315), no. 15 (12-January-1318); carp. 1733, no. 2 (20-November-1321), no. 20 (28-March-1332); carp. 1734, no. 1 (16-April-1332). In 1334 a peasant sold his land to the monastery of San Andrés de Arroyo and became its *vasallo solariego*. See also another example of selling and leasing the land right back in *Documentación del monasterio de San Salvador de Oña (1032–1284), FMCL*, 3: 64.

33. Freedman, *The Origins of Peasant Servitude*, 119–53.

34. See, for example, AHN, Clero, carp. 1667, no. 9 (13-April-1315); carp. 1033, no. 1 (15-April-1315), et passim in which Alfonso XI and/or his regents agreed to lower the number of taxpayers in the rolls. In 1316 John Ferrández burned and looted the village of Ribafrecha to the point that the surviving peasants migrated elsewhere. Because of this, the monks of Santa María de Nájera requested a tax moratorium for ten years. Alfonso XI (or his regents) granted it but only for seven years. See AHN, Codices, 105B, ff. 125–127v. The whole threat to these poor villagers continued into the late 1330s. In 1283, when the Infante Don Sancho confiscated the property of Juan García de Covarrubias, he ordered one of his men in Covarrubias to select the twelve richest men in the town and to force them to purchase the property. *Fuentes*, 2: 126–27.

35. For the Brenner thesis and the responses to his ideas, see T. H. Aston and C. H. E. Philpin, eds., *The Brenner Debate: Agrarian Class Structure and Economic Development in Pre-Industrial Europe* (Cambridge: Cambridge University Press, 1985).

36. *Propiedades del cabildo segoviano*, II, n. 1, 79–85.

37. AHN, Clero, carp. 1668, no. 5 (12-November-1316); carp. 383, no. 9 (8-April-1347).

38. AHN, Clero, carp. 234, no. 7 (6-October-1336).

39. *Documentación del monasterio de San Salvador de Oña (1285–1310)* in *FMCL*, 4: 78–79.

40. AHN, Clero, carp. 1732, no. 9 (22-July-1310).

41. *Albelda y Logroño*, 312–13. All other leases are found in 52, 62, 68, 77–78, 80, 104, 122, 135, 241, 250–51, 261, 268, 274, 276, 278, 280–81, 283–84, 286, 292, 300, 304, 312, 315–16.

42. *Fuentes*, 2: xlix ff.

43. *Documentación de la catedral de Burgos (1294–1316)*, in *FMCL*, 17: 193–94.

44. See, for example, *Vida económica*, 58–67. For property owned by peasants sold or auctioned to pay debts to Jews, see: AHN, Clero, carp. 354, no. 6 (12-January-1290), no. 7 (19-February-1290), no. 9 (7-December-1293); carp. 383, no. 10 (4-October-1347). See also Salvador de Moxó, "Los judíos castellanos en el reinado de Alfonso XI," *Sefarad* 35 (1975): 142–43.

45. MacKay, *Spain in the Middle Ages*, 52–53.

Part III

Urban Society in
Late Medieval Castile

The cities and towns on the northern plain differed as much from each other as did the agricultural regions. Urban society above the Guadarrama range was organized according to diverse economic, political, and social models. Historians of medieval northern Castile have long noted these differences and have emphasized the distinct character of cities along the road to Santiago de Compostela and north of the Duero and those municipalities further south. One criterion for analysis has been to look at their administrative organization. North of the Duero, the land had been organized in *merindades* (administrative units similar to shires in England or *bailliages* in France) since the twelfth century, and one finds few autonomous municipal councils or, to be more precise, cities under direct royal rule, such as Burgos or San Vicente de la Barquera. Instead, the lordship of most towns was held by secular and ecclesiastical lords. Santander and Silos, to cite just two examples, were ruled by abbots. South of the Duero, in the ancient Extremaduras, the so-called *comunidades de villa y tierra* (communities of town and land) were royal towns: Segovia, Ávila, Sepúlveda, Cuéllar. Moreover, while north of the Duero urban jurisdiction over the countryside seldom extended very far, the communities of town and land had urban centers that served as the administrative focal points for sprawling hinterlands.[1]

One could make further distinctions between those cities and towns which benefited economically from international commerce and those which served essentially as focal points for their surrounding hinterland. Furthermore, there were locations that rose to great prominence and power without strategic proximity to the pilgrimage road, without serving as a bishop's see, and without playing a role in long-distance trade, as Adeline Rucquoi has shown magisterially in her study of Valladolid.[2]

Institutionally, urban centers could be fairly autonomous, that is, they were under royal lordships or had to bear an ecclesiastic lordship (Palencia, Silos, Santander) or lay lordship (Aguilar de Campóo in the mid-fourteenth century). The thirteenth and fourteenth centuries witnessed a fair number of changes in lordships. Partly due to royal largesse but mostly due to the weakness of the crown and ecclesiastical institutions, *ricos hombres* (magnates) and princes of the blood royal appropriated royal jurisdiction over towns for their own benefit.

Relations between a city and its lord were often antagonistic and were complicated by the perennial confusion of overlapping and conflicting royal, seignorial, and municipal jurisdictions. For example, the town (*villa*) of Silos was under the lordship of the Benedictine monastery of Santo Domingo de Silos, and this lordship, with its concomitant exemptions from royal taxes and assorted privileges, was confirmed and reconfirmed by successive kings throughout the late Middle Ages. Yet royal officials often treated Silos as part of the royal domain, and representatives of its *concejo* had to travel first to Valladolid and later to Burgos to do homage to Ferdinand and Peter, sons and heirs of Alfonso XI, in the 1330s. Moreover, as I have already shown for Burgos, even powerful city councils were half paralyzed by jurisdictional disputes and by the overlapping exemptions and privileges of ecclesiastical and secular corporations, religious minorities, and individuals in their midst.[3]

Clearly, each city or town had its own unique history, each with its own local variations and ambitions. In spite of the difficulty in generalizing about such diverse localities, however, there is perhaps something to be learned in looking at urban life in Old Castile as a whole. Jean Gautier-Dalché has already done so for the period before 1250, and his book, *Historia urbana de León y Castilla en la edad media*, serves as a most valuable starting point for our inquiry. His study, however, examines urban life in Castile before the mid-thirteenth century and thus does not deal with the important political, social, and economic transformations that took place in the structure of urban life after that date, nor does it deal with the changing relations between the crown and the cities.

In attempting to describe the nature of urban life and municipal organization, one is faced with serious obstacles. My first area of research was the city of Burgos, and I have examined its history in detail for the period 1200–1350. Unfortunately, Burgos was unique in northern Castile not only because of its commercial orientation but also because of the wealth of its documentation before 1350. Municipal archives from northern Castilian cities before the mid-fourteenth century have been lost, as was the case in Ávila, or are sparse (less than twenty documents in Segovia), or have almost no manuscripts extant (Santander, Soria). Most of the information has to be weeded out from royal sources or from other types of documents: ecclesiastical records, land transactions, litigations, and references in the chronicles. The documents provide us with an occasional view of the social, economic, and political structures of towns. Often one is forced to borrow from the knowledge of later periods and assume, I believe almost always correctly, that they reflect conditions before 1350.

One last point should be made here before we turn in earnest to the problem at hand. I have been quite troubled by the words "city" and "town," or better yet "city" and "*villa*." The terms are not used here as synonyms. Juridically, there were few cities in northern Castile. Burgos was certainly one and had been a *ciudad* from an early period in its history. Segovia was not a city before 1300, and neither was Santander. It is not always clear what criteria were used to define one or the other, whether it was a papal or royal authority which determined the status of urban centers in Castile. Yet royal documents served as a touchstone, for in this period they carefully distinguished between city and *villa*. As far as possible, I will attempt to retain the distinction, but in truth, in terms of urban society and economy, such semantic distinctions meant little.

Notes

1. This distinction is made by Gonzalo Martínez Díez, *Las comunidades de villa y tierra de la extremadura castellana* (Madrid: Editora nacional, 1983), 9.

2. Adeline Rucquoi, *Valladolid en la edad media*, 2 vols. (Valladolid: Junta de Castilla y León, 1987), 1: 57.

3. For Silos, see below; for Burgos, see Ruiz, *Sociedad y poder real*, ch. 4.

6. The Institutional Organization of Castilian Towns

A study of each individual city and town in northern Castile would obviously require many volumes. Moreover, in many instances such enterprise would duplicate existing studies of important urban centers. Through the work either of antiquarians carried out long before the onset of the twentieth century or of enterprising historians in the last decade, we now have a formidable collection of local histories that allows for an attempt at synthesis.[1] But in our attempt we must begin by identifying the important urban nucleus of the region.

The Towns of Northern Castile

There are several approaches one could choose from the categories presented in the introduction to this section. A typology of cities would have to include economic, social, and political aspects. Nevertheless, for the sake of expediency, let us focus at present on those localities thrown into prominence at the beginning of the fourteenth century. In 1315, representatives of a large number of cities, towns, and *hijosdalgos* from throughout the realm met in Burgos to form a *hermandad* or league. They did so to protect their own interests against the rapacity of some of Alfonso XI's regents and of an unruly nobility. The charter of the *hermandad*, which has been published among the ordinances of the Cortes, lists the cities and towns represented as well as individual attendees. A few of the small localities sent one procurator, though the majority of the towns had two representatives. Ávila, on the other hand, had as many as sixteen procurators.[2]

Of the one hundred municipal councils in attendance, more than half came from northern Castile. They included most of the important urban centers—Burgos, Segovia, Ávila, Palencia, and Soria—but, pointedly, not Valladolid, which served as headquarters for the regency. Four of the important ports on the Bay of Biscay coast—San Sebastián, Guetaria,

Castro Urdiales, and Laredo—were present; significantly, Santander and San Vicente de la Barquera were not. Also missing were the great municipal councils of Toledo, Seville, and Córdoba. At first glance, the *Hermandad* of 1315 appears as a northern Castilian affair led by Burgos, with the strong support of Leonese towns and those on the pilgrimage road. (See Chapter 7 for a discussion of the importance of the road to Santiago de Compostela.) In addition, there was spotty participation from Extremaduran and Andalusi towns. Why some municipal councils were present and some were not is impossible to determine; one can only speculate as to the reasons. The presence of some of Alfonso XI's regents and their forces at Valladolid, for example, may have deterred the sending of procurators from that city. Toledo traditionally had been the center of its own league and must have been quite unwilling to give way to Burgos. There was a bitter and ancient strife between the two for precedence at the meetings of the Cortes. Seville was in the orbit of rebel princes of the blood royal, the enemies of María de Molina, grandmother of and regent for Alfonso XI, and of urban interests.[3]

Difficult to explain, however, is the presence of many small localities. Salinas de Añana must have been there only because it was an important source of salt; Orduña only because it was a toll station on the commercial route between the plain and northern ports. Arnedo may have been there because its strong castle commanded a strategic position on the eastern borders facing Aragon. But when all these explanations are given, they only point to the difficulties in defining what was an urban center and what was not. We know next to nothing about the conditions and internal structures of these small localities in 1315, although it is almost certain that most of them were little more than overgrown villages, engaged mostly in the cultivation of the surrounding countryside.[4]

What these last paragraphs point to is the impracticality of arriving at a set number of towns and cities which one could define as part of urban society. For medieval men and women, what was urban and what was rural was not always as clear as it is for us today. City dwellers, of course, lived somewhat differently from their country cousins, but in places such as Navarrete, Castrojeriz, and Aguilar de Campóo, the dividing line was not always sharp and well-defined; nor was it clear, for that matter, even in fairly large urban centers.

Why did the procurators of these small localities come to Burgos in 1315, when their interests seldom coincided with those of cities? Obviously, protection of life and property and pressure from nearby towns provided the greatest impetus for attendance and membership in the *Hermandad* of

1315. Using this criterion, we see that approximately fifty localities in northern Castile, for one reason or another, qualified as urban centers in the very loose sense of the word—though I must hasten to add that only a handful could be considered as having the characteristics that defined city life in other parts of the medieval West. But this discussion is somewhat unproductive, and we must focus our inquiry on specific cities and examine, as much as the documentation allows, their origins, different patterns of development, and resulting social and political structures.

Origins of Towns in Northern Castile

When the great Belgian historian Henri Pirenne published his pioneer work, *Medieval Towns*, most of his examples came from northern Europe, following his already classical distinction between Mediterranean and northern societies in the medieval West. Yet, many of the towns that rose in northern Castile faithfully followed Pirenne's model for the emergence of urban life in the north. Some Castilian towns, Burgos, Ávila, and Coca, among others, began their existence as strongholds, castles on a disputed frontier. Others emerged primarily as sees for the supposed restoration of ecclesiastical jurisdiction and religious life. Valpuesta, Silos, and Sigüenza are, to a certain extent, examples of towns which came to life because of the revival of religious life. A few others, Castro Urdiales, Vitoria, and Medina de Pomar, owed their growth to the settling of merchants within and without their walls and to their location along important trade routes or on the coast. These categories, however, were never exclusive of each other. Instead, they often overlapped to provide a hybrid confirmation of Pirenne's thesis. Burgos is, of course, the best example. Settled around a hill castle in the 880s, a stronghold on the new frontier line of the Arlanzón River, the city became the resting place for the peripatetic bishops of Oca-Valpuesta-Gamonal in the late eleventh century, and, last and most importantly, a commercial center from that date on.[5]

There were, however, other complex forces at work that led to the rise of towns in northern Castile. The history of these beginnings and of the structure of urban life in the region is a topic already dealt with by others, and with excellent results. As mentioned above, Jean Gautier-Dalché's *Historia urbana de León y Castilla en la edad media* is an excellent summary and a brave effort to provide an overall view of urban life until the early thirteenth century. Luis García de Valdeavellano's *Orígenes de la burguesía en la España medieval,* the appropriate sections in his monumental *Historia de España* (vol. 1) and in his *Curso de historia de las instituciones* are excellent efforts to explain how the "bourgeoisie" developed in northern Castilian towns and to define northern Castilian cities and towns in two broad categories: urban settlements along the road to Compostela and those which developed independently of the road. María del Carmen Carlé's *Del concejo medieval castellano-leonés* also provides a lucid description of the administrative and institutional structure of the Castilian *concejos* or city councils. Finally, a good number of older works and more recent monographs on specific cities or particular aspects of urban life provide a fairly good understanding of urban life in northern Castile.[6]

Institutionally, the urban centers of northern Castile rose anew from the ruins and desolation of the early Middle Ages. Though local historians and antiquaries have spent untold hours tracing the earlier history of their cities to their Celtiberian, Carthaginian, or Roman roots, few cities in the north of Castile could lay claim to such antiquity. Roman settlements in what is today northern Castile either were military encampments, such as León, or stood in strategic places, commanding troubled areas or military roads. The Visigoths were not urban dwellers, and the decline of civic life, which had begun before the collapse of Roman Spain, continued unimpeded in the peninsula. The Muslims brought new life to cities in southern Spain. Under their power, first Córdoba and later Seville reached heights unmatched by either Christian Spain or the West in the central Middle Ages. The rule of Córdoba did not reach northward, however, into the kingdoms of Asturias-León, Galicia, and, later on, Castile. There, the first signs of urban life appeared only slowly in the eighth century—as cities only in name, mere administrative centers for pettykings (Cangas, Oviedo) or, at most, as the embryonic beginnings of true urban life, as was the case for León around the year 1000.[7]

These new towns often shared charters of foundation. Kings, laymen, and ecclesiastical lords promoted the repopulation of their lands and the settlement of towns by the granting of *fueros* and *cartas pueblas.*[8] These charters spelled out the obligations and rights of town dwellers and the nature of the bonds between towns and their lords. Some of the *fueros* were later given to other towns. For example, the *fuero* given by Alfonso VI to Logroño in 1095 was extended to more than thirty other towns in the region of the Bay of Biscay and to interior settlements such as Miranda de Ebro (1099), Medina de Pomar (1181), Vitoria (1181), and Orduña (1229). The *Fuero juzgo,* the old Visigothic territorial law, was also widely given as a local *fuero* to cities and towns throughout León, Old and New Castile, and, after Ferdinand III's conquest of Andalucía in the first half of the thirteenth century, to Andalusi towns as well.[9]

By the early thirteenth century and into the later Middle Ages, urban centers in northern Castile were governed by *fueros* which, in spite of local variations, showed a fair amount of uniformity. Moreover, Alfonso X sought to further this uniformity by granting the *Fuero real* to many Castilian towns as a municipal body of laws. Though meeting with resistance in many parts of Castile, the king was on the whole quite successful.[10] During the thirteenth and fourteenth centuries the administrative and institutional structure of the Castilian city councils had come of age, and its basic composition can be seen in every community, from the largest commercial city to insignificant rural councils. This administrative unit, the *concejo*, had been emerging slowly since the ninth century and undergoing slow transformations through time. Earlier historians of Castilian institutional history and even recent ones had offered a typology for the identification of successive levels of development: *concejo abierto* (open council), *concejo cerrado* (closed council), and the *regimiento*. In theory, the *concejo abierto* dated from the initial phase of urban life on the Castilian and Leonese frontier and, as lyrically described, its main characteristic was the open assembly of all of the town's inhabitants with the exception of Jews and Moors. To these early meetings came all the inhabitants of the village. "There was no distinction among the neighbors, *villanos* [villains], and *infanzones* [noblemen], men and women, old and young."[11] Based upon the same egalitarian principle, any neighbor had the right to hold the different offices of the *concejo* and to attend its open meeting. These gatherings, which met usually on Sundays, took place within or in front of the church, summoned by the ringing of the church's bell.

In truth, extant medieval documentation and even municipal accounts of the late nineteenth century repeat again and again this powerful image of the council of neighbors (*vecinos*) being summoned to an assembly by the tolling of the church bell or by the voice of the town crier. Size had little to do with it. As seen in Chapter 2, small localities such as Matute, in the lordship of the Cistercian nuns of the monastery of La Asunción in Cañas, in 1340 called its *concejo*, "clerics and laymen, noblemen [*fijosdalgo*], and peasants [*labradores*] to a meeting at the church of San Román by the tolling of the bell as it was the usage and custom [*a campana tañida según el uso y costumbre*]." In 1318 the council of Covacardiel "*a campana repicada*" met in the portal of the church of San Cucufat to deal with its lord and master, the prior of Santa María la Real de Nájera, on the important matter of securing the village from noble attacks.[12] Even in large places, such as Burgos, Logroño, and elsewhere throughout Castile, bells and town criers also called the *concejo* to assembly. A long and angry meeting, held by the city council of Logroño in the cemetery of St. James on Saturday 14 May 1334, was called to session by the town crier the evening before and every evening for the next three days before the meeting moved on to the nearby village of Leza.[13]

In all these examples, the lists of those in attendance provide information about the number and composition of the council. In some instances, as when in 1351 the neighbors of Matute litigated over taxes with the abbess of La Asunción, it is clear that almost all the men who were *vecinos* of the village were present.[14] In Logroño, during that contentious dispute to which I have already referred, many men were present at the Saturday meeting as interested observers. In Burgos the meetings of the city council drew a crowd of male *vecinos*, and frequent complaints were sent to the king against city officials who conducted their official business at home or without proper announcements.[15]

And yet for all this I have found no evidence in the thirteenth and fourteenth centuries of real open councils. Nor have I seen any convincing proof of their existence in earlier centuries. Clearly, such an image of open and free town assemblies had long been dear to many historians of Castile, but it has very little real foundation in fact.[16] In truth, small rural villages had *concejos* in which *fijosdalgo*, *escuderos*, and *labradores* (petty noblemen and peasants or farmers) sat and worked together to protect their interests. Most probably, in those villages some decisions were taken with the concurrence of all the male *vecinos* (meaning property holders), as is done to this day in Castilian and Leonese villages. But it is also clear that women who owned property and had rights as *vecinas* (citizens) did not participate as either voting members or attendants, at least not directly.[17]

In larger towns and cities the council played an even more significant role. What we observe throughout most of Castile are administrative bodies that operated with the consent, although also at times with the opposition, of property owners. In contrast to the case in Andalucía, where noblemen lived and shared in city life and power, or in country villages in the north where they did likewise, nobles were, at least until the late fourteenth century, exempted from municipal jurisdiction but also excluded from rights of citizenship. Ruling elites in northern Castilian towns were thus more homogeneous, though still contentious and less "open" than the rural *concejos* just outside their walls. Though the open councils have been described as prospering under the relative openness of a frontier society, in practice the life of the new towns was marred by internal struggles between opposing factions of the ruling groups and by the frequent interference of local lords or the crown.

Factional struggles were not new in Castile. Not unlike towns in the rest of the West, northern Castilian urban centers (above all, those located on the pilgrimage road) in the twelfth century witnessed widespread "bourgeois" rebellions. The most notable ones took place in Sahagún and Compostela and were directed against ecclesiastic overlords. In the latter town, however, even Queen Urraca was pelted with stones and publicly humiliated.[18] These social revolts are not yet well understood, but they underlined existing political, social, and economic antagonisms. They did not lead to the extension of franchise in towns; rather, the "bourgeois revolutions" of the twelfth century signaled in Castile and elsewhere the entrenchment, even in defeat, of oligarchies within the city.

Whether open councils existed or not, it is clear that what we can describe from extant thirteenth- and fourteenth-century sources is a closed council. At this stage, franchise was restricted solely to Christian male *vecinos*. Citizenship (*vecinaje*) was defined somewhat differently from town to town, but essentially it required residence in the town for at least a year, ownership of a house within the city walls, some property, and concomitant military obligations.[19] In Segovia, residence and the fulfillment of property qualifications in one of the villages of the community of *villa y tierra* brought citizenship in the city. Women, as pointed out elsewhere, enjoyed citizenship rights, though without political rights or representation.

From the late twelfth to the mid-fourteenth century, two parallel processes were under way. First, oligarchical elites in most towns and cities of northern Castile were well on their way to monopolizing political and economic power within their respective urban centers. This they accomplished at the expense of less well-to-do groups within the bourgeoisie. Second, the transformation of the social and political structure of most of northern Castilian urban society was often accomplished with the tacit, and even active, support of the crown and led to the eventual direct intervention and royal takeover of municipal government. In later pages we will have the opportunity to examine this transformation in detail. For the time being, we must attempt to visualize the administrative structure of the Castilian *concejos* and those offices that became the objects of bourgeois political ambitions as well as bones of contention with other groups within the city.

The Institutional Organization of Northern Castilian Towns

From the smallest rural village to the largest urban center, the institutional structure of the Castilian *concejos* was fairly uniform. While the number of officials ranged widely from place to place, the offices themselves and their jurisdiction were similar. The first of these municipal offices to be considered was the *juez* or *justicia* (judge). In theory, the *juez* was the political, military, economic, and judicial head of the early medieval *concejo*. During the ninth and early part of the tenth century, when Castile was under Leonese rule, two *jueces* had acted as governors alongside the local counts. In the urban context, the *juez* represented the lord of the city or area, distinct from the council which, in theory at least, represented the citizens. The *juez* had the right to call the city council into session. Moreover, he carried the municipal banner into battle and, with the *alcaldes*, passed judgments on crimes not under royal jurisdiction. The *juez* received a salary from the council and a share of the fines, booty, and tolls collected at the town gate; in addition, he was exempted from most taxes.[20]

There are few references to *jueces* in the urban documentation of northern Castile for the thirteenth and fourteenth centuries. On 14 June 1283, the Infante Don Sancho addressed a letter to the council, *alcaldes, juez*, and *merino* of Covarrubias, and Blasco Blázquez, already mentioned in previous chapters, was a royal *juez* in late thirteenth-century Ávila. At Sepúlveda, the *fuero* reveals the existence of a *juez* into the thirteenth century, but no mention is found thereafter.[21] On the other hand, there were probably no *jueces* in Burgos, Segovia, or Logroño by 1300.

The powers which had been conferred earlier to the *juez* were, by the late Middle Ages, already in the hands of the *alcaldes* and, to a lesser extent, the *merino*. The word *alcalde* corresponds today to mayor, but in the Middle Ages the *alcaldes'* main function was judicial. Nevertheless, *alcaldes* in Castile performed a variety of administrative functions, which helps explain the term's evolution to its modern meaning. According to the *Fuero real*, the *alcaldes* had to be *omes buenos* (good men) and *vecinos* (having fulfilled all the requirements for urban citizenship), and they could not be of noble blood.[22] In theory, they sat as judges every day until Terce unless prevented by sickness or royal service. This, however, was not always the case, and citizens often protested to the king of the *alcalde*'s absence or of having to plead their cases in front of unqualified substitutes. Gradually, through the thirteenth and fourteenth centuries, the *alcaldes* were saddled with other duties. Together with the *concejo* they administered the city; they also led the urban militias, both in the royal campaigns against the Moors and against internal enemies. Led by its *alcaldes*, or at least by one of them, the militias of Burgos, Ávila, and other northern Castilian towns marched into battle in the mid-thirteenth century during the great conquest of Andalucía or (as had the militia of Ávila) joined in Alfonso X's short incursion against Navarre.[23] In 1334, the *alcalde* of Logroño, Johan Pérez, led the municipal contingents of that town in a successful campaign against rebellious noblemen fortified at the walled villages of Ribafrecha and Leza. Similar examples can be provided for most urban centers in northern Castile.[24]

Clearly, because of their judicial and administrative duties at the local level, the *alcaldes* also functioned as extensions of the royal administration. Again and again the crown ordered them to investigate disturbances in areas nearby, to help disgruntled citizens or religious establishments, and otherwise to be at the beck and call (when the king had enough authority to do so) of their royal master. We must keep in mind this dual function of urban *alcaldes*, both as local administrators and as auxiliary regional agents of the crown. As to the latter function, they complemented and sometimes supervised the jurisdiction of the unreliable royal bureaucracy.

On the other hand, the *alcaldes*' duties reinforce the vision of Castilian cities as centers of a sprawling rural area, tied by administrative, social, political, and economic connections to their urban centers. Thus, in 1278 Alfonso X ordered the *jurados*, (see below), *alcaldes*, and *justicia* of Sepúlveda to protect the rights of the abbot of Santo Domingo de Silos in Sanct Fructos from the attacks of the men of Sepúlveda. In 1326, Alfonso XI ordered the *alcaldes* and *merino* of Burgos to intervene in Quintanadueñas, a village under the lordship of the bishop of Burgos, and to impede the unlawful collection of taxes by a royal agent.[25] In these and in many similar interventions, the boundaries between town and country become vague and imprecise, with urban administrators intruding, acting, and litigating with small rural councils whether they were within their jurisdiction or not.

The *alcaldes*' frequent service to the king points to another aspect in the evolution of urban administration: the progressive symbiotic relationship between city elites and the crown which we will have the opportunity to explore in greater detail below. One should not be surprised, therefore, that in 1348 the Ordenamiento of Alcalá de Henares—the great legislative accomplishment of Alfonso XI's reign—restricted the office of *alcalde* to those citizens who owned horses and weapons for at least a year prior to their appointment.[26] This, however, may have applied mostly to large towns and cities—those which sent procurators to the meetings of the Cortes—for there were urban centers where the *alcaldes* may not have been non-noble urban knights.

What is clear, however, is that the functions and social status of the *alcaldes* had been greatly transformed over the previous century, and that by the 1330s the role of the *alcaldes*, both in the cities and the kingdom, went far beyond the limited definition of the office found in the *Fuero real*. Perhaps because of their diverse duties the number of *alcaldes* fluctuated from locality to locality and even in one single place over time. Burgos had two *alcaldes* in 1259, four from 1273 to 1305, eight in 1338, two in 1345, and six in 1366. The evidence from Logroño is that the *villa* had one *alcalde* in the 1330s, while the small town of Albelda near Logroño also had one *alcalde* in 1293 and the same number in 1343. Ávila had either four or six *alcaldes* in 1284; Cuéllar, with an extensive *alfoz* and a ranching economy, may have had six *alcaldes* or more in the second half of the thirteenth century. Local conditions, the expanse of territory under city jurisdiction, and, above all, the extent to which the *alcaldes* were drawn into performing duties for the crown probably dictated their number.[27]

By the late thirteenth century, growing demands for justice and the streamlining of the judicial system and of the royal bureaucracy led to the emergence of other *alcaldes*. One may call them supra-urban, for often their jurisdiction extended beyond the confines of the city. In ever increasing numbers, the documents refer to *alcaldes del rey* (royal *alcaldes*) to whom cases could be taken directly or appealed from the judgment of city *alcaldes*, without a costly and cumbersome trip to the royal court. We can see these *alcaldes* settling down in the important towns of Castile, the spearheads of royal intervention in civic life: Esteban Domingo in the 1260s, and Diego Pérez, Alfonso Fernández, and Galín Gílez in Ávila in the 1290s. Around this date we also find *alcaldes del rey* elsewhere throughout northern Castile. These royal *alcaldes* were either drawn from the local ruling oligarchies or had set roots in the towns to which they were assigned, marrying into prominent local families.[28]

Besides the regular *alcaldes* or *alcaldes de fuero*, as they were also known, and the royal *alcaldes*, we also find the *alcaldes* of the Mesta, charged with judging matters related to the transhumance, *alcaldes* of the *Herman-dades* with judicial responsibility on matters concerning the leagues of cities and lesser noblemen. Finally, after Ferdinand IV's institutional reforms of 1312, the extant documents refer to the *alcaldes* of the kingdom or of the court, a modified version of royal *alcaldes* but with permanent residence at court; this judicial innovation came to naught after the anarchy that followed Ferdinand's death in 1312. In late 1330s Burgos, we also find a certain Pero Alonso as an *alcalde dotor* (in charge of dowries), but this is a single reference not substantiated elsewhere.[29]

Although the *alcaldes* were the most important officials within the municipal council, they were not the only ones. They were supported in their duties by a bevy of other municipal officials. Of these, before 1345, the most important was the *merino*. One must distinguish, however, between the royal *merino* and the urban one. The former was a high royal official, and his jurisdiction was the *merindad*, roughly equivalent to a bailliage or shire. The urban *merino*'s jurisdiction, on the other hand, extended only as far as that of his town. The *merino* was exempted from taxes, as the *alcaldes* were, and was often a member of the ruling *caballero* elite. His duties, among others, were to carry out the sentences handed out by the *alcaldes*, to recruit the local militia, and to supervise weights and measures. Together with the *alcaldes*, one finds *merinos* settling litigations, leading armed raids, and also acting as minor royal agents in the Rioja, in the area of Burgos, and in other parts of Castile.[30]

In addition to the *alcaldes* and *merinos*, one must also mention the *jurados*, an administrative innovation of Sancho IV in the late 1280s, and the crown's means for exercising some control over municipal authorities. The *jurados*' duties complemented and even overlapped those of the *alcaldes*, and they served as watchdogs against the latter's tendencies to monopolize political power within the cities. In practice, Sancho's attempts did not always succeed. Nevertheless, *jurados* functioned as auxiliaries of the *alcaldes*, part of the city council, but in theory with the interest of the crown also at heart. We find *jurados* accompanying the *alcalde* in settling disputes in many parts of northern Castile, with strong indications that the institution had been adopted even in small towns. During the 1330s and until the mid-fourteenth century, when the structure of the *concejo* in many Castilian cities was radically altered by royal intervention, *jurados* were also known as *regidores*, a forerunner to the institutional developments of the mid-fourteenth century.[31]

Another group of urban officials one must mention are the *escribanos públicos* or public scribes. From the 1250s on, urban procurators at the meeting of the Cortes petitioned the king for the office to be restricted to the members of one social group, that is, to the rising non-noble knights vying for control of northern Castilian cities. Although in theory the *escribano mayor* (head clerk and other, lesser clerks) was elected for a year by the citizens of the town to keep royal charters and to record transactions and litigations, in practice *escribanos* held their offices for many years. Such was the case of Fernán Martínez, scribe of Ávila from at least 1285 to 1294, and of other scribes elsewhere throughout Castile. Scribes received their salaries from the same sources as the *alcaldes*, but it is clear that town clerks also had to compete with royal scribes assigned to specific towns and cities.[32]

In Ávila public clerks derived their authority from the royal scribe and functioned therefore as an extension of him. There, the king had a direct say, at least during periods of political stability, in the naming of scribes. Even though Ávila was, to a certain extent, an exception—being one of the most formidable strongholds north of the Guadarrama range and, thus, jealously kept under close royal control—the evidence from other urban centers points to the crown's desire to name scribes throughout the region or to profit from their nomination. In 1336 Alfonso XI requested payment from the municipal council of Silos in return for naming scribes. However, when Alfonso Sánchez de la Tomera, citizen and procurator of Silos, complained to the king, Alfonso XI recognized the right of the town's council to name scribes. What is peculiar about this occurrence is that Silos was a town under the nominal jurisdiction of the Benedictine abbot of Santo Domingo de Silos. Yet, in fact, the *concejo*, the abbot, and the king had long wrangled for control of the locality.[33] Moreover, local *escribanos*, certainly those of important urban centers, usually worked their way into the royal bureaucracy as scribes, tax collectors, and in other functions. Such was certainly the case at Burgos, often the site of the royal chancery, where the *escribano mayor* shared equal power with members of the *regimiento*, the *alcaldes*, and royal *merino* in Alfonso XI's administrative reforms of 1345.[34]

Municipal clerks, above all, the head clerk, were often people of some learning and some wealth, and there is good indication of their social mobility. We find clerks renting or purchasing urban and rural property in Ávila, Burgos, and other towns in northern Castile, such as Frías. In Burgos, John Maté or Mathé, clerk of the council in 1304 and a royal clerk (1293–94), was a member of one of the most influential families of the city and of the brotherhoods of non-noble knights. Obviously, not every clerk made it. Burgos had as many as thirty-eight scribes in 1345 and 1366, but only those with abilities, ambitions, and family connections could advance both within the city and the kingdom.[35]

Finally, we should refer in passing to such minor offices as the *sayón* or town crier, who called the council to session, watched over weights and measures, and functioned as doorkeeper whenever the council met behind closed doors.[36] Another official was the *fiel*. In theory the *fiel* was elected by the citizens of the parishes (*colaciones*) and collected fines for violations of rules on weights and measures. We find *fieles* acting as adjuncts to the *alcalde* of Albelda in 1339, and their role was probably of greater importance in smaller towns than in large ones. By the early fourteenth century, the election of *fieles* was one of the last vestiges of an open franchise, even though it had already been restricted to "good men" or *caballeros villanos*. In 1307 the city council of Burgos attempted to impose its own candidate as *fiel* in place of Sancho García, duly elected by the citizens of the parish of Sanct Llorente. After an angry appeal to Ferdinand IV by the neighbors of Sanct Llorente, the *concejo* rescinded its attempts and allowed Sancho to take office.[37]

Rounding out the offices of the urban councils, we find the *almotacén*. Chosen by the city council, the *almotacén* was the rough equivalent of a policeman or guard. He kept order in the market and enforced the regulations of the city.[38] More important, however, than these lesser officials was the procurator or representative of the *concejos* to the royal court, to the meeting of the Cortes, or to litigations with other urban centers or ecclesiastical corporations. The social and political standing of the *personero* varied with the importance of the business at hand. Sometimes they were drawn from among the members of the council or from among the most influential families as the issue merited it. In other instances and depending on the locality, the procurators came to represent special interest groups or factions. Those from Ávila representing the city at the meetings of the *hermandad* in 1315 clearly were drawn from contending *linajes* or patrician clans so as to provide representation for each. Segovia's procurators balanced the interest of town and rural villages in Segovia's *contado*. Those of Soria were chosen from the ruling oligarchy, the *común* (the common), and the rural villages around the town.[39]

This rather mechanical review of the administrative structure of the Castilian *concejos* does not do justice to the numberless variations in the functions, power, and social status of officials in Castilian towns. Examples from every corner of northern Castile would only make this a fruitless and tedious enterprise. Against this administrative background, we must now examine both the economic history of Castilian urban society and the role of the councils in furthering or, at times, hampering economic development.

Notes

1. See Jean Gautier-Dalché, *Historia urbana de León y Castilla en la edad media (siglos IX–XIII)* (Madrid: Siglo XXI, 1979), bibliography, 466–70; María Asenjo González, *Segovia: La ciudad y su tierra a fines del medievo* (Segovia: Excelentísima diputación provincial de Segovia, 1986), bibliography, 19–54; Adeline Rucquoi, *Valladolid en la edad media*, 1: 28–47; Carlos Estepa Díez et al., *Burgos en la edad media* (Valladolid: Junta de Castilla y León, 1984), 503–6.

2. *Cortes*, 1: 263–71; for the *Hermandad* of 1315, see Luis Suárez Fernández, "Evolución histórica de las Hermandades castellanas," *CHE* 16 (1952): 5–78.

3. See *Crónica de Alfonso XI*, 174–92; Joseph F. O'Callaghan, *A History of Medieval Spain* (Ithaca, N.Y.: Cornell University Press, 1975), 403–4; Mercedes Gaibrois de Ballesteros, *María de Molina: Tres veces reina* (Madrid: Espasa-Calpe, 1967), 193–239. On Burgos's disputes with Toledo over primacy at the Cortes, an issue not settled until 1348, see Manuel Colmeiro, *Introducción a las Cortes de los antiguos reinos de León y Castilla*, 2 vols. (Madrid: Establecimiento tipográfico de los sucesores de Rivadeneyra, 1883), 1: 281.

4. We have a sense of the small size of many of these localities in the *Censo de población de las provincias y partidos de la corona de Castilla en el siglo XVI*, 7: Laredo had 330 *vecinos*; 12: Medina de Pomar, 320 *vecinos*, etc.

5. On Burgos's origins and early developments, see Estepa Díez et al., *Burgos en la edad media*, 25–34 et passim.

6. See note 4 above. See also Luis García de Valdeavellano, *Orígenes de la burguesía en la España medieval* (Madrid: Espasa-Calpe, 1969); María del Carmen Carlé, *Del concejo medieval castellano-leonés* (Buenos Aires: Instituto de historia de España, 1968); María del Carmen Carlé, *La sociedad hispano medieval: La ciudad* (Buenos Aires: Celtia, 1984). The bibliography on urban history elsewhere in the medieval West is extensive enough, and a few recent titles will suffice here. See, for example, Rodney H. Hilton, *English and French Towns in Feudal Society: A Comparative Study* (Cambridge: Cambridge University Press, 1992); Jacques Heers, *La ville au Moyen Âge en Occident: Paysages, pouvoirs et conflits* (Paris: Fayard, 1990); Vito Fumagalli, *Citta e campagna nell'Italia medievale* (Bologna: Patron, 1985); Rita Costa Gomes, *Guarda medieval: posiçao, morfologia e sociedade (1200–1500)* (Lisboa: Livraria Sá da Costa Editora, 1987). See also below.

7. See, for example, Claudio Sánchez Albornoz, *Ruina y extinción del municipio romano en España e instituciones que le reemplazan* (Buenos Aires: Facultad de filosofía y letras, 1943); also his *Una ciudad hispano-cristiana hace un milenio: Estampas de la vida de León*, 5th ed. (Madrid: Rialp, 1966).

8. On *fueros*, see *Dictionary of the Middle Ages* (New York: Scribners, 1985), 5: 308–10; 7: 521–22.

9. Rogelio Pérez Bustamante, *Historia de la villa de Castro Urdiales* (Santander: Ayuntamiento de Santanders, 1980), 36–37; García Gallo, *Manual de historia del derecho español*, 1: 378–85, 393–98.

10. O'Callaghan, *A History of Medieval Spain*, 372–75; Eelco N. van Kleffens, *Hispanic Law until the End of the Middle Ages* (Edinburgh: Edinburgh University Press, 1968), 288–89; Ruiz, "The Transformation of the Castilian Municipalities," 24.

11. Carlé, *Del concejo medieval*, 33.

12. AHN, Clero, carp. 1025, no. 18a (30-March-1340); AHN, Códices, 106B, ff. 133–135a (23-June-1318); for modern examples, see Behar, *Santa María del Monte*, 125–59.

13. AHN, Códices, 106B, ff. 187–205.

14. AHN, Clero, carp. 1025, no. 19 (26-November-1351).

15. AMB, clasif. 2920 (8-November-1279); clasif. 2928 (2-May-1282).

16. See Ruiz, "The Transformation of the Castilian Municipalities," 3–4, n. 8.

17. Women, although frequently referred to as *vecinas*, never appear in the documents as witnesses to litigations, rural councils' decisions, or transactions of property.

18. For revolts in the twelfth century, see Bernard F. Reilly, *The Kingdom of León-Castilla under Queen Urraca, 1109–1126* (Princeton, N.J.: Princeton University Press, 1982), 124; Reyna Pastor, *Resistencias y luchas campesinas en la época del crecimiento y consolidación de la formación feudal: Castilla y León, siglos X–XIII* (Madrid: Siglo XXI, 1980), 122–41, where Pastor emphasizes the role of the peasantry in the rising. See also Reyna Pastor, "Las primeras rebeliones burguesas en Castilla y León (siglo XII)," in *Conflictos sociales y estancamiento económico en la España medieval* (Barcelona: Ariel, 1973), 15–101.

19. Carlé, *Del concejo medieval*, 35, 81ff.

20. Carlé, *Del concejo medieval*, 70–74; Antonio Sacristán y Martínez, *Municipalidades de León y Castilla: Estudio histórico-crítico* (Madrid: Rojas, 1877), 249–56.

21. *Fuentes*, 2: 126; *Silos*, 2: 259; Jean Gautier-Dalché, "Sepúlveda à la fin du Moyen Age: évolution d'une ville castillane de la meseta," *Le Moyen Âge* 69 (1963): 809; for Blasco Blázquez see *DMA*, 98 et passim.

22. *Fuero real*, 1: vii, 2, 3 in *Los códigos españoles*, 1: 353–55; also *Cortes*, 1: 585.

23. Carlé, *Del concejo medieval*, 114–17; Sacristán y Martínez, *Municipalidades de León y Castilla*, 257–66; AMB, clasif. 2610 (10-July-1279); the militia of Ávila fought in Jaén and Seville: see José M. Carremolino, *Historia de Ávila, su provincia y obispado*, 3 vols. (Madrid: Librería española, 1872–73), 2: 348ff.

24. AHN, Códices 106B, ff. 187–205a.

25. *Silos*, 2: 259; ACB, vol. 32, f. 143 (15-February-1326).

26. *Cortes*, 1: 585.

27. AMB, clasif. 683 (26-September-1259); IGR, *Texto*. "Primitiva regla," 158–64. AMB, clasif. 1444 (9-May-1345); clasif. 152 (18-April-1366); AHN, Códices, 106B, ff. 187–205a; *Albelda y Logroño*, 1: 138–39, 262–65; *DMA*, 100–6; Esteban Corral García, *Las comunidades castellanas y la villa y tierra antigua de Cuéllar* (Salamanca: Imprenta Varona, 1978), 294.

28. *DMA*, 75–77, 126–27, 145; Ruiz, "The Transformation of the Castilian Municipalities," 23.

29. On the *alcalde dotor*, see IGR, *Texto*, 18. For Ferdinand IV's reforms, see César González Mínguez, *Fernando IV de Castilla (1295–1312): La guerra civil y el predominio de la nobleza* (Vitoria: Colegio universitario de Álava, 1976), 318–19.

30. On the *merino*, see Atanasio Sinues Ruiz, *El merino* (Zaragoza: Consejo Superior de Investigaciones Científicas, 1954), 26, 81, 219, 223. AMB, clasif. 2473 (2-November-1281); ACB, vol. 63, f. 57 (3-September-1302); AMB, clasif. 1784 (2-April-1334); ACB, vol. 40, f. 212 (17-November-1335); IGR, *Texto*, 17; AHN, Códices 106B, f. 187 (11-May-1334).

31. Ruiz, "The Transformation of the Castilian Municipalities," 25; AHN, Clero, carp. 1032, no. 9 (26-October-1272), no. 19 (12-March-1304); and *Albelda y Logroño*, 235.

32. *Fuero real*, I, viii, 2, in *Códigos españoles*, 1: 355–56; Sacristán y Martínez, *Municipalidades de León y Castilla*, 272–73; *DMA*, 116, 126, 144, et passim.

33. *Silos*, 2: 371. See below for political developments in Silos.

34. AMB, clasif. 154 (9-May-1345).

35. For John Mathé and his family, see Benavides, *Memorias*, 2: 450; *Sancho IV*, 1: xxiii; "Primitiva regla," 163; IGR, *Texto*, 17. For Ferrant Pérez de Frías, scribe of Frías, moneylender, and philanthropist, see AHN, Clero, carp. 227, no. 2 (20-October-1334), no. 7 (13-April-1344). For the number of scribes in Burgos in 1345 and 1366, see AMB, clasif. 154; clasif. 152. For *escribanos* in Ávila purchasing or renting property, see *DMA*, 123, 226.

36. Carlé, *Del concejo medieval*, 119; Sacristán y Martínez, *Municipalidades de León y Castilla*, 277.

37. Carlé, *Del concejo medieval*, 120–21; AMB, clasif. 3145 (1-September-1307); *Albelda y Logroño*, 227.

38. Carlé, *Del concejo medieval*, 120.

39. *Cortes*, 1: 115. Some of the most important citizens of Burgos served as procurators to the Cortes or to the royal court. See, for example, the case of Rodrigo Ibáñez, member of the Sarracín family group, in AMB, clasif. 99 (25-March-1268), and that of Pedro Bonifaz, member of the other ruling Burgalese family, in AMB, clasif. 99 et passim.

7. Merchants, Trade, and Agriculture

We must turn here from the institutional structure of towns to their economic life. As with everything else, the variations from one urban center to another were significant indeed. For the sake of convenience we may adhere to one of the categories presented in the previous chapter and classify Castilian towns into two distinct types: those that derived their income from commerce and those that did not. In some respects, however, this may be a false dichotomy. It would be more accurate to say that the distinctions have to be made between cities in which the ruling oligarchies derived their income from trade and farming and those in which the hegemonic groups received most of their income from farming and/or ranching. But this again sets up a misleading image of a sharp break between these models; in fact, there was no such thing.

The evidence for the economic activity of urban centers in northern Castile is twofold: first, accounts of toll taxes that reveal what goods were traded and the nature of international trade, and second, incidental information that allows for a partial reconstruction of artisanal, commercial, and farming enterprises in northern Castilian towns. The pattern of trade (which I examine below), I must add, represented an important change from ancient commercial connections between Islamic Spain and the Christian north. Here, as was the case with other economic, political, and social aspects, the conquest of Seville altered long-standing trade patterns. What was traded, to whom, and how were all changed by the demise of al-Andalus as an independent political and economic entity.[1]

The Economic Foundations of Northern Castilian Society: Long-Distance Trade

Transmarine and regional commerce functioned roughly as follows: A large assortment of finished goods and, at times, agricultural products came through the ports of the Bay of Biscay on their way to the interior of

Castile. How the trade moved and where it eventually went tell us a great deal about commercial life in some of these towns. Clearly, localities with a stake in this commerce—as ports of entry, transfer points, or distribution centers—had developed a mercantile orientation. More important, we find, wherever the documentation allows, that the ruling oligarchies of these towns derived a good part of their income from trade and had, therefore, an understanding of regional and foreign economic exchanges. There are several clues to the common vision of these northern cities—and here I refer to the towns north of the Duero, for those further south had somewhat different economic goals. The evidence is both political and commercial.

In 1296, the procurators of the coastal towns of Santander, Laredo, Castro Urdiales, Bermeo, Guetaria, San Sebastián, Fuenterrabía, and the interior town of Vitoria met in Castro Urdiales to pool their resources and efforts. Their primary aim was to establish procedures for the peaceful settlement of their disputes, but the league's charter also prohibited the export of wine, bread and other foodstuffs, arms, horses, and other merchandise to Bayonne (in Gascony), England, or Flanders, as long as the war with France continued.[2] Seven of the eight towns were ports on the Bay of Biscay and, together with other smaller ports of Lequeitio, Portugalete, Plencia, and, above all, Bilbao after 1300, they served as entry and departure points for most of northern Castilian commerce. One finds a large number of merchants from interior cities, especially from Burgos, actively engaged in transmaritime trade, but in the port towns, local merchants and sea captains maintained a vigorous commerce with southern Spain, England, France, and the great Flemish textile centers.

Elsewhere I have already shown the activities of these Cantabrian and Basque shippers in terms of the Castilian–English trade, and Wendy Childs's book on the same topic explores their role in detail for the period between 1254 and 1485.[3] Between 1279 and 1354, one can document more than fifty-one merchants and thirty ships from the westernmost coastal towns of San Vicente de la Barquera, Santander, Castro Urdiales, and Laredo having been actively engaged in different aspects of trade with England.[4]

TOWNS ON THE BAY OF BISCAY
The evidence for commercial activity is even more extensive for the ports east of Laredo, in the Basque coast proper, and in the interior towns of Orduña, Miranda de Ebro, Valmaseda, Medina de Pomar, and Vitoria. The

documents reveal a well-defined pattern of trade: northward by sea to England, Gascony, France, and Flanders, and southward to Seville. Flemish goods, mostly textiles, were carried overland to Burgos and from there to other cities on the plain. The bulk of our evidence comes from English sources, the *Calendars of Close, Patent, and Fine Rolls*, with little information extant for the period before 1350 on direct trade between Basque ports and Flanders or Andalucía.

Merchants from coastal towns often served as agents or carriers for Burgalese commercial interests. Yet, although this is clear in many instances, some of the towns north of Burgos had commercial interests of their own, and at times they totally circumvented the Burgos connection to their own profit. Obviously, Santander, Castro Urdiales, Laredo, San Sebastián, Bermeo, Vitoria, and other locations on and near the coast had their own commercial elites, connected by trade interests to that of Burgos but often independent from it. Although small in number, these merchants and ship captains must have exerted a strong influence in the affairs of their respective communities since these towns probably did not exceed two to three thousand inhabitants at the turn of the thirteenth century, and some of them, towns such as Bilbao, fully came to life only after 1300. The overseas trade with Seville and the employment of Castilian merchants and sailors—who carried English goods to Gascon ports (mostly Bordeaux) and English wool to Italian cities—as hired merchantmen for the Bardi and the Peruzzi mercantile and banking firms point to their relative independence from the traditional trade routes and to their desire to circumvent the numerous inland tolls and charges of the overland routes.

Around 1300 and afterward, in spite of the long and perilous journey, merchants shipped cumin, cinnamon, honey, and hides from Andalusi ports on the Atlantic Ocean to northern markets. Following a route along the Portuguese–Galician and Asturian coasts, these products reached Castilian ports on the Bay of Biscay. There, some of the merchandise might have been sold locally. Other goods, mostly iron, were added to the cargo, and finally the ships sailed northward to English, French, and/or Flemish ports. In 1294, the goods of three Castilian merchants—1,500 *quintales* (hundredweight) of iron, thirty sacks of cumin, and twenty-four bales of tallow—were seized in England. In 1337, Domingo Pérez, in a ship of Santander, brought twelve butts of honey, one thousand cow and calf hides, fifty bales of hare and rabbit skins, twenty bales of cinnamon, and twenty pipes of fat. Unable to sell his merchandise at Sandwich, he was allowed to depart for Brabant and Zeeland. The same year Sancho Fernández de Frías also reached Sandwich with one thousand cow and calf

TABLE 7.1.   Merchants from Coastal
(Basque) and Interior Towns (1250–
1350).

Town	No. of Merchants (*mentioned in* Calendars)
Coastal	
Bermeo	12*
Bilbao	6*
Fuenterrabía	7
Guetaria	10
Lequeitio	2
Plencia	4*
Portugalete	2
San Sebastián	11*
Interior	
Medina de Pomar	3
Miranda de Ebro	1
Orduña	6*
Tolosa	2
Valmaseda	3
Vitoria	20*

Source: Ruiz, "Burgos y el comercio castellano en la baja edad media," *La ciudad de Burgos*, 40–41.

*Indicates that some of the documents mention merchants from these towns without specifying their names or numbers.

hides from Seville, dried and salted, fifteen tuns of honey, and eight pipes of grain. Upon meeting with the same difficulties in selling his goods in England, he also sailed to Flanders.[5]

By analyzing the English rolls that mention the Basque ports and interior trading stations—and I wish to make a distinction between Cantabrian (examined elsewhere) and Basque towns, since on the whole their trade came into the plain through different roads—we can compare the numbers of traders from coastal and interior towns (see Table 7.1).

At least thirty-three of the ships, which are recognizable by location—as, for example, the *Siente Johan* of San Sebastián or *La Nief Seint Sauver* of Bermeo—originated in Basque ports (see Table 7.2).

Designations of place of origin, however, did not always mean that the

TABLE 7.2.   Ships Originating in
Basque Ports (1250–1350).

Place of Origin	Number of Ships
Bermeo	10
Bilbao	3
Fuenterrabía	2
Guetaria	5
Lequeito	1
Plencia	3
Portugalete	1
San Sebastián	8

Source: Ruiz, "Burgos y el comercio castellano en la baja edad media," *La ciudad de Burgos*, 40–41.

ships were fitted in that specific location; rather it was perhaps an indication of the town providing the financial backing for its operation. The *St. Mary* of Burgos, owned by Juan Sánchez, a merchant of Castro Urdiales, probably served Burgalese mercantile interests, since Burgos was certainly not on the coast.

In any case, the ports of the Cantabrian and Basque coasts understood the commonality of their commercial and political interests. Coastal navigation must have also brought these small towns into close contact. We have what amounts to a list of the crew and passengers of *Le Holop* of Guetaria, which sailed from a Bay of Biscay port to trade in England in 1296. The ship carried four merchants: John Ortiz of Bermeo and Martín Johan, Lope, and Rodrigo of Valmaseda. The master, Bertram Pérez, was probably from Bermeo, but six of his crew came from Guetaria, four from Fuenterrabía, two from Bermeo, two from San Sebastián, and the last, "Edward le Engleys" as his name indicates, from England.[6] This motley group was probably representative of the commercial and seafaring enterprises of the northern Castilian coast. Commerce brought together merchants from inland towns—Valmaseda stood on one of the main roads to the plain—with merchants, sea masters, and sailors. And having an Englishman as a crew member was, perhaps, a common practice as well, for it probably made communication and travel across England a great deal easier.[7]

In order to look at the commercial enterprises that made Castilian cities more than just hubs for their extensive hinterlands, we must of necessity begin with these ports on the Bay of Biscay. They served as gateways to the transmarine trade that was the lifeline of Castile's urban mercantile elites. The nature of this trade, both incoming and outgoing, helps explain the peculiar structure of these commercial groups and of urban life in some of the cities in the region. Fortunately, we have extant royal accounts for the period 1293–94 which reveal to us what was exported and imported through a specific port for almost an entire year. In the *Cuentas y gastos del Rey Don Sancho IV*, we have a partial view of Castile's foreign trade. Unfortunately, these accounts cover a period of less than a year, and they are limited to a few ports: San Sebastián, Fuenterrabía, Oyarzún, Orio, Higur (Higuera), and La Nao. We know that import duties were collected all along the coast and in interior toll stations as well. In addition, Américo Castro's edition of the accounts of an interior toll station provides us with a list of goods for which custom duties were paid (or not paid) in Santander, Castro Urdiales, Laredo, and San Vicente de la Barquera.[8]

Imports can be divided into two groups: cloth and everything else. Gual Camarena has already examined aspects of the cloth trade from the aforementioned accounts of 1293–94, and the Table 7.3 reveals the origin, volume, and prices of cloth imports.

The amount and price of cloth imported in less than one year and through a limited number of locations is staggering. These figures, in fact, represent only the tip of the iceberg of Castile's import trade. The bulk of it corresponded to the so-called *valencina* cloth, originally from Valenciennes but produced elsewhere as well by the late thirteenth century. According to Miguel Gual Camarena, this type of fabric was purchased to clothe servants, squires, and other retainers, people usually dressed by their masters at considerable expense.[9] On the other hand, wills, inventories of goods, and, above all, the sumptuary legislation of the thirteenth and fourteenth centuries show the importance of luxury cloth (primarily *escarlata*) and the social prominence associated with the wearing of these fabrics. In fact, because of cost and sumptuary legislation, these cloths were carefully restricted to those on top of the social hierarchy.[10]

We can follow the pattern of imports through the port of San Sebastián almost day by day, from 20 January 1293 to 1 October of the same year. The accounts provide information on the type of goods imported, their quantity, their estimated price, the names of merchants importing cloth,

TABLE 7.3.   Castilian Textile Imports (1293).

Origin or Type	Amount of Cloth (in pieces unless otherwise noted)	Price (in mrs.)
Narbonne	305	28,010
Valenciennes	1,820	407,480
Saint Omer	853	126,292
Saint Denis	5	1,250
Recambort	1	300
Dovarada	3	900
Toulouse	1 gross and 4 dozens	130
Rennes	2	600
Montpellier	12 *cuerdas*	180
Razes	221	54,080
Ypres	102	31,210
Châlons	3	450
Rouen	3	750
Lille	31	10,850
Carcassonne	31	6,120
Bruges	8	2,340
Commines	16	5,400
Ghent	18	4,970
Tournai	59	14,660
Langemarck	11	1,550
Malines	8	1,120
Blaos	85	25,360
Ensayes	10	2,960
Camelines	29	9,990
Tornaes	78	17,220
Cabicoas	54	8,320
Barrandetes	25	4,000
Contrafechos	143	21,130
Paños tintos (red)	247	131,230
Luca	19	150
Venice	10	650
England	11	2,060
Scarlet cloth	2	2,400
Purple cloth	2	160
Cendales	2	360
Total	3,906 pieces	897,072

Source: Miguel Gual Camarena, "El comercio de telas en el siglo XIII hispano," *Anuario de historia económica y social,* 1 (1968): 104–5. Totals are as reported by Gual Camarena. The correct total is over 4,000 pieces and more than 900,000 *mrs.*

TABLE 7.4. Ship Arrivals at the Port of
San Sebastián (1293).

Month	No. of Arrivals
January (12 days)	3
February	34
March	10
April	6
May	14
June	8
July	16
August	13
September	11
October (1 day)	2
Total	117

Source: Cuentas, iii–xiii.

and, often, the place of origin of these merchants as well as the amount of
the tithe paid to royal agents. At San Sebastián, merchandise entered into
Castile at an uneven pace (see Table 7.4).

February was the busiest month. Royal fiscal officials collected dues on
thirty-four (actually thirty-five, as one merchant had two different lots)
customs declarations during that month. Although we do not have entries
for November and December or complete entries for either January or
October, we may deduce from the evidence of Fuenterrabía and La Nao
that February was indeed the most active month for the arrival of imports
all along the coast. Custom declarations, however, were not evenly distributed throughout the month. In fact, they were limited to a few days
between 12 and 21 February.[11]

These figures suggest, I believe, that most of the merchandise came in
ships sailing in a convoy from Flemish and French ports. A few sailed ahead
and a few others straggled behind. We are not to think, however, that each
entry represented a ship. Although most of the merchandise for the entire
year arrived on just one day, 17 February, the goods declared at the customs
of San Sebastián—cloth, needles, otter furs, salted and dried sardines, and
other goods—were not very bulky items. Ships must have been hired to
carry the cargo of several merchants. Nor does it follow that all of the
merchants listed in the accounts traveled back and forth between northern

ports, San Sebastián, and their final inland destinations. Juan de Beunza, for example, for whom we have entries on 25 May, 8 July, 21 August, and 10 September, obviously did not have enough time to go abroad and return to the Basque coast. Instead, he must have been permanently or semi-permanently at San Sebastián as an agent or receiver of transmarine trade.[12]

We must return to 17 February 1293 for, although it was an exceptional day, the entries for that date are representative of commercial activity throughout northern Castile. The extant information for that day also allows us to reconstruct aspects of the life of urban elites in the region. Nineteen different merchants are listed with their goods. The total value of their merchandise amounted to 307,249 *mrs.* or around 43 percent of the monetary value of all the merchandise imported through San Sebastián that year: 714,487.5 *mrs.*, 28 *ss.*, and 10 *ds.* Moreover, almost every one of these declarations exceeded 10,000 *mrs.*, but for the rest of the year there were only four entries over 10,000 *mrs.* and none over 20,000 *mrs.*

One can visualize a convoy of Castilian ships leaving Flemish ports together and reaching the Cantabrian coast more or less as a group. On 26 October 1293, eleven merchants paid tithe on their merchandise at the Figuer of Fuenterrabía. Their goods, cloth from Bruges, Ghent, Lille, Tournai, Saint Omer, Valenciennes and elsewhere, were valued at 167,510 *mrs.*, with one importer bringing a rich haul of precious cloth worth 53,910 *mrs.*[13] Whether in February or October, Castilian ships, like most seafarers in the period, sailed in groups, probably to support each other in the rough waters of the Bay of Biscay and the English Channel, but also perhaps to provide some protection against the pirate-infested Bay of Biscay.

What we know about the merchants themselves is not always enough to provide a full account of their lives and activities. Some of the merchants' names are mentioned once, with no indication as to their place of origin. Of the nineteen merchants bringing goods into Castile on 17 February, there are some, however, who can be traced back to the local documentation. Giralt de Prestines, who brought cloth valued at 17,500 *mrs.*, was a member of the Prestines-Bonifaz family group, one of the most important in Burgos in the early fourteenth century. In 1293, he was probably in his twenties. Twenty years later, he lent money to the municipal council of Burgos for the rebuilding of the city walls, and by 1338 (already an aged man, as shown by his portrait), he was a member of the patrician brotherhood of the Real Hermandad.[14] Another merchant, Juan Pérez de Carrión, imported goods valued at 8,790 *mrs.*; he belonged as well to one of the influential *caballero* families of Burgos, the Cambranas-Pérez de Carrión clan. Juan had been a member of the *concejo* in 1273, one of the king's men in 1293, *alcalde* of Burgos in 1303, and with his brother, García Pérez de Carrión, the largest contributor to the building of the walls in 1313. Members of his family held important positions in the administration of Burgos and membership in the exclusive brotherhoods of non-noble knights and merchants.[15] These examples should suffice to point to the close connection between the merchants' commercial enterprise and the social and political power they wielded back in their respective cities. These were not the only Burgalese merchants in San Sebastián, and I have been able to identify eight (and possibly ten) merchants for whom we have additional information in Burgalese archives.[16]

That there were such large numbers of Burgalese merchants in San Sebastián—at least one-tenth of the total number of merchants coming through that port during a period of ten months—is remarkable indeed. It is not surprising, of course, to find merchants from Vitoria in San Sebastián, such as Fernán Iváñez and others, but the assumption has long been that Burgalese trade arrived through the ports of Castro Urdiales, Laredo, and Santander and traveled inland through the direct roads linking those ports to the interior. Perhaps Burgalese merchants brought their goods to San Sebastián to serve the Basque and Rioja markets. On the other hand, sailing in the Bay of Biscay was not easy, and San Sebastián might have been the first port safely reached.

San Sebastián, like most of the other ports, attracted merchants from all over the region. We find there men from Guetaria, prominent among them Johan de Ochoa, from Castro Urdiales; French merchants, mostly Gascons but at least one from Carcassonne; two English traders; Navarrese merchants; and others from Burgos, Vitoria, and elsewhere.[17] The wide range of the trade, especially in cloth, which moved inland from San Sebastián can be illustrated by the activities of Lop de Roncesvalles. Either alone or with his partner, Miguel Sanz de Roncesvalles, Lop received or brought merchandise to San Sebastián on 28 January, 21 April, 6 June, and 10 September. His imports were modest: 12,000 dried sardines, valued at 480 *mrs.* for the entire lot, and 70 pieces of reinforced cloth from Valenciennes, the popular and inexpensive *valencina* of medieval documents, at 170 *mrs.* per piece, for a total of 12,380 *mrs.* One can visualize Lop carrying his goods from San Sebastián in a southwesterly direction to Vitoria, where he paid tolls in one of his trips, and then eastward to Navarre.[18]

This brief glance at Lop de Roncesvalles's trading activities leads us to consider again in greater detail the patterns of imports and exports. As pointed out earlier and as studied by Gual Camarena, the bulk of the imports that entered Castile through Basque and Cantabrian ports were cloth. As seen before, most of the imports consisted of the low-priced *valencinas e Santomer* (cloth from Valenciennes and Saint Omer or types of cloth similar to those produced there).

Table 7.5 shows that most of the volume of cloth imported through San Sebastián was of the inexpensive kind, but, at the same time, luxury cloth, *pannos tintos* (red cloth, perhaps an expensive imitation of the fabled scarlet cloth?), *camelin, blaos,* and *blanqueta* of Commines, represented an important part of the entire cloth trade. And, in this particular case, *escarlata* (scarlet cloth), the most fashionable and costly of imported fabrics, is not even included.

Related to the commercial activities of northern Castilian merchants is the issue of a market for luxury and moderately priced cloth. One must assume that the high nobility and well-to-do bourgeois purchased large quantities of cloth imports, while the poor, whether rural or urban, wore local textiles or very inexpensive imported cloth. In this connection the crown's allocation of funds for the clothing of the royal household reveals, in this single example of 1293–94, the conspicuous consumption of imported textiles, which was a constant drain on royal finances. It also shows us the dynamics of commerce in late medieval Castile. Johan Matheo, an official in the court of Sancho IV, was granted an allocation to clothe his men, ten horsemen and ten footmen. Each of the horsemen received nineteen *varas* (almost a yard per *vara*) of *viado* for cloaks and *pellotes* (long robes), plus three and one-half *varas* of *panno* (*paño,* cloth) *tinto* for *sayas e calzas* (tunics and breeches); each footman received nine *varas* of *viado* and one *vara* of *paño tinto*. Foot messengers (thirty of them) were given eleven *varas* of *viado* each, and thirteen *varas* of *paño tinto* were given to one of the royal scribes. The head crossbowman, an important official, was given eleven *varas* of *paño tinto* and one of the precious *escarlata* cloth. Yet the court juggler (*saltador*), a Moor, also received twelve *varas* of *paño tinto*. The list goes on to include almost the entire royal household. Most of them received what may be considered expensive cloths for their garments, but there were also large quantities of *valencinas* and *santomers* given to clothe lesser royal servants and those of court officials; and in some cases the cloth was used for saddles, covers, and so forth.[19]

Altogether, the accounts of Don Bartolomé, an official sent by Queen María de Molina to pay for the clothing of the king's household, showed an expense of around 139,813 *mrs.* Almost 140,000 *mrs.* were spent in a single

TABLE 7.5.   Cloth Imported through San Sebastian (1293).

Origin and Type	Quantity (in pieces)	Price per piece (in mrs.)	Total
Expensive Cloth (*more than 300* mrs. *per piece*)			
Pannos tintos (red cloth)	155	550	85,250
	6	530	3,180
Camelins from Lille	2	450	900
from Ypres	2	400	800
from Lille	19	350	6,650
Blaos (mostly from Ypres)	76	350	26,600
	7	330	2,310
	13	300	3,900
Blanquetas de Camua (Commines)	11	300	3,300
Viado from Ghent	1	350	350
from Ypres	2	300	600
Viadillo	2	300	600
Total	296		134,440
Inexpensive to Intermediate Cloth (*less than 300* mrs. *per piece*)			
Pannos tintos (imitation)			
from Carcassonne	10	150	1,500
from Narbonne	24	150	3,600
Camelins pardos	2	270	540
from Ghent	4	180	720
small	4	160	640
Blaos	2	150	300
Blanquetas (imitations) from Narbonne	190	90	17,100
	22	80	1,760
	25	70	1,750
Tintas	40	150	6,000
Grolos (?)	8	50	400
Raz (cloth from Arras)	88	270	23,760
	5	260	1,300
	5	250	1,250
	1	240	240
	3	230	690
	19	220	4,180
From Tournai	7	240	1,680
	79	220	17,380
	40	200	8,000

TABLE 7.5.   *Continued*

Origin and Type	Quantity (*in pieces*)	Price per piece (*in* mrs.)	Total
Viados from Ghent	1	160	160
from Ypres	10	140	1,400
Viadillos	4	140	560
from Ypres	4	103	412
From Valenciennes	60	200	12,000
	825	180	148,500
	244	170	41,480
	202	160	32,320
	30	150	4,500
	30	140	4,200
Valenciennes (*cuerda*)	211	150	31,650
	156	140	21,840
Valencinas of Maubeurge	52	150	7,800
(plus 11 *valencinas*, price not stated)			
Saint-Omer	516	150	77,400
	120	140	16,800
Baradetes of Ypres	4	165	660
	33	160	5,280
Total	3,080		499,752

Source: Cuentas, iii–xiii. Gual Camarena, "El comercio de telas en el siglo XIII hispano," 104–5.

year on the king's household, and that figure did not include the expenses in clothing the royal family itself, the queen's household, the large retinues of magnates and prelates present in the court, or the lavish gifts in clothing to ecclesiastical establishments or royal officials.[20] A few things are obvious from this data. First, of course, is the exaggerated display of the royal court, a display which, as shall be seen later, sharply contrasted with the dire economic conditions of the realm and of most of its inhabitants. Second, and far more important, the huge expenses of the royal court served as an engine for the commercial activities of northern Castilian merchants, or to be more precise, of one specific aspect of their trade, the import of luxury cloth. This last point is worth emphasizing again. The bulk of the cloth imported may have been *valencinas*, low-priced and poor quality cloth, but in monetary terms this was not as important as the luxury cloth.

As shown in Table 7.5, expensive cloth represented only 8.8 percent of the total volume but 20.8 percent of the total cost. Of the king's household expenses only 5,030 *mrs.* corresponded to Valenciennes and *santomer* cloths, or less than 3 percent of the total. And here is, of course, the key. Luxury cloth, the *paños tintos*, the *escarlata*, left great profits with far less work. Merchants, to be certain, sold wherever they could, whatever they could, and thus in 1302 the Dominicans of Saint Paul in Burgos were exempted of tolls on their imports of 550 *varas* of sackcloth every year.[21] Sackcloth may have been used by the friars, but it was also the cloth given to the poor in ceremonial funeral feasts. Even the destitute in Castile wore imported clothes. But there was no great profit in sackcloth, and a great deal in *escarlata*. We cannot conclude this section, therefore, without a brief look at cloth prices and their change over time, for they provide an explanation for the dynamics of Castilian commercial life.

In examining cloth prices over a period of more than a century we are faced with serious difficulties. We have comprehensive information on prices for just a few years: 1252, 1258, 1268, 1293–94, 1351, and 1369. In most instances the information for those years reflects not the market price, but rather the crown's attempts to impose a ceiling on prices. We must assume that merchants often sold their goods at prices much higher than those set by the ordinances of the Cortes. With that caveat, Table 7.6 provides a brief glimpse of trends in cloth prices. I have included only the most popular fabrics.

Table 7.6 provides some indication of a significant rise in the price of expensive cloth with little or no increase for inexpensive imported textiles. One should also take into account that the real value of money in 1293–94 was only one-sixth of what it had been in the mid-thirteenth century, and even the crown admitted to the weakening of the coinage in royal charters. Debasing of coinage and economic difficulties had led to a marked decrease in the strength of the *maravedí*.[22] Under such circumstances, the price of expensive cloth still increased, though not as dramatically, while that of inexpensive cloth actually decreased in real price. However, since we do not have hard data on salaries throughout the period, it is difficult to estimate whether the common people were keeping up with inflation and the numerous devaluations of coins. One's first impression is that they were not.

Two points are worth mentioning here. First, the accounts of the Cortes of Toro in 1369 do not provide a list of textiles fully corresponding to those of 1268 and 1293–94 because by the second half of the fourteenth century, as Verlinden has pointed out, textiles from Brabant had entered the Castilian market in direct competition with Flemish, English, and French imports.[23] Cloth from Malines, Brussels, and elsewhere in Brabant gained a lion's share of the Castilian market. Second, the difference in prices between

TABLE 7.6.   Prices of Imported Cloth (in *maravedíes* per *vara*).

Origin or Type of Cloth	1268	1293	1303	1369
Escarlata of Montpellier	6	50	100	120
of Malines				110
of Douai				150
Paño tinto of Cambrai	3–3.5	22–25		
Camelin of Ghent	1.5	15		
Blaos	1.5	15		80
Blanqueta	1.5	15		
Saint-Omer	8	8		
Valenciennes	6.5	8		
Viado of Ghent	8	15		40
Bruneta of Douai	3		58	80

Source: Cortes, 1:66–67, 2:172–73; *Cuentas*, iii–xiii; Carlé, "El precio de la vida"; Carlé, "Mercaderes en Castilla."

imported and local cloth was indeed extraordinary. The prices for local textiles as recorded in the Cortes of Jerez provide a good indication of this disparity (see Table 7.7).

Only one type of local cloth is mentioned in the accounts of 1293–94, and none is mentioned afterward. For all practical purposes, imported textiles almost monopolized the Castilian market, and local production must have been reserved in this period for the basest use. Even when one considers the expense of transportation, import tithes, and the risks of sea travel, the profits to be gained by selling imported luxury textiles were considerable. This explains why Castilian merchants were never anxious to invest in local production, and why perhaps the crown, which derived substantial income from dues on imports and from extorting merchants, never really encouraged local production. We must now leave this long discussion of cloth and look to other aspects of Castilian commerce.

CASTILIAN COMMERCE: FINISHED GOODS AND FOODSTUFFS
Other goods besides cloth that were imported through the Bay of Biscay included finished goods and foodstuffs. Of the latter, dried sardines were imported in large quantities. At least 121,000 sardines, at an average price of 35 *mrs.* per thousand, came through the port of San Sebastián in just ten months (1293). Fish was consumed in large quantities then (as it is today)

TABLE 7.7.   Price of Cloth Produced in
Castile in 1268 (in *sueldos* per *vara*).

Type of Cloth	Price
Cardenos	2
Viado	2
Llano blanco	4
Segoviano cardeno viado	4
Segoviano of Segovia	18
Marfaga	5
Blanqueta of Ávila	4
Burel of Ávila	7
Frisa	4
Pardo (1293)	8

Source: *Cortes*, 1:66.

throughout the region, and not just for liturgical reasons.[24] Other items imported in far lesser quantities but at prices much higher than sardines were pepper, at around 5 *mrs.* per pound; sugar, at between 3 and 5 *mrs.* per pound; saffron, in very small lots of twenty-five pounds, at the high price (though certainly less expensive than at present) of 12 *mrs.* per pound; ginger, at 4 *mrs.* per pound; and dates, at 2.5 *mrs.* per *ponz.* Although not mentioned in the 1293 entries of the port of San Sebastián, we also know that grain was imported in times of dearth, as was the case in 1346 when Castilian merchants brought from England 160 tons of wheat in one instance and 1,000 quarters of wheat in another.[25]

Except for dried fish, an occasional cargo of wheat, and, of course, textiles, most of the imported foodstuffs had a definite meridional origin. Pepper, ginger, dates, and saffron came from Andalucía by way of Seville, or even from farther east through Mediterranean ports to Seville, and afterwards from there to northern ports. All this information points to a steady trade between the Bay of Biscay and southern markets. We know that a well-traveled maritime route existed and that the patterns of commerce were far more sophisticated than the shipping of a few spices and tropical products. Andalusi commercial centers also sent hides, wool, and wines north, and received in return iron and hemp. Such was the cargo of two Burgalese merchants, Pero (Pedro) de la Riba and Pero Pérez, who were ordered by the king to carry 2,500 *quintales* of iron and hemp to Seville in 1293.[26] Economic exchanges between north and south by sea also included a whole range of Mediterranean finished goods. Italian luxury cloth, including purple from Venice and Lucan gold brocade, dyed textiles from Montpellier, and rich silk fabrics made the difficult journey through the Straits of Gibraltar to Andalusi ports, on to the north of Castile, and beyond to English, Flemish, and northern markets. Thus we see northern Castilian merchants and sea captains carrying pomegranates to Eleanor, the Castilian queen of Edward I or, as carriers for the Bardi and Peruzzi companies, transporting English wool to Italian manufacturing centers or Gascon wine to England. In this trade, Italian merchants played a vital role as intermediaries and as sources for capital to finance commercial ventures. It is worth emphasizing, however, that although Genoese and other foreign merchants were able to establish a strong foothold in Seville—where they had already established a strong presence under Muslim rule—and control its international trade, such was not the case with northern Castilian urban centers. In the north, the foreign merchants settled in Castile, and they and subsequent generations became Castilians.[27] Of course, maritime links with Andalucía and the Mediterranean did not replace the overland trade routes across the Castilian plain, but they did open another possibility, especially in the troubled thirteenth and fourteenth centuries, for the enter-prise of northern Castilian commercial groups.

What else was imported into Castile? Again the entries of San Sebas-tián are representative of the overall nature of Castilian trade. Large amounts of needles (at 3 *mrs.* per thousand), combs, toothpicks (half a gross for 6 *mrs.*), knives and other dinnerware, swords, hemp, buttons from Paris, hats from Toulouse, rings, thimbles, and a whole range of bric-a-brac were imported in 1293. On the whole, these were low-priced items, and it is remarkable that such goods as toothpicks would be imported. Some of the merchandise, such as, for example, hats from Toulouse, may have been brought overland to Bordeaux or Bayonne and then shipped to San Sebas-tián. Others, such as swords and knives, probably came from Andalucía.

EXPORTS

Trade, however, could not consist only of imports. The halcyon days of wool export were more than two generations away in the late thirteenth century. The 1293–94 accounts show us that Castile suffered from a severe trade deficit, and booty or tribute money—the little that there was of it in this period—found its way to northern European pockets. In truth, medi-eval men and women, and indeed medieval rulers, thought of trade deficits

TABLE 7.8.   Iron Exports from San Sebastián Area (1293).

Toll Station	Dates	Amount (*in* quintales*)
Segura	1 March through 5 May	213
Oyarte	13 February through 28 April	3,285
Orio	30 January through 30 September	4,493
Total		7,991

Source: Cuentas, xvii–xxii.

*One *quintal* equals approximately one hundred pounds.

and exports and imports in ways that were radically different from the way we see them today. There was always a tendency to restrict the export of precious commodities, including horses, falcons, and so forth.

If we choose ports around San Sebastián to serve as case studies of Castilian exports, we must begin by acknowledging that they are not representative of overall Castilian sales abroad. For the sake of brevity, we will concentrate on one commodity, iron, and on the role played by merchants in the marketing of that commodity.

The entries for the small toll stations of Orio, Oyarte, and Segura cover only a few months in 1293, and iron is almost the only item in the entries (see Table 7.8).

Almost 800,000 pounds of iron passed through these three small localities in only a few months; thus, it is reasonable to assume that the total volume must have been in the millions of pounds. Bilbao's great ironworks did not become important until after 1300, and its ore went directly abroad from its own ports. Of the ore exported from Segura, Oyarte, and Orio, some, as we saw above, was shipped to Andalucía. Small amounts must have been employed locally, especially in shipyards, as were the twenty-nine *quintales* of iron that Pero Johan de Aperrequín shipped to San Sebastián for the window frames of a ship on 3 August 1293. The bulk of the iron exports, however, must have gone north to England, Flanders, and northern France in order to offset, at least in part, the great cost of purchasing rich cloth. The accounts of Segura also include the export of small quantities of hides, wool, hemp, and iron tools, and we know from other sources that horses, when their export was allowed by the king and Cortes, were one of Castile's most precious commodities.[28]

There are no surprises when we come to the merchants controlling the export of iron. A good number of them—John Ochoa de Guetaria, Miguel de Buenga, Pero Ortiz d'Osunsulo, John Bono, Martin Orduña, Domingo de Berrio, and John Yenequez de Vitoria—were active as both importers of fine cloth and exporters of iron. A few of them enjoyed what may be considered a monopoly over iron exports throughout Orio, Oyarte, and Segura. Pero Ortiz d'Osunsulo, for example, imported thirty pieces of *valencina reforzadas*, eight pieces of Tournai cloth, and ten pieces of *valencina de cuerda* valued at 7,500 *mrs.* through San Sebastián on 31 January 1293. On five different days in 1293–94, Pero Ortiz exported 1,476 *quintales* of iron, or more than one-eighth of the total iron exported through the already mentioned ports. As was the case for the cloth trade, the merchants' place of residence or origin did not prevent them from traveling back and forth along the coast, buying and selling wherever a profit was to be made.[29]

We cannot conclude this discussion of Castile's international trade without mentioning, once again, its importance to the fiscal well-being of the crown. The large amount (more than 368,860 *mrs.*) depicted in Table 7.9 represents only a few selected ports and does not include the many other tolls collected inland, as the goods were transported to the interior. As can be seen, San Sebastián was not the largest entry port, but it was nevertheless quite representative. We are left with the puzzle of San Vicente de la Barquera. None of its merchants is mentioned in the English documentation or, as far as I know, in the 1293–94 accounts. Since the documentation for that port is scant, little can be said, except that against all reason the accounts show it to be the busiest entry port. Did San Vicente serve as entry port for Asturias, the region of Campóo, and the Tierra de Campos? Was its trade so dominated by outsiders, Burgalese, men from Santander and elsewhere, that its local merchants and sailors were completely eclipsed? This we cannot know.[30] To return to my initial point, although the crown had alienated a good part of its tithe income in the ports of San Vicente de la Barquera, Santander, Castro Urdiales, and Laredo to the cathedral of Burgos, the profit from international trade made them responsive to the political and economic needs of northern Castilian commercial elites. An analysis of what these elites were like and how they related to those below them in the city and to other social groups in the realm should be our next task. Before addressing this, however, we should look briefly at the commercial activities of interior towns.

TABLE 7.9.   Tithes Collected in Selected Ports (1293–94).

Port	Amount Paid	Total in mrs., ss., and ds.
Castro Urdiales	64,237 mrs. plus 35.5 baskets of dry sardines at 446 mrs.	64,683 mrs.
Laredo	13,235.5 mrs.	13,235.5 mrs.
Santander	64,973 mrs. plus 24.5 baskets of dry sardines at 535 mrs.	65,508 mrs.
San Vicente de la Barquera	144,071.5 mrs.	144,071.5 mrs.
Guetaria	6,370 mrs.	6,370 mrs.
San Sebastián	68,402 mrs.	68,402 mrs.
Fuenterrabía	6,167 mrs., 18 ds.	6,167 mrs., 18 ds.
Orio	170 mrs.	170
Segura	253 mrs., 6 ss.	253 mrs., 6 ss.
Total		368,860 mrs., 6 ss., 18 ds.

Source: Cuentas, iii–xxiv.

Towns of the Plain: Commerce and Agriculture

In the previous pages, our attention has been focused mainly on coastal towns, even though a good number of the merchants doing business in the area of the Bay of Biscay came from interior cities. We have seen how these trading and fishing localities joined in economic and political leagues, with Vitoria often acting as a link to inland communities. There are no similar alliances for the cities on the plain. The great *hermandades* of the late thirteenth and early fourteenth centuries were essentially political in nature and included urban centers with little or no long-distance trade. We have, however, a series of royal grants in the early 1280s which reveal the structure of Castilian trade and the financial foundations for oligarchical government in some northern Castilian towns.

INTERIOR TOWNS

On 13 February 1281, Rodrigo Ibáñez de Zamora and Pero de la Riba Gordón, acting as representatives for the native and foreign merchants in the realm, presented Alfonso X, then in Burgos, with a long list of griev-

Figure 2. View of the Castilian countryside from the Alcazar of Segovia. (Photo by Scarlett Freund)

ances. Their complaints, which can be gathered from the royal response delivered shortly afterward, voiced the usual protests against the greed of customs and toll collectors and the endemic violence imperiling their liveli- hood. The early 1280s were a time of growing conflict between the old king and his ambitious son, the Infante Don Sancho. Both the violence in the countryside and the official violence in the form of illegal exactions im- peded, as the king was willing to admit, the free flow of merchants and their trade through the realm. In his response, Alfonso X promised to address these complaints and to protect merchants from the unjust collection of debts by municipal officials and individuals. Moreover, merchants were allowed to export goods up to a value equal to the amount of their imports, but if the merchants exceeded that limit, then security had to be provided. In addition, the king ordered that the merchants pay the tithe in silver— this at a time when the coinage of the realm was being savagely debased.[31]

In the royal grant of 13 February, as well as in one issued two days later, Alfonso X exempted merchants from the payment of tolls on their personal belongings or on goods imported for the personal use of the merchant's family. The descriptions found in the royal charters allow us to see how, in most cases, almost every item of clothing, bed sheets and covers, the very basins in which merchants washed their hands came from abroad.[32] On 15 February, the king also met with a delegation of merchants representing northern Castilian and foreign commercial interests. In this instance, the merchants faced charges of exporting banned goods through San Vicente de la Barquera and Fuenterrabía; they were also accused of failing to make the required deposit in silver to guarantee their transactions. The roster of merchants meeting in Burgos provides a summary of trading towns in the north of Castile and of their prominent citizens. Pero de la Riba Gordón and Rodrigo Ibáñez de Zamora, as pointed out earlier, represented foreign merchants in Castile. Asencio García and Guillén Trapaz spoke for the merchants of Burgos and Martín de Salzedo and Don Ochava for those of Castro Urdiales. Bernard Pelegrín came from Laredo; Domingo Pérez de Precianes from Santander; Don Quirze from Aguilar de Campóo; John Martínez de Çamarra and Lope Yuánez from Vitoria; and Don Bartolomé and Domingo Pérez from Medina de Pomar. They agreed to pay 101,000 *mrs.* to the king as settlement. Pero de la Riba and Rodrigo Ibáñez de Zamora paid for themselves, as well as for the other merchants. In return the king promised to stop the ongoing investigations.[33]

Several things can be deduced from this affair. First, one sees once again the regional nature of Castilian trade. Those merchants present at Burgos from Aguilar de Campóo, Medina de Pomar, and Vitoria represented intermediate distribution centers for the maritime trade coming through the Bay of Biscay. Burgos was the joining link in all the commercial routes flowing from the northern ports and plain into the markets further south. Second, the profits derived from international trade must have been quite high indeed. These merchants were willing to pay a rather large sum in silver to stop an investigation into their activities. Finally, regardless of how much profit these Castilian merchants derived from the import trade, their high profits could not be sustained unless they could also export. At a time when Castile's currency was utterly debased and little gold came into the royal treasury from either tribute by Muslim vassals or from booty, buying cloth in the textile centers of northern Europe required hard currency or suitable goods in exchange. Therefore, in spite of the often enacted restrictions on the export of certain items, including horses, other kinds of livestock, silk, grain, wine, falcons, beeswax, and other goods, Castilian merchants continued to export them (most likely in order to partially finance their large cloth purchases).[34]

A close look at some of the merchants meeting with Alfonso X in 1281 also provides insights into other aspects of commercial life in northern Castile. We have already seen Pero de la Riba Gordón at the meeting held two days earlier, when he acted as representative of foreign merchants in Castile. We know that he had settled in Burgos and become a citizen, that is, he owned a house within the walls, enjoyed a certain income, and probably served in or contributed to the city's militia. Between 1 February 1293 and 31 January 1294, Pero de la Riba, together with Pedro Pérez, *alcalde* of Burgos, collected the royal tithe in Castro Urdiales, Laredo, Santander, and San Vicente de la Barquera. As royal officials, they also supervised the work and accounts of local collectors. On 14 July 1294, both men presented to the crown an account of the amounts collected, as well as those payments they had made in the king's name: expenses for transporting iron and hemp to Seville in a ship of Laredo and for the painting of the chapel of Saint Barbara in Burgos. Almost four decades later, in 1338, we find a Pero de la Riba, possibly a son or grandson of the 1294 Pero, as a member of the Real Hermandad, the prestigious fraternity of non-noble knights, and a resident of the street of Sanct Llorente, the neighborhood of the well-to-do and politically influential elite of Burgos. Rodrigo Ibáñez de Zamora, also a merchant and royal official, was equally influential in the commercial life of Burgos.[35]

Asencio García had collected royal taxes, probably as a tax farmer, in 1279, 1281, and 1293, when he received 2,000 *mrs.* from the royal treasury. This money was a partial payment for the 13,000 *mrs.* which Asencio and other men of Burgos had advanced to Abraham el Barchilón for the king's use. In 1280 Asencio purchased what must have been a substantial and important vineyard within the walls of Burgos, since he gave in exchange another vineyard plus 233 *mrs.* Guillén Trapaz, the other Burgalese representative to the above-mentioned meeting between Castilian merchants and the king, was a member of one of the most influential families in the city, with a strong foothold in the political and economic realms of the city. Domingo Pérez, the representative of Medina de Pomar, may have been one of the important cloth merchants mentioned prominently in the royal accounts of 1293–94.[36]

Clearly, commercial centers such as Burgos or Vitoria attracted enterprising men from other parts. Conditions still might have been fluid enough in the late thirteenth century to allow foreign merchants and those from nearby cities to settle in Burgos and gain citizenship and political influence there. We find merchants and city officials in Burgos and other important towns whose names point to a place of origin outside of Burgos: Carrión, Frías, Santo Domingo de Silos, Zamora, and other places. This, I believe, shows the mobility of commercial elites, at least before 1300, and their integration into the economic structures of other towns—if they were capable of contributing with their capital and enterprise. Regional movement and the constant contacts between urban centers and their community of interests made for cooperation up to a point.

In times of crisis, this cooperation was often expressed in powerful political alliances, such as the *Hermandad* of 1315 referred to in the previous chapter. Moreover, the northern Castilian elites, specifically those north of the Duero River, were able to integrate those foreign merchants transacting business in their respective cities without losing their preeminence in the region. This was not a commercial life controlled by Italian mercantile interests, as was the case in Seville, nor is there any evidence of Jewish or Muslim participation at the international or interregional level. Stereotypes and commonplaces, however, are hard to overcome, and the picture of Jewish merchants and tax collectors running the economic and financial life of medieval Castile, although incorrect for this period, remains a powerful image in popular history.

The commercial elites that came to dominate the life of some northern Castilian cities were autochthonous or were the descendants of eleventh- and twelfth-century merchants who, coming down into Castile along the pilgrimage road to Compostela, settled in the towns along the road and over time became Castilians. Sometimes, of course, the weight of tradition and ancient customs preserved the distinctions between *francos* (people from north of the Pyrenees) and Castilians well into the fourteenth century, but this was mostly a formulaic tradition. Such was the case in 1345 when, in a long document ratifying the monastery of Santo Domingo de Silos's lordship over the town of Silos, Alfonso XI confirmed two *merinos* for Silos: one a Castilian, the other a *franco*, but both in fact citizens of the town and vassals of the abbot.[37] Silos had been and was still in the fourteenth century one of the important shrines just off the main pilgrimage route. As such Silos must have had a good number of foreign merchants in an earlier period; yet there is no evidence that by 1350 foreign merchants played any important roles there or elsewhere in the region.

Overland Trade: The Road to Compostela

Up to this point we have examined trade from the sole perspective of maritime commerce, that is, of goods—mostly cloth—imported from northern Europe through the Castilian ports on the Bay of Biscay. We have also glimpsed the exports of Castile to English and Flemish markets: iron, hides, fat, horses, and other raw materials. Moreover, the transfer of goods from Andalucía to northern Castile and the rest of Europe through the labors of Castilian merchants and sea captains was yet another aspect of the complex exchanges between coast, mountain, plain, and transmaritime regions. This is, however, only a partial view of Castilian commercial activities. We must consider now, if only in its outline, trade that moved overland along ancient routes. These roads of northern Castile dictated, to a large extent, the direction of trade. The region was linked, held together as it were, by a series of highways and smaller roads. These byways, many of which dated from an even earlier era, provided access to the world beyond the mountains encircling Castile. Map 3 shows only the main thoroughfares of northern Castile; thus, it gives us also a sense of the manner in which goods moved across the northern plain.[38]

THE ROAD TO COMPOSTELA AND URBAN LIFE

Commercial life in northern Castile began in earnest with the economic activities generated by the pilgrimage to the tomb of Saint James in far-off Galicia. Underlying the numerous works written on this topic and their careful examination of the social and economic aspects of the pilgrimage is the impact it had on the development of urban life in the area.[39] Before the coastal towns of Cantabria and Biscay had come into being, the people from northern Castile had already come to appreciate and purchase the fine woolens from Flanders, as well as a host of other imported products from northern Europe. Enterprising pilgrims, with one eye on salvation and the other on profits, did not come to or leave Spain empty-handed. The similarities among the cities and towns that grew along the road to Santiago de Compostela (elongated urban centers oriented on an east–west axis), as well as their common pattern of settlement and charters of foundation (*fueros*), in towns with large neighborhoods of *francos* and extensive commercial life, speak forcefully to the importance of the road in the awakening of commercial life in Castile. Yet if the urban model at the inception of town life along the road to Santiago de Compostela or the French Way was in fact a common one, subsequent developments were not.

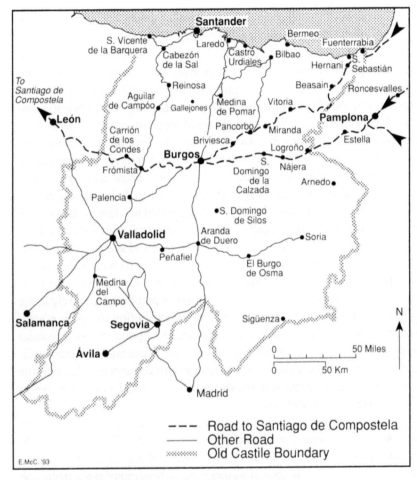

Map 3. The main roads of late medieval northern Castile.

Some urban centers failed to fulfill their promise, others were relegated to the seasonal commercial activity of pilgrimage life, while a few struck new and successful commercial ventures wholly independent of the road. In spite of these distinctions, it may prove useful to examine some of the towns along the road and to compare their structures and the tenor of urban life with those of some of the towns examined previously. We should also draw comparisons with urban centers south of the Duero, the communities of *villa y tierra*, towns with extensive hinterlands and a different economic orientation.

The story of the pilgrimage to the tomb of the apostle James in Compostela is well known to medieval historians. Since the mid-tenth century (950) when Gotescald, bishop of Le Puy, made the first recorded trans-Pyrenean pilgrimage to Compostela, the road has beckoned millions of the faithful, the adventurous, and the profit-seeking from almost every corner of western Europe.[40] Westward on the road from the kingdom of Navarre into Castile proper was Logroño, the first important urban center. Here we have a good example of a town that rose to prominence because of the pilgrimage but which was unable after the decline in the number of visitors to maintain or develop its long-distance trade. Whatever commercial life Logroño and its network of adjacent small towns (Santo Domingo de la Calzada, Navarrete, Briviesca, Nájera, and Arnedo) had depended to a large extent on the traffic of the road. Only later, after 1250, did Logroño acquire some commercial orientation as a center for the Rioja wine trade and as a regional market. But the town's attempt to sell its wine in the region met with stiff competition from Navarrese wine producers, and there is no evidence that merchants from Logroño or any of its nearby towns participated actively in the profitable international cloth trade, nor in its distribution along the north–south roads into New Castile and Andalucía.[41] In point of fact, I wonder what link there was between the decline of the pilgrimage to Compostela and the opening of the Bay of Biscay to northern commerce. Although the evidence is almost nonexistent, the chronological coincidence of both events raises intriguing possibilities.

Burgos, on the other hand, with its own constellation of dependent and semi-dependent towns (Belorado, Castrojeriz, Frías, Medina de Pomar, Silos, and others), retained its commercial importance by opening new markets for its imports and maintaining its hegemony as a distribution center for the region. Logroño was unable to do the same. As the number of pilgrims decreased, their trading spirit also waned. In truth, the road, for all of its early importance, had serious limitations. It led only into specific areas of Castile that did not have the commercial potential of the north–south trade. Trade prospects along the east–west axis of Castile were indeed poor. To the west, Galicia was too backward to hold any interest; besides, most of its trade went by sea through the ports of Noya, Pontevedra, and La Corunna. To the east, Aragon was not easily accessible by land. Moreover, the Aragonese were in the commercial orbit of Barcelona and the aggressive Catalan merchants with their access to Mediterranean markets.[42]

We do not know as much as we should about Logroño, but the few extant documents point to a limited commercial activity. The town therefore mostly sold its agricultural goods, particularly wine. We can see to what extent the Rioja in general and the area of Logroño in particular had become specialized in a single agricultural product. A quick glance at the percentage of vineyards included in extant records of land transactions and leaseholds of the area of Logroño and a comparison with the rest of Castile (see Chapter 5) makes this specialization in wine quite evident. Of the twenty-nine extant lease contracts, twenty were of vineyards; of the twenty-nine transactions of land, fifteen involved vineyards.[43]

Where could all this wine be sold? During this period, most lords in northern Castile, regardless of how unsuitable their lands were for viticulture, encouraged the cultivation of the vine. At the same time, most towns jealously enforced laws that favored local wine production. Moreover, Navarre, just across the Ebro River, sought to market its own wine in direct competition with that of the Rioja. One can gather as much from a letter by Sancho IV (25-April-1286), commanding the town councils of the frontier with Navarre not to import wine from that kingdom. This order was later confirmed by Alfonso XI in 1315, an indication of the probable disregard of the royal ban. But it was not only from abroad that Logroño faced stiff competition. In 1305 the municipal officials of Logroño protested vehemently against the actions of the city council of Vitoria, which had forbidden its citizens to buy any goods, above all wine, from the men of Logroño. This is one further example of economic rivalries unraveling the obvious political advantages of close cooperation.[44]

In 1336 the councils of Logroño, Navarrete, Nájera, Treviño, Santa Cruz de Campeço, Haro, Briones, and other small localities near the Navarrese frontier wrote to the king because "que en las dichas villas e en otras villas que son en sus comarcas *que no son villas mercaderas* [which are not trading towns] que an mucho vino de suyo e que non pueden dello aprovechar nin a correr para se mantener,"[45] and requested that the king ban the import of Navarrese wine. Recognizing that they were not mercantile towns, these urban centers also complained of their excessive supply of their most important commodity—wine—of the lack of markets, and of competition from across the Ebro. Vitoria, a commercial center with international connections and markets in Navarre for its imported cloth, was once again the culprit, purchasing Navarrese wine rather than wine from nearby Rioja.

The Way South: Commerce, Ranching, Agriculture, and Urban Life

Overland trade, initially oriented along the road to Santiago de Compostela, followed a different direction in the later Middle Ages. There is ample evidence for this commerce, mostly on muleback, to and from the northern plain, south into the lower Duero region, and across the Guadarrama range into New Castile, Extremadura (the present geographical area), and Andalucía. In 1285 the merchants of Burgos were exempted from *portazgo* when traveling from Burgos to Palencia by the royal road. By the early fourteenth century, the merchants of Burgos and those of other northern cities were also granted the right to move freely throughout the kingdom with their *carretas e acemilas* (carts and mule trains); this they did carrying *todas sus mercadurías et viandas et pannos* (all their merchandise, and foodstuffs, and cloth).[46]

It would be repetitious to list all the royal privileges that attest to the north–south overland trade. One must point out, however, the prohibitive cost of land transport between regions. Carts pulled by oxen could be used in the plain along the roads described in an earlier chapter, but they had to be abandoned once one crossed into New Castile or moved north into the mountains. Moreover, transportation by cart moved far too slowly for the needs and ambitions of Castilian merchants. With no waterways and the access to other regions made difficult by mountain barriers, mules remained the best means of transport in medieval and early modern Castile.[47] The high prices paid for mules at the end of the thirteenth century, ranging from 40 *mrs.* for a mule to carry merchandise to Seville, to 700 *mrs.* for a mule for Doña Sancha, nursemaid of the Infante Don Fernando, to as much as 1,200 *mrs.* for a mule for the king of Aragon, as well as the high salaries paid to muleteers in the royal service—the 6,922 *mrs.* paid to Pero Martínez, the head muleteer, and his men for expenses, or the 150 *mrs.* per month to the muleteer of the queen—reveal the importance of mules and those in charge of mules in the overall pattern of transportation.[48]

In addition, mules were the favorite mount in Castile, especially on long journeys. Sure-footed in mountain passes and stronger than horses, mules were not only the best means of transporting goods and, at times, even for plowing, but also the preferred mount for everyone from those of the blood royal to enterprising merchants. On the other hand, horses, so jealously protected by royal legislation, were also used for carrying goods. In the case of both horses and mules, the range of prices and thus of the quality of mounts was quite wide. In 1294, a man and mule transporting goods for the royal household between Valladolid and Logroño cost 150 *mrs.* for a five-week period, while the royal treasury paid just 70 *mrs.* for two mules and one muleteer carrying cloth between the same two localities.[49] These prices do not really look excessive, except when considered in the context of the overall pattern of prices in late medieval Castile. In 1338, 70 *mrs.* would have purchased almost eighteen *fanegas* of wheat, or enough bread to feed two people for almost an entire year, and a plowman was paid only between 12 and 16 *ds.*, plus a ration of wine for a day's work in 1351.[50]

In spite of the costs and of the numerous inland and gate tolls that merchants had to bear in their treks across Castile, mule trains were capable of moving quite fast, a necessary quality if one was to maximize profits. In the accounts of Navarrese envoys (1351), one can follow the movement of the company and its daily expenses. Led by two merchants, Per Álvarez de Rada and Gil García de Iañiz, riding on mules, the group also included ten more men on mules, another mule that carried their provisions, six footmen, and ten servants also on foot. They traveled around 1,800 kilometers back and forth between Estella and Seville in thirty-two days of actual traveling, though Gil García was ill during the journey and delayed them a day in Valladolid and another in Burgos. They moved at an average rate of about 55 kilometers per day; since the pace was dictated by those on foot and by the mule carrying provisions, this was a good pace indeed.

On their journey, however, they did not proceed at a steady pace. We find days in which they traveled as many as 120 kilometers, and other more leisurely days of only 19 or 20 kilometers. One can calculate roughly the expenses of travel by mule as the company crossed northern Castile. (Expenses in Navarre are accounted in Navarrese money and were, on the whole, lower than northern Castilian or Andalusi prices.) In fourteen days of travel between Nájera (the first important Castilian town) and their destination, Seville, Per Álvarez and Gil García paid 628 *mrs.*, 25 *ds.* for barley, plus 83.5 *mrs.*, 15 *ds.* for straw to feed the thirteen mules. In addition, 40 *mrs.*, 60 *ds.* were needed for shoeing the mules, fixing harnesses, and other expenses. Tolls came to only 9 *mrs.*, which may indicate that as ambassadors the Navarrese merchants might have been exempted from tolls, or that the endless complaints about the expense of internal tolls was much ado about nothing. During the twenty-nine days they remained in Seville, the keep of the mules, repair of harnesses, shoeing, bleeding of sick animals, and other expenses were as follows: barley, 1,776 *mrs.*, 5 *ds.*; straw, 257 *mrs.*, 6 *ds.*; shoeing, 49 *mrs.*, 8 *ds.*; equipment and miscellany, 37.5 *mrs.*, 72 *ds.*

On their return trip, which also took fourteen travel days but which included some rest days, the expenses were similar to those of the first part of the journey: barley, 594 *mrs.*, 2 *ds.*; straw, 78.5 *mrs.*, 30 *ds.*; shoeing, 35.5 *mrs.*, 30 *ds.*; equipment and miscellany, 2 *mrs.*, 56 *ds.* Altogether the direct expenses of mule transportation to and from a stay in Seville for fifty-seven days amounted to 3,596 *mrs.*, 304 *ds.* (including 15 *mrs.* in tolls), with most of the expenses, 3,417 *mrs.*, 78 *ds.*, dedicated to the feeding of the thirteen animals. Although at first glance these costs appear excessive, they actually come to be under 5 *mrs.* per day per mule. This is still high when compared to wages and prices in the mid-fourteenth century, but not excessively so.[51]

We can not leave this account of the Navarrese journey to Seville without commenting, if only in passing, on some of the items they purchased along the way. The variety of products these merchants bought and consumed during their voyage reveals to us a well-regulated system of exchanges between the different regions of the realm and the regular provisioning of the northern towns with products from al-Andalus. On the road from Navarre to Seville, pepper could not only be found in large cities such as Burgos but also in small towns and villages. Saffron, cumin, and ginger could be obtained easily in Dueñas, a small locality on the road between Burgos and Valladolid. There is, of course, nothing surprising about this, but it is obvious that these travelers were accustomed to seasoned food and that spices and sauces were found all along the road without too much hardship.[52]

We should, before leaving behind the commercial aspects of northern Castilian society, attempt to describe those levels of exchanges connecting different regions with each other and with the exterior. These transfers of goods, both east–west and north–south, bound together foreign markets, coastal towns, the northern mountains, the plain, the Central Sierras, and Andalucía. They also allowed for the distribution of finished goods from abroad and of agricultural products over a wide region. Salt from the great wells of Salinas de Añana, Rucio, and elsewhere—not as profitable perhaps as imported cloth but certainly a far more vital a commodity—moved on muleback throughout the region. Mules, oxen, bulls, and cows were raised in the mountains north of Burgos and exchanged alive or as hides and tallow in the plain below for grain, from as far away as the Tierra de Campos, and for wine, from the region of the Rioja or elsewhere. Spices, silk, and iron products from Andalucía or from the forges of Toledo were exchanged for agricultural products from the northern plain and, above all, for rich cloth from Flanders, the very blood of Castilian commerce. Dried and salted fish entered the realm through Cantabrian and Basque ports and made its way inland across mountain divides. Iron and hemp were also shipped from northern coastal towns to Andalusian markets. And, perhaps, although not as often, Castilian merchants carried their wares eastward, as did merchants from Burgos in 1339, when Alfonso XI granted them the right to export one workhorse (*rocín*) each to Flanders and Montpellier.[53]

Beyond these interregional and international links of thirteenth- and fourteenth-century Castilian commerce, the transhumance already held a promise of great profits to merchants and crown alike. Soon after the disasters of the mid-fourteenth century and beyond the chronological boundaries of this book, Castile opened its dams to an endless river of wool. Out of Burgos, retracing the routes that brought imported cloth into the realm, wool made its way overseas to the textile centers of Flanders, Brabant, and elsewhere. With this commerce also came a growing demand for carts, muleteers, and beasts of burden from the northernmost parts of Old Castile.[54] Yet even before the rise of wool exports, the Mesta already fueled a modest textile industry in Segovia, Ávila, and Soria.[55] The Mesta also provisioned the markets at Burgos and Valladolid with large quantities of lamb and goat meat. Between 1 August and 13 November 1294, the royal household bought 1,513 rams for a price of 8,990.3 *mrs.*, an indication of the commercial and dietary importance of the transhumance in the economy and life of Castile. Not surprisingly, the Rastro, a Burgalese market for lamb meat, operated in Burgos from Michaelmas through Christmas, probably so that animals would not have to be kept through the winter or left behind by the transhumance.[56]

All of this points to a sophisticated system of interdependence and exchanges vital to the economic survival of the realm and closely related to its rural economy. If, as pointed out earlier, agricultural subregions in northern Castile were quite distinct from each other, these differences were bridged by commerce. Here, then, in the goods that were carried on muleback to and from the northern plain, lies the explanation for the single destiny (although there were local rivalries) of the region. Economic interdependence could only foster the progressive centralization of political power in Castile; thus the Castilian kings sought to control those outlets: the northern and Andalusi ports by which the flow of exports and imports maintained Castilian commercial life.

INTERNAL MARKETS

We must not leave this section without mentioning local markets, fairs, and artisanal activity, although in many respects this is a bit redundant. There is no need to muster the extant documentation to illustrate how towns, whether large or small, had their usual complement of butchers, carpenters, storekeepers, and so forth. Elsewhere I have already examined such evidence for Burgos, and the same can be done or has already been done for most urban centers in northern Castile. In some instances, such as Ávila or Santo Domingo de la Calzada, elaborate surveys of urban property held by the local cathedral chapter provide us with a fairly comprehensive view of local commerce.[57]

In the case of Ávila, a city which lost most of its municipal archives to a fire in the 1350s, the ecclesiastical *apeo* (survey) of property (1303) allows us to reconstruct most of the layout of the city, the number of houses, and the nature of local commerce. Obviously, the chapter did not own all the urban property in the city, and we may suppose that the largest commercial concerns may have owned their shops outright. Regardless, the 1303 census gives us a representative view of trading activities in Ávila. Altogether the census lists forty-one retail shops and stores spread throughout almost every neighborhood of the city. In addition, twenty-four more local businesses, including inns, blacksmiths, and fishmongers (there was a street of them and another for shoemakers) are mentioned in the extant cathedral documentation. By the thirteenth century and in succeeding centuries, a large market, the *mercado mayor*, operated near the cathedral, probably on a weekly basis. It brought together merchants from Ávila with farmers from the surrounding countryside, as occurs to this very day during the Friday market held in the San Esteban quarter of the city. Other small neighborhood markets also provided a place for daily exchanges of goods. For the period, however, there is little one can say about the size, volume, and modes of operation of these businesses, but they do allow us to see something of the pace of commercial life in a city that had a strong rural orientation.[58]

The streets leading to the "great market" were inhabited by Jews, Moors, and Christians; houses there commanded handsome prices, as did houses around the central markets in Valladolid and elsewhere. Around the mid-fourteenth century Fernando Mathos, a canon of the cathedral of Ávila, sold houses in the area of the market for the rather large sum of 1,000 *mrs*.[59] The high prices paid for houses and stores located in the commercial areas of Ávila is a telling sign of the importance of local business. Ávila, which as we know was not a distribution center for long-distance trade, was nevertheless a center for regional commerce. Unlike Burgos, however, where long-distance commerce as well as artisanal pursuits were solidly in the hands of Christian merchants and artisans, Ávila has enough evidence to

TABLE 7.10.   Urban Property Transactions* (1230–1350).

Price range (in *mrs.*)	*Ávila* No. of Transactions	*Burgos* No. of Transactions
0–100	3	8
101–500	15	9
501–1,000	7	3
1,001–5,000	7	9
5,001–8,000	0	3
Not stated	2	1
Total	34	34
Highest price per transaction	1,800 *mrs.*	8,000 *mrs.*
Lowest price per transaction	40 *mrs.*	33 *mrs.*
Average price per transaction	578.1 *mrs.*	1,594.9 *mrs.*

Source: DMA, 222–32. AHN, Clero, carps. 23–30. *ACB* and *FMCL*, vols. 13, 14, 16, 17.

*Items sold included houses, stores, urban mills, mill rights, and urban gardens.

show the active participation of Moors and Jews in local business. This is not to say, of course, that in Ávila and other towns with a ranching and/or rural economic base the ruling urban groups did not partake in the profits of commerce—they did. Fortún Blázquez, *alcalde* of Ávila, paid rent to the chapter for four stores in the centrally located neighborhood of Saint Thomas, and we find other members of Ávila's oligarchy as tenants, owners, and operators of local businesses throughout the city. From the mid-thirteenth century on there is a marked tendency toward buying out Jewish property in the city and toward the concentration of that property into the hands of a few privileged individuals of selected areas of the city. Table 7.10 provides a partial view of the market for urban property in late medieval Ávila and a comparison with that of Burgos.[60]

We must return, however, to our central point of inquiry, that is, what was the role of commerce in a city such as Ávila, with its agricultural and ranching orientation? Presiding over a large territory, holding jurisdiction over important towns, such as Arévalo, Barco de Ávila, and others, with impressive and inexpugnable walls and the see of a sprawling diocese, Ávila held its own in spite of being removed from the main international and regional trade routes. Moreover, the presence of dyers and weavers, mostly Moors and Jews, points to a modest textile industry, which produced low quality cloth, probably for distribution within its immediate region. Cloth from Ávila, the *blanqueta* and *burel*, is mentioned in the ordinances of the *ayuntamiento* or Cortes of Jerez in 1268, but its low price (4 *ss*. per *vara* of *blanqueta*, 7 *ss*. for *burel*) reveals its low demand in the face of a flood of foreign textiles. In Ávila, Segovia (where we have even stronger evidence for cloth manufacturing), Frías, and, to a lesser extent, Burgos we find embryonic textile centers producing cloth for a limited and often poor clientele. The *tiendas de pannos* (cloth stores), mentioned so prominently in the extant documentation, were most probably retail stores for the much-valued foreign imports.[61]

What one can say for Ávila, a city with a large number of stores, artisan shops, wine cellars, and other small commercial enterprises, can also be said for any city or town with sufficient extant documentation. In Burgos, the streets of San Juan, Sanct Llorente, and Tenebregosa, which formed part of the road to Santiago de Compostela as it made its way through the city, were filled with stores and tradesmen, and many of the Burgalese merchants and well-to-do artisans also lived in these commercial thoroughfares. In addition, the crown sought to promote commercial life throughout urban centers in Castile by granting to many localities the right to hold annual markets and fairs. Weekly markets have already been well studied, and they were a common feature of medieval economic life throughout the West. From important urban centers, such as Ávila with its "great market" and Burgos with its grain market of the Llana or its meat market, the Rastro, to the small weekly markets of large villages, these gatherings of merchants and farmers were of great importance for economic exchanges.

We know little about fairs in the period before 1350. The available information has already been summarized in magisterial fashion by Ladero Quesada. A fair granted to Burgos in 1339 by Alfonso XI, lasting fifteen days from the feast of Saint John on, never became a successful operation, nor did fairs succeed anywhere else, for that matter, until the rise of the town fairs of Medina del Campo and Medina de Rioseco in a later period.[62] Perhaps special fairs held no attraction in an economy that had a well-established pattern of commerce. If the fair held at San Esteban de Gormaz, a small town on the Duero River, is any indication, the volume of merchandise exchanged at such gatherings was minuscule. The *sisa* (sales tax) imposed on the fair held at San Esteban came only to 555 *mrs*., 7 *ss*., and 3 *ds*. for a period of twelve days. The tax collected on 22 November 1293 amounted to the paltry sum of 2 *mrs.*, 6 *ss.*, with most of the sales concentrated in one or two days.[63]

We must turn now to other aspects of urban life and to examine the social structure of northern Castilian towns and the manner in which those above, based upon their economic well-being, exercised their social and political power over those below.

Notes

1. On the commercial relations between al-Andalus and western Europe, see Olivia Remie Constable *Trade and Traders in Muslim Spain: The Commercial Realignment of the Iberian Peninsula* (Cambridge: Cambridge University Press, forthcoming 1994); also Francisco Hernández, "Las cortes de Toledo de 1207," in *Las cortes de Castilla y León en la edad media* (Valladolid: Cortes de Castilla y León, 1988), 219–63.

2. Pérez Bustamante, *Historia de la villa de Castro Urdiales*, 47–50.

3. Teofilo F. Ruiz, "Castilian Merchants in England, 1248–1350," in *Order and Innovation in the Middle Ages. Essays in Honor of Joseph R. Strayer*, ed. William C. Jordan et al. (Princeton, N.J.: Princeton University Press, 1976), 173–85. There is a Spanish edition with an appendix listing sailors and merchants from Cantabrian ports, "Mercaderes castellanos en Inglaterra, 1248–1350," in *Anuarios del instituto de estudios marítimos Juan de la Cosa*, vol. 1 (1977): 11–38; see also Wendy R. Childs, *Anglo-Castilian Trade in the Later Middle Ages* (Manchester: Rowman and Littlefield, 1978), 11–39 et passim.

4. See appendix to Ruiz, "Mercaderes castellanos," 31–38.

5. *C.C.R.* (1288–96), 365 (21-August-1294); Ruiz, "Castilian Merchants in England," 176.

6. For the types of ships sailing in the Bay of Biscay, see José Luis Casado Soto, *Arquitectura naval en el Cantábrico durante el siglo XIII* (Santander: Bedia, 1976), 18–33. For the names of sailors and passengers in the *Holop* of Guetaria, see *C.P.R.* (1292–1301), 207 (16-September-1296), cited in Ruiz "Burgos y el comercio castellano." Most of what follows on coastal towns is a revised version of this article.

7. For the activities of Castilian merchants within England, see Ruiz, "Castilian Merchants in England," 176–81.

8. Américo Castro, "Unos aranceles de aduanas del siglo XIII," *Revista de filología española* 8 (1921): 1–29, 325–56; 9 (1922): 266–76; 10 (1923): 113–36.

9. Miguel Gual Camarena, "El comercio de telas en el siglo XIII hispano," *Anuario de historia económica y social* 1 (1968): 96.

10. *Cortes*, 1: 451; AMB, clasif. 1391 (12-October-1252) et passim.

11. *Cuentas*, iii–vi.

12. *Cuentas*, ix (25-May-1293): Juan de Beunza imported cloth for the amount of 1,170 *mrs.*; (8-July-1293I), cloth valued at 2,000 *mrs.*; xii (21-August-1293), cloth valued at 3,800 *mrs.*; xiii (10-September-1293), cloth valued at 1,350 *mrs.*

13. *Cuentas*, xiv–xv.

14. *Cuentas*, v; AMB, clasif. 652 (19-December-1313); IGR, *Texto*, 17.

15. *Cuentas*, v; *Sancho IV*, 1: lxxiv; AMB, clasif. 652 (19-December-1313); AHN, Clero, carp. 185, no. 11 (17-March-1303); for his brother García Pérez, see ACB, vol. 30, f. 594 (21-September-1324); *Cortes*, 1: 406 (1329); IGR, *Texto*, 17; "Primitiva regla," 160–64.

16. See, for example, *Cuentas*, lxxiii, xcv, cxxxix; Antonio Ballesteros, *Alfonso X el Sabio* (Murcia, 1963), 933; AMB, clasif. 806 (4-August-1273); AMB, clasif. 2690 (15-February-1281); *Cuentas*, vi; *Cortes*, 1: 263 et passim.

17. *Cuentas*, iv–xxi.

18. *Cuentas*, iii, vii, ix, and xii.

19. *Cuentas*, lxxiii ff.

20. *Cuentas*, cvi–cviii. See also payment by Don Bartolomé de Monresin for 18 November 1294.

21. AHN, Clero, carp. 185, no. 9 (25-July-1302).

22. See below for manifestations of the late medieval Castilian crisis, including inflation.

23. Charles Verlinden, "Draps des Pays-Bas et du nord de la France en Espagne au XIVe siècle," *Le Moyen Âge*, 8 (1937): 22 et passim. See also his *El comercio de paños flamencos y brabanzones en España durante los siglos XIII y XIV* (Madrid: Cátedra de la fundación del excelentísimo señor Conde de Cartagena, 1952).

24. *Cuentas*, iii–vi. In two days Castilian merchants imported 111,000 sardines. For the consumption of fish in Benedictine monasteries, see *Vida económica*, 92.

25. *Cuentas*, ix–xi; Ruiz, "Castilian Merchants in England," 182, n. 75.

26. *Cuentas*, xliii.

27. Ruiz, "Castilian Merchants in England," 180, n. 54. Ruiz, "The Transformation of Castilian Municipalities," 12–13; Miguel Ángel Ladero Quesada, *Historia de Sevilla: La ciudad medieval* (Sevilla: Universidad de Sevilla, 1976), 126–30.

28. On the accounts of Orio, Segura, and Oyarte, see *Cuentas*, xvii–xxii; Ruiz, "Castilian Merchants in England," 181–82.

29. See examples in *Cuentas*, iii, xix–xx, et passim.

30. On San Vicente de la Barquera, see Valentín Sáinz Díaz, *Notas históricas sobre la villa de San Vicente de la Barquera* (Santander: Institución cultural de Cantabria, 1973), 5–77, and documents edited therein.

31. AMB, clasif. 134 (13-February-1281). On the debasement of coinage, see Felipe Mateu y Llopis, "En torno a las acuñaciones de Sancho IV de Castilla," *Boletín de la Comisión de Monumentos de la Provincia de Burgos* 109 (1949): 334–40; Octavio Gil Farrés, *Historia de la moneda española* (Madrid: n.p., 1959), 204–8. On the political conflict in this period, see Antonio Ballesteros y Beretta, *Alfonso X, el Sabio* (Barcelona: Salvat, 1963), 927–1056.

32. AMB, clasif. 2689 (15-February-1281).

33. AMB, clasif. 2690 (15-February-1281).

34. Restrictions on exports can be found in the Cortes of Jerez (1268), Haro (1288), etc. See *Cortes*, 1: 71, 105, et passim.

35. *Cuentas*, xl–xliii; IGR, *Texto*, 16–18; AMB, clasif. 683 (26-September-1259); clasif. 99 (25-March-1268); clasif. 2574 (22-December-1275); ACB, vol. 50, p. 2, f. 150 (5-June-1290) et passim.

36. *Cuentas*, xlii; AMB, clasif. 2572 (20-February-1279); clasif. 2689 (15-February-1281); ACB, vol. 49, f. 80 (11-February-1280). On the Trapaz family, see Ruiz, "The Transformation of the Castilian Municipalities," 31, appendix. See also Ballesteros y Beretta, *Alfonso X*, 933; AMB, clasif. 806 (4-August-1273); clasif. 2690 (15-February-1281); *Cuentas*, lxxiii, xcv, cxxxix.

37. On foreign merchants settling in Burgos and elsewhere, see Ruiz, "The Transformation of the Castilian Municipalities," 10–11; García de Valdeavellano, *Orígenes de la burguesía*, chs. 4–5; *Silos*, 2: 413.

38. For roads in northern Castile, see Gonzalo Menéndez Pidal, *Los caminos en la historia de España* (Madrid: Ediciones cultura hispánica, 1951); Pero Juan Villuga, *Repertorio de todos los caminos de España* (Medina del Campo, 1546; reprint, New York: Hispanic Society of New York, 1902). The indispensable guide to northern roads is Jean Pierre Molénat, "Chemins et ponts du nord de la Castille au temps des rois catholiques," *Melanges de la Casa Velázquez* 7 (1971): 115–62.

39. See García de Valdeavellano, *Orígenes de la burguesía*, 21–83, 129–210; Jean Gautier-Dalché, *Historia urbana de León y Castilla*, 67–210. See also *Villes médiévales du chemin de Saint-Jacques de Compostelle (de Pampelune a Burgos): villes de fondation et villes d'origine romaine* (Paris: Editions recherche sur les civilisations, 1984).

40. On the pilgrimage to Compostela, see Luis Vázquez de Parga, J. Ma. Lacarra and J. Uría Riu, *Peregrinaciones a Santiago de Compostela*, 3 vols. (Madrid: Consejo Superior de Investigaciones Científicas, 1949); Luciano Huidobro y Serna, *Las peregrinaciones jacobeas*, 2 vols. (Madrid: Instituto de España, 1950).

41. On Logroño's wine trade and its networks of dependent towns, see below.

42. For examples of Galician trade with England, see *C.P.R.* 1292–1301 (London, 1895), 203; Vázquez de Parga et al., *Peregrinaciones a Santiago de Compostela*, I, 77–79. On the Crown of Aragon, see Thomas N. Bisson, *The Medieval Crown of Aragon: A Short History* (Oxford: Oxford University Press, 1986), 72–103.

43. See Chapter 5. Also *Albelda y Logroño*, 52, 64–65, 68, 77–78, 98, 138, 143–44, 146, 175, et passim.

44. Diego Ochagavia, "Notas para la historia de los vinos riojanos," *Berceo* 10 (1949): 12–17.

45. Ibid., 14–17.

46. AMB, clasif. 120 (21-May-1285); clasif. 104 (28-January-1303).

47. Ringrose, *Transportation and Economic Stagnation in Spain*, 43–48.

48. *Cuentas*, xli, xxxiii, xxxv, liii; Carlé, "El precio de la vida," 152.

49. *Cuentas*, xli.

50. Carlé, "El precio de la vida," 146–47; *Cortes*, 2: 116 et passim. *Vida económica*, 68, 93.

51. *Desde Estella a Sevilla*.

52. Ibid.

53. For Alfonso XI's privilege to the merchants of Burgos, see AMB, clasif. 96 (28-November-1339). For other exchanges, see above.

54. Carla Rahn Phillips, "Spanish Merchants and the Wool Trade in the Sixteenth Century," *Sixteenth Century Journal* 14 (1983): 259–82; Manuel Basas Fernández, *El consulado de Burgos en el siglo XVI* (Madrid: Escuela de historia moderna, 1963).

55. Juan de Contreras, Marqués de Lozoya, *Historia de las corporaciones de*

menestrales en Segovia (Segovia: Mauro Lozano editora, 1921), 43–63; Asenjo González, *Segovia: La ciudad y su tierra*, 197–208; Paulino Iradiel Murugarrén, *Evolución de la industria textil castellana en los siglos XIII–XVI: Factores de desarrollo, organización y coste de la producción manufacturera en Cuenca* (Salamanca: Universidad de Salamanca, 1974), 15–50.

56. *Cuentas*, cxxxvii–cxxxix; Julián García Sáinz de Baranda, *La ciudad de Burgos y su concejo en la edad media*, 2 vols. (Burgos: Tipografía de la editorial El Monte Carmelo, 1967), 1: 288.

57. See, for example, Asenjo González, *Segovia: La ciudad y su tierra*, 184–211; Ruiz, *Sociedad y poder real*, 54–60, 163–70; *DMA*, 222–32; *Colección diplómatica calceatense*, 27–31. See also below.

58. Barrios García, *Estructuras agrarias y de poder*, 2: 62–63; *DMA*, 222–32.

59. For Jews and Moors, see below. For prices of houses located close to the central markets in Ávila, Valladolid, Aguilar de Campóo, and elsewhere, see *DMA*, 147–48 (1291); 165–68 (1297); Ajo, 105–6 (1314); AHN, Clero, carp. 29, no. 8 (1347); carp. 1672, no. 11 (1338), no. 12 (1339), et passim.

60. *DMA*, pp. 222–32. For Moors and Jews, see below.

61. *Cortes*, 1: 66. See also above. In the ACB, *Cuadernos de contabilidad*, there is a reference to a woman weaver renting a house from the cathedral chapter.

62. See Cristobal Espejo and Julián Paz, *Las antiguas ferias de Medina del Campo* (Valladolid, 1912); Miguel Ángel Ladero Quesada, "Las ferias de Castilla, siglos XII a XV," *CHE* 67–68 (1982): 269–315.

63. *Cuentas*, lvi–lvii. Compare with Brihuega, where between 5 and 28 November, 8,464 *mrs.*, 13 *ss.* were collected (lvi).

8. Society and Politics
in Urban Northern Castile:
The Non-Noble Knights

The social and political dynamics of urban northern Castile cannot always be observed in their entirety. Not unlike the case for other topics in late medieval Castilian history, the paucity of documents at key points makes difficult the careful description of urban social structures. Moreover, our knowledge about the largest segments of the urban population—the petty bourgeoisie increasingly disfranchised after 1248, the religious minorities, and the urban poor—is often sparse or nonexistent. The urban poor, for example, emerge in the documentation of the period only as nameless recipients of ecclesiastical, municipal, or private largesse, or when their violent actions bring them into contact with those upholding the law and the structures of power. In many respects, without enough demographic data, without parish records, our story must remain of necessity incomplete: our vision of life in medieval urban Castile a blurred picture of a long gone reality.

Yet, in spite of our lack of information, we can deduce a rather full outline of the diverse social groups found within city walls and describe with some accuracy the interaction between these groups. An examination of urban social structure provides another approach to a typology of urban experiences in northern Castile. Here, again, diversity is the key word. Although in a broad sense most towns in the north followed the same patterns of development, there were noticeable differences between them. The inner dynamics of each city or town in the region dictated its final mode of social and economic organization, its relationship to the crown, and its political destiny.

We must begin with a commonplace and accept, without forgetting the numerous exceptions, that by the thirteenth century and certainly before the Black Death, urban oligarchies had come to control the economic, political, and social life of most northern Castilian cities. The process by which this was accomplished was not the same everywhere, nor was the outcome similar. While in places such as Ávila and Burgos the urban elites were capable of securing a fairly strong hold on municipal offices and political power, elsewhere, as was the case in Soria, political authority had to be shared to a certain extent with the commons. In Segovia, a community of "town and land," elites in the Segovian hinterland participated, to some degree, in the government of the community and land, and they enjoyed representation in the Cortes. Moreover, in many towns throughout the region, power was apportioned to contending factions or family groups within the ruling elites.

In defining social groups,[1] one must pay close attention to the economic structure of each locality. In large (by Castilian standards) and commercially oriented urban centers such as Burgos, the mercantile groups were successful in keeping the nobility from interfering with their monopoly of the towns' economic resources, political life, and lordship over the surrounding countryside. Yet such an appraisal is a bit deceiving. Indeed, from the late twelfth to the end of the fourteenth century, the aristocratization of urban elites became a reality throughout the land. This was a twofold process accomplished either by the settlement of noblemen in the cities, as was the case early on in Andalusi towns, or much later in Cuéllar or Valladolid, where, after the ascent of the Trastámaras (1369), many of the great magnates built large town houses; or, as occurred in Burgos, by the eventual and progressive accession of the oligarchy to the ranks of the nobility.

In Burgos, the non-noble knights (*caballeros villanos*) began to monopolize municipal offices in the late twelfth century and gained complete political hegemony within the city by 1300. In this context, Alfonso X's privileges of 1255 and 1256, granting tax exemption to the non-noble knights of Burgos and those of other Castilian cities, were a turning point in the social and economic development of the Castilian patriciate. The link between commercial activity—mostly long-distance trade—and social and political prominence or, in the case of Ávila, between rural property and power, was central to the complex relationship between the crown, urban elites, high nobility, and disfranchised groups which developed, after the mid-thirteenth century, within Castilian towns and the realm as a whole. This led to the alliance of the crown with the non-noble knights against noble violence and ambitions, but also against the rightful claims of the petty bourgeoisie. In this dual conflict, the oligarchy of Burgos and other towns welcomed, albeit probably reluctantly, royal control of municipal affairs in return for royal acknowledgment of their privileges and protection against the excesses of the high nobility.[2] I have argued in the past that developments in Burgos could be seen, with some modifications, as a model for the rest of northern Castile. Here I wish to demonstrate, despite the differences between commercial- and rural-oriented towns, that such was the case.

The Making of an Urban Elite: The Non-Noble Knights

Although we do not have as abundant documentation for other northern Castilian cities as we do for Burgos, the transformation of the institutional, social, and economic structures of Castilian municipalities can be illustrated in a fairly broad manner. Our point of departure in Burgos and elsewhere in the region is the martial character of these towns. The military role of the so-called bourgeoisie is a well-known aspect of the history of urban medieval Europe and is by no means unique to Castile. We are well acquainted with the combative nature of medieval burghers. Throughout the West, they armed themselves in "Leagues of Peace" to combat feudal violence. They rose against oppressive lords and dealt crushing defeats to mighty kings and emperors, as the Flemish townspeople did to the French noblemen at Courtrai in the early fourteenth century, and as the Italians did much earlier to the imperial troops at Legnano in 1176.[3] This reality clashes with the well-ordered tripartite division of society into those who pray, those who fight, and those who work. Even one who should have known better, the Infante Don Juan Manuel (1282–1348), frequently defeated by city militias during his many years of rebellion, could not avoid applying a well-worn stereotype and placing merchants on the same level as rustics.[4]

What was commonplace throughout the medieval West, the citizen soldier or the merchant ready to take arms, was in Castile an ancient and well-established tradition. In a "society organized for war" military service was long a necessary aspect of life. From free peasants to merchants everyone was subject either to serve or, at least, to contribute financially to the war effort. City militias served again and again on the frontier, sometimes many days away from home, and they often carried, as the militia of Ávila did at Jaén, the brunt of the campaign. More important, urban contingents stood between the crown and a rebellious nobility. It was not unusual for urban contingents to fight against violent magnates or for cities to join in *hermandades* to protect the throne from noble anarchy in times of minorities. More than in any other place in western medieval Europe, in Castile the kings depended on urban military resources for their campaigns against foreign enemies and, far more significantly, to keep at bay internal threats against their authority. Not surprisingly, most of the royal privileges to Castilian cities stated explicitly that they were granted as rewards for specific military service.[5]

Within the municipal militias those with enough wealth to fight on horseback and to purchase arms (the knights, *caballeros villanos*) had long gained great social and political advantages over those who fought on foot (*peones*). The nature of warfare in medieval Iberia, involving long-distance raids against al-Andalus or travel to faraway strongholds, made mounted militias far more important than archers or infantrymen, at least in the period before 1492. Consequently, from the mid-twelfth century on, the crown had bestowed numerous privileges on these non-noble knights. These concessions, in turn, brought the non-noble knights into prominence within their respective towns and cities.

By the late twelfth century and afterward, the extant documentation of Burgos, Valladolid, Ávila, and other localities allows us to see how a few families began to monopolize political offices and to acquire substantial urban and rural properties. We must realize that this social and political prominence was directly related to their military service and to their ownership of horses and weapons. Moreover, their status as knights was subject to annual review, the *alarde*—a ceremony in which urban knights paraded before municipal officials to demonstrate the fitness of their mounts and weapons—and depended as well on their availability for military campaigns. Here we must note, if only in passing, the symbolic and real social impact of these annual displays. Through them those in power administered a powerful lesson to those below, through a visual depiction of the gulf that separated those who went to war with spirited war-horses, finery, and a full complement of offensive weapons from those who fought on foot or not at all. Similar displays were also present in late medieval and Renaissance Italy and elsewhere throughout the medieval West.[6]

One's military service as a knight depended on one's wealth. The maintenance of a war-horse and weapons was a costly enterprise in the late twelfth century and became even more so in succeeding centuries. Long-distance merchants, successful local traders, and prosperous master craftsmen were among those capable of affording such expenses in places such as Burgos. In towns with little commercial life—Cuéllar, Sepúlveda, Ávila, and other agricultural and ranching communities—income derived from the land or from livestock served to furnish horse and weapons. We must distinguish thus between those knights whose social and military place within the city rested on their commercial endeavors and those whose standing resulted from income derived from the land. Although this dichotomy is somewhat artificial—most successful merchants or their descendants eventually became landholders and abandoned the city and their former trade—there were differences between the two groups. The aristocratization of rural knights or urban knights with incomes from the land was swifter than that of the city-bound bourgeoisie, and the dynamics of political change and social stratification, even the dealings with religious minorities, were different as well. Moreover, in towns such as Ávila, Soria, Salamanca, and Valladolid, founded or resettled late in the eleventh century, the leading families were soon organized in *linajes* (familial clans) of marked noble character. Two such groups dominated the political and economic life of Ávila. In Soria we find as many as twelve *linajes*, while there were two in Segovia, and seven in Salamanca. Two large family groups, the Tovar and the Reoyo (each comprised of five different families) ruled Valladolid.[7]

Unlike the case of Burgos, where some of the dominant families had foreign origins—the descendants of foreign merchants who had settled in the city in the eleventh and twelfth centuries and for whom trade was the road to political and economic power—there is little evidence that similar developments occurred south of the Duero. There, income from farming and ranching provided the backbone for social and political hegemony. But again these distinctions must be tempered. After all, farmers and ranchers still depended on commerce to turn their products into cash. As Adeline Rucquoi has shown, and as the documentation from Ávila demonstrates, members of the elite of Valladolid, Ávila, and other towns were not reluctant to try their hands at commerce if necessary or to invest some of their income from land rents into local and/or long-distance trade.[8]

A further turning point in the fortunes of non-noble knights was marked by the extensive privileges granted to the *caballeros villanos* of most Castilian towns by Alfonso X in 1255 and thereafter. Some of the problems that led the king to grant such generous concessions included an increase in the power of the nobility, the political opposition from Alfonso X's brother, the Infante Enrique, and the restructuring of the Castilian economy due to the conquest of al-Andalus.

Exempted from most taxes were those citizens who owned houses within the city walls and who had horses and weapons fit for combat.

Grazing rights for their livestock, tax exemptions for their servants, and other economic and social benefits altered the relationship between non-noble urban knights and other social groups within Castilian cities. We have direct or indirect evidence of the granting of these privileges to knights in towns and cities throughout northern Castile. This included large urban centers, such as Valladolid, Segovia, Ávila, and Burgos, as well as such small localities as Buitrago, Peñafiel, and other towns that could be best described as large rural enclaves. Knights in commercial centers or in ranching locations, as for example, Cuéllar and Sepúlveda, benefited equally from Alfonso X's generosity and from successive confirmations and extensions of these grants by later kings. Soon, canons and clerics in these same towns, who, after all, often belonged to non-noble knights' families or had been in their youth members of the mounted urban militias, perceived the economic and social significance of these grants and petitioned the king for similar exemptions. Thus, in 1259 Alfonso X exempted forty clerics, "citizens of Ávila and their servants of all taxes, in the same manner enjoyed by the *cavalleros* of Ávila." Similar grants were extended to the clergymen of Cuéllar, Sepúlveda, and elsewhere.[9]

Those *caballeros villanos* who missed out in Alfonso X's first round of privileges were not reluctant to petition the king. In 1282 the city council of Logroño—whose city militia engaged rebellious nobles in the service of the crown again and again—sent two of its representatives, Miguel García and Domingo Velasco, to Alfonso X. They complained that in the past they had had many men with horses and weapons, but such was not the case at present because Logroño's knights had not been exempted from taxes. If the king would deign to grant them such privileges, they would be able to "service and honor" the king. A privilege soon followed, freeing from taxes all those citizens of Logroño who owned houses within the walls, horses, and weapons.[10] Obviously, the city was dominated by non-noble knights, since it is hard to imagine those without houses within the city and without horses and weapons petitioning the king to exempt their betters.

The other side of the coin is, of course, that royal exemption of taxes for the urban patriciate brought important benefits for the crown as well. In the particular case of Logroño the returns were immediate. In 1283, the town's militia wrested the castle of Clavijo from John Alfonso de Haro, one of the magnates in rebellion against the king. The Infante Don Sancho granted the lordship of the castle to the *concejo* of Logroño, which in reality meant that the town was saddled as well with the expense and risk of defending it from the influential and violent Haro family. The Haros were not to be dismissed lightly. John Alfonso was the most important lord in the region and controlled several important strategic areas along Logroño's trade routes. There he made sure that the town's merchants paid tolls, even if they had been exempted by royal privileges.[11]

Alfonso X's privileges to the non-noble urban knights merit a closer look. Almost without exception, the tax privileges to the urban knights were accompanied by a granting—or perhaps we should say imposition—of the *Fuero real* on most Castilian cities. This is not the place to examine the scope of Alfonso X and Sancho IV's legal reforms or the extent of royal interference in the institutional structure of the city.[12] It suffices to say, however, that the widespread concession of economic advantages to the urban mounted militia (with its concomitant social and political benefits) was paralleled by a bold restructuring of municipal law and by a concerted effort to provide a uniform legal code to most urban centers throughout the realm. With its strong debt to Roman legal concepts and to the revival of jurisprudence in twelfth-century Italy, the *Fuero real* defined the duties and qualifications of municipal and royal officials, established ground rules for litigation, set terms for business transactions, wills, donations and other transfers of property, and, above all, extended secular jurisdiction over matters, such as adultery, homosexuality, and even religious transgressions, formerly reserved for ecclesiastical courts. As was to be expected, the *Fuero real* met with stiff resistance throughout the land; yet, the grants to the non-noble knights must be placed within the context of this legal transformation. Its acceptance and implementation in the cities of Castile could not have occurred without the acquiescence and support of urban elites.

Moreover, this radical change in the structure of the Castilian municipalities was not limited to the mid-thirteenth century. In the following decades, the crown sought to further its control over urban centers—whenever political conditions allowed for it and not always without resistance from some urban elites—until the royal will was imposed on cities throughout the land.

We must return, however, to the matter at hand, that is, the privileges granted to the urban knights. A closer examination of a few of them reveals small but significant differences, and they tell us a great deal about the peculiarities of each locality. There is much one can learn from a close reading of these charters, above all, that sweeping generalizations, including my own, are essentially misleading. Although a large number of these privileges—those to the *caballeros* of Segovia, Burgos, Buitrago, Peñafiel, and other towns in northern Castile—were granted to non-noble knights,

in New Castile and Andalucía urban noble knights received similar concessions. Alfonso X bestowed the same advantages already enjoyed by the
lower nobility (*fijosdalgo*) of Toledo to the noble knights settling in Arcos
de la Frontera in 1268. At the same time, the non-noble knights of Arcos
received rights similar to those of their counterparts in Seville. In the latter
city, the distinctions between noble and non-noble knights turned on an
exception from *moneda forera* (in theory a tax paid every seven years for
preservation of the coinage). Both groups were exempted: the former's
privilege depended on blood and place in the social order, the latter's on the
possession of horses and weapons. Nevertheless, the prohibition to confis-
cate the horses of non-noble knights because of debts and the extension of
tax exemption to their widows and surviving children (up to the ages of
sixteen or eighteen depending on the region), and further concessions
throughout the next century eventually turned the non-noble knights into a
hereditary and, by now, noble group: their position was no longer subordinated to their military role.[13]

In most Andalusi cities, noble and non-noble knights shared the risks
and profits of frontier war, political power, and social status on a more or
less equal basis before 1350. In most urban centers of Old Castile, on the
other hand, mercantile groups as well as those urban elites deriving their
income from ranching and farming were able to keep the nobility at bay. By
the early fourteenth century they were, for all practical purposes, indis-
tinguishable from the vast class of *hijosdalgo* (lesser nobility). This blurring
of distinctions is not difficult to understand. Both groups dressed and
behaved in similar fashion, served as cavalry, and, at times, shared the same
political aims: to neutralize magnate violence and excesses.[14]

As we have already seen, in villages throughout northern Castile,
hijosdalgo and farmers often joined in litigation against their common lord.
But, surely, in rural Castile distinctions between the lower nobility and the
peasantry must have been evident. In towns, especially in places such as
Sepúlveda, Cuéllar, and Ávila, where both noble and non-noble knights
made their living from land rents and livestock, the differences between
both groups must have been minimal. In a sense, the conflict between Peter
I and Henry of Trastámara in the late 1350s and early 1360s was a watershed.
The dynamics of civil war, economic change, and the emergence of a new
magnate group led to a further aristocratization of urban life in the late
fourteenth century. The new nature of warfare, with its dependence on
mercenary and foreign troops, also led to a decline in the military role of
urban oligarchs. Their position, therefore, came to depend increasingly on
their economic and social standing and on birth.[15]

The comparison I have drawn above between the lower nobility and the urban patriciate is that of two groups that were already not very different. That certainly was not the case with the magnates. They constituted a world unto themselves. Their power helps explain somewhat the political connections between the other two groups. The lower nobility— seldom well-off, dependent on jobs in the royal armies or bureaucracy, unless they were in the service of great noblemen and fed from magnate rapacity—understood well the aspirations of non-noble urban elites. The *hijosdalgo* married freely with urban oligarchs and often were their allies against the excesses of the upper aristocracy or of the regents. One hundred and two of these *hijosdalgo* joined the procurators from the cities of northern Castile in the *Hermandad* or League of 1315 to protect the crown and urban interests during the troubled minority of Alfonso XI. Some of them, García Lasso de la Vega, John Martínez de Leyva, Diego Gómez de Sandoval, and others, later figured prominently among Alfonso XI's officials. One of them, Gonzalo Díaz, was *alcalde* of Talavera, showing how urban nobles were also capable of assuming municipal offices. Talavera is located south of the Guadarrama and, like Toledo and the Andalusi cities, beyond the geographical boundaries of this study; but we also have evidence from northern Castile as to the willingness of the lower nobility to settle in towns—or perhaps I should say the willingness of the crown to provide incentives for such settlement. In 1273, to cite just one example, Alfonso X granted tax exemptions to *hijosdalgo* willing to settle in the *puebla* of Vergara, a new settlement on the trade route between Vitoria and San Sebastián.[16]

I do not need to emphasize again the impact which the gradual aristocratization of the Castilian bourgeoisie had on the social, political, and economic structures of northern Castilian towns. Growing social and economic differences within individual cities led to conflict between those who had horses and armor and those who did not. This internecine fighting between the rising urban oligarchy and the petty bourgeoisie would not come fully to a head until the 1320s and 1330s, but the charters of tax exemption crystallized and defined the boundaries of enmities. Although it is quite difficult to describe these antagonisms for an earlier period, they probably had been on the rise since the late twelfth century. And it was not just the tax exemption—which must have seemed utterly unfair to those who paid—but the patriciate's display of their well-being, their aping of the nobility, their social exclusiveness, which led to deeper divisions within urban society.

In this sense, the example of Escalona, a small town on the road from

Ávila to Toledo, shows the swift impact the charters had on civic relations. On 5 March 1261, Alfonso X granted the *Fuero real* to the *villa* of Escalona and extended the town's civil and criminal jurisdiction over the surrounding countryside, while at the same time carefully defining the boundaries of Escalona with the *alfoces* or jurisdictions of nearby towns. This was followed by the charter exempting from taxes those with horses worth more than 30 *mrs.* and owning shields, lances, swords, and armor. In addition, the knights of Escalona were expected to own and inhabit houses within the city from at least eight days before Christmas to the feast of Saint John the Baptist. A detailed series of further privileges followed, providing tax exemptions for the knights' livestock and for their servants. These differed from those found in the charters granted to the knights of northern Castilian towns, thereby serving as further evidence of the economic foundations of Escalona's patriciate. Three months later, on 23 June 1261, Alfonso X responded to the complaints of the good men (who in this case were *not* members of the knightly groups) of Escalona. These *omes buenos* had protested against those who, without meeting all the prerequisites for knightly status, still claimed exemption from taxes. Moreover, they requested the king's protection from the abuses perpetrated by the *alcaldes* and the *caballeros* of Escalona against nearby villages.

In the 1260s the *concejo* of Escalona still included people other than the knights, but their power was on the wane and they had, as their only recourse, to appeal to the crown to check the ambitions of the rising non-noble knightly group. Access to *caballero* status was most desirable, and one can see from Alfonso X's letter how many urban dwellers, whose income placed them in between the two social groups, sought to claim membership in the *caballería villana* and thus exemption from taxes. This, of course, meant a further reduction of the tax rolls and an added burden on the *omes buenos* or *pecheros*: those lower-middling citizens and inhabitants of Escalona who shouldered the brunt of taxation. Furthermore, Alfonso X's letter of June 1261 reveals to us the abuses which the well-to-do—especially those on horseback and wearing armor—committed against the rural population of medieval Castile. The king, therefore, emphasized once again the need to comply with the *alarde*, the annual showing of horses and armor on 1 March, as well as a tighter control of the activities of the knights.

Three years later, in 1264, the knights and good men of Escalona petitioned the king for the right to name their own *alcaldes* and *justicia*. With the king's assent, Johan de Coca and Gonzalo, the son of Martín Rodrigo, were named *alcaldes*, and Gil Ponce was appointed *justicia*. The

document does not provide any clues to the dynamics of political development in the town. Had the knights of Escalona gained the upper hand and
monopolized municipal offices? Was there a compromise between *caballeros*
and good men to divide political power within the locality? Alfonso X's
rather plaintive letter to the council of Escalona five years later reveals,
however, the kind of urban violence with which one is well-acquainted in
medieval Italian urban history, but for which there is little evidence in
Castile. The conflict, however, was no longer between knights and non-
knights, but rather between factions of *caballeros*, including nobles, who
fought for a larger share of the income from town taxes. Alfonso X's
solution, to divide them into two groups (excepting the vassals of the
magnates), each one every other year (in turns) collecting two-thirds of all
the taxes for their own profit, reveals the swift rise of cavalrymen, noble and
non-noble, to political and social prominence. Moreover, the king encouraged them to attend the town's festivities and weddings with their horses
and lances, a display of their privileges that further emphasized social
distinctions.[17]

The charters to Escalona, as well as those granted to other towns
throughout Castile, provide further clues as to the social and economic
structure of urban life. All the privileges emphasized the obligation of the
knights to own and maintain a house within the town walls. One expects
that anyone wealthy enough to afford a war-horse and full armor could also
keep a town house. Ownership of property was the first qualification for
urban citizenship (*vecinaje*). Indeed, purchase of a house within the town
walls was often the first step toward admission to the ranks of citizens, with
all the concomitant rights to the use of the commons and assorted legal
privileges. In Burgos and elsewhere, profitable land purchases outside the
city walls were often followed by the acquisition of more expensive urban
property and admission to citizenship.

There is, however, another important aspect to this residence requirement. On this issue the charters differed. In Burgos, Cuéllar, Peñafiel,
Buitrago, and other places, the knights had to reside in town at least from
eight days before Christmas to eight days after Quinquagesima Sunday. At
Escalona, as we have seen, this period extended as far as 23 June, while the
charter to the knights of Valladolid—which was granted in 1295, forty years
after the initial privileges—did not have any time limits. One can gather
from this the intimate relationship between town and country. Even in
commercially oriented cities such as Burgos, the ruling knight elite owned
land in the surrounding countryside and, seemingly, preferred to live out-

side the city rather than in town houses. The period during which residence was required coincided roughly with those of lessened agricultural activity or reduced livestock migration. During harvest time, the high point of the agricultural cycle, all those who had a stake in the countryside wished to be present in their lands, confirming the strong rural orientation of most northern Castilian towns, even those that had a strong commercial life. It could be argued that the city is never a favorite residence for the rich during hot summers. Alternating between rural (summer) and urban (the rest of the year) is a common pattern in most of Spain to this day. The village of my relatives, almost deserted through most of the year, fills with families from June to September, when gardens and fruit trees are once again carefully tended.

Elsewhere in medieval Castile, the demands of urban life went even further. In 1254 Alfonso X expanded the *fuero* of Treviño. In his letter, the king insisted once more that the citizens dwell within the town walls from fifteen days after Saint Michael's Day until Easter. From March to 29 September—although they were allowed to be absent during the day—the citizens of Treviño had the obligation to spend their nights in town.[18]

We must not be surprised by this royal interest in urban life. Towns throughout northern Castile, regardless of size and of the absence of any Muslim threat, were busily erecting or improving their walls after the 1250s. Urban centers often stood as bastions of royal power against noble rebellions; furthermore, the crown probably found it easier to collect taxes and to muster military contingents from urban centers than from dispersed rural settlements. Sometimes, of course, the latter could not be avoided.

In Segovia, with its vast hinterland, the privileges granted the non-noble knights included not only those with houses within the walls, but also those with horses and weapons in the villages under Segovia's jurisdiction. In this particular case, political development followed a somewhat different path. Although in Segovia a few influential families eventually gained control of the city's political and religious life (while investing heavily in the adjacent countryside), the non-noble rural knights retained a certain amount of input into the political decision-making process. They sent procurators to the meeting of the *Hermandad* in 1315 and were included, if only enjoying a minority representation, in the *regimiento* of 1345.[19]

The privileges granted to the non-noble knights also laid the foundations for a hereditary elite. Economic and political privileges were dependent on the maintenance of horse and weapons, but widows as well as children up to the age of sixteen or even eighteen were allowed to retain their status in the expectation of future service. The crown expanded these and other, similar privileges—such as forbidding the confiscation of horses because of outstanding debts—throughout the next hundred years, thus guaranteeing the knights their privileged position even in the face of financial adversity.[20] By following these policies the crown promoted its own interests, since the grants were aimed at keeping a fairly reliable and ready contingent of mounted soldiers.

In this respect, the importance of the charters of tax exemption of the mid-thirteenth century lies in the fact that they sought to rationalize a long-standing policy of promoting and maintaining mounted urban militias, rather than in any radical innovation of the urban social order. For quite a long time the kings of Castile had pursued these ends in specific localities, either through *fueros* or local privileges. The non-noble knights of Soria, to mention one instance, were granted a charter in 1256, but they had long benefited from special considerations. In 1285, Sancho IV confirmed an ancient privilege of Alfonso VIII which bound the kings of Castile to provide, on the first year of their rule, enough shields, harnesses, lances, saddles, and other equipment to fit one hundred cavalrymen chosen from the twelve *linajes* (lineages) of Soria.[21]

This concession, renewed on the ascent of each new king, enhanced the power of the twelve family groups within Soria, making their position, to a certain extent, independent of their economic status. Sancho IV's confirmation of this privilege reveals to us the lasting grip of these twelve family groups on Soria. Their fiscal exemption and judicial advantages dated back to the resettlement of the city in the early phases of the Christian advance on the Duero valley; they were further enhanced in the late twelfth century by Alfonso VIII's lavish concession of horses and weapons, and successively reconfirmed by later kings. It also gives us a starting point from which to calculate the number of knights in Soria, one of the few places in the peninsula for which we have some reliable data on population so early on. Of the 777 *vecinos* or citizens that Esther Jimeno has calculated for Soria in 1270, probably more than one hundred were *caballeros*. Together with their wives, children, and retainers, they constituted a large percentage of Soria's estimated total population of around 4,000 inhabitants.[22]

Their strength, however, resided in more than just numbers. The few documents extant for Soria in this period offer glimpses of *caballeros* serving as *alcaldes* and judges in the city and actively policing and enforcing the regulations of the town's guilds. In Soria, weavers, muleteers, and other tradesmen had organized themselves quite early and quite well by Castilian standards, but a *caballero maior* (one of the main knights) of the city council kept a watchful eye on their activities. By 1290 Sancho IV increased the number of knightly overseers to two. As indicated above, the knights of Soria seem to have reached a compromise, at least in the thirteenth and early fourteenth centuries, with the good men (probably the aforementioned merchants, muleteers, and weavers). Men from the *común* (commons) and from the villages around the town had a minority representation in the delegation sent to Burgos for the formation of the *Hermandad* of 1315.[23]

We must again underline the political changes that led Alfonso X to grant extensive rights to the urban knights. Troubled by noble violence, by the rebellion of one of his own brothers (the Infante Enrique) and, later on, his son Sancho, Alfonso X granted privileges granted to the *caballería villana*, while also promoting forcefully the fortification of towns throughout Castile. One policy paralleled the other, pointing to the king's long-term planning. Wherever we turn, city walls were being improved, rebuilt, or enhanced at high cost to both the royal treasury and the cities. From Burgos, where Alfonso X granted the income of the *alcabala* (sales tax) to subsidize the building efforts, to Roa, where in 1295 the construction of the wall still went on amid bitter strife between the town and the surrounding villages whose inhabitants were forced to work for free, the ruling knightly elites and the crown sought, not always successfully, to dot the realm with fortified cities.[24] It is within this context that the promotion of non-noble knights and their eventual absorption into the lower nobility went hand in hand with their economic, social, and political hegemony.

Economic Power and Social Prominence

We must conclude this examination of the privileges granted to the urban knights by outlining the variations that permit us to observe the diversity of economic and social conditions found in Castilian cities. Although earlier charters of exemption to the *caballeros villanos* were, on the whole, fairly uniform, later ones, such as that granted to the non-noble knights of Valladolid, took into account the pastoral interests of the ruling urban elite. One clear indication of this economic orientation toward pastoral and ranching activities, at least during this period, can be gathered from the prominent role played by Jewish merchants and shopkeepers in the Valladolid documents. As in Ávila, the Jewish neighborhood in Valladolid was adjacent to the main market of the city. In 1283 Doña Franca, the widow of Yago Verrox, and her children sold three *corrales* and twelve stores (*tiendas*) on the street of the Old Synagogue for 800 *mrs*. Jewish contributions in head taxes amounted to 69,520 *mrs*. in the late thirteenth century, in further evidence of their numerical importance.[25]

Without the beneficial influence of the road to Santiago de Compostela, Christian commercial activity lagged behind in the valley of the Duero and in the areas between Burgos and the Central Sierras. By the late twelfth and early thirteenth centuries, when Andalusi trade connections promised good incentives for mercantile activities, knightly oligarchical groups must have been well entrenched in specific economic activities. We must assume that the non-noble knights of Valladolid, although not entirely reluctant to engage in trade or to accept into their ranks those who did, derived most of their income from land rents and from livestock. We can gather as much from the charter of 1265. In it the king, after closely following the pattern of previous charters, proceeded to spell out the different exemptions conferred on knights owning more than one hundred cows, between one hundred and one thousand sheep, or more than the latter figure. Knights with more than twenty mares, with between one hundred and one thousand beehives, or with one hundred pigs benefited from tax exemptions for their servants. In addition the king granted to them the right to fence pasturelands in their rural holdings, so long as this activity did not harm the economic well-being of nearby villages. These concessions and those of a similar nature granted to Cuéllar confirm the varied economic bases of knightly power. Although the tax-exemption grants to the knights of Burgos, Segovia, and elsewhere also contained rights of pasture and exemption for sheepherders and other rural laborers in the service of knights, it is also clear from them that ownership of livestock in those towns did not play the same role it did in Valladolid.[26]

If the economic basis of knightly power differed somewhat in the early thirteenth century, the desire for social distinction and political and ecclesiastical hegemony within the city and the surrounding countryside did not. Wherever we have extant evidence, we see the knights organizing into brotherhoods. At first, these social groupings were not too restrictive, but by the mid-fourteenth century they began to exclude those without horses and weapons from their ranks. In Valladolid, the knights had formed brotherhoods quite early, giving evidence, as Armando Represa has pointed out, of their corporative spirit. Among these fraternities we find those of Esgueva, Casas, Corral (1182), Rehoyo (1188), Castellanos (1208), and Cuadra (1255), which, identified by the family name rather than by their patron saints, gathered large family groups or clans, as well as those with political and economic affinities. The early dates of these brotherhoods (*cofradías*) of knights points to the uneven character of urban elite formation in northern Castile: early in Ávila and Valladolid, late in Vitoria and Logroño.[27]

In Burgos, where admission to knightly status depended to a large extent on wealth generated by trade or artisanal pursuits, the evidence points to a much later date for the emergence of sharp social distinctions. Yet, even there, the process took almost one hundred years and, moreover, access to *caballero* status in this period was never a closed affair. The city offers a valuable model for social change within other northern Castilian cities.

In Burgos two *cofradías*, Our Lady of Gamonal and the Real Hermandad, served as vehicles for the segregation of those of lower social standing or economic position in the period between the early thirteenth century and 1338. The extant rules of both brotherhoods and their membership lists provide valuable information on the social structure of the city, as well as a convenient census of the number of knights in Burgos between 1305 and 1338. "The first of these brotherhoods, Our Lady of Gamonal [also known as the brotherhood of non-noble knights], was founded in 1285 by Don Miguel Estevan and his wife Doña Ucenda Prestines." The latter was a member of the Prestines family (we have already met a member of this family, Giralt de Prestines, as an importer of Flemish cloth into Castile). The rules of the brotherhood

> described the festivities peculiar to the organization, set the amount of the admission fee (2 *mrs.* and a pound of wax) and established procedures for the funerals of members and their families. . . . In 1305 Our Lady of Gamonal had ninety-nine members with their occupations or trades listed, in most cases, next to their names. Two members of the Bonifaz family—the most important *caballero* family in the city—headed the membership list, followed by knights from other important families. All the *alcaldes* of the city in 1305 were members of the brotherhood, as well as former and future officials of the city council.[28]

Although one cannot claim that all the knights of Burgos belonged to the brotherhood of Our Lady of Gamonal or that all those listed were knights, this first documented attempt at grouping the city officials and merchants of the city into a semi-exclusive confraternity was a sure step toward social differentiation. The final step toward the emergence of the knights as a distinctive group came with the foundation of a new brotherhood, the Real Hermandad or Real Cofradía del Santísimo y Santiago: "Founded by Alfonso XI in 1338 [a non-nobiliary counterpart to his order of La Banda] the Real Hermandad explicitly excluded those who did not possess fighting horses and weapons, restricting membership to those who had the proper equipment and belonged to the right families." The brotherhood of Our Lady of Gamonal did not disappear, and one must assume that most knights retained membership in both *cofradías*. The early brotherhood kept them in touch with the commercial pulse of the city and brought them into contact with representatives of the petty bourgeoisie and the trades, while the Real Hermandad allowed them to enhance further their social aspirations.

In open imitation of the noble military order of Santiago, the beautiful depictions of most of the members which accompany the original charter of 1338 show conclusively how difficult it was to differentiate them from the nobility. By the mid-fourteenth century, the principal families of Burgos already displayed proudly their coat of arms.[29] (See Figure 3.) In their ostentatious behavior, the non-noble knights of Burgos followed a pattern already common to other towns in Castile and elsewhere in thirteenth- and fourteenth-century Europe. In Ávila, Valladolid, and other localities, neighborhoods were beginning to be segregated not only by religion but also according to social and economic status. In Burgos, the non-noble knights resided exclusively in a few streets around the cathedral and the main square of the city—the religious, political, and commercial centers of the town.[30]

SOCIAL DISTINCTIONS: HOUSING AND CIVIC DISPLAYS
We must return here to a point raised earlier only in passing but which deserves closer examination. Social differentiation was not only enforced by exclusive confraternities, it was also a manifestation of everyday life. Knights, noble and non-noble, had from early on claimed the best houses and neighborhoods in their respective cities. The privileges granted to the non-noble knights of the mid-thirteenth century already mentioned the *casas mayores* (great houses), and we find these knights owning or purchasing expensive urban property. In an earlier chapter we have already seen the evidence for a high-priced urban real-estate market; individual examples also confirm this. In 1228 Ramón Bonifaz, who later led the naval siege of Seville (1248), and his cousin Guiralt Almeric invested 6,000 *mrs.* in build-

Figure 3. Non-noble knights of the Cofradía de la Real Hermandad or del Santísimo y Santiago (1338). (Archivo municipal de Burgos; photo by the author)

ing houses in the neighborhood of Sanct Llorente in Burgos. The price is so outrageously high for the period that one might conclude that the houses must have been palatial.[31] In Ávila, where a 1303 census of property owned by the chapter provides partial information on the distribution of the population throughout the city, we can see certain areas in which most of the houses either had been donated by knights or were inhabited by them. A present-day street of the *caballeros* may be a reminder of its former habitation by knights.[32]

The houses of the urban oligarchs stood in marked contrast to those of other groups within the cities. Kings, queens, and important visitors were not reluctant to seek accommodation in these dwellings. In Segovia, where some of the houses of the urban patriciate of the fifteenth and sixteenth centuries still stand, one can catch a glimpse of the past. It would not be too far-fetched to draw similarities here to Italy, where powerful aristocratic and mercantile clans built their proud towers as bastions and symbols of their power. Indeed, in northern Castilian towns frictions existed not only between different social groups—exempted knights and taxpayers (*pecheros*)—but also within the ruling patrician groups. Thus, in Segovia the membership of the *regimiento* of 1345 consisted of five representatives from each of the ruling lineages, two from the *pecheros* and three from the inhabitants of the Segovian hinterland.[33] Alfonso XI's compromise nominations sought, probably, to end factional struggles between the two ruling groups, between knights and taxpayers, between city and country. In the end, however, the houses of the *caballeros* were bigger, easier to defend; they towered over the humble dwellings of the common.

Furthermore, the charters provide additional evidence as to the possible size of these households. We know that the non-noble knights, or at least a good number of them, kept a rather large number of servants and retainers. Although most of them worked the lands of the urban knights outside the city or tended to their flocks, there is also evidence for servants living in knightly houses. In Burgos the family group of Bonifaz-Prestines owned and occupied at least eleven houses in a two-block area of the street of Sanct Llorente. Together with their families and servants, they must have constituted a distinctive presence on the street.[34]

Unlike most modern cities, sprawling and densely populated, where neighborhoods are often carefully segregated by class or race, northern Castilian towns and cities, with populations ranging from 4,000 to 10,000 inhabitants, contained non-noble knights and the poor in close proximity, mixing daily in the bustle and squalor of commercial streets and in churches and civic festivals. It is not too difficult to see why the knights sought to group in exclusive brotherhoods and to emphasize the distinctions among those who rode through the streets of the city on the day of the *alarde* and on holidays and weddings. They paraded with their multicolored garments of imported cloth, their spirited horses, their lances, their shields. What feelings did they evoke among the urban poor, among the lower-middling groups? We do not know fully, for the evidence on this matter is mostly literary.[35]

There are indications, however, of growing resentment at the displays of these urban elites and of growing antagonism between rich and poor in city and country alike.[36] In the *Dance of Death*, the merchant laments his own coming death and plaintively wonders to whom he would leave his wealth. His fortune, the harsh poem reminds us, has been earned by trickery and transgressions, and Death admonishes him to worry no longer about crossing to Flanders, but to stay quietly and examine Death's wares: the buboes and lacerations of the plague. Noble authors—Don Juan Manuel and Pedro López de Ayala, among others—could not avoid their contempt for these bourgeois upstarts and for their noble pretensions.[37]

Yet, within the walls of towns throughout northern Castile and in the surrounding countryside, these urban oligarchical groups ruled. They and their wives and children, dressed in fashionable garments of colors and fabrics forbidden to those below them, were living representations of the growing gulf between those above and those below. Not surprisingly, in towns where their wealth did not derive from land rents or ranching, the urban knights acquired rural holdings at an increasing pace from the 1250s onward. Knightly status and land purchases or estate building went hand in hand in the social promotion of the urban knights to noble status. Similarly, political power—both the political influence of a few individuals and families within the city and the corporate sway of the city over its hinterland—is partly to be explained by the intrusion of urban wealth into the countryside.[38]

Urban Oligarchies and the Town's Hinterland

These developments have important implications. We must remember that from an early period urban knights often divided their time between town and country. The charters reveal as much, and this seasonal pattern of habitation was a fact of life even in essentially commercial cities such as Burgos. Thus, to give just one example, from the twelfth century on, the Sarracín family—which for more than a century dominated the economic, political, and ecclesiastical life of Burgos—acquired extensive holdings in and around Burgos.[39] The pattern of land buying in the thirteenth and fourteenth centuries was very clear. The apparent random and fragmented purchase of land of an earlier period was now replaced by a rational effort to consolidate holdings into unified and more easily managed estates. In these efforts, the bourgeoisie moved more swiftly and with more decisiveness than ecclesiastical corporations with their still dispersed and inefficient estates. Moreover, knightly investment in land aimed at maximizing profits by concentrating their investments on either vineyards or on urban property, both of which were capable of bringing good returns. The initial distinctions between urban knights in rurally oriented towns and urban knights in commercial centers tended to be less pronounced after 1300. By then, both types of ruling urban groups had an important stake in the rural world. By the same token, when the status of *caballero* was almost always accompanied by ownership of rural property, the distinctions between lower nobility and non-noble knights were, for all practical purposes, no longer relevant.

We must attempt to visualize these knights returning after the harvest to their town houses, bringing with them a haul of grain and wine (which, to add insult to injury, they could bring into the city for their own use free of taxes), filling their barns and cellars to the brim, supplied throughout the year with meats, cheeses, and honey from their farms nearby. The Sarracíns, to return to our earlier example, had extensive estates in Villatoro, a mere ten kilometers north of Burgos. Exempted from the daily struggle for bread, these *caballeros*, both noble and non-noble, dressed and ate differently from the rest of the population. Nor were they as vulnerable as small landholders and tenant farmers were to the vicissitudes of bad harvests and inclement weather. Commercial profits and connections assured them of survival. And in times of pestilence and epidemic, it was easy for them to escape to the relative security of their farms.

Urban Oligarchies: The Church and the Land

The extant records of land transactions, above all, the records of the purchases made by urban oligarchs, from the late twelfth into the fourteenth century also provide evidence for the close relationship between holding office, either in municipal or royal government or in the Church, and landowning. I have made this point repeatedly in previous pages, but it is worth stating again. Those with knightly ambitions sought to dominate every important office, secular and spiritual, within the city and to exercise influence in the wider setting of the realm as well. By the mid-thirteenth century and in succeeding years, members of prominent non-noble knightly families—often university-trained, as their titles indicate—captured many of the important benefices in cathedral and collegiate churches throughout northern Castile. In some towns, such as Burgos and Ávila, they were elected to the deanship of their chapters and even became serious contenders for the episcopate.

One can discern a certain pattern in the lives of some of these knights, at least for those with a commercial background. They often began their climb to prominence as merchants abroad, in their youth making perilous journeys to English and Flemish commercial centers. This was followed by a stint in municipal and royal service, which coincided with investments in the land and real-estate markets. Later in life we may find some of them, especially those who had lost their wives, as archdeacons, archpriests, canons, and even deans. Clearly, in many cases an ecclesiastical benefice was a royal reward for services rendered to the crown. In Castile, where kings kept a tight rein on the church, the assignment of ecclesiastical plums to aging royal servants was a common practice, as it was in other medieval kingdoms. Yet this was not always the case, and assignment to a canonry or a deanship was also directly related to one's economic and social standing within the city. Thus Pedro Sarracín, a widower with a university degree, the son and brother of *alcaldes* of the city and of important landholders in the region, was a likely candidate for a profitable ecclesiastical benefice. For all their assumption of a clerical state, their subsequent investment—in this particular case, that of Pedro Sarracín—reveals the continuity of family designs and not a newfound piety. Most of these urban oligarchs, now in the church, could not avoid the pious donation, but, with a few exceptions, the interests of the familial clan came first.

My previous work on Burgos shows in detail the activities of some of these knights, above all, those of Pedro Sarracín and Pedro Bonifaz in the market for land and in their ecclesiastical careers. In both instances, the acquisitions were not made to further the well-being of the church (the cathedral of Burgos) but, essentially, for their own and their families' benefit. I am inclined to think that the misfortunes that befell the Castilian church in the late Middle Ages and its mounting economic ills, vividly depicted by Peter Linehan, were due as much to royal extortion as they were to this privatization of church wealth and the redirecting of ecclesiastical income—certainly in the case of Burgos, Ávila, Segovia, and Salaman-ca—to private ends.[40]

There are many examples of evidence for this assertion; a few of these will suffice here. Above, we have already examined the activities of Blasco Blázquez and referred to the purchases made by Pedro Sarracín and Pedro Bonifaz. In these three instances, we deal with members of the most powerful families of Ávila and Burgos. What has been written about them, however, can also be said about less influential men. Such was the case of Master Sancho in Ávila. In 1329 he purchased *algos* in Castellanillos, near Ávila, for 300 *mrs*. By 1334 Sancho was already prebendary of the cathedral of Ávila, and four years later he is mentioned as archdeacon of Olmedo. In 1341, the last entry extant on Master Sancho records his purchase of a vineyard in Vellacos for 30 *mrs*. He died sometime before October 1341. For the period between 1329 and 1341 we have eighteen extant transactions recording his purchases of lands, houses, vineyards, and even a row in a garden for the minuscule amount of 6.5 *mrs*. Ten of these acquisitions took place in the village of Vellacos, where he concentrated his investments from 1334 on. He also bought two houses in Ávila proper and land elsewhere in Ávila's hinterland. Altogether he invested about 5,900 *mrs*, with most of the expense concentrated on a large purchase of land and two teams of oxen in the village of Muño Sancho.[41]

When we turn to knights who did not enter the church, it is also easy to illustrate the seignorialization of the urban hinterlands. In Burgos, even those without important family connections—people such as Martín Mar-tínez, a butcher, Pedro Pérez, and Sancho García, a goldsmith—were able to invest profitably in the land market and, thus, to rise to a higher social rank. Whenever financial conditions permitted it, artisans and merchants invested their money in land with an alacrity that did not speak well of their urban vocation. The census of property of Ávila (1303) is filled with the names of petty bourgeois and artisans who rented or bought property outside the walls of the city.

In the region of Segovia, we have already seen the example of Miguel Pérez, a citizen and inhabitant of Oter de Herreros. Between 30 October 1341 and 24 November 1358, he bought houses, hemp fields, vineyards, and land in Oter de Herreros. The size of the land purchased, seldom more than one or two *obradas*, and the prices paid indicate the modesty of these transactions as compared to those examined above, but also reveal that rational desire, found elsewhere in this period, to concentrate property within a certain region.

One could go on piling up examples of the way in which those above monopolized political and ecclesiastical offices, purchased lands and houses, and, by excessive display, represented their power to others in the city. However, we must turn now to those below, to those who seldom bought anything or commanded any civic responsibility, but instead bore on their shoulders the burden of those above.

Notes

1. Although my approach may be thought of as Marxist (which I am not), I have purposely avoided the term "class" throughout the text. In truth, in Castile and elsewhere in the medieval West there were already stirrings of what may be called class conflict. Yet most Castilians thought of themselves as members of an order and not a "class" in the sense in which the term is understood today. There is, of course, a strong current in Castilian medieval historiography that seeks to explain the history of the region in terms of class. See, for example, the works of Julio Valdeón Baruque, Salustiano Moreta Velayos, and others cited below.

2. Teofilo F. Ruiz, "The Transformation of the Castilian Municipalities," 3–32; "Expansion et changement," 548–65. For other cities, see below.

3. See Henri Pirenne, *Medieval Cities: Their Origins and the Revival of Trade* (Princeton, N.J.: Princeton University Press, 1969), 227–28; Fritz Rörig, *The Medieval Town* (Berkeley: University of California Press, 1967), 90–91, 161–73; for Castile, see James F. Powers, *A Society Organized for War: The Iberian Municipal Militias in the Central Middle Ages, 1000–1284* (Berkeley: University of California Press, 1988).

4. Infante Don Juan Manuel, *Libro de los estados* (Madrid: Biblioteca de autores españoles, vol. 51, 1952), 337; José R. Araluce Cuenca, *El libro de los estados: Don Juan Manuel y la sociedad de su tiempo* (Madrid: Ediciones José Porrua Turanzos, S.A., 1976), 102–11.

5. See Elena Lourie, "A Society Organized for War: Medieval Spain," *Past & Present* 35 (1966): 54–76; Powers, *A Society Organized for War*, 136–61; AHN, Códices 106B, ff. 187–205a; for Ávila, see below.

6. On the types of armor and horses, see Powers, *A Society Organized for War*, 126–34; AMB, clasif. 1391 (12-October-1252). For displays in a later period, see Teofilo F. Ruiz, "Festivités, couleurs et symboles du pouvoir en Castille au XVe siècle: Les célébrations de mai 1428," *Annales E.S.C.* 3 (1991): 521–46; and Ruiz, "Elite and Popular Culture in Late Fifteenth Century Castilian Festivals: The Case of Jaén" (forthcoming from the University of Minnesota Press).

7. Asenjo González, *Segovia: La ciudad y su tierra*, 285–95; Adeline Rucquoi, *Valladolid en la edad media*, 1: 236–67; Manuel González García, *Salamanca en la baja edad media* (Salamanca: Universidad de Salamanca, 1982), 101–9. González García identifies non-noble knights as part of the nobility. Such was not the case in the thirteenth and early fourteenth centuries. See Barrios García, *Estructuras agrarias y de poder*, 2: 133–54; for Soria, see below.

8. Rucquoi, *Valladolid en la edad media*, 1: 243–53; for Ávila, see Chapter 7.

9. On the privileges to the *caballeros villanos*, see Carmela Pescador, "La caballería popular en León y Castilla," *CHE* 33–34 (1961): 101–238; 35–36 (1962): 156–201; 37–38 (1963): 88–198; 39–40 (1964): 169–260; Ruiz, "The Transformation of the Castilian Municipalities," 7–9; *MHE*, 1: nos. 43, 44–45, 48 (clerics in Ávila), 102, 109, 132, et passim. *Sepúlveda*, 1: 34–40; *Cuéllar*, no. 21.

10. AHN, Microfilm, Caja 1, rollo 12925, no. 8 (2-January-1282).

11. AHN, Microfilm, Caja 1, rollo 12925, nos. 12 (17-July-1283); no. 17 (16-December-1288): John Alfonso de Haro had the right to collect the *portazgo* in Logroño, Calahorra, Arnedo, Agreda, Berlanga, Alfaro, and other places. He attempted to collect them from the municipal council of Logroño even though the *concejo* had a royal exemption from *portazgo*.

12. On Alfonso X's legal reforms, see the insightful synthesis by Joseph F. O'Callaghan, "Image and Reality: The King Creates His Kingdom," in *Emperor of Culture: Alfonso X the Learned of Castile and His Thirteenth-Century Renaissance*, ed. Robert I. Burns (Philadelphia: University of Pennsylvania Press, 1990), 14–32. See also Joseph F. O'Callaghan, *The Learned King: The Reign of Alfonso X of Castile* (Philadelphia: University of Pennsylvania Press, 1993). See Ruiz, "The Transformation of Castilian Municipalities," 8, n. 22.

13. *MHE*, 1: no. 109, 240–41 (27-January-1268); no. 132, 292–93 (3-June-1273). For the privileges to the widows and children of *caballeros* see *Cuéllar*, doc. no. 16 (21-July-1256); *Cortes*, 1: 518 (Ordenamiento de Alcalá de Henares).

14. On fashions of dress, see illustrations to the rules of the *cofradía* del Santísimo y Santiago of Burgos (1338).

15. On the Castilian civil war and the transformation of Castilian society during the reigns of Peter I and Henry II, see Julio Valdeón Baruque, *Enrique II de Castilla: la guerra civil y la consolidación del régimen (1336–1371)* (Valladolid: Universidad de Valladolid, 1966); for the rise of a new nobility, see Salvador de Moxó, "De la nobleza vieja a la nobleza nueva: La transformación nobiliaria castellana en el siglo XIV," *Cuadernos de Historia: Anexos de Hispania* 3 (1969): 1–271. For the development of noble urban elites after 1350, see Casado Alonso, *Señores, mercaderes y campesinos*, 451–510; Asenjo González, *Segovia: La ciudad y su tierra*, 263–99. See also below.

16. The list of knights joining the *Hermandad* of 1315 is found in *Cortes*, 1: 261–63; for officials of Alfonso XI, see Salvador de Moxó, "La sociedad política castellana en la baja edad media de Alfonso XI," *Cuadernos de Historia: Anexos de Hispania* 6 (1975): 187–326. See also below for García Lasso de la Vega and other officials. *MHE*, 1: no. 131, 292.

17. For the entire discussion on Escalona, see *MHE*, 1: nos. 83, 175–80; no. 86, 187–90; no. 94, 210ff.

18. *MHE*, 1: 23, 44–50; no. 24, 52–53.

19. On the building of walls see, for example, Burgos, which received a royal incentive to rebuild its walls in 1276. AMB, clasif. 2914 (27-November-1276). The city was still paying off the debt in 1313: AMB, clasif. 652 (19-December-1313). For Segovia see *Cortes*, 1: 267 (1315): there were three representatives of the city and two from the *pueblos*: Miguel Ffechor and Don Simón del Colmenar Viejo. See also the

setting of the *regimiento* in Segovia in a confirmation of Juan I, AMS, carp. 7, no. 3 (5-November-1379); Armando Represa Rodríguez, "Notas para el estudio de la ciudad de Segovia en los siglos XII–XIV," *Estudios Segovianos* 2 (1949): 281–84.

20. See Pescador, "La caballería popular," *CHE* 35–36 (1962): 76–93.

21. *Osma*, 1: no. 83, 221–22 (12-May-1285).

22. Esther Jimeno, "La población de Soria y su término en 1270, según el padrón que mando hacer Alfonso X de sus vecinos y moradores," *Boletín de la Real Academia de la Historia* 97 (1958): 207–74; Josiah Cox Russell, *Medieval Regions and Their Cities* (Newton Abbot, Eng.: David and Charles, 1972), 189. See a comparison with Burgos in Ruiz, "The Transformation of Castilian Municipalities," 20, n. 66.

23. For royal grants to the *caballeros villanos* of Soria, see *Osma*, 1: no. 50, 86–182 (12-July-1256); no. 51, 182–84 (19-July-1256); no. 81, 217–21 (18-May-1283); no. 83, 221–22 (12-May-1285); no. 88, 230–31 (26-August-1290), et passim. *Cortes*, 1: 266.

24. For Burgos, see above. For Roa, see *Osma*, 1: no. 79, 231–33 (7-March-1295). See also below.

25. *Documentos de la iglesia colegial de Santa María la Mayor de Valladolid*, ed. Manuel Mañueco Villalobos, 3 vols. (Valladolid: Imprenta castellana, 1917), 3: 33–34. See also vol. 2: 376–77 (25-February-1271); Amador de los Ríos, *Historia social, política y religiosa de los judíos en España y Portugal* (reimpresion, Madrid: Aguilar, 1960), 916. Rucquoi, *Valladolid en la edad media*, 1: 318–20, where she notes the importance of livestock in the economy of the city. For the tax-exemption charter to the *caballeros villanos* of Valladolid, which included provisions dealing with grazing and livestock, see *MHE*, 1: no. 102, 224–28 (19-August-1265).

26. See note 23 and 25. *Cuéllar*, xxvii and doc. nos. 16 (21-July-1256), 21 (29-April-1264).

27. Armando Represa Rodríguez, "Origen y desarrollo urbano del Valladolid medieval (siglos X–XIII)," in *Historia de Valladolid II. Valladolid Medieval*, ed. J. M. Ruiz Asencio et al. (Valladolid: Ateneo de Valladolid, 1980), 86.

28. For this quote and preceding one, see Ruiz, "The Transformation of the Castilian Municipalities," 18–20.

29. For previous quote and most of the discussion following, see Ruiz, "The Transformation of the Castilian Municipalities," 18–20. For the Real Hermandad in a later period see Estepa et al., *Burgos en la edad media*, 365–69.

30. Ruiz, "The Transformation of the Castilian Municipalities," 19–20.

31. *Las Huelgas*, 1: 397–98 (14-December-1228). The highest price paid in Burgos for a house in the decade of the 1220s was 210 *mrs*. ACB, vol. 70, no. 90 (?-August-1223).

32. *DMA*, 222–32. For patterns of habitation in the south, see *Repartimiento de Jérez*, lx; the *caballeros villanos* were distributed fairly uniformly throughout Jérez.

33. Diego de Colmenares, *Historia de la insigne ciudad de Segovia y compendio de las historias de Castilla*, 2 vols. (Segovia: Academia de historia y arte de San Quirce de Segovia, 1969–70), 1: 479–80.

34. IGR, *Texto*, 17–18. On the exemption to servants, see above.

35. For display in the fifteenth century, see Ruiz, "Festivités, couleurs et symboles du pouvoir," 533–39.

36. On social antagonisms, see Reyna Pastor, *Resistencias y luchas campesinas en*

la época del crecimiento y consolidación de la formación feudal: Castilla y León, siglos X–XIII (Madrid: Siglo XXI, 1980), 113–250; Represa, "Notas para el estudio de la ciudad de Segovia en los siglos XII–XIV," 284; Julio Valdeón Baruque, *Los conflictos sociales en el reino de Castilla en los siglos XIV y XV* (Madrid: Siglo XXI, 1975), 46, 73–74, 76–79, et passim.

37. *La danza de la muerte* in *Poetas anteriores al siglo XV* (Biblioteca de autores españoles, 57: Madrid, 1966), 382. For Don Juan Manuel, see above. Also see the bitter reproaches hurled against merchants by Pero López de Ayala in his *Rimado de palacio*, ed. Germán Orduña (Madrid: Castalia, 1987), 179–82.

38. See above, Chapter 5. See also Barrios García, *Estructuras agrarias y de poder*, 1: 202–18; 2: 133–86; Casado Alonso, *Señores, mercaderes y campesinos*, 325–404; Juan Antonio Bonachía Hernando, *El señorío de Burgos durante la baja edad media (1255–1508)* (Salamanca: Biblioteca de Castilla y León, 1988), 357–66.

39. Teofilo F. Ruiz, "Prosopografía burgalesa," *Boletín de la institución Fernán González* 184 (1975): 467–81.

40. Linehan, *The Spanish Church*, 101–87.

41. AHN, Clero. carp. 27, no. 16 (24-March-1329); Ajo, no. 55, p. 107 (6-March-1329); AHN, Clero. carp. 27, no. 20 (16-April-1331); carp. 28, no. 1 (1-June-1332); no. 2 (27-October-1332); no. 4 (28-March-1333); no. 5 (21-March-1334); no. 7 (23-November-1335); no. 10 (9-March-1338); no. 12, two transactions (9-December-1338 and 29-June-1339); no. 15 (29-June-1339); no. 16 (26-September-1339); no. 20 (1-April-1341); no. 21 (12-April-1341); no. 22 (16-April-1341); carp. 29, no. 1 (26-April-1341); no. 2 (2-May-1341). Similar evidence can be provided in Salamanca for the activities of Don Martín, the dean of the cathedral chapter for whom we have twelve purchases between 1245 and 1263, and for the deans Pedro Pérez and Juan Martín. See evidence in *Salamanca*, doc. nos. 214, 221, 225, 227, 228, 229, 252, et passim.

9. Society and Politics in Urban Northern Castile: *Peones*, the Poor, and the Religious Minorities

Up to this point I have focused mostly on the oligarchical groups that ruled the Castilian towns: the non-noble urban knights. Occasionally, the documents allow us to see petty merchants and artisans, above all, those who rose to the rank of *caballeros* and who, like them, bought and/or rented houses and land in and around the city. In this chapter, I will examine other urban social groups and their places within the economic, political, and social structures of city life. Unfortunately, there is not a great deal of information about those below the urban ruling groups, and their respective histories are no more than fragments of a rich past which, at least for northern Castile, cannot be fully recovered. Those below interacted daily with the urban elites of northern Castile: sometimes in uneasy partnership, often in open conflict with them.

Those Below: Good Men, *Pecheros*, and *Peones*

The process of social stratification in Castilian towns was uneven and not always complete during this period. Although in every important city or town mercantile and landholding urban elites rose to social, political, and economic prominence, this was not always accomplished without concessions to other groups or without internecine and debilitating conflict. Just below the urban knights, we find a combative group sometimes identified by the term *omes buenos* (*omnes bonos*) or, more often, as *pecheros* or tax-payers. From time to time, the documents also refer to this group as *peones*, that is, the foot soldiers of the city militias. Royal charters often made a distinction between good men and knights, while the term *pecheros* is used continuously throughout the period under examination in royal documents and in the ordinances of the Cortes. As to the last designation, *peones*, our best examples come from the books of *repartimientos*, specifically that of Jerez, where the *peones* (mostly farmers, artisans, and petty merchants with some military obligations) constituted more than 80 percent of those settled in the town with rights of *vecinaje* or citizenship.[1]

This social grouping—which for the sake of convenience may be defined as the petty bourgeoisie and artisanal groups (and in agriculturally oriented towns as citizen farmers)—was, in many respects, a fluid element within the urban social structure. At the top we find the fairly prosperous shopkeepers and artisans not too far removed from the ranks of the urban knights. In fact, there is ample evidence for their promotion to the status of *caballeros*. Social mobility worked in two ways: vertically, from the top echelons of the petty bourgeoisie to the tax-exempted benefits of the *caballería villana*; horizontally, from one town to another, as seen in the example of those merchants from Frías, Santo Domingo de Silos, and other small localities in northern Castile admitted into the Burgalese *caballero* elite.[2]

These "good men" at the top appeared prominently in the documents of the period as witnesses to wills and real-estate transactions, as buyers and sellers of small urban and rural holdings. We know a great deal less about the lower ranks of this social group. They do not appear in the documents as much as other elements of the population, and it seems that in this period they were under great economic and social pressure, their status as *vecinos* imperiled by a downturn in the economy and by the excessive burden of taxation. One can guess, without being too far off the mark, that a large number of them owned small rural holdings close to the cities or held them under a variety of leasing arrangements.

Once again, our best data on the social and economic structures of these *pecheros* come from Burgos, although it can also be verified by sources from elsewhere. In 1270 Alfonso X confirmed the ordinances of the shoemakers of Burgos (which dated originally from 1259). The rules of the guild provide some sense of the internal organization of artisanal groups in the city while stating the usual pious obligations of its members, the types of material to be utilized in the trade, as well as measures to prevent unfair competition. The four master shoemakers named by the guild to supervise compliance with the rules were John Esperq, Don Domingo Raedo, Roy Pérez, and Pedro Moro, whom we may safely assume were not knights but rather "good men." Of the four, we can follow in some detail the fortune of one of them: Pedro Moro. Another Pedro Moro, either his father or a relative, owned land in Sotrajero, a village near Burgos, in the 1180s. In

1224, another Pedro Moro exchanged a house in Burgos for land and 95 *mrs.* Ten years later, our Pedro Moro appears as owner of several houses in Rabe, a town in the *alfoz* of Burgos. By 1273, some of Pedro's properties in Villagonzalo de Quintanadueñas were sold by the *merino* of Burgos to pay for his outstanding debts to the *concejo.* This particular document reveals to us that Pedro had farmed some of the city taxes for which he had failed to pay in full, drawing therefore the judicial wrath of the Burgalese authorities. His son, García Pérez (also listed as witness to Alfonso X's confirmation), was the father of John García of Burgos. The latter, together with his wife Marina Gutiérrez, bought several vineyards in Pampliega—a town under the jurisdiction of Burgos—for 630 *mrs.* in 1301.[3]

Shoemaker and landholders, Pedro Moro and his descendants do not seem to have entered the ranks of the urban knights, probably because their wealth may not have been sufficient to support the required horse and weaponry. Nor should we think that their name, which may or may not imply Moorish origins, could have barred them from entering the ranks of the *caballería villana.* A certain Domingo Moro, perhaps even a relative of Pedro Moro, was named *fiel* (a low municipal post) of the rich and influential parish of Sanct Llorente in 1301, but not, we should add, without the vehement protest of the neighbors.[4]

Although apart from the shoemakers we do not have for Burgos the extensive information on guild organizations that we have for other parts of western Europe, two other guilds operated in the city: the blacksmiths and the sheath and harness makers. One may assume that in both cases members formed part of the artisanal and petty merchant groups. Significantly, the representatives of the blacksmiths, Pedro Pérez de la Llana and Pero de Sopriellos, protested against the attempts of the *caballero*-controlled *concejo* to tax their activities.[5] It would be quite difficult to attempt to identify local merchants and artisans who were not *caballeros* in northern Castilian cities. Once again, in Jerez, where the excellent edition of the *repartimiento* provides a census of the inhabitants, we can find the breakdown according to social status and military service (see Table 9.1). The number of tradesmen and artisans identified in the *Repartimiento* (157) represented about 8.6 percent of the total male military population of Jerez de la Frontera.[6]

Jerez, a new frontier town, was not a commercial center, and the proportion of artisanal and local merchants must have been a bit higher in some, but not all, of the northern Castilian cities. In Soria, for example, a city with a strong ranching economy, there are indications that middling groups below the ranks of the urban knights were able to resist quite

TABLE 9.1.   Social/Military Makeup of Jerez Population (1260s).

Social Category	No.	Percent of Total Male Military Population
Noble knights	42	2.3
Non-noble knights	212	11.6
Royal crossbowmen	38	2.1
Almogávares (light troops)	14	0.8
Adalides (troop leaders)	5	0.3
Almoçadenes (infantry captains)	24	1.3
Crossbowmen and archers	28	1.5
Peones	1,467	80.2
Total	1,830	

Source: González Jiménez and González Gómez, *El libro del repartimiento de Jerez de la Frontera*, LVII–LIX.

successfully the urban knights' political and economic pressure. Soria, as seen above, was a small town with only 777 *vecinos* in 1270. Of those, at least one hundred or more belonged to the twelve knightly lineages that had been established in the city in an earlier period. Since the knights of Soria had a far more aristocratic profile than did urban non-noble knights elsewhere, one must assume that social mobility of good men and *pecheros* was somewhat more restricted than it was in other places.

In spite of these differences, or most probably because of them, Soria seemed to have had some of the strongest guilds north of the Guadarrama. A center for ranching and the terminus for one of the Mesta's *cañadas* (transhumance paths), Soria was located strategically on the trade route from the Rioja south and on the east–west road running from Zaragoza to Valladolid. Not surprisingly, Soria had a well-established guild of muleteers. In 1290, the "good men" of the *cofradía* of muleteers of Soria protested to Sancho IV that their privileges had been violated. Since 1219, when Ferdinand III had granted them rights and privileges, they were allowed to bring goods freely into town and to have their own measures, supervised by two knights and four "good men" of the *cofradía*. Although the urban knights exercised a growing control over the economic activities, specifically through the active policing of their measures, Sancho IV's charter reveals the resistance of the muleteers, acting as a group, against the encroachment of the non-noble urban knights. In addition, the document provides further confirmation for the existence of a well-organized and, by 1290, almost a century-old wine trade from Logroño southward, carried by Sorian interests.[7]

Earlier, in 1283, Alfonso X had confirmed an agreement between the city council and the "good men" representing the brotherhood of weavers of Soria. The ordinances of the weavers, confirmed again in 1314, 1315, 1332, and 1378, provide useful information on the guilds of Soria and on the town's textile industry. The ordinances contain the usual dispositions against unfair competition and those working at night, as well as regulatory measures on the quality of cloth. The charter also reveals that the group of weavers, made up of men and, it seems, a large number of women, produced low quality woolens, burlap, and linen cloth.[8] Similarly, the *cofradía* of Saint Michael, established by the sellers of wax, oil, and "other things," had its ordinances confirmed by Ferdinand IV in 1302. Besides the usual pious, philanthropic, and burial dispositions, the regulating of weights, and self-policing of their commercial activities, these small shopkeepers insisted on their tax-exempted status dating back to the reign of Alfonso VIII. That merchants of wax and oil were so numerous as to organize a *cofradía* points once again to the importance of Soria as a transfer point for oil and beeswax from Andalucía to the markets of the Rioja and, perhaps, to western Aragon. In another sense, the existence of these corporations, which the charters reveal to be in uneasy competition with the *caballeros villanos* of Soria, points to the stratification of social groups there.[9]

In Burgos, mobility between the upper levels of the *pechero* social groups and the lower levels of *caballería villana* can be easily documented, but this was not the case for Soria. In Burgos, almost as late as the mid-fourteenth century, the criteria for membership in the ranks of the non-noble urban knights remained ownership of a horse and weapons, that is, membership was essentially dependent on wealth; in Soria, however, membership in the ruling oligarchy depended on wealth, but it was also conditioned by blood. This may help explain in part why in Burgos the *caballeros villanos* were able to monopolize political offices, whereas in Soria, the good men, the *pecheros*, retained a foothold in the administration of the city. As mentioned above, Soria's representatives to the meeting of the *Hermandad*, held in Burgos in 1315, included four knights, two from the *común* (the commons), Diego Pérez and Ferrán Pérez, and one from the small villages in Soria's hinterland.[10]

These digressions into political relations within the towns will be explored in further detail shortly, but we must at present return to those middling groups just below the urban knights. If for Soria we have evidence of at least three strong and well-organized *cofradías* of shopkeepers, muleteers, and weavers, we may assume that the number of petty merchants and artisans, out of roughly 800 *vecinos*, exceeded the 8.6 percent calculated for Jerez. In Ávila, where the number of *pecheros* in the sixteenth century was only 2,826, and which probably did not have more than 5,000 inhabitants altogether in the pre-plague period, we do not find as many Christian shopkeepers and artisans as we do in Burgos. Yet, from the partial information provided by the 1303 census of property owned by the cathedral chapter, one can see the economic activities of these Christian merchants in Ávila's market. Although there is no evidence of long-distance merchants, as in Burgos, or of organized artisanal brotherhoods, as in Soria, the large number of *tiendas* (stores) and of artisans points to a lively internal commercial life in Ávila. Few of the Christian shopkeepers, however, seemed to have played a role in the political life of Ávila or to have enjoyed the kind of social mobility we witness in Burgos. On the other hand, few of the ruling *caballero* elite appeared to have had any commercial ties. One who did was Fortún Blázquez, brother of Blasco Blázquez and *alcalde* of the city from 1303 to 1305. Fortún owned or held at least four stores within the city walls, but this, in a manner similar to the ownership of stores by canons, was probably an investment in real estate for rental to others rather than an example of his mercantile pursuits.[11]

The large number of local merchants and artisans who, because of their religion, were excluded from political power or social prominence and the local nature of Ávila's trade may have precluded the development of a dynamic mercantile-oriented oligarchy (as had developed in Burgos); however, they did not prevent the antagonism between *pecheros* and tax-exempted knights peculiar to other Castilian cities. While many of the conflicts generated in the region of Ávila in the 1330s appear to have been the result of factional struggles between knightly families or lineages, there is also evidence that the knights of Ávila expropriated commons belonging to the village councils. We do not know fully how these tensions were resolved, but by 1330 power in the city was divided between two *cuadrillas* or lineages: those of Esteban Domingo and Blasco Jimeno. This stands in marked contrast to the sixteen representatives (all knights) Ávila sent to the meeting of the *Hermandad* (1315), a reflection, perhaps, of the need to represent every patrician family in the city.[12] These two lineages still dominated the life of the city in the sixteenth century, emphasizing their social distance from the *pecheros* as well as the purity of their ancestry and blood. Thus, in 1517, a local chronicle stated that "the knights, as far back as the twelfth century, had never married into artisan, *ruanos* (tradesmen), or any other families, except those of noble knights," facts that point to their distance from merchants as well.[13] Other evidence also points to the exclusion of the *pecheros* from a political role in Ávila, unlike Soria, Segovia, or Madrid, where they retained a small political role. Paradoxically, by different routes Burgos and Ávila reached the same point. While in the former, the urban knights were on the whole willing to admit well-to-do middling groups to their ranks (once they were capable of maintaining horses and weapons, thus coopting the upper echelons of the petty bourgeoisie), in Ávila access to the oligarchy seems to have depended, once again, on blood, on rural holdings, and on tradition. Yet the end result—a municipal council fully monopolized by urban knights—was essentially the same.

The Lower Ranks of the *Pechero* Social Group

I have fallen once again into a discussion of political developments, because the extant documentation tends to make that easier than a full treatment of social history. Such an enterprise becomes even more difficult when one attempts to reconstruct the mentality and lives of the lower stratum of the *pechero* group. The three *ortelanos* (gardeners, ortolans), John García de Medina de Pomar, his brother, Asencio Pérez, and John Pérez de Valmaseda, *moradores* (residents, but not citizens) of Burgos, who appeared as witnesses to Doña María García's will in 1337, probably belonged to a category of daily laborers near the bottom of the social hierarchy. They were employed by María to tend her gardens and house near the convent of Saint Augustine in Burgos, and, as her employees, they witnessed her testament.[14]

Since the level of industrial activity in northern Castilian towns in this period was never very high, the workers in urban society must have provided most of the labor for the tending of farms, gardens, vineyards, mills, and for other rural activities in and around Castilian cities. Perhaps one may also argue, though the evidence for this is not extant, that many of these people also inhabited the city on a seasonal basis. As the masters and employers, the non-noble urban knights, returned to their farms by late spring, their servants, agricultural laborers, and hangers-on may have followed suit. They would, then, move back and forth between country and town in a cycle dictated by agricultural need. It is not improbable that some of these *pecheros*, both those at the top as well as those at the bottom of this social group, owned or held some land outside the walls. There is evidence for this in the later period, and similar patterns survive into the present. In the village of my ancestors, factory workers in Bilbao and Tolosa (but once inhabitants in Gallejones), still own farms and fruit trees in the valley which they and their families tend carefully on weekends and during vacations.[15] If I am correct, the boundaries between rural and urban, always vague in Castile, become even less clear. I think it is important to emphasize this point once again. In an earlier chapter, we witnessed the intervention of urban capital into the rural land market, but the ties binding city and country went beyond economic exchanges. This fluidity was most evident among the lowly *pecheros*: urban dwellers by necessity who, still in this period, nevertheless had deep roots in the surrounding countryside.

THE POOR

In the last decade a great deal of work has been done on the questions of poverty and the conditions of the poor in medieval Iberia. Many of these works deal with literary and legal responses to the problems of poverty; we know, however, little about the actual number and conditions of the poor for the period before 1350.[16] The working poor and the destitute did not pay taxes and seldom, if ever, bought or sold property. They did not participate in the political life of the city; they wrote no books and did not discuss the great issues of the day. Without exception they were illiterate and probably far too concerned with the pressing task of survival to engage in intellectual pursuits. Nevertheless, although silent, they were indispensable witnesses to and actors in the making of urban Castilian history.

Unlike the case in England, France, and other parts of western Europe, in Castile we do not witness the widespread uprisings of either the peasantry or the urban workers which brought the oppressed into the limelight of history. There were, of course, "social conflicts," localized antagonisms between peasants and lords, urban dwellers and patrician elites, Christians and Jews which were manifested, especially in the last case, in acts of violence.[17] Yet there was no Jacquerie, no Ciompi, no John Ball to ignite the popular mind and to provide us with an idealized or, at times, distorted image of the peasantry and/or urban workers and their acts of defiance. Instead, we can approach the questions of who the poor were and how many there were from the perspective of charity and welfare. Valdeón Baruque has already proposed a typology of the poor (based on Mollat's work) and an estimate of their number in Utrera. We also know that in 1384 the so-called poor constituted only a small percentage of the population of Seville, but that year's census may have not reflected real conditions.[18]

The number of the urban poor obviously varied from locality to locality and oscillated in response to changing economic conditions or political upheavals. It seems common sense to suppose that towns with commercial and some manufacturing orientations experienced types of poverty that were somewhat different from towns with a ranching- or agricultural-based economy. Likewise, the number of the poor must have been larger in the former than in the latter. There seems to be a correlation between the economic structure of towns and the number of hospitals and philanthropic foundations aimed at the poor, with more in commercial towns than in those with a ranching or agricultural economy. There are, of course, a host of variants that recommend caution in drawing such conclusions. At the same time, it is also quite clear that by the thirteenth century hospitals, once dedicated to the care of pilgrims, were turning their energies and resources toward the needs of the poor. This development and the increase in testamentary, confraternity, and municipal dispositions for the feeding and clothing of the poor point to changes for the worse in the number and conditions of the poor in northern Castile's urban centers.[19]

For the end of the twelfth century and the beginning of the next, wills provide a good guide to this new concern with the care of the poor. There was a noticeable difference between wills in which pious donations were confined mostly to ecclesiastical institutions in return for masses for the donor and his family, and wills which, while not neglecting this important aspect of personal expiation, also included philanthropic provisions.

Most importantly, hospitals were urban institutions; thus they did not isolate the poor fully, at least during this period, from the rest of the urban population. Moreover, in Burgos and probably in other Castilian cities, the poor and the handicapped, who were often one and the same, took the initiative in petitioning municipal authorities for relief. Thus in 1312 the destitute blind requested that the city council of Burgos build a hospital for them. Erected shortly afterward near the tanning shops in the neighborhood of San Gil, the hospital soon became a place of refuge for other poor people. In 1338 Alfonso XI ordered the *alcaldes* and *merino* of the city to bar the use of the hospital to anyone but the blind; yet in 1366 the hospital was crowded with lame and other disabled poor men and women who often robbed and abused the blind.[20] Clearly, in a city such as Burgos, where at the end of the fourteenth century a German pilgrim, Herman Künig, counted thirty-two hospitals, there was a growing need for organized assistance to the poor. Not surprisingly, a good number of the hospitals, especially those founded in the thirteenth and fourteenth centuries, were endowed by either urban patricians or by brotherhoods of knights and/or merchants and administered, in some cases, by lay institutions or persons. As in the case of the hospital for the blind in Burgos, charity was no longer the sole responsibility of the church.

In this respect, the two wills of Ferrant Pérez de Frías, one of the town's scribes, and his wife Catalina Royz—the first drawn in 1334 and the other after Catalina's death ten years later—provide information on the number of the poor even in small towns such as Frías, as well as on the new concern of the bourgeoisie for the indigent. In 1334 Ferrant was already a prosperous municipal official with properties in and around Frías, including shares in the mill of Ascucha. The first will was a modest affair. Small amounts of money and wax were assigned to different churches and to the hospital of Santa María de Frías in return for masses and burial at the hospital. Catalina's will also included provisions for the clothing (one half burlap, the other half sackcloth) of fifteen poor people.

The next will, after Catalina's death, shows that Ferrant's fortunes had undergone a most favorable change. The large outstanding debts that he left for his executors to collect all around the region and his financial transactions with Jewish moneylenders in Pancorbo and elsewhere identify him as an important usurer and, probably, a tax farmer. His pious donations to monasteries were, in some cases, tenfold those of a previous decade. Among them, Ferrant assigned 1,000 *mrs.* for the building of a stone hospital to house ten poor people, as well as additional money to dress and feed 310 poor men and women in the region of Frías. If in the late sixteenth century the entire archpriesthood of Frías had only 588 *vecinos*, it is doubtful whether in the mid-fourteenth century the entire population surpassed 2,500 inhabitants. This will, therefore, provides a sense, albeit imprecise, of the number of the poor and their visibility in Castilian urban society.[21]

If our knowledge of the life and conditions of the poor is limited, that is not the case with our last category of those who lived in Castilian urban centers. I refer here to the religious minorities of Jews and Moors. We find both groups, especially the Jews, placed along a broad spectrum of social positions: from privileged places in the royal administration, to the cultural and financial spheres, to a humble and fragile standing in the life of the city.

Jews and Moors in Urban Medieval Castile

THE JEWS

The history of the Jews in medieval Spain and of their peculiar relationship with the dominant Christian majority has long attracted the attention of historians.[22] Thanks to their work, we now know the general outline of Jewish life in the Iberian peninsula before 1492, as well as the patterns of Jewish political, social, and economic organization. There is also an abundant literature on the impact of forced conversion on the Jews at the end of the fourteenth century, the introduction of the Inquisition in Castile in 1484, and the tragic exile of the Jews from *Sefarad* eight years later.[23]

My aims here are far less ambitious than the discussion of such momentous events. Instead, I would like to focus on the social and economic structures of Jewish life in some sample northern Castilian urban centers in the thirteenth and fourteenth centuries. The standard and, by now, dated view has been that Jews monopolized artisanal, mercantile, and money-lending operations in Castile, but the extant sources show conclusively that Jews in each city had their own peculiar history, reflecting the diverse economic and social structure of the particular locality. As to the question of the relations between Christians and Jews and the widespread violence against Jews and, to a lesser extent, Moors, one should note that the nature of Christian responses and attitudes toward Jews depended to a large extent on the location in the social hierarchy of both the persecutors and the persecuted. Each order in Castile's tripartite society related to Jews, at least before 1350, in its own way. Although in the end Jews and Moors became the targets of all, the way in which the nobility, clergy, bourgeoisie, and common people reacted to them differed widely. It is improper, therefore, to speak in general terms of Christian-Jewish relations or anti-Jewish sentiments. Rather, we must examine these relations and antagonisms in each specific context.[24]

The internal structure of Jewish communities throughout northern Castile was fairly uniform, but the relations between Jews and local ecclesiastical and municipal authorities, and the nature of their economic activities and social life varied from place to place. These differences depended mainly on the type of economic organization prevalent in each locality. Directly dependent on royal authority, the Jewish communities of northern Castile were theoretically exempted from ecclesiastical and municipal jurisdictions. These communities or *aljamas* were organized institutionally along lines paralleling the municipal council, often with their own special *alcaldes* or judges. Litigations between Christians and Jews on civil and criminal matters came under royal law and followed procedures (the taking of the oath on the Torah, having an equal number of Jewish and Christian arbitrators) which, if they did not favor the Jews, were at least not overtly hostile to them.[25] We can see how Jews fared in Castilian urban society by comparing their roles in two cities of northern Castile: Burgos and Ávila.

Burgos had one of the largest and richest *aljamas* in the kingdom. The number of Jews living in the city at the end of the thirteenth century has been estimated between 120 and 150 families or between around 540 and 675 people altogether. The entire population of the city in that period probably did not exceed 6,500 inhabitants, thus as many as 10.4 percent of them may have been Jewish.[26]

Regardless of their number, this was a rich community indeed. Jews were purchasing substantial properties in and around Burgos, although we do not know exactly what kinds of property or how much they paid for them. The number of acquisitions and their monetary value can only be gathered from the protests of the city council of Burgos to the king in the late 1270s and early 1280s, as was the case elsewhere in the realm as evidenced by the *cuadernos* of the Cortes. On 20 April 1280, the Infante Don Sancho answered the complaints of the *concejo* of Burgos and ordered the moneylenders, the inhabitants of San Felices (a Jewish quarter), the Jews of Burgos, and the residents of La Llana (an area in the center of the city) to pay taxes on those recently purchased *heredamientos e terras* (lands and properties bought outright and held free of any seigniorial claims). The Infante was simply confirming an earlier privilege granted by his father Alfonso X. Five years later, the city council of Burgos complained again that the Jews were buying *heredades pecheras* (taxable property) from its citizens and refusing to pay taxes on them. The city procurators argued that the consequent reduction in tax revenues was such that the city was unable to pay its own dues to the crown. Sancho IV ordered that taxes be paid by the Jews as they had been in the time of his grandfather, Ferdinand III, and his father, Alfonso X.[27]

We must assume that the ruling elite of Burgos was probably exaggerating the situation and seeking to shift the blame, either partly or fully, to the Jews for its own resistance to royal financial demands. We know that in 1278–79 the Burgalese oligarchy had been engaged in a bitter conflict with both Alfonso X and his son Sancho over its unwillingness to meet a heavy fine imposed by the crown on the city council for the usurious activities of some of its prominent Christian citizens.[28] Moreover, at the end of the 1270s the position of the Jews in Castile had begun to deteriorate rapidly, culminating with the assassination of Zag de la Maleha, an important Jewish royal financial agent, in Seville, and growing restrictions on Jewish economic and social activities. The Jews were, therefore, an easier target for municipal complaints. Most probably, Jews and the Castilian towns were caught in the middle of the open war between Alfonso X and the Infante Don Sancho for control of the realm. Often Jews and municipal authorities joined the wrong camp, at the cost of their lives and fortunes.[29] This does not explain, however, why we know so little about how much property the Jews owned within the city and in the Burgalese hinterland.

The Burgalese sources, the richest in northern Castile, do not include a single extant record of a Jew buying property in the area during the years between 1200 and 1350. They are also as laconic when it comes to Christians buying from Jews, with only a single, albeit important, entry extant. Although the evidence from the real-estate and land markets is scant, however, we have other ways of assessing the economic well-being of the Jewish community of Burgos. In 1290 the Jews paid a head tax of 87,760 *mrs.*, plus 22,161 *mrs.* in *servicio* (an extraordinary tax voted for by the Cortes), or a total of 109,921 *mrs.* Only Toledo, with its huge contribution of 216,505 *mrs.*, paid more. The amount indicated for Burgos represented only the contribution of Jews living in the city. Jewish communities elsewhere in the dioceses of Burgos—in towns such as Pancorbo, Muño, Briviesca, and others—paid additional sums.[30]

If one considers that in addition the *aljama* of Burgos made special payments to the cathedral chapter and paid gate tolls, sale taxes, and a whole range of other fiscal dues, including 12,000 *mrs.* annually to the city council after 1301, then its contribution came to more than 800 *mrs.* per family. This would have been enough, barring the legal restraints on Jews, to qualify them for membership in the knightly oligarchy ruling the city. But this is not to say, of course, that all the Jewish families were rich. The taxes were assessed on the community and apportioned by the Jewish leadership to those able to pay. In fact, Francisco Hernández has found instances in Leonese *aljamas* in which a single individual paid the tax for the entire community. Yet, regardless of whether paid by the community or not, this financial burden pales when compared with the one-million-*maravedíes* fine imposed on the *aljama* of the city after Henry of Trastámara captured the city from his brother, Peter I, in 1366.[31]

These references to the wealth of the Jews in Burgos require some explanation, albeit tentative, regarding its sources. Among the commonplaces found in Castilian medieval history, one of the most persistent is that Jews dominated mercantile, artisanal, and financial activities. This assumption is incorrect. In Burgos and in other commercially oriented towns in Castile, Christian merchants had monopolized the economic life of their respective cities. The extant sources show conclusively that in Burgos, Vitoria, Medina de Pomar, the port towns of the Bay of Biscay, and other towns, Christian merchants had an exclusive monopoly on long-distance and international trade. They also dominated high-volume moneylending and shared in the profits of local tax-farming operations. We can state categorically that in commercial centers in Castile (mostly towns located along the road to Santiago de Compostela or those engaged in the import of textiles from Flanders), the Christians held the upper hand in financial and commercial matters.[32]

Still, this does not answer our early query regarding Jewish sources of income in Burgos. We could begin to formulate a tentative response by noting that some of the most important tax farmers in the kingdom, among them Abraham el Barchilón and Yuçef Pimintiella, had their headquarters in the city. This is to be expected, inasmuch as Burgos was the unofficial capital of Castile and the see of the royal chancery. Perhaps the wealth of the Burgalese Jews depended on their kingdomwide economic role as royal financiers, while at the local level they had been effectively blocked by enterprising Christian merchants. This was also the case in Seville, where Genoese merchants gained control over the commercial and financial life of the city.[33]

Burgalese Jews did have other sources of income. There are the usual references to Jewish butchers in the city, and one must assume that these shops served both Jews and Christians alike. Moreover, in 1270 Alfonso X granted jurisdiction over the Jews of Santa Cecilia in Briviesca to the nuns of the powerful nunnery of Las Huelgas, as well as the right to employ a Jewish physician to attend to the nuns. According to Anselmo Salvá, the city council of Burgos had a Jewish or a Muslim doctor throughout this period. We can safely assume that in late medieval Burgos and elsewhere in Castile, Jews and Moors held an important place in the medical profession, and that their care was often sought by those who could pay well. A few other scant references from Burgos allow us additional glimpses of Jewish economic life there. In 1286, Juçef Haraçon and his wife Ledizia sold two parts in a vineyard at Villalgamar to Pedro Sarracín, dean of the cathedral chapter of Burgos, for 2,000 *mrs*. As indicated above, this is the only extant transaction in Burgos before 1350 in which Jews appear, although we do know that they bought and sold land and houses in this period. In spite of being just one piece of evidence, this transaction is quite revealing indeed. Two thousand *maravedíes* was an extraordinary amount to be paid for a vineyard. In fact, there are serious doubts as to whether any vineyard, traditionally restricted to small plots, could command such prices in the 1280s. Was there a hidden charge, a different kind of economic transaction taking place in this transfer of parts of a vineyard? In any case, the document does show a Jewish couple holding lands in the Burgalese hinterland and transacting business with Pedro Sarracín, dean of the cathedral and member of the most powerful family in the city.[34]

The possibility of a hidden surcharge, perhaps for money borrowed previously, in this purchase—even though it is not revealed directly in the extant sources—provides tangential evidence of the Jewish role in moneylending in the area of Burgos. The testament of Ferrán Pérez, a Christian scribe, landholder, and usurer in Frias, a small town north of Burgos, offers a clear indication that Ferrán worked very closely with Jewish moneylenders in Pancorbo. He borrowed from them and lent the capital, one supposes at a higher interest rate, to other Christians; at times, Ferrán Pérez and his Jewish counterparts in Pancorbo engaged in joint ventures.[35] Similarly, there is enough evidence of an active and important Christian role in moneylending in Burgos: perhaps Jews and Christians there also engaged in joint ventures. On the other hand, although the existing evidence does not verify this, it is possible that Jews and Christians served a different clientele altogether. Some Jews concentrated on petty loans, while others tended to the large financial operations of the realm. Christians too may have engaged in petty loans, but their financial activities may have been directed toward financing long-distance trade and lending to ecclesiastical institutions in the area. It is clear, however, that by the fifteenth century, after the pogroms of 1391, the financial position of the Burgalese Jews had been severely crippled.[36] Finally, as was the case throughout northern Castile, we also find a few Jews in Burgos in the royal service; for example, Abraham el Levi, Yuçaf Cordiella, and Çag Abenbeniste, all from the *aljama* of Burgos, collected royal taxes in the lands of the dioceses of Burgos in 1343.[37]

Although the evidence from Burgos is scant when dealing with Jewish life, conditions in other towns in Castile differed markedly. In Sepúlveda, Ávila, Valladolid, and Salamanca, to mention just a few urban centers in northern Castile and León—towns where the ruling oligarchical elites derived their income mostly from ranching and/or agriculture—the extant evidence shows a strong Jewish and Muslim presence in local trade and agricultural and artisanal occupations. We also find differences in living patterns in northern Castilian towns: In Burgos, for example, Jews had been fairly segregated in their own quarters, the *judería*, with its synagogue and its own gate opening in the city walls. In Ávila, Valladolid, and Salamanca, although most Jews lived in neighborhoods that were predominantly Jewish, one also finds them living throughout the entire city. The 1303 census of the property owned by the cathedral chapter of Ávila, which provides only an incomplete record of patterns of habitation in the city, shows more than fifty Jews (twelve of whom were women, mostly widows) renting houses, stores, and other urban property from the chapter. The neighborhood of the Yuradero in Ávila, with its Jewish butcher shops, comes very close to being a Jewish neighborhood, although Christians and Moors also lived there; but we also find Jews living in every other part of the city, including the areas around the cathedral, the preferred abode of Ávila's ruling families. In Valladolid, Aguilar de Campóo, and elsewhere, Jews lived around the central market, an area in which the merchants and knights of the city also chose to reside.[38] The census of 1303 and the extant records of urban real-estate transactions throughout northern Castile allow us to identify Jewish economic activity in Ávila and elsewhere (see Table 9.2).

In Ávila we find strong Jewish participation in artisanal and local mercantile activity, and this presence was directly related to the fact that Ávila's ruling elite derived its income from ranching and land rents.[39] Moreover, the number of Jews in artisanal activities vividly contrasts with the far smaller number (15) of Christian artisans mentioned in the extant documentation. Yet, similar tables for Burgos, Vitoria, Fuenterrabía, and other towns involved in long-distance trade yield mostly Christian names for traders and shopkeepers.[40]

When we turn to exchanges of property between Christians and Jews, our sources for Ávila are also far more revealing than those for any other town in northern Castile before 1350. As was the case nearly everywhere else, in Ávila there is almost no extant evidence of Jews buying from Christians. What we have are records of sales of Jewish property. This can be explained in part by the exclusive ecclesiastical nature of the documentation, which includes only records pertaining to property willed to, sold to, or ending up in the hands of the church during this period. Unlike Burgos, however, Ávila and other cities in northern Castile reflect, in the wealth of their documentation, a greater acceptance of the important economic con-

TABLE 9.2.　Jewish Trades and
Economic Activity in Ávila (1240–1360).

Trade/Activity	Number of Jews Identified
Blacksmith	5
Shopkeeper	5
Money-broker	3*
Locksmith	2
Shoemaker	2
Packsaddle-maker	2
Chipelero (?)	2
Weaver	2
Tailor	1
Taper of cloth	1*
Butcher	1
Quiltmaker	1
Chairmaker	1
Goldsmith	1
Cloth shearer	1
Carpenter	1
Dyer	2
Shopkeeper (ludes)	1*
Total	34**

Source: DMA, AHN, Clero, carps. 23–30.

*Number includes one female.
**Twenty-nine of these references come from the 1303 census, reflecting Jews who rented their places of business from the cathedral chapter of the city.

tributions made by the Jews. In Table 9.3 we can see the role played by Jews in the urban real-estate markets of Ávila and Salamanca between 1240 and 1360, as well as the considerable amount of property they owned within the city walls.

One example from Ávila helps illuminate the position of Jews and their role in the economic life of those urban centers that lacked a well-established Christian bourgeoisie. In 1297 Menahen, a dyer, and his wife Cimha sold a pair of houses in the main market of Ávila to Pascual Sánchez, a cleric of the church of Saint Vincent, for 1,300 mrs. Menahen and Cimha had resided in one of the houses, and the transaction provides us with a very good description of the house and of the neighborhood. Menahen's house

TABLE 9.3.   Urban Real-Estate Markets of Ávila and Salamanca (1240–1360).

	Ávila	*Salamanca*
Total number of extant transactions	34	60*
Number of transactions involving Jews	14	13 (1 purchase**)
Percentage of total	41	22
Lowest price paid for Jewish-owned property	143 *mrs.*	15.5 *mrs.*
Highest price paid for Jewish-owned property	1,300 *mrs.*	450 *mrs.*
Average price per transaction	620 *mrs.*	174.6 *mrs.*
Average price per transaction not involving Jews	601 *mrs.*	

Identity of Jewish Sellers	No. of Transactions	
Couples	5	5
Female (single)	2	4
Male (single)	6	2 (including a rabbi)
Siblings	1 (brothers)	1 (brother and sister)

Source: AHN, Clero, carps. 23–30; carps. 1886–1888; *DMA*, and *Salamanca*.

*These transactions reflect activity mostly up to 1300. The extant sources for Salamanca at the Archivo histórico nacional in Madrid are meager. The documentation of the cathedral archive of Salamanca has been published only up to 1300.
**In the only extant transaction in which the buyers were Jewish, the couple paid 32 *mrs.* for their purchase.

had two doors: one opened onto the market and the other toward the cathedral. On one side of Menahen's houses stood the house of Mosse Merdohay; on the other side, we find a store selling women's ornaments(?), owned and run by Ledicia, wife of Mosse Amariello. Nearby, we also find the houses and stores of Rabbi Yhuda, also a dyer, and of Mencia. The man surveying the property was Pedro Pérez, a Christian, together with Don Çag Franco, a Jew of Ávila. Caçon and Mira, the children of Menahen and Cimha, as well as their son-in-law Mosse served as guarantors of the sale. Christian judges and Menahen testified to the closing of the contract and drew up the appropriate documents. This example of the complex relations of Christians and Jews in an urban setting ought not to obscure the Jewish role in rural life. The evidence from Calahorra and from the area of Aguilar de Campóo also shows Jews as owners of vineyards, gardens, mill rights, and cereal-growing lands.[41] Nevertheless, in the single document examined above, we can see a microcosm of Jewish and Christian relations in medieval Castile. And yet the document also underlines significant changes in these relations.

Although we must assume that Jews also purchased property during this period, the property they were selling, the prices these houses commanded, and, far more importantly, the identity of the buyers, already point to important transformations in the making. After 1250 there are indications that most of the important urban properties owned by Jews were purchased by members of the rising urban oligarchies in northern Castile. Were Jews facing such economic difficulties after 1250 that they were forced to sell some of their properties to Christians? Or were the dynamics of change within northern Castilian towns—evident especially in the appropriation of economic, political, and social power by a narrow group of non-noble knights—pressuring Jews into selling?

The second half of the thirteenth century was a hard period for almost everyone. Our evidence for the internal economic conditions of Jewish communities is scant, and we know little about poor Jews, except that their numbers must have also been increasing, as reflected by philanthropic activities. Luis Suárez Fernández has already pointed out that most fifteenth-century Castilian Jews were of modest means, and the Inquisition records from the latter part of the century show that as well. While a few rich men remained the pillars of the Jewish *aljamas*, there is the possibility that the late thirteenth century already witnessed a decline in the economic well-being of most Jews. This would explain the emphasis laid on communal responsibility for taxes and loans, by means of which "big and small" supported one another in carrying the burden of royal taxation.[42]

On the other hand, the heightened millenarian activities and expectations of northern Castilian Jewish communities in the 1280s and 1290s may have been partly a reflection of that dual burden of growing economic difficulties and antagonism to which we referred above, but again our evidence is mostly tangential. Whether because of financial duress or hardening attitudes from the Christian urban oligarchies, the results were essentially the same. What we witness here is the transfer of economic power to noble and non-noble urban knights. This dramatic transformation marks the ascendancy of new social groups within the city and the growing distance and animosity between these Christian urban oligarchs and the Jews.

MOORISH LIFE IN LATE MEDIEVAL CASTILE

When we turn to the *moriscos* or Moors living under Christian rule in northern Castile, we encounter a sorry and melancholy state. Their number small, often relegated to menial occupations, the Moors in the urban centers north of the Guadarrama did not enjoy either the economic or political standing of their Jewish counterparts. Thus the municipal councils had more or less a free hand in controlling these communities. Not unlike the Jews, the Muslims were restricted in the style and types of clothes they wore, the fashion of their hair and beards, the areas they lived, and in their contacts with Christians and their political and financial lives. The head tax paid by these communities—for example, only 1,092 *mrs.* in Burgos as compared to the 87,760 *mrs.* paid by the Jews—is a further confirmation of their limited resources and numbers.[43]

Although not as completely as can be done for the Jews, Moorish quarters can be identified in a good number of towns in northern Castile. Their neighborhoods or *morerías* were found adjacent to the Jewish quarters. At times, as was the case in Ávila, Moors and Jews lived in the same area of the city. The documents of the period and the secondary sources tell us of Mudejares communities composed of a few rich men and a vast group of laborers. We are told, again and again, that most of the Moors in northern Castile served as agricultural hands, masons, and construction workers.[44] Even if the sources did not already confirm this, the Mudejar style of churches, city gates, and other public and private buildings in late medieval Castile give witness to Moorish contributions to the making of Castilian urban spaces. But Moors also filled other occupations, often in direct competition with Jews and Christians.

In Burgos, where Jews had been, for all practical purposes, excluded from artisanal pursuits, we find a certain Andalla, the dyer and son of Don Inza of Pampliega. In 1305 Andalla and his wife, Doña Cienzo, sold houses in the street of the Salinera of Burgos for the large sum of 5,000 *mrs.* There was at least one Moor of substance in Burgos before the Black Death. Twelve Moors also served as officers of the monastery of Las Huelgas in the thirteenth century. In Ávila the extant documentation contains less than twenty-five references to Moors in the period before 1350, but these references must represent only a partial view of Moorish life in the city.

I do not wish to conclude this section with a pessimistic assessment of how these minorities were treated. In the thirteenth and fourteenth centuries, Jews and Moors were often oppressed and exploited. The next century would bring even greater evils, but we should lighten this somber image by evoking those rare happier times, when Christians, Jews, and Moors shared, each from the peculiar perspectives of his or her own religion and culture, in the public rituals of Castilian life. In Briviesca, a small town in northern Castile, we witness the entrance of Doña Blanca, a princess of Navarre, who, accompanied by her royal mother, traveled to Valladolid in the mid-fifteenth century to marry the future Henry IV. Great lords and knights met her at the outskirts of the town; one hundred knights—fifty dressed in red and fifty in white—fought fierce jousts in her honor. Once these festivities were concluded, her cortege entered the town, where Christian artisans and shopkeepers received the royal entourage with their banners and *tableaux vivants*. And joining them in the streets of Briviesca were the Jews dancing with the Torah and the Moors with the Koran, as was the custom, the chronicler wrote, when foreign princes came to rule Castile.[45]

Notes

This chapter includes a section on Jewish history for which I received the assistance of Ms. Scarlett Freund. The work was divided as follows: Ruiz undertook research in Castilian sources and wrote an early draft. Freund researched sources in Hebrew and German found in Baer, *Die Juden*. In addition, she thoroughly revised, edited, and rewrote sections of the final text. More importantly, Freund looked at the historical question raised here from both a Jewish and a Christian perspective. We wish to thank Mr. David Nirenberg for his help and for his graceful sharing of his unpublished research on "Jews and Muslims in the Crown of Aragon."

1. For "good men," see Evelyn S. Proctor, "The Interpretation of Clause 3 of the Decrees of Leon," *English Historical Review* 85 (1970): 45–53; María del Carmen Carlé, "Boni homines y hombres buenos," *CHE* 39–40 (1964): 133–68; Ruiz, "The Transformation of the Castilian Municipalities," 3–33; examples from Cortes in *Cortes*, 1: 132 (1293), 374 (1325), et passim; *Repartimiento de Jerez*, liv.

2. See Ruiz, "Burgos y el comercio castellano en la baja edad media," 55. For other examples, see Chapter 6.

3. ACB, vol. 70, no. 219 (1183); vol. 70, no. 240 (1187); vol. 70, no. 253 (1224); vol 5, p. 1, f.33 (1234); vol. 49, f. 75 (1273); vol. 42, f. 105 (1301); AMB, clasif. 683 (10-May-1270).

4. Named *fiel* in 1307, Domingo Moro married into the Pérez-Sarracín family, one of the most influential in the city. He was on the list of those holding a contract for the city wall in 1313. AMB, clasif. 3145 (1-September-1307); clasif. 652 (19-December-1313); ACB vol. 50, p. 1, f. 62b (16-February-1262).

5. Ruiz, *Sociedad y poder real*, 112.

6. *Repartimiento de Jerez*, LIX.

7. *Osma*, 1: no. 88, 230–31 (26-August-1290).

8. *Osma*, no. 81, 217–21 (18-May-1283).

9. *Osma*, no. 97, 245–48 (23-May-1302).

10. *Cortes*, 1: 266.

11. *DMA*, 223. Barrios García, *Estructuras agrarias y de poder*, 2: 133–54.

12. Barrios García, *Estructuras agrarias y de poder*, 2: 152–54; José Mayoral Fernández, *El municipio de Ávila. (Estudio historico)* (Ávila: Diputación provincial de Ávila, 1958), 38; *Cortes*, 1: 267.

13. Abelardo Merino Alvarez, *La sociedad abulense durante el siglo XVI: La nobleza* (Madrid: Imprenta del patronato de huérfanos, 1926), 32, 135.

14. AHN, Clero, carp. 177, no. 4 (24-March-1337).

15. Casado Alonso, *Señores, mercaderes y campesinos*, 480–84.

16. See, especially, the articles in *A pobreza e a assistencia aos pobres na peninsula iberica durante a idade media*, 2 vols. (Lisboa: Centro de estudos históricos, 1973); Carmen López Alonso, *La pobreza en la España medieval* (Madrid: Ministerio de trabajo y seguridad social, 1986). For the rest of Europe, see Michel Mollat, *The Poor in the Middle Ages: An Essay in Social History* (New Haven, Conn.: Yale University Press, 1986).

17. See Valdeón Baruque, *Los conflictos sociales en el reino de Castilla*.

18. Julio Valdeón Baruque, "Problemática para un estudio de los pobres y de la pobreza a fines de la edad media," in *A pobreza*, 2: 889–918; Antonio Collantes de Terán, *Sevilla en la baja edad media: La ciudad y sus hombres* (Sevilla: Ayuntamiento de Sevilla, 1977), 296–303.

19. On the feeding and clothing of the poor and on the changes in the nature of wills, see Teofilo F. Ruiz's forthcoming monograph on daily life in Castile.

20. ACB, vol. 44, f. 178 (15-September-1312); vol. 44, f. 179 (20-April-1338); vol. 44, f. 180 (2-December-1366).

21. AHN, Clero, carp. 226, no. 17 (20-August-1334); carp. 227, no. 2 (20-October-1334), no. 7 (13-April-1344); *Censo de población de las provincias y partidos de la corona de Castilla en el siglo XVI*, 224.

22. The bibliography on Jewish life in medieval Spain is lengthy indeed, and there is no need to review all of it here. For the standard histories of the Jews in Spain, see Y. Fritz Baer, *A History of the Jews in Christian Spain*, 2 vols. (Philadelphia: The Jewish Publication Society of America, 1961–66); relevant documentation is found in Baer, *Die Juden im Christlichen Spanien*, 2 vols. (Berlin: Akademie-Verlag, 1929–36; new printing, Farnborough, Eng.: Gregg, 1970). See bibliography by H. Beinart in the 1970 printing. See also A. Neuman, *The Jews in Spain: Their Social, Political and Cultural Life during the Middle Ages*, 2 vols. (Philadelphia: The Jewish Publication Society of America, 1944); and the old but still valuable J. Amador de los Ríos, *Historia social, política y religiosa de los judíos de España y Portugal*; and the more recent work by José María Monsalvo Antón, *Teoría y evolución de un conflicto social: El antisemitismo en la corona de Castilla en la baja edad media* (Madrid: Siglo XXI, 1985), see bibliography, pp. 337–42. See also the numerous articles published in *Sefarad*, the journal of Iberian Jewish history.

23. The bibliography on the pogroms of 1391 and of the mid-fifteenth century,

on the *conversos*, and on the Inquisition is even more extensive. A considerable amount of new and challenging research on the topic has been published in the last ten years. For a standard survey of the Inquisition and the Jews, see Henry Kamen, *The Spanish Inquisition* (London: Weidenfeld, 1965); also Angel Alcalá et al., *Inquisición española y mentalidad inquisitorial* (Barcelona: Ariel, 1984), 9–19; for a review of recent scholarship, see William Monter, "The New Social History and the Spanish Inquisition," *Journal of Social History* 7 (1984): 705–14; Sara T. Nalle, "Inquisitors, Priests and People during the Catholic Reformation in Spain," *The Sixteenth Century Journal* 18, no. 4 (1987): 557–87. See n. 1 in Nalle's article for a bibliography of recent work on the Inquisition.

24. See my "Relaciones entre judíos y cristianos en Castilla, 1200–1350: Avila y Burgos," in *Actas del congreso de judíos y cristianos en la historia*, forthcoming in 1994.

25. Baer, *A History of the Jews*, 1: 212; Amador de los Ríos, *Historia social, política y religiosa de los judíos de España y Portugal*, 2: 72–74. See also illustrative documents in Baer, *Die Juden*, 2: no. 70. An example of the swearing on the Torah by Jews and on the Bible (probably the New Testament) by Christians can be found in AMB, clasif. 4125 (10-August-1274).

26. For the population of Burgos, see Ruiz, "The Transformation of the Castilian Municipalities," 20; also Estepa Diez, et al., *Burgos en la edad media*, 117–19, 150–51.

27. For protests, see AMB, clasif. 118 (20-April-1280); AMB, clasif. 2509 (25-May-1285). See also *Sancho IV*, 3: xlix. For the legislation of the Cortes against the tax exemption of Jews, see *Cortes*, 1: 99 (Haro, 1288); 111–12, 115 (Valladolid, 1293), et passim. See 115: "Otrossi alo que nos pidieron que los iudios e los moros non ouieses los heredamientos delos christianos por conpra nin por entrega nin en otra manera, que por esto se astragaua muy grande pieca delos nuestros pechos et perdiamos nos ende nuestro derecho."

28. Estepa Diez, *Burgos en la edad media*, 167.

29. Amador de los Ríos, *Historia social, política y religiosa de los judíos*, 261ff.; Baer, *Die Juden*, 2: no. 84, 66–69.

30. Amador de los Ríos, *Historia social, política y religiosa de los judíos*, 299–302. The Jews in the entire diocese of Burgos paid 209,482 *maravedíes* (*mrs.*) in 1290. For a more detailed breakdown of who benefited from Jewish taxes, see pp. 916–31. For example, the money assessed on the *aljama* of Burgos found its way into the coffers of the Infante Don Fernando, heir to the throne, the powerful Infante Don Juan Manuel, as well as other important magnates and royal officials. The recent discovery by Francisco Hernández of a hitherto unknown account book (late thirteenth century) in the archives of the cathedral of Toledo will provide us with a clearer understanding of Jewish contributions and of Jewish population in late thirteenth-century Castile. The forthcoming publication of these accounts will radically modify our understanding of this topic.

31. On the 800 *mrs.* needed to qualify for *caballero* status, see Ruiz, "The Transformation of the Castilian Municipalities," 12–16. On the assignment of 12,000 *mrs.* from Jewish taxes to the city council of Burgos, see AMB, clasif. 154 (9-May-1345). On the fine on Burgos, see Baer, *A History of the Jews*, 1: 365.

32. See Chapter 6. See also Ernesto Pastor Díaz de Garayo, *Salvatierra y la llanada oriental alavesa (siglos XIII–XV)* (Vitoria: Diputación foral de Alava, 1986), 102–13; for the absence of references to Jews in commercial activities, see pp. 156–57.

33. For Seville, see Ramón Carande, *Sevilla, fortaleza y mercado* (Sevilla: Universidad de Sevilla, 1975), 53–81; Ladero Quesada, *Historia de Sevilla*, 73–130. On Abraham el Barchilón and other important Jewish financiers, see Francisco Cantera Burgos, "Burgos y don Yucef Pimintiella," *Boletín de la Institución Fernán González* 31, no. 118 (1952): 1–4; Klein, *The Mesta*, 13; Sancho IV, 1: 143–44.

34. See Chapters 7 and 8; see also *Las Huelgas*, 1: 160: ". . . et que los metan [Jews] en aquellas casas que ovieran menester las duenas que enfermaren en el monasterio." Anselmo Salvá, *Cosas de la vieja Burgos* (Burgos: Excelentísimo ayuntamiento de Burgos, 1892), 62. ACB, vol. 49, f. 85 (22-April-1286). On vineyards, see Chapter 3.

35. AHN, Clero, carp. 226, no. 17 (20-August-1334); carp. 227, no. 7 (13-April-1344).

36. One of Burgos's leading citizens, Simón González, lent a considerable amount of money to the monastery of Santo Domingo de Silos. See *Silos*, 418. See also Estepa Diez et al., *Burgos en la Edad Media*, 349; María del Carmen Carlé, "Mercaderes en Castilla, 1252–1512," *CHE* 21–22 (1954): 295.

37. Francisco Cantera Burgos, "La judería de Burgos," *Sefarad* 12 (1952): 71.

38. *DMA*, 211–481. For Jewish life elsewhere, see Asenjo González, *Segovia: La ciudad y su tierra*, 322–23; Rucquoi, *Valladolid en la edad media*, 1: 228: Rucquoi finds Jews cohabiting with Christians throughout the city and employed in diverse trades and occupations. See also José R. Díaz de Durana, *Álava en la baja edad media: Crisis, recuperación y transformaciones socioeconómicas, 1250–1525* (Vitoria: Diputación foral de Álava, 1986), 300.

39. On Ávila see Barrios García, *Estructuras agrarias y de poder*, 2: 133–259. On references to Jews in trade elsewhere in an earlier period and during the late Middle Ages, see Baer, *Die Juden*, 2: 1–3, et passim.

40. See Ruiz, "The Transformation of the Castilian Municipalities," 12–16; also my *Sociedad y poder real*, ch. 2.

41. *DMA*, 165–68. On transactions elsewhere, see Francisco Cantera Burgos, "La judería de Calahorra," *Sefarad* 15 (1955): 355–58; and his "Documentos de compraventas hebráicos de la catedral de Calahorra," *Sefarad* 6 (1946): 37–62. See also Luciano Huidobro y F. Cantera Burgos, "Los judíos en Aguilar de Campóo," *Sefarad* 14 (1954): 335–53; Salvador de Moxó, "Los judíos castellanos en el reinado de Alfonso XI," *Sefarad* 35 (1975): 142–43, and documents in 36 (1976): 37–120.

42. See Luis Suárez Fernández, *Judíos españoles en la Edad Media* (Madrid: Rialp, 1980), 237 et passim. Although the evidence is from Barcelona, see evidence of Jewish poverty in A. Cardoner, "El 'hospital para judíos pobres' de Barcelona," *Sefarad* 22 (1962): 373–75. See also the social class of Toledo *conversos* brought to the Inquisition tribunals in Toledo, in Teófilo F. Ruiz, "La Inquisición medieval y la moderna. Paralelos y contrastes," in Alcalá et al., *Inquisición española*, 62; Baer, *Die Juden*, 2: 137.

43. Luciano Huidobro y Serna, "Los moros de Burgos y su influencia en el arte," *Boletín de la comisión de monumentos de la provincia de Burgos* 105 (1945): 222–25.

44. See, for example, *DMA*, 438; Miguel Ángel Ladero Quesada, *Los mudejares de Castilla y otros estudios de historia medieval andaluza* (Granada: Universidad de Granada, 1989), 11–132, and bibliography therein.

45. *Crónica de Juan II*, ed. C. Rossell (Madrid: Biblioteca de autores españoles, vol. 68), 565.

Part IV

The Crisis of Late Medieval Castilian Society: Continuity and Change

In previous chapters I have examined the general patterns of Castilian rural and urban life and also sought to examine in detail specific regions in the realm. In the concluding chapters and epilogue, however, I would like to take a different tack. My aims here are threefold: (1) to examine the changes—most of them catastrophic—in rural and urban life over time; (2) to attempt to explain why and how this transformation took place; (3) to place the crisis of northern Castile within the context of the general crisis of European society in the late Middle Ages.

Several years ago I suggested some explanations for the problems that afflicted Castile in the late thirteenth and fourteenth centuries. I argued then that the Castilian conquest of Seville in 1248 and the subsequent Christian expansion into and settlement of al-Andalus marked a turning point in the institutional, economic, social, and cultural life of the Castilian realm.[1] Although I still believe that my overall argument is essentially correct, it is clear that many of the points I had advanced in 1979 require further elaboration and, in some cases, modifications. My analysis was an impressionistic one, based on a small documentary base and restricted, to a large extent, to the area around the city of Burgos. The main thesis of my article was that the conquest of Seville led to a rearrangement of political forces in Castile, with just a passing reference made to the crisis in agriculture and demography. In the preceding chapters I have attempted to amend this neglect and to examine the social and economic transformations of Castilian life. Two more points should be made here by way of introduction.

Historians suffer, at times, from the tendency to emphasize one specific historical event as a catalyst for later developments. The conquest of Seville in 1248 and the Christian resettlement of Andalucía appear to form such an "event." But in reality, 1248 marked only one more stage on the long road of Castilian expansion. This process of expansion, conquest, and settlement had begun almost five centuries earlier, and it continued in the peninsula, in North Africa, in other parts of Europe, and in transoceanic colonies for centuries afterward. In a sense, northern Castilian society had to adapt to the perennial drawing off of men, women, and material resources to the beckoning needs of its many frontiers. This continuous readjustment of labor supply, this ceaseless peeling off of the region's limited demographic resources, was not a new challenge, but an old and well-known process, met quite successfully throughout the previous centuries. This constant drain of manpower—or what can be better described as an ebb and flow of population (since some emigrants to the south sometimes returned north)—was a permanent feature of Castilian life, shaping its economic and social structure. This is not to say, of course, that the majority of the population moved to and fro across the Castilian plain. Those who migrated were never in the majority, and for most Castilians their horizon did not extend beyond nearby villages or towns. But very much as the Mesta—another instance of long-term movement on the north–south axis of Castilian history—could not but deeply affect the development of Castilian and Spanish history, so too did this almost millennium-long movement of people across the land.

The other point is an obvious one. Looking back into the past, putting together documents, we construct a running story—a sequence of events that lead us to speak of crises and changes. But for the peasant scratching a living from an ungrateful soil, if this year was bad and the next terrible, then the one after next might be better. What for us are long-term crises, seen developing over time, may have been for contemporaries, the stuff of daily life—not very different from the hunger and violence endured by their ancestors. In this sense, change was seldom radical and noticeable at close view. If in previous works I have emphasized the swift transformation of Castilian society, then the change was swift only when seen through the distorting lens of time.

Note

1. Teofilo F. Ruiz, "Expansion et changement," 548–65.

10. The Conquest of Seville Revisited: Demography and Fiscal Oppression

Changes in the Rural Structure of Castile: Territorial Expansion, Agriculture, and Demography

We know, in a general manner, the patterns of population movement, demographic dislocation, climatic changes, and endemic violence that plagued Castile in the late Middle Ages. We also know the general outline of the corollaries to these disasters: shortages of food, rises in grain prices, and the slow and not always successful readjustment of northern agriculture to these problems.[1] But these factors did not come about suddenly. The year 1248 is only a convenient benchmark along the road of an ancient process of agricultural transformation.

We must begin with an assumption which, even though it cannot always be fully illustrated, is, I believe, incontrovertible. I refer here to the demographic limitations of the northern plain. Most indications we have for the thirteenth century point to a small and scattered population.[2] By the mid-fourteenth century, conditions had worsened considerably under the blows of aristocratic violence, deteriorating rural conditions, and, finally, the Black Death. Thus in the thirteenth century, when the expansion of the arable and the size of medieval populations were reaching their high points in certain areas of England and France, there was no noticeable expansion of settlements in northern Castile, and possibly some indications of a contraction of the arable in most parts of the region.[3] One must remember those descriptions of late medieval and early modern travelers paraphrased in an earlier chapter. They provided a vision of human enclaves, hugging urban centers or water courses, divided from each other by the sparsely populated and often forbidding plain. The plain was, of course, not always sparsely populated nor entirely forbidding, but the human capital was always in short supply, and by the thirteenth and fourteenth centuries it was getting shorter. This was not a world in crisis due to Malthusian pressures.

In previous chapters, I have already provided examples of the labor shortages and population decline in the lands of the monastery of Santa María la Real, as well as of the small percentage of the available arable cultivated in the lands of the chapter of Segovia in the 1290s. Angel García Sanz has pointed to the evidence of abandoned vineyards and underutilized arable in the region of Segovia, and he dates the shrinking of the areas of cultivation to early in the thirteenth century. In examining this and other, similar assertions about northern Castilian agriculture, we are on rather shaky ground. Conditions favoring rural production in the thirteenth century may not have been as favorable as those in the previous century, and the fourteenth century was certainly worse. But, again, some specific areas were less affected by the problems of the later Middle Ages. Luis Martínez García reports population pressure in the lands of the Hospital del Rey in Burgos in the 1330s. This took place at a time when the evidence from elsewhere shows a different trend.[4] Ecclesiastical domains probably fared worse than seignorial ones, or so it seems, for before 1350 we know little about the latter, and, above all, we know far too little about general economic conditions in twelfth-century rural Castile to undertake any comprehensive comparison.[5]

As a result of these contractions, by 1300 many ecclesiastical lords were facing problems cultivating their lands. One may assume as much from the growing tendency to enter into rental agreements (*arriendos*), which at least helped generate a stable, even if low, income in money or in kind. A good number of these *arriendos* emphasized the cultivation of lands that were, as the documents state, uncultivated or abandoned. Likewise, land and real-estate transactions sometimes involved waste or uncultivated land. Significantly, the mention of *tierras yermas* in such exchanges of property decreased dramatically after 1300, an indication, I would argue, that by the fourteenth century any hope of putting new lands under cultivation had been abandoned. Wherever in Castile we can trace property over time, we see no growth, no attempt at expansion. Once a house or a mill had fallen down, or land had gone out of production, there was seldom any attempt to rebuild it or to plow it.

The account books of the cathedral of Burgos—one of the most formidable sources for the economic history of Castile—has a running inventory of ecclesiastical property, both urban and rural, from 1267 into the fifteenth century. Every five years or so, at fairly regular periods, long inventories of houses, rural income, mills, and other revenue-producing property are listed. Houses that were down by 1267 remained down into the fourteenth century, with no efforts made to repair and rent them. In 1272

TABLE 10.1.   Mills Held by the Cathedral Chapter of Burgos.

Year	Total Number of Mills	Empty	Fallen Down
1277	17	1	1
1279	16		1
1280	17		1
1282	13		1
1314	11? (unreadable)		1
1325	17		1
1344	15		1
1350	18		1

Source: ACB, Cuadernos de contabilidad.

the chapter held outright or had a majority interest in seventeen mills in and around Burgos, of which one was vacant and another, the mill of the Holy Sepulcher, had fallen down.

Over a period of nearly one hundred years, the number of mills did not change very much (see Table 10.1). The eighteen mills in 1350 included a very recent donation of a mill by the dean of the chapter, Pedro Bonifaz, who had died that same year. The mill of the Holy Sepulcher, first reported as "fallen" (caída) is in succeeding years described as "destroyed" (destruída); obviously, the chapter did not have the financial resources for, or there was no demand meriting, the rebuilding of the mill. Moreover, the chapter was most willing to reduce rents to maintain the occupied mills. Indeed, the flexibility of the chapter to adapt to changing conditions was worthy of praise, and we could almost follow the changing fortunes of the realm in the changing pattern of rent. Years of crisis brought lower rents (in real money); the promise of improving conditions brought the reverse.[6]

Regardless of other reasons, the chapter did not wish to or could not repair a fallen mill; rather, it sought to consolidate, to improve, and to hold on to existing property. That is usually the pattern we find wherever we turn in this period. There is little or no expansion throughout northern Castile, although, of course, exceptions can be found. In some areas of the Rioja, to give just one example, vineyards brought good returns, and there were incentives to put more land under cultivation.[7]

There is no single explanation for the stagnation of northern Castilian agriculture. Clearly, the crises of the late thirteenth and early fourteenth centuries in Castile, as elsewhere in the West, resulted from a combination of factors that varied from place to place. However, the reasons that have been advanced for similar crises in northern Europe—overextended arable, cultivation of marginal lands, a drop in food production, and, ultimately, a reverse in demographic growth—cannot be accepted for Castile, with the exception of some specific and nonrepresentative subregions.

In Castile, even though most lands did not yield abundant crops and may have even been considered marginal elsewhere, the problem was certainly not a shortage of suitable arable land. The difficulties resided in the availability of human and animal labor, with their scarcity—a fact of life since the early thirteenth century and probably earlier—leading to reduced production or acting as impediments to the expansion of cereal-growing lands. Yet scarcity of labor cannot be blamed for all the evils plaguing Castile. The swift increase in the price of food in the 1260s, which I had previously attributed to the partial abandonment of grain-producing lands in the north by peasants migrating to Andalucía, seems also to have been caused by the debasing of the coinage. The higher cost of food, cloth, and other luxury items reflected, among other things, the unwise minting of a limited issue of silver coins, followed by the excessive issue of debased coinage; the sharp increase in magnate wealth, with its accompanying conspicuous consumption; and a sharp decrease in the crown's income with the termination of tribute money from al-Andalus. I am certain that demographic dislocations produced by migration to the south and the resettlement of Castilian peasants, urban dwellers, and noblemen in Andalucía had a lasting impact on the institutional, social, and economic structure of the realm, but not the sort of food shortages or sharp decline to which I subscribed several years ago.

We are, for all practical purposes, at the same point as where we began. On the one hand, I speak of a general crisis with an emphasis on agricultural production; on the other, I argue that there were no spectacular famines or food shortages to justify this assertion.[8] Though at first sight this appears a bit contradictory, I think the explanation is not, and that it can be presented in a straightforward and coherent manner.

Although the opening of al-Andalus to Christian settlement may not have directly caused a rise in food prices or even led to food shortage, the impact, though more subtle, was nonetheless as dramatic. What we witness throughout the century after the battle of Las Navas de Tolosa and the conquests of Córdoba (1236) and Seville (1248) was the slow realignment of commerce and agriculture in Castile, both north and south, accompanied by a redistribution of the Castilian population. Local expansion, so evident in the later part of the twelfth century and even in some parts of northern Castile into the early thirteenth, came to an end as the kingdom doubled its size by the acquisition of the rich lands of Andalucía. I do not think it is too difficult to imagine how grain production may have declined—as it is evident in the documentation of Segovia, Ávila, Burgos, and elsewhere, which report uncultivated fields and reduced numbers of taxpayers—and yet since the population, which was scarce to begin with, had also decreased, one development did not bring the scourge of famine, which was so familiar elsewhere. Segovia and Ávila, which were, in a sense, on a double frontier (toward the kingdom of Toledo and Andalucía and toward the region of Extremadura), showed signs of contraction and abandonment of at least part of the arable much earlier than the northern regions of Campóo, Burgos, or even more stable regions in the mountains, such as Oña.

Nevertheless, the attraction of the south was far too strong, the promise of what could be gained there too bright, to be ignored for long. The final expulsion of the Muslims from al-Andalus after the Mudejar revolt (1264–66) is a crucial moment in the economic history of Castile. I did not fully understand before the connection between the expulsion of the Mudejars and the reforming Cortes of Jerez (1268), nor did I emphasize enough the strong economic interdependence between al-Andalus and northern Castile. After 1248 and more markedly after the early 1260s, Castile went through a painful (as we judge in retrospect) period of population readjustment and economic distabilization.

In this respect, the repopulation and *repartimiento* of Jerez de la Frontera are representative of the conditions that still existed almost two decades after the conquest of Seville, a period that coincided with the rising and expulsion of the Mudejars. The successes and failures of this *repartimiento*, as well as those of other, similar distributions of urban and rural property in Andalucía, serve almost as a guide to the flux and reflux of Castilian economic and institutional life in the first twenty-five years after the conquest of Seville. The movement of people from the northern plain to the south meant the further scattering of a population that was already small when compared to the size of the kingdom.[9]

Northern peasants and estate managers might not have understood very well or, what is more probable, did not wish to understand the special techniques of Muslim agriculture, or the different demands of Andalusi rural life and economy. With the expulsion of the Mudejars from the countryside, the cycle of misfortune was completed, and the Christians failed often in their attempts to till the land according to patterns learned and employed long ago in the northern dry lands. Many returned north in defeat, and the upheaval of migration from the north, resettlement in the south, desertion of newly settled lands, return to the north, or descent into the ranks of the landless peasantry created havoc in the realm. Manuel González Jiménez has already shown this reverse migration to the north by peasants from the area around Seville, and Glick's description of the problems northern Christian peasants confronted in the area of Murcia and in the Campo de Cartagena points to the widespread difficulties faced in their task of resettling the newly conquered lands.[10]

That such was the case is not difficult to understand. We have examples from modern and contemporary history that show how difficult it is for peasants to adopt new agricultural techniques. The long refusal of European peasants in the eighteenth century to accept the potato and of third world farmers to plant more resistant strains of wheat points to the barriers in changing long-standing traditions in planting, eating habits, and dress. Moreover, the basic economic structures of Andalucía were different from those of northern Castile. It must have taken a while for Christian settlers to understand the culture of the olive and what was required to grow and export spices and fruits, as well as how to employ the distinct techniques of irrigation and grape growing prevalent in al-Andalus. The Muslims had also practiced dry-farming, but only on a limited scale. A comparison with Valencia (conquered 1238), where Moorish peasants were retained as farm labor, even though under a changed status, provides a good example of a different pattern of conquest and resettlement. The fabled Valencian gardens and Valencia's ancient irrigation works did not suffer the damage or the setbacks that occurred in Andalucía. Christians there were able to learn and to adapt to the needs of the land and to the techniques of Muslim agriculture over a period of centuries.

The Castilian Crisis: Decreased Income and Resistance to Taxation

The scattering of the population of Castile over a large territory and the accompanying reduction in the size of cultivated land in specific areas of the realm had a long-lasting impact. Before we see the first signs of crises in northern Europe—perhaps as early as 1285 in some parts of France—Castile was already caught in a tailspin. The conquest of the south by the Christian armies, a task begun much earlier than the twelfth century but highlighted by the decisive battle of Las Navas de Tolosa (1212), and the conquest of most of western Andalucía by 1264, brought a long-term redistribution of population throughout the realm. The migration of lords and peasants to the south to resettle the lands deserted after the expulsion of the Mudejars meant a retrenchment of agriculture in northern Castile. This is most evident in the records of monastic and cathedral institutions and in land and real-estate transactions that show the underutilization of land in the north.

In the south, the very low prices of land in and around Seville—land which at first impression seemed to have been easily accessible to the city—point to the abundant supply of good farming land.[11] The higher salaries paid to agricultural laborers in the region, enforced by the legislation of the Cortes, already give an indication of the shortage of labor and the difficulties of bringing Andalusi production back to its original level.[12] It is very difficult to recapture the confusion of those years, but it is clear that it was not an easy adjustment. This movement of people from north to south, with a subsequent ebb northward, must have brought untold problems: first, social and economic difficulties when they moved out, and second, further problems when they returned, seeking to recover what they had left behind. John Domínguez of Burgos and his wife María Fernández came to Jerez and received houses in the *repartimiento*, but within a short time he was back north in Logroño. Caught stealing horses, he was killed, and his wife was able to keep only half of the houses in Jerez; these she sold immediately so that she could return, one must assume, to northern Castile.[13] Others must have had experiences not unlike those of John and María, even if they did not meet a similar tragic end.

Such instability in the overall population of the realm, but particularly in the north, must have meant that monasteries and cathedral chapters suffered a decrease in the income they received from their rural holdings. We have abundant documentary evidence for the impoverishment of the church, but the nobility must also have suffered from these economic changes. We must remember that these transformations occurred before the takeoff of the Mesta and of the wool exports, which, after 1350, provided a large income for some magnates and ecclesiastic corporations. The upper segments of the society, however, were not the only ones affected, and the middling groups, *caballeros villanos* and merchants and artisans, suffered as well. From the 1260s on, the economic difficulties were reflected in growing resistance to taxation, numerous petitions for remission of taxes, commutations of debts to Jews, and reduction in the number of taxable units in secular and ecclesiastic villages and domains.

The history of Castile in this period is marked by increased competition for shrinking resources, in which the crown, nobility, church, and municipal councils fought bitterly and often violently to preserve or to gain access to tax monies and to grasp control over ever-decreasing sources of income. This requires a lengthy and well-documented explanation, but first several comments should be made which are necessary for understanding the complexities of Castilian history in the mid-thirteenth century and the nature of the crisis that beset Castile in succeeding decades. As the first impact of the conquest of Andalucía was beginning to affect its economic structure, Alfonso X, the reigning king, embarked on an ambitious program of legislative and economic reforms. This also included an expensive, harmful, and eventually failed candidacy for the imperial crown.

My own evaluation of Alfonso X has been undergoing a slow change. While a few years back I condemned his policies as a complete failure and, in many ways, as being responsible for many of the ills that plagued Castile in following years, I am at present more inclined to think, following O'Callaghan, that Alfonso X was as much a victim of circumstances as of his own limitations as a ruler. Perhaps a more capable or prudent king would have been able to mitigate the impact of the expansion into the south, but it is doubtful that anyone could have prevented or even understood exactly what was going on. The fact remains, however, that the newly conquered lands had to be resettled to prevent their falling back into Muslim hands, and that the patterns of conquest and occupation employed in Andalucía had a long historical tradition from which Alfonso X, or even a better man, could not have escaped.[14]

The key here, of course, is that the conquest of Córdoba and Seville and the large donations, grants, and booty which this expansion generated provided the high nobility of Castile with the economic wherewithal to play a greater role in the political affairs of the realm. Whereas, in spite of some troublesome minorities, specifically that of Alfonso VIII (1158–1214), the magnates had cooperated with the crown in the task of the reconquest, after the 1250s this was no longer the case. The temporary halt of the reconquering advance after the 1260s put an end for a while to what had been easy pickings since 1212.

Coincidental with the hiatus in the Christian advance, the legislative and institutional program of Alfonso X threatened the special *fueros* or privileges of the nobility and sought, as kings were doing elsewhere in the medieval West, to establish the authority of the king and his laws throughout the realm and above the local interests and customary rights of lords, prelates, and municipal councils. On the other hand, the establishment of financial frontiers, by the creation of custom houses, the rationalization and more efficient collection of royal taxes, and the admission into the royal bureaucracy of a greater number of the bourgeoisie, could have only brought resentment toward the king.[15] The sumptuary legislations of 1252 and 1258—measures aimed exclusively at the nobility and, above all, against the magnates—show the growing antagonism between the king and the *ricos hombres* and Alfonso's determination to be independent of magnate influence.

One of the consequences of the conquest of the south was the dramatic realignment of political forces within the realm. The kings of Castile sought and obtained support from the non-noble knights of Castile against the pretensions of the nobility and, in return, granted to these urban oligarchs extensive economic and political rights. The results of this alliance have already been seen in a previous chapter: the rise of patrician elites to political power in cities and towns of Castile with the acquiescence and even active support of the crown. In exchange, the kings of Castile obtained the non-noble knights' military support and eventual control of the political and financial resources of the cities.[16] Here, however, what ought to be emphasized is that Alfonso X's reforms, together with his extravagant gifts to foreign princes and to Castilian ecclesiastical institutions, as well as his imperial ambitions led to open confrontation with the nobility. To a large extent, the history of Castile from this point until the reign of Isabella and Ferdinand was shaped by constant aristocratic unrest and, more often than not, by challenges to the crown's authority.[17]

There is yet another factor that ought to be mentioned here and which constitutes a topic worthy of careful and separate study. To anyone acquainted with the workings of the English and French administrations in the Middle Ages, the Castilian bureaucracy seems, at best, rudimentary.[18] The lack of administrative records and the disorganization of its financial accounts are just vivid examples of its weakness. Even if some of the records were lost in the fires at the *alcazares* of Madrid and Segovia (neither of the two towns an important administrative center in the Middle Ages), their absence does not explain fully the limitations of Castile's administration. In a realm with a peripatetic court, with no real administrative center, always at war against internal and external enemies, the extant documentation often provides the impression that the left hand did not know what the right hand was doing. A feeble administrative base and a bureaucracy that lacked the levels of specialization found in other parts of the West reflected in part a failure of leadership, but, most importantly, it denied Castile the luxury that other realms, such as England or France, had during the tenure of an incompetent king or in the absence of a ruler. In a previous chapter, we saw how municipal officials and merchants were drawn on an ad hoc basis to carry diverse duties for the crown. There is no evidence of what may be described as the "professionalization" of certain branches of the administration to deal with specific aspects of government. It is therefore against this backdrop of human limitations and failings that we must set the development of Castilian history in the late Middle Ages.

DEALING WITH THE FINANCIAL CRISIS

The conquest of Andalucía by the Christians also had its positive aspects, and we should not ignore them. There were immediate as well as long-term benefits to the occupation of the south. On the one hand the economic links between northern Castile and al-Andalus, which had existed for a long time, were now strengthened and expanded. The commercial network discussed in an earlier chapter and the sea voyages between Andalucía and the Bay of Biscay ports, with further links to English and Flemish ports, point to the closer integration of regional markets and the establishment of commercial ties that had a long and beneficial impact on the Castilian economy. For example, in 1292 Sancho IV ordered the shipping of arms and siege machinery from Castile, Asturias, and Galicia to the armies investing Tarifa, attesting to the easy communication between the two regions.[19]

By sea and land, northern merchants traveled south in search of new products and new forms of economic exchanges. Furthermore, the opening of the southern grazing lands marked the official beginnings of the Mesta. As is well known, the history of transhumance on the Iberian Peninsula dates back to prehistoric times, but it was only in 1273 that Alfonso X's privilege to the sheepherders guild turned transhumance into a truly kingdom-wide enterprise. In many respects, the expansion of the Mesta and its privileged position after 1273 indicate the failure of agricultural interests in certain parts of Andalucía that were unable to defend the primacy of agriculture over livestock grazing. It also reveals the vast expanses of uncultivated and unpopulated land in both the north and the south. The conquest of the south brought victory to the ranching interests which for centuries had fought an indecisive battle against farming. While there are many criticisms that could be levied against the Mesta and against its long-term influence on the development of Castile and Spain, the fact remains that through the late Middle Ages and most of the early modern period the income from the Mesta represented an important component of royal finances. Thanks to transhumance, the kings of Castile and, after 1474, of Castile and Aragon counted on a reliable source of income to finance, in part, their ambitious foreign programs.

Last but not least, through the conquest Castile gained Atlantic and Mediterranean ports and the eventual control of the Straits of Gibraltar. This opened Castile to a wider world, brought foreign merchants (mostly Italians) to Andalusi cities, and, after the union with Aragon, thrust Castile into the world of Mediterranean politics. Dominion over Andalucía meant the establishment of important economic links with Mediterranean and North African markets. Finally, the region served as a natural springboard for Castile's western expansion: first in the Canary Islands, and then across the ocean to the discovery and conquest of the New World.

REMISSION OF TAXES

In the mid-thirteenth century, the high hopes of empire and glory lay still in the future, and it did not take very long for contemporaries to realize that things were not going quite right. The hostile author of the chronicle of Alfonso X, writing almost a century afterward, placed the blame squarely on the shoulders of the king. He charged that the income of the *parias* (tribute exacted from Muslim kingdoms in the peninsula) paid by the king of Granada to Ferdinand III amounted to 600,000 *mrs.* of such "strong value that one counting *maravedí* was worth almost as much as a gold *maravedí*."[20]

While Alfonso had devaluated the coinage and received only 250,000 *mrs.* of the new, weaker coinage, it was precisely this debasing of the coinage then circulating in Castile that the chronicler blamed for the rapid increase in prices and subsequent failure of price and wage control. In many respects, the kingdom never fully recovered from these first adversities.

What follows can be easily illustrated in two ways: (1) in the general requests for tax and debt relief because the land was poor and empty, and (2) in the individual petitions in northern Castile for the reduction in the number of those on the tax rolls for the same reasons. These pleas tell a vivid story of the progressive shrinking of tax rolls and the collapse of royal, seignorial, and ecclesiastic income.

Fighting over taxes or struggling to control the power of taxation does not always reflect a deteriorating economic condition. There is no doubt,

however, than in Castile in the late thirteenth and early half of the fourteenth century, the ordinances of the Cortes read almost as a medical chart,
and in them we could read the worsening conditions of the realm. This was
most evident in the numerous petitions that procurators of the urban
centers of Castile addressed to the king seeking some form of regulation of
taxation and control over illegal collectors. Obviously, the urban oligarchies, which dominated Castilian cities, were also prompted by their political ambitions and the need to protect their economic interests, but there
was clearly a great deal more than this. Miguel Ángel Ladero Quesada has
given us the first outline of royal financial structure in this period. As he
points out, the reign of Alfonso X marked a starting point for attempts to
develop a somewhat orderly fiscal system. Unfortunately, the king sought
to enhance his income at a time when, due to the expansion into the south,
there had been a downturn in the available financial resources of the
kingdom.[21]

Not unlike other medieval rulers in this period, the kings of Castile
suffered from a chronic shortage of money. In their case, this problem was
compounded by excessive royal largess and by the inefficiency of their half-
developed bureaucracy. Alfonso X sold the arrears of several taxes to Jewish
tax farmers for 1,670,000 *mrs.* in 1277,[22] and his successors followed this
practice on many occasions. Cities also found it easier to farm taxes than to
collect them. This was the case in Burgos in 1281, when Arnalt de Sanchester
and other members of the city's ruling oligarchy farmed the taxes on the
sale of wine. Of course, the practice of farming taxes was not exclusive to
Castile, nor in the context of the Middle Ages was it a sign of financial
weakness, but what was evident is that the financial apparatus required to
make the collection of revenues efficient did not exist.[23]

Adding to these problems, political upheaval over taxes—as when two
hostile factions laid claim to the same fiscal resources in Burgos in 1279, or in
the whole kingdom in 1295 and 1313—did not make for an orderly system of
taxation.[24] On the other hand, taxes became difficult to collect not only
because of economic difficulties, but for other reasons as well. The migration of taxpayers from one region to another—with the subsequent confusion that ensued—could have been an important reason for the failure to
raise the proper amount of income. But it did not help either that the
numerous and indiscriminate exemptions from taxes granted by the king
further eroded royal income. Urban non-noble knights, who already enjoyed some tax exemptions from an earlier period, were almost completely
freed from taxes after 1256, as were their servants. Clerics in Castilian cities

demanded and received similar grants in the second half of the thirteenth century. Nobles, who had been excused from most exactions because of their military functions and privileges, refused the "levying of extraordinary taxes [the *servicios*] upon their dependents, although they had previously given their consent in 1272."[25] As we examine the evidence available for the mid-fourteenth century, the most cursory glance at the *Becerro de behetrías* would show that numerous rural communities in northern Castile enjoyed exemption from even the most basic royal taxes, and this often resulted from petitions from the nobility, who sought to enhance their own incomes by exempting their dependent peasants from royal exactions.[26]

In 1292 Sancho IV received the paltry sum of 35,400 *mrs.* in *fonsadera* from the entire dioceses of Palenzuela, Palencia, Burgos, and Calahorra, that is, from almost all of northern Castile. It seems that, for all practical purpose, almost everyone was exempted from this particular obligation. In addition, as I have indicated above, the extravagant gifts to monasteries and individuals—as, for example, the 60,000 *mrs.* that Alfonso XI reconfirmed as a grant to Las Huelgas on the occasion of his crowning in 1332—were a constant drain on the treasury or, worse yet, on the future, since most gifts were given against projected tax revenue, tying the crown into perpetual donations.[27]

It is not surprising, then, that the Castilian kings seldom had enough money with which to carry out their policies.[28] With traditional sources of revenue drying up or alienated to the nobility or to ecclesiastic establishments, the crown was forced to look elsewhere. I have already mentioned that the income received from transhumance and from taxes on the Jews were important substitutes for the shortcomings of a regular taxation system. According to the *cuadernos* of the Cortes, the contribution of the Jews alone amounted to 6,000 *mrs.* daily in the late thirteenth century or more than 2,000,000 *mrs.* annually around 1300.[29] Yet, to supplement these sources of income, the crown had to ask for special subsidies (*servicios*) from the cities. These subsidies were voted by the Cortes, but unlike the case in France, where the assemblies argued with the crown over the right of the king to collect such extraordinary taxes, the Castilian Cortes appear remarkably meek. There is no evidence that the cities ever questioned the legality of the *servicio*, nor was the amount to be paid a matter of contention. Traditionally, a *servicio* was equal to a payment for *moneda forera*. If the urban procurators protested, it was essentially over the frequency of these subsidies, or because they sought to gain some advantages and concessions from the king in return for their acquiescence.[30]

YANTAR (PURVEYANCE)

These revenues, however, were not sufficient, and the king's efforts to increase royal income by other means led to conflict. The abuse of the royal right to *yantar* (purveyance) was the reason for many grievances. The king, his family, royal officials, and magnates used and abused this right. Even though, as was the case in other parts of the medieval West, purveyance had often been commuted for money payments, a royal visit could bring havoc to any town. The language of the demands presented by the urban procurators to the Cortes is quite vivid in its detailing of official abuse: "that you say that our officials wreck your houses and take bread, wine, fish, straw and firewood. . . ."[31] But magnates and royal officials behaved very much like the king, and the language of the petition evokes the image of a realm where the powerful lived off the land as if in an enemy's country.

The urban procurators sought to define and restrict their obligations to the crown and to end abuses through legislation. The Cortes of Palencia (1286) set an annual purveyance obligation of 600 *mrs.* for the king and of 200 *mrs.* for the queen. Purveyance for the royal *merino* was to be given only once a year. In spite of these ordinances, complaints were voiced again in 1293 and in 1295. At the later date, the regent, María de Molina, in dire need of municipal support, promised to pay for those provisions appropriated for the use of the royal court rather than to exercise her right of *yantar*.[32]

In 1298 the regent queen agreed to defer her claims of *yantar* until custom had been rightly established.[33] This was, of course, no guarantee that either the magnates or the royal officials would cease in their attempts to extort money from cities, towns, and villages. Once Ferdinand IV reached his majority, he sought to assert his rights of purveyance at the Cortes of Medina del Campo (1305) and Valladolid (1307). The response of the urban procurators was to protest against the abuse of *yantar* at a time when, as the language of the *cuadernos* of the *Cortes* stated, the land was "poor and uncultivated." Disregarding their pleas, Ferdinand IV set his income from *yantar* at 1,000 *mrs.* and that of his queen at 400 *mrs.* His mother, María de Molina, and the king's uncle, the Infante Don Juan, both former regents, were also assigned 400 *mrs.* annually from each city owing purveyance.[34]

In spite of the crown's promises, the regularity with which the urban procurators complained about abuses of *yantar* through the next fifty years serves as a telling sign of the economic—and political—ills derived from this policy. At Valladolid (1312), the two Cortes of Palencia (1313), Burgos (1315), Carrión (1317), Valladolid (1322 and 1325), Madrid (1329), and Alcalá de Henares (1348), the cities protested against the financial burden of purveyance. Even when Alfonso XI agreed to lower purveyance contributions to 600 *mrs.* in 1325—and this came at a time when, ready to assume personal control of the realm, he required the support of the cities—in reality the urban oligarchies derived little from all their protests.[35]

TAXES AND RESISTANCE TO TAXATION

The important issues regarding who should be a tax collector and how taxes were to be collected were also debated at the meeting of the Cortes. As income fell, the scramble for control of tax revenues and for the profits derived from tax collection intensified. At the Cortes of Palencia (1286), the urban procurators asked and received the right to collect taxes, and the local administrative units, the city councils, acquired responsibility for taxes raised within their jurisdictions. Between 1286 and the late fourteenth century, the *concejos* made their right to collect taxes one of the outstanding questions discussed at the meeting of the Cortes. As has been seen in previous chapters, in northern Castile a significant number of those collecting the tithe in the northern ports or the *fonsadera* in the *merindades* of Castile belonged to the ruling urban elites. This made the question of taxation one of vital interest for certain segments of Castilian society, since their income and political position very often depended on their position as collectors of the royal taxes from which they were themselves exempted.[36]

There is no doubt as to why this was an important issue. As the need for money grew, the cities suffered numerous abuses at the hands of royal tax collectors. The language of innumerable individual petitions throughout this period, as well as the pleas of the procurators to the Cortes, reveal a population hounded by tax collectors pressing, most often illegally, for contributions. In the countryside, monastery after monastery, year after year, spent a great deal of energy and money in appealing to the king against the illegal demands of the royal bureaucracy. In fact, the overwhelming number of royal letters to northern Castilian monasteries in the first half of the fourteenth century were answers to pleas for relief from illegal taxation. The king, of course, always expressed his indignation at such actions, but they continued unabated throughout the period. These actions by royal agents were not uncommon in other realms and were part of the long and tortuous process of state building. In the case of Castile, however, the difference lies in the arbitrary character of these exactions and in the fact that the income collected illegally, more often than not, did not end up in the royal coffers.[37]

The royal tax collectors rode into the cities and villages, imprisoning citizens, calling taxpayers to testify at all hours of the day, and more than once, even though this was forbidden by the *fueros*, confiscating and selling the properties of those unable to pay. Between 1340 and 1346, the king, Alfonso XI, his officials, and the city council of Cuéllar engaged in a protracted struggle over taxes and claims on former Templar properties in the region. When the council refused to pay, property was confiscated and sold forcibly to the "three or four richest men in the town."[38] The same complaints also emerged from monastic establishments that had to stand by while their property and their vassals' properties were confiscated not only by royal officials but by the agents of independent and unruly magnates engaged in fierce competion for stagnant or decreasing sources of revenue.[39]

Protests against tax farming were almost as widespread as the claims of non-noble urban knights and "good men" to collect taxes and were usually linked in the same petition. Rather than reflecting a growing poverty, these petitions were most probably linked to the urban oligarchs' competition with Jewish tax farmers for access to the profits of such activities. This competition continued, with some success for Christian financiers, in the next century and a half.[40]

Economic Conditions and Borrowing Money

Tied also to the anti-Jewish sentiment of the urban oligarchs, but even more popular in a time of crisis, were the demands to control the rates of interest in loans made by Jews (Christians are not mentioned, although there were a good number of Christian moneylenders) as well as for partial commutation of debts to Jews because of adverse economic conditions and because the land and people were poor. In addressing these issues, the ordinances of the Cortes also provide significant information as to the economic and political conditions of the realm. Obviously, the kings of Castile were in a bind. Income obtained from the Jews was an important component of royal finances, and frequent cancellation of Christians' debts to them could only diminish royal income. On the other hand, petitions for such cancellations or regulations of interest rates, specifically against Jews, came at times of great distress when the king truly needed urban support.

The problems, however, went beyond remission of debts. In 1312, the Cortes complained that during the reigns of Alfonso X and Sancho IV the Jewish *aljamas* of Castile contributed 6,000 *mrs.* daily; no Jew then was exempted from paying a fifth of his or her income to the crown, whereas at the end of Ferdinand IV's reign (1312) more than 5,000 (surely an inflated figure!) rich Jews were exempted from taxes. The result was that the tax burden fell heavily on fewer and poorer Jews, and the *aljamas* were "*astragadas*" (poor and empty)—a diagnosis that probably fit the entire kingdom.[41]

Because Christians were poor or alleged to be poor, again and again debts to Jews were partially canceled and interest rates were set at a maximum of 33 percent. For every 3 *mrs.* borrowed, one more should be paid as interest; for every three *fanegas* of wheat, one extra should be paid as compensation. The cost of borrowing, whether money or grain, was indeed quite high, and one must suspect that these rates were nothing but an artificial ceiling. Also implicit in the petitions of urban procurators to the Cortes is the role of Jews in lending grain or the equivalent in money to farmers. We had an inkling of this in an earlier section, when we saw the liquidation sales of some small farms to satisfy outstanding debts to Jews. It is not very difficult to visualize the lending of a few *fanegas* of wheat or barley at seeding time or, most probably, after an inadequate harvest to support a family through the winter.[42]

Even more directly linked to the economic conditions were the demands for reduction or outright cancellation of taxes at almost every meeting of the Cortes from 1286 on. Again the reason advanced for such petitions was that the land was poor and desolate and/or that the wars and civil disturbances affected the economic well-being of the realm.[43] Clearly, many of these complaints were part of the political jockeying of urban procurators, as were the king's responses, but they also provide a vivid chart of Castile's economic problems.

DEMOGRAPHIC DECLINE AND REDUCTION IN REVENUES

More revealing of these economic ills and of the demographic difficulties that Castile faced before the plague are the numerous petitions of monastic establishments, cathedral chapters, and municipal councils for lowering the number of their dependents and neighbors on the tax rolls. These were not demands for exemption from taxes, but rather a plea for revision of the tax rolls to reflect accurately the new demographic situation. Since, in many cases, this meant a serious diminution in royal income, the crown's acquiescence to these petitions was often preceded by inquests conducted by royal officials. The extant documents show the king's willingness to accept this reduction of the tax base in most of northern Castile. It could be argued that if the number of taxpayers was reduced in the north, new sources of revenue opened in Andalucía. One must remember, however, that settlers in the south had received generous exemptions from most taxes as an enticement to migrate there.

Most of the reductions in the number of those owing taxes occurred after 1300, and the explanation most often given for such actions was the impact of war and of noble violence.[44] Peasant communities may have been left better off by the migration of some neighbors to the south. In theory, peasants could concentrate their farming on the best lands available, and migration would have diminished the competition for nearby grazing lands and wooded areas, which were always in short supply. This, however, was handicapped by onerous fiscal demands and by the violence brought about by two successive minorities.

In 1304 Ferdinand IV agreed to reduce the *fonsadera* of the *concejo* (city council) of Silos from 4,000 to 3,000 *mrs.* He took this action since, because "of the many evils and harm that the said town received during the times of war" during his minority, the territory was "very diminished" (*muy menguado*) and "very depopulated" and, thus, could no longer pay fully the royal taxes. Alfonso XI confirmed this tax reduction in 1329, an indication that conditions had not really changed a great deal in the quarter of a century after the 1304 grant.[45] In 1306, two years after he had reduced their taxes by 1,000 *mrs.*, Ferdinand IV once again made extensive concessions to the city council of Silos. As a compensation for the damages received in the last war from rebellious noblemen, as well as for the expense of building a wall around the town, the king exempted the inhabitants of Silos from all taxes except *moneda forera* and *martiniega*, so that the lands of the *villa* (town) would not become "waste and uninhabited.[46] As we saw in an earlier chapter, Silos had an uneasy relationship with its lord, the abbot of the monastery, and the kings—above all, Ferdinand IV—made bids to wrest the town from its monastic overlords.

In 1311, when some semblance of order had been restored to the kingdom, Ferdinand IV agreed to fix the number of *pecheros* (taxpayers) of Villalvilla, a village in the lordship of the bishop of Burgos, at four. He did this because the villagers were poor and in need. The same year the town of Covarrubias, claiming poverty, had the number of taxpayers on its rolls reduced to just fifty-four, a number accepted three years later by Alfonso XI's regents. If Covarrubias, an important small town in northern Castile, had only fifty-four taxpayers, one can certainly imagine that conditions were quite dismal throughout the region.[47]

In 1315, John Martínez de Leyva, an official of the Infante Don Pedro, petitioned the king, Alfonso XI (that is, the regents Don Pedro and the queen María de Molina), for a reduction in the number of taxpayers in Ventosa (in the area of Logroño). The villagers of Ventosa were vassals of John Martínez de Leyva, and because of war and the attacks of local noblemen—above all, of John Alfonso—they could no longer pay taxes. Moreover, the situation had deteriorated to such an extreme that the peasants threatened to form a brotherhood and to leave the land. The regents agreed to reduce the number of taxpayers from twenty-eight to ten, requesting those keeping the tax rolls to remove eighteen names from their lists.[48]

Obviously, the reduction of the numbers of taxpayers did not have great effect. In 1326 García Lasso de la Vega, *merino mayor* of Castile, wrote to the king about the conditions of villages around the kingdom, most of them poor and half desolate, the land going to waste. These were the consequences of the wars and upheavals during Alfonso XI's minority, of noble violence and excessive taxes. The land everywhere lay uncultivated, and the people were migrating to other kingdoms. Thus inquests were ordered to determine the true number of taxpayers. A tax collector was to visit villages and request four or five "good men" of the village to state under oath how much they had to pay in taxes for *servicio* (subsidies). Among these inquiries, we find one undertaken by Sancho Ferréndez (Ferrández) de Agreda, tax collector in the *merindad* of Logroño. In 1326, he traveled to Ventosa with four other good men (probably from Logroño itself). He carried with him a copy of the 1315 grant reducing the number of taxpayers to ten. On arriving at the village, he found it uninhabited, the land uncultivated. Its inhabitants had migrated to Navarre and to other places.[49]

Sancho Ferréndez determined that Ventosa was still liable for ten taxpayers; however, since there was no longer anyone there, I find it difficult to imagine who would have paid this tax. The case of Ventosa is not an isolated one. In 1315 John Alfonso de Haro, one of the magnates most responsible for the desolation of the area of the Rioja, successfully petitioned the king for a reduction of the number of taxpayers in Bezares from twenty-two to fifteen, claiming once again that the peasants there were "few, poor and deprived of the few things they had by the assaults of magnates and other noblemen."[50] Even in the mid-1320s, when Alfonso XI had already assumed personal control of the kingdom, the reduction of the tax base proceeded apace. In 1324, the twenty-two *pecheros* of the village of the Aguilera, in the jurisdiction of the bishop of Burgos, were reduced to ten. Two years later, the forty-one *pecheros* of Quintanadueñas (also in the region of Burgos) were cut in half. As late as 1347, a period of serious economic problems, the crown was forced to reduce taxes. That year the monks of Santa María in Bujedo de Juarros, in the *merindad* of Burgos, pleaded with the king to reduce their contribution of purveyance because they were poor, they could not pay, and their monastery "*se yermaba*" (was becoming waste). Alfonso XI lowered their payments from 400 to 200 *mrs*. This royal order was later confirmed in 1367 by Henry II, who finally canceled the whole payment four years later.[51]

Many similar examples can be given for other areas of northern Castile, although clearly some areas in the region were more adversely affected by changing economic conditions and violence than others. On the whole, however, the symptoms of the general crisis appear uniformly distributed throughout most of northern Castile. One can argue that petitions to reduce the number of taxpayers were prompted as much by the natural tendency to resist paying taxes, regardless of how well-off one is, as by real troubled conditions, but the language of these protests is far too vivid and the outcome of the inquests far too revealing to doubt the veracity of these accounts. Long before the Black Death struck Castile, villages were being deserted, the tax base eroded. Those who were left to pay could not but suffer under the increased demands of their secular and ecclesiastical lords.

Notes

1. The discussion of the impact of the conquest of Seville on Castilian society is found in my "Expansion et changement," 548–65. References to the mid-thirteenth-century Castilian crisis are found in note 5 of my "Expansion et changement." A critique of my position on the emergence of the latifundia system in Andalucía is found in Manuel González Jiménez, *En torno a los orígenes de Andalucía*, 2d. ed. (Sevilla: Universidad de Sevilla, 1988), 115–40; he points out, correctly I must add, that the purpose and first outcome of the *repartimientos* was to establish a system of medium and small properties. The latifundia was the result of later developments. A direct critique of my views on demographic decline is found in García de Cortázar, *La sociedad rural en la España medieval*, 198, although García de Cortázar has been one of my sources, upholding a contrary opinion to his present one, for demographic dislocations. See his *La época medieval*, 200–201.

2. See above (Part II) and below. Also *Propiedades del cabildo segoviano*, 87–95.

3. On the crisis of late medieval society elsewhere, see E. Perroy, "Les crises du XIVe siècle," *Annales E.S.C.* (1949): 167–82; Georges Duby, *Rural Economy and Country Life*, 289–311. For the density of population in the late thirteenth century, see Joseph R. Strayer, "Economic Conditions in the County of Beaumont-le-

Roger, 1261–1313," in *Medieval Statecraft and the Perspectives of History*, 13–27. See also *Cortes*, 1: 373; *Crónica de Alfonso XI*, 197.

4. Luis Martínez García, *El Hospital del Rey de Burgos*, 291–331.

5. Most of our information on rural life in the twelfth century is limited to specific studies of ecclesiastic domains. Thomas Glick's work and that of García de Cortázar are the only attempts at a comprehensive examination of the earlier period. See references in Part II, Chapters 2 and 3.

6. On mills in general and the mill of Atga in particular, see above and Ruiz, "Tecnología y división de la propiedad: Los molinos de Burgos en la baja edad media," 73–93, especially, 91–93. Many other factors, which are not apparent to us from the account books, might have also influenced the rent structure of these mills. The mill of Atga, for example, was greatly enhanced by the addition of grinding stones. For a view of the fluctuation of rents, see Table 5.6.

7. *Albelda y Logroño*, 1: 144–47, 219–20, et passim. See above.

8. We must remember that in some instances Castile was able to export grain to England. See *C.C.R.*, 1313–18, 452 (31-January-1317); *C.P.R.*, 1330–34, 419, 487, 542; *C.P.R.*, 1345–48, 58; Renée Doehaerd, *Les relations commerciales entre Gênes, la Belgique et l'Outremont*, 2 vols. (Brussels: Palais des académies, 1941), 1: 225–26.

9. See above, but also González, ed., *Repartimiento de Sevilla*; and *Repartimiento de Jerez*.

10. González Jiménez, *La repoblación de la zona de Sevilla durante el siglo XIV*, 25–29; Glick, *Islamic and Christian Spain*, 102–3.

11. See published documents of land transactions in González, *Repartimiento de Sevilla*, vol. 2. Compare prices to those in northern Castile around the same time in Chapter 5, above.

12. González Jiménez, *En torno a los orígenes de Andalucía*, 121–23.

13. *Repartimiento de Jerez*, lxxvi, 8.

14. A valuable preliminary, general assessment of Alfonso X's reign is provided by Joseph O'Callaghan, "Image and Reality: The King Creates His Kingdom," in *Emperor of Culture: Alfonso X the Learned of Castile and His Thirteenth-Century Renaissance*, ed. Robert I. Burns (Philadelphia: University of Pennsylvania Press, 1990), 14–32. For a complete and detailed examination of Alfonso X's reign, see O'Callaghan's monumental study, *The Learned King: The Reign of Alfonso X of Castile*.

15. On Alfonso X's reforms, see O'Callaghan, "Image and Reality," 16–22, and his *The Learned King*; see also his *A History of Medieval Spain*, 433–58; *Curso de historia*, 604–6.

16. See Ruiz, "Expansion et changement," 555–60.

17. One should also take into account the misfortunes that plagued the realm between 1252 and 1474. In this period, there were four minorities, for a total of thirty-six years. Eight of the eleven kings and queen who occupied the throne in this period had their rule contested. A number of them can be described as incompetent. See Teofilo F. Ruiz, "Une royauté sans sacre: la monarchie castillane du Bas Moyen Âge," *Annales E.S.C.* 3 (mai–juin 1984): 435.

18. For the workings of the French and English bureaucracies, see Joseph R. Strayer, *The Reign of Philip the Fair* (Princeton, N.J.: Princeton University Press,

1980); and his *The Administration of Normandy under St. Louis* (Cambridge, Mass.: The Medieval Academy of America, 1932), as well as his work on the English administration.

19. *Crónica de don Sancho IV*, 86.

20. *Crónica del rey don Alfonso X*, 4.

21. Miguel Ángel Ladero Quesada, "Ingreso, gasto y política fiscal de la corona de Castilla. Desde Alfonso X a Enrique III (1252–1406)," in *El siglo XV en Castilla: Fuentes de renta y política fiscal* (Barcelona: Ariel, 1982), 13–44.

22. *MHE*, 1: 308–24.

23. AMB, clasif. 2925 (12-July-1281). The *Cuentas* of 1293, so often cited in previous chapters, are among the few examples of regional tax collection.

24. For Burgos, see Teofilo F. Ruiz, "Una nota sobre la estructura y relaciones fiscales del Burgos bajomedieval," in *En la España medieval: Estudios en memoria del Profesor D. Salvador de Moxó*, 2, ed. Miguel Ángel Ladero Quesada (Madrid: Universidad Complutense, 1982), 391–93; see also *Cortes*, 1: 133–35, 248–49; González Mínguez, *Fernando IV de Castilla*, 29–119.

25. O'Callaghan, *A History of Medieval Spain*, 373.

26. *Becerro de behetrías*, 1: 254–57 et passim. Here I have just cited a handful of examples of villages where peasants were exempted from *martiniega, fonsadera*, and *yantar*. Most villagers paid only *moneda* and *servicio*, that is, extraordinary taxes.

27. *Sancho IV*, 3: CCXCVI–CCXCVII (18-December-1292): The tax had been estimated at 54,000 *mrs*. ACB, vol. 47, f. 224 (12-March-1312); vol. 47, ff. 225–26 (15-April-1332): The grant was a confirmation of a previous grant from Ferdinand IV, and the income was to be drawn from the tithe on imports through the port of Castro Urdiales.

28. See Joseph F. O'Callaghan, "The Cortes and Royal Taxation during the Reign of Alfonso X of Castile," *Traditio* 27 (1971): 380–81.

29. *Cortes*, 1: 220 (Valladolid, 1312): ". . . quelas mis aljamas delos judios delos mios rreynos ssolian pechar al rey don Alfonso mio auelo e al Rey don Sancho mio padre, sseys mill mr. cada dia. . . ."

30. On taxes, see a brief summary in Appendix I and also *Curso de historia*, 600–605.

31. *Cortes*, 1: 110 (Valladolid, 1293).

32. *Cortes*, 1: 96–97 (Palencia, 1286); 96–97 (Valladolid, 1293); 132 (Valladolid, 1295).

33. *Cortes*, 1: 138 (Valladolid, 1298).

34. *Cortes*, 1: 174 (Medina del Campo, 1305); 187–89 (Valladolid, 1307).

35. *Cortes*, 1: 210, 212–13 (Valladolid, 1312); 227 (Palencia, 1313); 242 (Palencia, 1313); 279, 287 (Burgos, 1315); 311 (Carrión, 1317); 366 (Valladolid, 1322); 384 (Valladolid, 1325), et passim.

36. For petitions for the right to collect taxes, see *Cortes*, 1: 97 (Palencia, 1286): "Et otrossi que quando yo quiere a poner cogedores que ponga omnes buenos delas villas . . . ," 104 (Haro, 1288); 110 (Valladolid, 1293), et passim.

37. For the protest of urban procurators against excessive taxation or unauthorized collections, see O'Callaghan, *The Cortes of Castile-León*, 136–42, and above. For petitions of monasteries and villagers to the king against abusive levies

see AHN, Clero, carp. 1033, no. 8a, 8b (25-July-1330): the men of Alencon complained that tax collectors were demanding taxes from them, even though they were exempted. Also ACB, vol. 32, f. 141 (9-December-1266); vol. 2, part 1, f. 52 (2-April-1274); vol. 2, part 2, f. 33 (8-April-1283); vol. 2, part 1, f. 41 (26-April-1288); vol. 17, f. 428 (19-December-1292), et passim. These documents deal with violations of tax exemption enjoyed by the bishop and chapter of Burgos. AHN, Clero, carp. 171, no. 2 (18-April-1338): tax collectors still demanded mules and silver goblets from the nuns of Our Lady in Bujedo, despite their exemption. For a similar protest from the monks of Gumiel de Izán, see AHN, Clero, carp. 233, no. 9 (28-December-1300) et passim.

38. *Cuéllar*, doc. nos. 93, 94, 95, 97, 98, 99, 100, 103 (20-February-1340 to 14-May-1346). See also *Cortes*, 1: 458–59 (Madrid, 1339); 481 (Alcalá de Henares, 1345).

39. In one of the examples cited above, the monks of San Pedro in Gumiel de Izán complained to the king that "magnates, *merinos, infanzones*, knights" demanded mules and silver goblets from them. When they refused to comply, since they had a royal exemption from this contribution, these men took the tribute from them by force. AHN, Clero, carp. 233, no. 9 (28-December-1300).

40. Miguel Ángel Ladero Quesada, "Los judíos castellanos del siglo XV en el arrendamiento de impuestos reales," in *El siglo XV en Castilla: Fuentes de renta y política fiscal*, 143–67.

41. *Cortes*, 1: 220 (Valladolid, 1312).

42. For an example of the lending of wheat or most probably money expressed in grain measures, see AHN, Clero, carp. 355, no. 5 (12-October-1330): the cleric Don Pedro de San Esteban owed the Jews of Medina de Pomar ninety-eight *almudes* of bread.

43. See Valdeón Baruque, "Aspectos de la crisis castellana"; *Cortes*, 1: 102–3 (Haro, 1288), 184 (Medina del Campo, 1305), 185, 187, 191 (Valladolid, 1307), 217 (Valladolid, 1312), et passim.

44. I am presently at work on a companion volume to this book. It will deal with daily life and such topics as violence, charity, family structure, and so forth.

45. *Silos*, 1: 321 (12-III-1304).

46. *Silos*, 1: 325 (26-VI-1306).

47. ACB, vol. 37, f. 9 (10-October-1311); *Fuentes*, 2: 153 (8-February-1311), 158 (2-October-1315).

48. AHN, Clero, carp. 1033, no. 1 (15-April-1315).

49. AHN, Clero, carp. 1033, no. 6 (26-May-1326).

50. AHN, Clero, carp. 1033, no. 2 (13-June-1315).

51. ACB, vol. 25, f. 309 (?-August-1324); vol. 32, f. 143 (15-February-1326); AHN, Clero, carp. 171, nos. 13, 14, 15, 16 (26-February-1347 to 15-November-1371).

11. Epilogue to an Age

Although I have depicted Alfonso XI as fairly removed from the reality of everyday life and from the suffering of Castilians, the king took some steps to remedy the adverse economic and fiscal conditions of the realm and to restore order. If a good number of his measures came to naught or served only as a stopgap to an increasingly deteriorating condition, then perhaps he failed because it was not humanly possible to succeed. And then, there was always that beckoning frontier, where the kings of Castile were to prove their worth. If the campaigns of Alfonso XI in Algeciras and Gibraltar and his victory at the Salado River prevented him from attending to problems in the northern part of Castile, it also gave him a very good reason for demanding yet another payment from his overburdened subjects.

Dealing with the Castilian Crisis: Royal Policy and the Needs of the Realm

For the period between 1100 and 1468, Alfonso XI remains one of the few kings who has not received a full-fledged study. The late Salvador de Moxó wrote a series of insightful essays on different aspects of Alfonso XI's administration and was in the process of editing a diplomatic collection, but his untimely death left unfinished a necessary and long-awaited important work.[1] The son of Ferdinand IV, Alfonso was born in 1311, shortly before Ferdinand's death, and became king in 1312, when he was barely a year old. His reign, from 1312 to 1350, is one of the longest in Castilian history, but the length is deceiving. Thirteen out of his thirty-eight years of rule corresponded to a divided and disputed regency. When he died, the only king in Europe to fall victim to the Black Death, Alfonso was only thirty-eight or thirty-nine years old, and thus still in the prime of his life.

Alfonso XI's reign must be divided into two distinct periods. The first, running from 1312 to 1325, witnessed the successive regencies of his mother,

Queen María of Portugal, and of his energetic and capable grandmother (Sancho IV's widow), María de Molina. His uncles, granduncles, and cousins, especially the Infante Pedro, joined warring camps in a disputed regency, and Castile was torn by factional war and lawlessness. Indeed, it was precisely this anarchy, highlighted by the excesses of the high nobility and their retinues, that led some members of the lower nobility (*fijosdalgo*) and numerous cities to join in a defensive brotherhood. Although aimed specifically against magnate violence and to protect urban commercial interests, the *Hermandad* of 1315 proved to be, as had been the case with previous brotherhoods in 1295 and 1296, an important bulwark for an imperiled monarchy. In spite of serious threats to his rule, the king came of age in 1325 and took personal control of the realm at the age of fourteen.

His twenty-five years of personal rule, from 1325 until his death at the siege of Gibraltar in 1350, also could be subdivided into two periods. The first, from 1325 to 1332, was an ambivalent time when the young and inexperienced Alfonso searched for ways to consolidate his rule, either by violently suppressing hostile magnates or by bribing them into submission. In 1332, however, the king chose to be anointed with holy oil, crowning himself at Las Huelgas of Burgos, and receiving knighthood from a mechanical sculpture of Santiago at the cathedral of Saint James at Compostela. From then on his rule, although contested still by rebellious nobles, did not face any serious challenge. He was finally lord and master of the realm.[2]

His policies can be grouped into four broad areas, all of them closely interrelated:

1. The taming of magnate ambition and controlling noble violence.
2. The end of the last vestiges of municipal autonomy and access to urban fiscal resources. This also meant a greater control of the Cortes.
3. Renewal of the war effort against Islam and the territorial expansion of the kingdom.
4. Legal and administrative reform, culminating in the Ordenamiento of Alcalá de Henares.

Many aspects of these reforms have already been examined elsewhere or require more detailed study. Here, for the sake of brevity, I will limit my comments to some specific issues.

In studying the reign of Alfonso XI, one is first impressed by the sharp drop in the extant documentation. This is not a phenomenon confined to royal documents but one present in every corner of Castile and in every type of archive: royal, ecclesiastical, and secular. The number of documents coming out of the royal chancery drops considerably after 1312. Although one should not expect the feverish activity of Alfonso X's scribes, there are long spans of time between 1312 and 1350 in which the only royal charters extant in the holdings of important monasteries and municipalities are the perfunctory confirmations of previous royal privileges. Those were often conferred at the request of either monasteries or municipal councils. There are great bursts of activity between 1312 and 1315, when the regents, in the king's name, confirmed existing privileges to the different estates of the realm and, then again, in 1325 when the king came of age. Afterward, there is little else except responses to specific requests or crises. Yet those few royal charters that were not confirmations of previous royal largess were almost, unfailingly, of great significance. Some of them, such as the royal charters establishing the *regimiento* in 1345, transformed the institutional structure of the realm.[3]

In the same vein, the Cortes, which had met with increasing frequency under the previous three kings and during Alfonso XI's minority, and which were on the way to becoming active partners in government, were called to session only sporadically after 1325.[4] Even the language of the ordinances underwent a subtle change, indicating the new relationship between the king and the urban procurators. Although the sessions of the Cortes after 1325 were often of great importance, it was clear that, at least under Alfonso XI, the urban procurators could not flex their muscles as they had done in 1295 and 1315.

We are faced, therefore, with an apparent contradiction: on the one hand, a king who gave signs of attempting to rule forcefully and to bring violence to an end, and on the other hand, a marked absence of any evidence that would indicate an active royal bureaucracy or attempts to extend royal power into certain areas of the realm.

TAMING THE NOBILITY

Our best guide to Alfonso XI's policies toward the nobility can be found in the chronicle of his reign and in the *Poema de Alfonso XI*. These two important sources help fill some of the vacuum created by the scarcity of the royal documentation. These narratives ought to be read carefully, since their obvious partiality to the figure of Alfonso XI glosses over some of the real difficulties the king faced, or, worse yet, they highlight his successes when other contemporary documents reveal otherwise. What these sources tell us is that, once Alfonso XI came of age, he boldly moved to assert his authority and to break the magnate coalition that threatened his rule. This he did with a two-prong policy of suppressing his enemies while attempting to entice some of the rebellious noblemen back into the king's service through marriage alliances and financial rewards. In the first years after 1325 it was a carrot-and-stick policy, with the stick often doing its work after the bait of the carrot had been taken. Regardless, however, of the encomiastic tone of the chronicle and of the *Poema*, the story they tell is one of continuous warfare and unrest.[5]

The indecisive struggle against the magnates had its successful counterpart in the effective royal control of the Castilian municipalities. This provided Alfonso XI with greater access to the financial resources of the towns. More importantly, it made available to the crown the kind of military muscle that was indispensable in dealing with the nobility. It also meant a greater control over what cities were to attend the Cortes, who was to represent specific towns, and what sort of issues were to be raised at these meetings. We have already seen how the militia of Logroño helped combat noble unrest even if not under direct royal prompting. Furthermore, by tradition and taste, the king was committed to the renewal of the campaigns against the Moors. A founder of the chivalrous order of the Banda, Alfonso XI was deeply taken with the courtly ideals of his age. The crusade against the infidels was also a convenient excuse to demand tribute from his impoverished subjects and a way, not always successful, of siphoning noble violence elsewhere.

The king's program, for all the violence and economic problems, may have succeeded in the long run, but the foundations upon which Alfonso XI's reforms rested were structurally unsound, and the next king and the realm had to bear the brunt of the debacles that plagued Castile after 1350.

Epilogue to an Age

In spite of Alfonso XI's program of reforms, conditions continued to deteriorate in the last part of his reign. The perennial unrest and greed of the nobility, more than matched by royal excesses, placed an even greater burden on a peasantry weakened and decimated by the loss of crops and by the adverse changes in the climate in the 1340s. The drain of the war against the Moors—a campaign that was not proving particularly profitable or successful—as well as the expense of the siege of Gibraltar could not help but undermine further the economic stability of the realm. In addition, by the late 1340s Alfonso XI's numerous bastards, the children of Leonor de Guzmán, were already demanding their place in the sun, receiving from their doting father the best ecclesiastical benefices and secular lordships. Besides antagonizing part of the nobility, Alfonso XI's largess toward his illegitimate children helped compromise even more the finances of the crown. Although, as I have already pointed out elsewhere, Alfonso XI sought to become independent from the fiscal restraints of the Cortes by seeking other sources of revenue—taxes on the Mesta and on the income of the Jews, custom taxes, and sales taxes (*alcabala*)—these new resources only amounted to so much and could barely keep pace with the increased cost of war and the rapacity of the Trastámara bastards.[6] In 1350, the fate of the realm seemed uncertain, and then the plague struck.

In previous chapters, I have sought to present an image of Castile before the mid-fourteenth century: a country weakened by war, violence, and excessive taxation, a realm with deserted villages and decreasing arable. The crisis of late medieval Castile was not the result of the Black Death. In fact, the crisis preceded the plague's onslaught. Thus, the impact of the Black Death must be seen in the context of severely deteriorating conditions. Unfortunately, we do not have the detailed statistical research for Castile that we have for other parts of medieval western Europe. Nor do we have the vivid descriptions of the effects of the bubonic plague that one finds in Boccaccio, Agnolo the Fat, and others. For Castile, the evidence is mostly implicit. The chronicles of Alfonso XI and Peter I mention the coming of the pestilence to Castile and León in the mid-fourteenth century but give no description of its impact or of how it spread throughout the realm.

There are just a few short studies of the plague's impact on the Iberian Peninsula as a whole and fewer still on the course of the Black Death in Castile or in specific regions of the kingdom. None of them adds much specific information to what we already know from other parts of western Europe. Jaume Sobrequés i Callicó, in his article, "La peste negra en la península ibérica," argues that the plague was the *coup de grâce* to a society already deeply troubled. Agreeing with Verlinden, he identifies royal policy favorable to the upper aristocracy as one of the consequences of the Black Death. Likewise, the plague led to an increase in prices and wages, or, at least, to the peasants and laborers' heightened expectations of a better income. The response of the crown and of those in power was the imposition of wage and price controls to contain increases in the cost of labor. These were, of course, the same responses of hegemonic groups in England and elsewhere.[7]

Although Sobrequés i Callicó does not offer documentary evidence to prove this point, it is reasonable to agree with him in that, quite likely, the towns on the plain suffered a great deal more from the plague than did the isolated mountain villages, and that centers of population in the great commercial networks were more vulnerable to the spread of the sickness than those outside the networks. Sobrequés i Callicó's hypothesis that the plague influenced the development of the Mesta and led to an increased struggle between the crown and nobility must be accepted only with great reservations.

When one turns from a general overview of the Iberian Peninsula to specific treatments of a region or regions, the accounts still lack a sharp focus. Rather than fault the authors, one must once again bemoan the lack of documentary evidence. Indeed, one of the most extraordinary things about the impact of the plague on Castile is the sharp drop in documents of any kind from 1350 to the early years of the 1360s. While royal charters, private contracts, donations, and other written agreements had been decreasing in number from 1300 on, after 1350 the number of documents in many monastic and cathedral chapters seems to drop off dramatically. Although the few extant documents do not mention the plague, it seems that in most localities, especially in the countryside, life had come to a standstill. As we saw above (Chapter 5), fewer lands were sold or rented, or at least we have fewer records of those transactions. The years between 1350 and 1360 are lost years, often bereft of the simplest reference to economic activity. Most of the documents are simply the confirmations of existing privileges upon the ascent to the throne of Peter I. A few examples of this dearth of documents will suffice (see Table 11.1). In a sense our evidence is, with a few exceptions, negative or implicit. Only occasionally does the extant documentation provide direct evidence of the onslaught of the plague and its impact on Castilian life and on seigniorial rent.

The first evidence comes from the often-cited *Becerro de behetrías* and has to do with the large number of deserted villages in the Castile of the *merindades*, that is, northern Castile. The inquest was undertaken at the petition of secular lords because of the many villages left deserted by the plague. As Gonzalo Martínez Díez, the editor of the *Becerro*, argues, the noblemen did not wish for a new distribution of *behetrías*, but rather for their conversion into *tierras solariegas*, that is, lands in which they would

TABLE 11.1.   Number of Documents Extant in Select Archives (Northern Castile).

Place	1330–39	1340–49	1350–59	1360–69
Burgos cathedral*	76	68	41	34
Monastery of San Juan	9	7	1	2
Santo Domingo de la Calzada	13	4	9	8
Collegiate churches of Albelda and Logroño	15	27	19	17

*There are no documents for the period between 2 October 1349 and 9 March 1350, and only two documents for the entire year of 1350.

enjoy enhanced seigniorial rights and, thus, a better guarantee of peasant labor and dues.[8]

In his introduction to the edition of the *Becerro*, Martínez Díez has calculated the total number of villages mentioned in the inquest as well as those still inhabited or deserted. The figures are nothing short of astonishing (see Table 11.2).

A bit more than 20 percent of all the villages and hamlets listed in the *Becerro* were deserted. A significant number of these places were probably already deserted or sparsely populated before the coming of the plague, but the number is still staggering. Moreover, we have no way of knowing the extent to which the villages that were not deserted remained inhabited, whether their populations were also reduced drastically by the deteriorating conditions before 1348 and, finally, by the Plague. This appears to be the case, since the nobility felt immediately the impact of falling income and promptly protested at the Cortes of 1351.

As Sobrequés i Callicó had assumed, the *merindades* on the plain suffered a great deal more than those *merindades* that extended wholly or partly over mountainous areas. In the jurisdictions of Cerrato, Infantazgo de Valladolid, Aguilar, Monzón, Carrión, Castrojeriz, and Saldaña, located on the plain and traversed by the road to Santiago of Compostela and other commercial roads, the percentages of deserted villages fluctuated from 50 percent in Cerrato to 17.6 percent in Santo Domingo de Silos (for which we have only a partial entry). On the other hand, in the *merindades* of Asturias de Santillana, Castilla la Vieja, and Liébana, located almost exclusively in the mountains of the north, the rate of desertion ranged from 16.3 percent in Castilla la Vieja (a region crisscrossed by trade routes from the ports of

TABLE 11.2. Deserted Villages in the *Becerro*.

Merindad	Location	Total Number of Villages	Number of Villages Deserted
Cerrato	Plain	112	56
Infantazgo de Valladolid	Plain	98	35
Monzón	Plain	97	22
Campos	Plain	71	21
Carrión	Plain	119	41
Villadiego	Plain	107	21
Aguilar	Plain and mountain	262	40
Liébana	Mountain and plain	131	15
Saldaña	Plain	195	42
Asturias de Santillana	Mountain	207	12
Castrojeriz	Plain	121	30
Candemuño	Mountain	79	18
Burgos-Ubierna	Mountain	121	22
Castilla la Vieja	Mountain	534	87
St. Domingo of Silos (partial)	Plain	148	26
Total		2,402	488

Source: Becerro, I, 78–79.

the Bay of Biscay) to as low as 5.8 percent in the somewhat more isolated region of Asturias de Santillana.

As revealing as these figures are, they still do not bring us close to a complete understanding of the problems caused by the plague. But while we cannot visualize or quantify the human carnage, there are at least two instances in which the sharp decline of seigniorial rent is quite evident.

At Pie de Concha, one of the toll stations on the road between Santander and Aguilar de Campóo, a place under the jurisdiction of the bishop of Burgos, the king had three *solares* that had been deserted for a long time. In addition, before the *mortandad* (great death), the king had collected 3,000 *mrs.* annually in toll dues. And now, as the *Becerro* implied, he collected nothing. Was the impact of the plague such that for at least two or three years even trade in cloth and metals diminished to a trickle on the road between Santander and Campóo?[9]

The account books of the cathedral of Burgos are even more revealing. Early on we saw the fluctuations in the rental income the cathedral chapter received from its mills. We also saw that the incomes from three different periods—1325, 1344, and 1350—provide insights into northern Castile's economic upheavals. While in 1325 the expectations were that rents were to be decreased, in 1344, in the midst of a serious economic crisis, the chapter had reduced the rents it charged with the expectation of raising them if there was an upturn in the economy. By 1350, however, prices had fallen by more than half in most cases and by almost two-thirds in others.

This radical decrease in the chapter's income was not unique to Burgos; it is reflected in the few rental agreements extant for the post-plague period. In most of them the scarcity of agricultural labor led to rather generous conditions favoring those willing to work the land. After 1348, the monks of the collegiate Church of Albelda gave a good number of vineyards at what seems, in comparison to previous rental agreements, very attractive rates. As late as 1357, when the scarcity of labor had not yet improved, we find a contract in which a woman granted uncultivated land to a farmer with the obligation of turning it into a vineyard. After five years, they would divide the property, each keeping half. She was thus willing to relinquish half of her property in order to obtain labor for the other half.[10]

As was the case in England, where the onslaught of the plague and the scarcity of agricultural laborers led to a Statute of Laborers, in Castile the upheavals of the Black Death moved the crown, the magnates, the prelates, and the urban oligarchies into action. Late in 1351, the Cortes of Castile and León met in Valladolid and, in a series of far-ranging actions, sought to mend the ills afflicting Castilian society. Although mostly prompted by the drastic drop in seigniorial rents resulting from the plague, the Cortes of 1351 and Peter I's legislation were aimed, above all, at remedying the ills caused by violence and general lawlessness. In many respects, the ordinances of the Cortes of 1351 reflect far more the long-standing malaise of the realm than the swift and sharp impact of the plague. In fact, the Cortes of 1351 completed the cycle begun a century earlier in 1253, and many of the measures adopted at Valladolid in the mid-fourteenth century faithfully resembled the ordinances drafted in the same city almost one hundred years before. Those entries on violence and the more elaborate sumptuary legislation, which paralleled earlier measures, are almost a clinical chart of the Castilian crises through the previous century and serve as a benchmark for this study. The meeting of the Cortes at Valladolid in 1351 stands as an epilogue to the previous century and as a revealing indictment of the partial failure of the late medieval kings of Castile and/or Castile's parliamentary institutions to deal with the greater complexities of government and statesmanship required by the age.

The experiences of France and England in this period were not dissimilar, for in the kingdoms north of the Pyrenees the new requirements of warfare and the unbounded ambition of the nobility, among other things, almost wrecked existing institutions. And yet, both of these realms, which for so long served as models in Castilian historiography, had developed fairly complex bureaucracies and administrative techniques. Their capitals, Paris and London, functioned as rallying points for the emergence of the nation-state. In the realm of the castle and the lions, demographic decline, administrative inadequacies, a peripatetic monarchy, and the endless requirements of frontier warfare and of the vaunted Reconquest delayed the emergence of a centralized monarchy until the end of the fifteenth century.[11] The almost unbearable violence of the late fourteenth and fifteenth centuries, the substitution, by the crown, of substance with the ever more elaborate celebration of secular rituals, pageantry, and festivals were the prices to be paid for these shortcomings. This is indeed the sorry story of northern Castile. Its peasants and merchants stood valiantly against the tides of adversity. And, regardless of the wanton violence of the economic and social crises, they stood their ground and continued doggedly at their tasks: the prosaic and boring deeds of everyday life, the sustaining labor of the powerless and oppressed, building in obscurity and misery the basis for Castile's future glory.

Notes

1. Alfonso XI's documents extant in the Archivo histórico nacional have been published by one of Moxó's students, Esther González Crespo, *Colección documental de Alfonso XI*. See pp. 27–28 in González Crespo for a bibliography of Moxó's works on the reign of Alfonso XI. Peter Linehan, who knows more about Alfonso XI's reign than anyone alive, has just completed a book on history and historians of Spain (forthcoming, Oxford University Press), which includes important original information on the king and his rule.

2. The narrative for the reign of Alfonso XI is still best gathered from the chronicle of his reign: *Crónica del rey don Alfonso XI*. On his coronation see Ruiz, "Une royauté sans sacre," 429–30. Peter Linehan's formidable forthcoming book, *History and Historians* deals in-depth with royal ideology in the reign of Alfonso XI. See also his "Alfonso XI of Castile and the Arm of Santiago (with a Note on the Pope's Foot)," in *Studi D. Maffei*, ed. P. Weimar and A. García y García (forthcoming 1994).

3. See above, Part III, and Ruiz, "The Transformation of the Castilian Municipalities," 26–29.

4. Joseph F. O'Callaghan, *The Cortes of Castile-León, 1188–1350* (Philadelphia: University of Pennsylvania Press, 1989), 36–39.

5. See *Poema de Alfonso XI*, strophes 152–342; *Crónica de Alfonso XI*, 197ff.

6. On the impact of war on the medieval economy see Joseph R. Strayer, "The Costs and Profits of War: The Anglo-French Conflict of 1294–1303," in *The Medieval City*, ed. Harry Miskimin et al. (New Haven, Conn: Yale University Press, 1977), 269–91.

7. Jaume Sobrequés i Callicó, "La peste negra en la península ibérica," *Anuario de estudios medievales* 7 (1970–71): 67–102. See also Angel Vaca Lorenzo, "La estrúctura económica de la Tierra de Campos a mediados del siglo XIV," *Publicaciones de la Institución Tello Téllez de Meneses* 39 (1977): 229–398; 42 (1979), 203–387; Nicolás Cabranilla, "La crisis del siglo XIV en Castilla: la peste negra en el obispado de Palencia," *Hispania* 28 (1968): 245–58; and the pioneering work of Charles Verlinden, "La grande peste de 1348 en Espagne: Contribution a l'étude de ses conséquences économiques et sociales," *Revue belge de philologie et d'histoire* 17 (1938): 103–46.

8. *Becerro*, 1: 18–21.

9. *Becerro*, 2: 179–80.

10. *Albelda y Logroño*, 312–13.

11. Although the genesis of the nation-state is an undeniable historical fact in the late Middle Ages, I do not wish to imply here that the emergence of a centralized monarchy in Castile and elsewhere was a beneficial and necessary step, nor do I believe that the nation—despite its probable inevitability—is the best solution to the problems of mankind.

Appendix 1. Partial List of Taxes Collected by the Kings of Castile

Ordinary Taxes

a. *Forum, Foro, Pectum*, or *Infurción*: Tithe, a territorial tax. It was paid by those living and working in the royal domain. Roughly equivalent to the tenth, the taxable unit was the household or hearth.

b. *Infurción*: Transformed into a public tax after the eleventh century. *Martiniega* was paid on Saint Martin's Day and *marzadga* was paid in March.

c. *Montazgo*: A tax paid to the crown for the use of forests. Eventually, it became associated with the Mesta and was one of the most important source of income as a tax on transhumance.

d. *Caloñas*: The income from fines.

e. *Fonsadera*: In the early medieval period, the refusal to serve in the royal host was punished with a fine known as *fonsadera*. By the thirteenth century, *fonsadera* was paid in lieu of or in addition to military obligation.

f. *Anubda*: A tax paid in lieu of guard duty in the royal castles.

g. *Yantar*: Purveyance. See Part IV, Chapter 10.

h. *Moneda forera*: A tax paid every seven years as guarantee that the king would not devaluate the coinage.

i. *Servicios*: Subsidies voted by the Cortes; the equivalent of *moneda forera*.

j. *Capitación*: A head tax on Jews and Moors.

k. *Diezmos de los puertos*: A tithe on imported and exported goods.

l. *Peaje*: A tax on the transit of people and goods.

m. *Portazgo*: A tax paid for goods brought within the walls of cities.

n. *Alcabala*: A sales tax.

o. *Tercias reales*: A third of the ecclesiastical tenth.

Extraordinary Taxes

p. *Quinto del botín*: One-fifth of all the booty taken in the wars against the Moors.

q. *Parias*: Tribute paid by the Moorish kingdoms to the kings of Castile.

r. Forced loans.

Source: García de Valdeavellano, *Curso de historia*, 599–612.

Appendix 2. Glossary of Coins, Weights, and Measures

Money*

Maravedí: (from the Arabic *murābitī*) A Castilian coin in use in Castile and Spain into the early modern period. Although there were limited mintings of gold and silver *maravedíes* in the mid-thirteenth century, thoughout the period examined in this book the *maravedí* was mostly a fictitious coin, used for counting purposes. The *maravedí de oro* was a gold *maravedí*, worth six *mrs.* of silver; the *maravedí alfonsí* or *blanco* was the silver *mr. Maravedí de los buenos* was a copper coin with some silver content.

Sueldo: (from the Latin *solidus*). In theory, 1 *sueldo* was equal to 12 *dineros*; in the *Becerro*, 1 *sueldo* was worth 1.3 *dineros*.

Dinero: (from the Latin *denarius*) Money of exchange in the fourteenth century. An ordinary *maravedí* was worth 10 *dineros*.

Weights and Measures

Almud: A measure of grain (about 4.6 liters). Also a measure of land under cultivation of about half an acre. In the *Becerro*, the *almud* was equivalent to one *fanega* and four *celemines*, or four *cuartas*.

Aranzada: (from the Latin *arantia*) A measure of land under cultivation of around 3,866 square meters. In the late Middle Ages, it usually meant the land that could be plowed by a team of oxen (two oxen) in one day.

Cántara: A measure for wine and other liquids (around 1.6 centiliters). In late nineteenth-century Spain, one *cántara* (16.1 liters) was equal to

*The value of coins fluctuated widely in the thirteenth and fourteenth centuries and from locality to locality within Castile.

eight *azumbres*, and the *azumbre* (2 liters) had four *quartillos*, or half a liter per *quartillo*.

Celemín: A measure of grain (around 4.6 mililiters in the late nineteenth century). Also a measure of land under cultivation (around 537 square meters). In some parts of Castile in the Middle Ages, one *almud* was equal to six *celemines* or half a *fanega*.

Cuarta (Cuarto): A measure of grain equivalent to four *celemines* or one-fourth of an *almud*. In the *Becerro* there is a value for a *cuarto* of six *celemines*.

Emina (Hemina): A tax and also a measure for liquids equivalent to half a *sextario* (in León, around eighteen liters). Also a measure of land under cultivation of about 939 square meters. As a measure of grain, the most common use in the documents referred to in this book, the *emina* was equal to a *celemín* of Toledo (in the *Becerro*). Elsewhere, one *emina* was equal to one *cuarto* or one-fourth of a *fanega*.

Fanega: A measure of grain (around 1.5 bushels). Also the land required to sow a *fanega* of seed (about 1.6 acres). One *fanega* was equal to twelve *celemines*. In the monastic accounts of 1338, one *fanega* was equal to two *almudes*.

Moyo (Modius): A measure of grain and of liquids (about 57 gallons). For grain, the value changes with location but was, more often than not, equal to one-half of an *almud*. The *moyo* had four *quartarios* and six *sextarios*.

Obrada: Labor done by a team of oxen (two oxen) in one day's work. Also a measure of land (between one and one-and-a-half acres).

Vara: Linear measure; close to a yard.

Yugada: The amount of land that could be worked by a team of oxen in one day (about 32 hectares). In some regions of Castile the *yugada* was the euivalent of fifty *fanegas*.

Addendum: Some values from the account of Benedictine monasteries in 1338.

Santo Domingo de Silos:	one *carga* = three *almudes* = four *fanegas*
	one *almud* = four *cuartos*
	one *cuarto* = four *celemines*
San Zoilo de Carrión:	one *carga* = eight *cuartos*
	one *cuarto* = six *celemines*
San Pedro de Arlanza:	one and one-qurater of *fanega* = one *almud*

Bibliography

Included are references to books and articles dealing with northern Castilian history. References to studies of other regions in Europe and Iberia in the late Middle Ages are restricted to those cited in the text. The bulk of my research was undertaken at the Archivo histórico nacional in 1979–80. Since then, most of the documentation for northern Castile has been published in the *Fuentes medievales castellano-leonesas*. This is a remarkable project which, once completed, will make available the rich documentation of medieval Castile—sources that have been hitherto neglected or ignored by most medieval historians.

SOURCES AND SOURCE COLLECTIONS

Archivo de la catedral de Burgos (ACB).
Archivo histórico nacional (AHN).
Archivo municipal de Burgos (AMB).
Archivo municipal de Segovia (AMS).
Ávila: Fuentes y archivos. Edited by Candido M. Ajo González y Sáinz de Zuñiga. 2 vols. Madrid: Artes gráficas Arges, 1967.
El becerro del monasterio de San Juan de Burgos. Burgos: Ayuntamiento de Burgos, 1950.
Biblioteca nacional (BN).
Calendars of the Close, Patent, and Fine Rolls. See "Abbreviations."
Cartulario de Santo Toribio de Liébana. See "Abbreviations."
Cartulario real de la provincia de Álava (1258–1500). Edited by Esperanza Iñurrieta Ambrosio. San Sebastián: Sociedad de estudios vascos, 1983.
Los códigos españoles concordados y anotados. See "Abbreviations."
Colección de fueros municipales y cartas pueblas. Edited by Tomás Muñoz y Romero. Madrid: Imprenta de don José M. Alonso, 1847.
Colección diplomática calceatense. Archivo catedral, 1125–1397. See "Abbreviations."
Colección diplómatica de Cuéllar. See "Abbreviations."
Colección diplomática de las colegiatas de Albelda y Logroño. See "Abbreviations."
Colección diplomática del concejo de Burgos (884–1369). Edited by Emiliano González Díez. Burgos: Institutos de estudios castellanos, 1984.
Colección diplomática del concejo de Segura (Guipuzcoa) 1290–1500. Edited by Luis M. Díez de Salazar Fernández. San Sebastián: Sociedad de estudios vascos, 1985.
Colección diplomática de San Salvador de Oña. See "Abbreviations."
Colección diplomática de Sepúlveda. See "Abbreviations."

Colección documental de Alfonso XI. See "Abbreviations."

Colección documental del archivo municipal de Piedrahita (1372–1549). Edited by Carmelo L. López. Ávila: Excelentísima diputación provincial de Ávila, 1987.

Colección diplomática del archivo municipal de Santander. Edited by Manuel Vaquerizo Gil and Rogelio Pérez Bustamante. Santander: Ayuntamiento de Santander, 1977.

Cortes de los antiguos reinos de León y Castilla. See "Abbreviations."

Crónicas de los reyes de Castilla. See "Abbreviations."

Cuentas y gastos (1292–1294) del rey D. Sancho IV el Bravo (1284–1295). Edited by Asunción López Dapena. Córdoba: Publicaciones del Monte de Piedad y caja de ahorros de Córdoba, 1984. (This is a new and better edition than the one by Mercedes Gaibrois de Ballesteros, cited throughout the book. It was not available to me until recently.)

Descripción histórica del obispado de Osma. See "Abbreviations."

Desde Estella a Sevilla. See "Abbreviations."

Die Juden im Christilichen Spanien. Edited by Y. Fritz Baer. 2 vols. Berlin: Akademieverlag, 1929–36. Reprint Farnborough, Eng.: Gregg, 1970.

Diplomatario andaluz de Alfonso X. Edited by Manuel González Jiménez. Sevilla: El Monte, Caja de ahorros de Huelva y Sevilla, 1991.

Diplomatario de Salinas de Añana, 1194–1465. Edited by Santiago López Castillo. San Sebastián: Sociedad de estudios vascos, 1984.

Documentación medieval de la catedral de Ávila. See "Abbreviations."

Documentación medieval de la catedral de Segovia (1115–1300). Edited by Luis M. Villar García. Salamanca: Universidad de Salamanca, 1990.

Documentación medieval del archivo municipal de San Bartolomé de Pinares (Ávila). Edited by Gregorio del Ser Quijano. Ávila: Excelentísima diputación provincial de Ávila, 1987.

Documentos de los archivos catedralicio y diocesano de Salamanca, siglos XII–XIII. See "Abbreviations."

Documentos inéditos de Alfonso X el sabio y del Infante su hijo Don Sancho. Edited by Juan M. del Estal. Alicante: Cirilo industrias gráficas, S.L., 1984.

Fuentes medievales castellano-leonesas. See "Abbreviations."

Fuentes para la historia de Castilla. See "Abbreviations."

Fueros locales en el territorio de la provincia de Burgos. Edited by Gonzalo Martínez Díez. Burgos: Caja de ahorros municipal de Burgos, 1982.

Historia de la diócesis de Siguenza y de sus obispos. See "Abbreviations."

Historia del reinado de Sancho IV de Castilla. See "Abbreviations."

Libro becerro de las behetrías. See "Abbreviations."

El libro del repartimiento de Jerez de la Frontera: Estudios y edición. Edited by Manuel González Jiménez and A. González Gómez. See "Abbreviations."

Memorial histórico español. See "Abbreviations."

Memorias de Fernando IV de Castilla. See "Abbreviations."

Palencia: Panorámica foral de la provincia. Edited by Justiniano Rodríguez Fernández. Palencia: Merino A.G., 1981.

Poema de Alfonso XI. See "Abbreviations."

Primera crónica general. Edited by Ramón Menéndez Pidal. Madrid: Nueva biblioteca de autores españoles, V, 1906.
"Primitiva regla escrita de la Cofradía de Nuestra Señora de Gamonal." See "Abbreviations."
Propiedades del cabildo segoviano: Sistemas de cultivo y modos de explotación de la tierra a fines del siglo XIII. Edited by Angel García Sanz et al. See "Abbreviations."
El real monasterio de Las Huelgas y el Hospital del Rey. See "Abbreviations."
Recueil des chartes de l'abbaye de Silos. Edited by Marius Ferotin. See "Abbreviations."
Repartimiento de Murcia. Edited by Juan Torres Fontes. Madrid: Consejo Superior de Investigaciones Científicas, 1960.
Repartimiento de Sevilla. Edited by Julio González. 2 vols. Madrid: Consejo Superior de Investigaciones Científicas, 1951.
Texto cronológico de las tres "Reglas," por las que sucesivamente, rigió su vida corporativa esta Real Hermandad fundada por el rey Alfonso XI en la era de 1376 [año de Cristo de 1338]. See "Abbreviations."
Viajes de extranjeros por España y Portugal. Edited by José García Mercadal. See "Abbreviations."
Vida económica de los monasterios benedictinos en el siglo XIV. Edited by Juan José García González. See "Abbreviations."

SELECTIVE SECONDARY SOURCES

Abel, Wilhelm. *Agricultural Fluctuations in Europe: From the Thirteenth to the Twentieth Centuries*. London: Methuen, 1980.
Albarellos, Juan. *Efemeridades burgalesas (Apuntes históricos)*. 2d. ed. Burgos: Diario de Burgos, 1964.
Alfonso, María I. "Las sernas en León y Castilla: Contribución al estudio de las relaciones socio-económicas en el marco del señorío medieval." *Moneda y credito* 129 (1974): 153–210.
Álvarez Borges, Ignacio. *El feudalismo castellano y el libro Becerro de las Behetrías: La merindad de Burgos*. León: Junta de Castilla y León, 1987.
Álvarez Palenzuela, Vicente Ángel. *Monasterios cistercienses en Castilla (siglos XII–XIII)*. Valladolid: Universidad de Valladolid, 1978.
Araluce Cuenca, José R. *El libro de los estados: Don Juan Manuel y la sociedad de su tiempo*. Madrid: Ediciones José Porrua Turanzos, S.A., 1976.
Ariz, Luis de. *Historia de las grandezas de la ciudad de Ávila*. Alcalá de Henares: L. Martínez Grande, 1607.
Asenjo González, María. "'Labradores ricos': Nacimiento de una oligarquía rural en la Segovia del siglo XV." *En la España medieval: Estudios en honor del profesor D. Angel Ferrari*. Madrid: Universidad Complutense, 1984.
———. *Segovia: La ciudad y su tierra a fines del medievo*. Segovia: Excelentísima diputación provincial de Segovia, 1986.
Aston, T. H., and C. H. E. Philpin, eds. *The Brenner Debate: Agrarian Class Structure and Economic Development in Pre-Industrial Europe*. Cambridge: Cambridge University Press, 1985.

Ayala Martínez, Carlos de. "La monarquía y Burgos durante el reinado de Alfonso X." *Cuadernos de historia medieval* 7 (1984): 9–63.

Baer, Y. Fritz. *A History of the Jews in Christian Spain.* 2 vols. Philadelphia: The Jewish Publication Society of America, 1961–66.

Ballesteros, Enrique. *Estudio histórico de Ávila y su territorio.* Ávila: Tipografía de M. Sarachaga, 1896.

Ballesteros y Beretta, Antonio. *Alfonso X, el sabio.* Barcelona: Salvat, 1963.

Barrios García, Ángel. *La catedral de Ávila en la edad media: Estructuras socio-jurídica y ecónomica. (Hipótesis y problemas).* Ávila: El diario de Avila, 1973.

———. *Estructuras agrarias y de poder en Castilla: El ejemplo de Ávila (1085–1320).* 2 vols. Salamanca: Universidad de Salamanca, 1983–84.

Basas Fernández, Manuel. *El consulado de Burgos en el siglo XVI.* Madrid: Escuela de historia moderna, 1963.

Behar, Ruth. *Santa María del Monte: The Presence of the Past in a Spanish Village.* Princeton, N.J.: Princeton University Press, 1986.

Benton, John F., and Thomas N. Bisson, eds. *Medieval Statecraft and the Perspectives of History: Essays by Joseph R. Strayer.* Princeton, N.J.: Princeton University Press, 1971.

Bilbao, Luis M., and E. Fernández Pinedo. "En torno al problema del poblamiento y la población vascongada en la edad media." In *III symposium de historia medieval del señorío de Viscaya.* Bilbao: Excelentísima diputación provincial de Viscaya, 1973.

Blanco, Flor. *Belorado en la baja edad media.* Madrid: Hijos de Santiago Rodríguez, 1973.

Bloch, Marc. *Feudal Society.* 2 vols. Chicago: University of Chicago Press, 1966.

Bolens, Lucie. *Les méthodes culturales au Moyen Âge d'après les traités d'agronomie andalouse: Tradition et techniques.* Geneva: Droz, 1974.

———. *Agronomes andalous du Moyen Âge.* Geneva: Droz, 1981.

Bolos y Capdevila, María de, Antonio Paluzier, and Angela Guerrero. *Geografía de España.* Barcelona: de Gasso Hermanos editores, 1969.

Bonachía Hernando, Juan Antonio. *El concejo de Burgos en la baja edad media (1345–1426).* Valladolid: Universidad de Valladolid, 1978.

———. *El señorío de Burgos durante la baja edad media (1255–1508).* Salamanca: Biblioteca de Castilla y León, 1988.

Bonoudo de Magnani, Marta. "El monasterio de San Salvador de Oña: Economía agraria y sociedad rural." *Cuadernos de historia de España* 51–52 (1970): 42–122.

Braudel, Fernand. *The Mediterranean and the Mediterranean World in the Age of Phillip II.* 2 vols. New York: Harper-Torchbooks, 1975.

Bustamante Bricio, José. *La tierra y los valles de Mena: Biografía de un municipio.* Bilbao: Gráficos Ellacuria, 1971.

Cabero, Valentín. *El espacio geográfico castellano-leonés.* Valladolid: Ambito, 1982.

Cabrillana, Nicolás. "La crisis del siglo XIV en Castilla: La peste negra en el obispado de Palencia." *Hispania* 28 (1968): 245–58.

———. "Los despoblados en Castilla la Vieja." *Hispania* 119 (1971): 485–550; 120 (1972): 5–60.

Camacho, Ángel M. *Historia jurídica del cultivo y de la ganadería en España.* Madrid: Establecimiento tipográfico de J. Ratés, 1912.

Cantera Burgos, Francisco. "Documentos de compraventas hebráicos de la catedral de Calahorra." *Sefarad* 6 (1946): 37–62.
———. "La judería de Burgos." *Sefarad* 12 (1952): 59–104.
———. "Los judíos de Calahorra." *Sefarad* 15 (1955): 353–72.
———, and L. Huidobro. "Los judíos de Aguilar de Campóo." *Sefarad* 14 (1954): 335–52.
Carlé, María del Carmen. "El precio de la vida en Castilla del rey sabio al Emplazado." *Cuadernos de historia de España* 15 (1951): 32–156.
———. "Mercaderes en Castilla, 1252–1512." *Cuadernos de historia de España* 21–22 (1954): 146–328.
———. "Boni homines y hombres buenos." *Cuadernos de historia de España* 39–40 (1964): 133–68.
———. *Del concejo medieval castellano-leonés*. Buenos Aires: Instituto de historia de España, 1968.
———. *La sociedad hispano medieval: la ciudad*. Buenos Aires: Celtia, 1984.
Caro Baroja, Julio. "Los arados españoles: Sus tipos y reparticion. (Aportaciones críticas y bibliográficas)." *Revista de dialectología y tradiciones populares* 1 (1949): 3–96.
Carremolino, José M. *Historia de Ávila, su provincia y obispado*. 3 vols. Madrid: Librería española, 1872–73.
Casado Alonso, Hilario. *La propiedad eclesiástica en la ciudad de Burgos en el siglo XV: El cabildo catedralicio*. Valladolid: Universidad de Valladolid, 1980.
———. *Señores, mercaderes y campesinos: La comarca de Burgos a fines de la edad media*. Valladolid: Junta de Castilla y León, 1987.
Casado Soto, José Luis. *Arquitectura naval en el Cantábrico durante el siglo XIII*. Santander: Bedia, 1976.
Casas Díez, Ángel. *Villada en Tierra de Campos: Historia, economía y costumbres*. Palencia: Excelentísima diputación provincial de Palencia, 1976.
Castro, Américo. "Unos aranceles de aduanas del siglo XIII." *Revista de filología española* 8 (1921): 1–29, 325–56; 9 (1922): 266–76; 10 (1923): 113–36.
Childs, Wendy R. *Anglo-Castilian Trade in the Later Middle Ages*. Manchester: Rowman and Littlefield, 1978.
Contreras, Juan de, Marqués de Lozoya. *Historia de las corporaciones de menestrales en Segovia*. Segovia: Mauro Lozano editora, 1921.
Corral García, Esteban. *Las comunidades castellanas y la villa y tierra antigua de Cuéllar*. Salamanca: Imprenta Varona, 1978.
Díaz de Durana, José R. *Álava en la baja edad media: Crisis, recuperación y transformaciones socioeconómicas, 1250–1525*. Vitoria: Diputación foral de Álava, 1986.
Díez Espinosa, José R. *Santa María de Palazuelos: Desarrollo, crisis y decadencia de un dominio monástico*. Valladolid: Diputación provincial de Valladolid, 1982.
Dillard, Heath. *Daughters of the Reconquest: Women in Castilian Town Society, 1100–1300*. Cambridge: Cambridge University Press, 1984.
Duby, Georges. *Rural Economy and Country Life in the Medieval West*. Reprint. Columbia, S.C.: University of South Carolina Press, 1990.
Dufourcq, Charles E., and J. Gautier-Dalché. *Histoire économique et sociale de l'Espagne chrétienne au Moyen Âge*. Paris: Armand Colin, 1976.

Elliott, John H. *Richelieu and Olivares*. Cambridge: Cambridge University Press, 1984.

Esteban Recio, María A. *Palencia a fines de la edad media: Una ciudad de señorío episcopal*. Valladolid: Universidad de Valladolid, 1989.

Estepa Díez, Carlos. "El alfoz y las relaciones campo-ciudad en Castilla y León durante los siglos XII y XIII." *Studia historica* 2, no. 2 (1984): 7–26.

——— et al. *Burgos en la edad media*. Valladolid: Junta de Castilla y León, 1984.

Faci, Javier. "Vocablos referentes al sector agrario en León y Castilla durante la alta edad media." *Moneda y credito* 144 (1978): 69–87.

Férotin, Marius. *Histoire de l'abbaye de Silos*. Paris: Leroux, 1897.

Ferrari Núñez, Ángel. *Castilla dividida en dominios según el Libro de las Behetrías*. Madrid: Ograma, 1958.

Fisher, W. B., and H. Bowen-Jones. *Spain: A Geographical Background*. London: Chatto and Windus, 1958.

Freedman, Paul. "The Enserfment Process in Medieval Catalonia: The Evidence from Ecclesiastical Sources." *Viator* 13 (1982): 225–44.

———. *The Diocese of Vic: Tradition and Regeneration in Medieval Catalonia*. New Brunswick, N.J.: Rutgers University Press, 1983.

———. *The Origins of Peasant Servitude in Medieval Catalonia*. Cambridge: Cambridge University Press, 1991.

Gacto Fernández, María T. *Estructura de la población de la extremadura leonesa en los siglos XII y XIII*. Salamanca: Consejo Superior de Investigaciones Científicas, 1977.

García de Cortázar, José Ángel *El dominio del monasterio de San Millan de la Cogolla (siglos X a XIII): Introducción a la historia rural de Castilla altomedieval*. Salamanca: Universidad de Salamanca, 1969.

———. *La época medieval: Historia de España Alfaguara*. 2. Madrid: Alianza editorial, 1973.

———. "La economía rural medieval: Un esquema de análisis histórico de base regional." *Actas de las I Jornadas de metodología aplicadas a las ciencias históricas, II*. Santiago de Compostela: Universidad de Santiago de Compostela, 1975.

———. *La historia rural medieval: Un esquema de análisis estructural de sus contenidos a través del ejemplo hispanocristiano*. Santander: Universidad de Santander, 1978.

———. *La sociedad rural en la España medieval*. Madrid: Siglo XXI, 1988.

——— et al. *Organización social del espacio en la España medieval: La corona de Castilla en los siglos VIII a XV*. Barcelona: Ariel, 1985.

García de Valdeavellano, Luis. *Historia de españa. Desde los orígenes a la baja edad media*. Madrid: Revista de Occidente, 1952.

———. *Orígenes de la burguesía en la España medieval*. Madrid: Espasa-Calpe, 1969.

———. *Curso de historia*. See "Abbreviations."

García Fernández, Ernesto. *La Guardia en la baja edad media (1350–1516)*. Vitoria: Diputación foral de Alava, 1985

García Fernández, Jesús. *Organización del espacio y economía rural en la España atlántica*. Madrid: Siglo XXI, 1975.

———. *El clima en Castilla y León*. Valladolid: Ambito, 1986.

García González, Juan José. "Rentas de trabajo en San Salvador de Oña: Las sernas (1011–1550)." *Cuadernos burgaleses de historia medieval* 1 (1984): 119–94.

García Sahagún, Javier. *La organización del espacio agrario en Liébana durante la edad media*. Santander: Ediciones tantín, 1986.

García Sáinz de Baranda, Julián. *La ciudad de Burgos y su concejo en la edad media*. 2 vols. Burgos: Tipografía de la editorial El Monte Carmelo, 1967.

García Sanz, Ángel. *Desarrollo y crisis del antiguo régimen en Castilla la Vieja*. Madrid: Akal, 1986.

Gautier-Dalché, Jean. "Le domaine du monastere de Santo Toribio de Liébana: Formation, structure et modes d'explotation." *Anuario de estudios medievales* 2 (1965): 63–117.

——. "Moulin à eau, seigneurie, communaté rurale dans le nord de l'Espagne (IXe–XIIe siècles)." In *Etudes de civilisation médiévales, IXe–XIIe siècles: Mélanges offerts à E. R. Labande*. Poitiers: C.E.S.C.M., 1974.

——. *Historia urbana de León y Castilla en la edad media (siglos IX–XIII)*. Madrid: Siglo XXI, 1979.

Glick, Thomas F. *Irrigation and Society in Medieval Valencia*. Cambridge, Mass.: Harvard University Press, 1970.

——. *Islamic and Christian Spain in the Early Middle Ages: Comparative Perspectives on Social and Cultural Formation*. Princeton, N.J.: Princeton University Press, 1979.

González, Julio. *Reinado y diplomas de Fernando III*. 3 vols. Córdoba: Publicaciones del Monte de Piedad y caja de ahorros de Córdoba, 1980–86.

González, Nazario. *Burgos: La ciudad marginal de Castilla (estudio de geografía urbana)*. Burgos: Imprenta de Aldecoa, 1958.

González Bartolomé, Mariano. "Riaza: Datos históricos y documentos." *Estudios segovianos* 27 (1957): 385–691.

González Díez, Emiliano. *El concejo burgalés (884–1369): Marco histórico-institucional*. Burgos: Imprenta de Aldecoa, 1983.

González García, Manuel. *Salamanca: La repoblación y la ciudad en la baja edad media*. Salamanca: Consejo Superior de Investigaciones Científicas, 1973.

——. *Salamanca en la baja edad media*. Salamanca: Universidad de Salamanca, 1982.

González Jiménez, Manuel. *La repoblación de la zona de Sevilla durante el siglo XIV*. Sevilla: Universidad de Sevilla, 1975.

——. *En torno a los orígenes de Andalucía*. 2d. ed. Sevilla: Universidad de Sevilla, 1988.

González Mínguez, César. *Fernando IV de Castilla (1295–1312): La guerra civil y el predominio de la nobleza*. Vitoria: Colegio universitario de Álava, 1976.

Gual Camarena, Miguel. "Para un mapa de la industria textil hispana en la edad media." *Anuario de estudios medievales* 4 (1967): 109–68.

——. "El comercio de telas en el siglo XIII hispano." *Anuario de historia económica y social* 1 (1968): 85–106.

Guiard Larrauri, Teófilo. *Historia de la noble villa de Bilbao*. Bilbao: Editora de la gran enciclopedia vasca, 1971–74.

Hernández, Francisco. "Las cortes de Toledo de 1207." *Las cortes de Castilla y León en la edad media*. Valladolid: Cortes de Castilla y León, 1988.

Herrera Nogal, Alfredo. *El concejo de la villa de Tardajos: Fueros e historia*. Burgos: Caja de ahorros municipal de Burgos, 1980.

Homans, George C. *English Villages of the Thirteenth Century.* Cambridge, Mass.: Harvard University Press, 1941.

Huetz de Lemps, Alain. *Vignobles et vins du nord-ouest de l'Espagne.* Bordeaux: Bibliothèque de l'école des hautes études hispaniques, 1967.

Huidobro y Serna, Luciano. "Los moros de Burgos y su influencia en el arte." *Boletín de la comisión de monumentos de la provincia de Burgos* 105 (1945): 222–25.

———. *Las peregrinaciones jacobeas.* 2 vols. Madrid: Instituto de España, 1950.

———. *Breve historia de la muy noble villa de Aguilar de Campóo.* Palencia: Excelentísima diputación provincial de Palencia, 1980.

La investigación de la historia hispánica del siglo XIV: Problemas y cuestiones. Barcelona: Consejo Superior de Investigaciones Científicas, 1973.

Iradiel Murugarrén, Paulino. *Evolución de la industria textil castellana en los siglos XIII–XVI: Factores de desarrollo, organización y coste de la producción manufacturera en Cuenca.* Salamanca: Universidad de Salamanca, 1974.

Jimeno, Esther. "La población de Soria y su termino en 1270, según el padrón que mando hacer Alfonso X de sus vecinos y moradores." *Boletín de la Real Academia de la Historia* 97 (1958): 207–74, 365–94.

Kantorowicz, Ernst H. *The King's Two Bodies: A Study in Medieval Political Theology.* Princeton, N.J.: Princeton University Press, 1981.

Klein, Julius. *The Mesta: A Study in Spanish Economic History, 1273–1836.* Cambridge, Mass.: Harvard University Press, 1920.

Ladero Quesada, Miguel Ángel. *Historia de Sevilla: La ciudad medieval.* Sevilla: Universidad de Sevilla, 1976.

———. "Las ferias de Castilla, siglos XII a XV." *Cuadernos de historia de España* 67–68 (1982): 269–315.

———. *El siglo XV en Castilla: Fuentes de renta y política fiscal.* Barcelona: Ariel, 1982.

Layna Serrano, Francisco. *Historia de la villa de Atienza.* Madrid: Consejo Superior de Investigaciones Científicas, 1945.

León Tello, Pilar. *Judíos de Ávila.* Ávila: Excelentísima diputación provincial de Ávila, 1963.

Linehan, Peter. *The Spanish Church and the Papacy in the Thirteenth Century.* Cambridge: Cambridge University Press, 1971.

———. *Spanish Church and Society, 1150–1300.* London: Variorum, 1983.

———. "The Toledo Forgeries c. 1150–c. 1300." *Falschungen im Mittlealter.* Vol. 1. Hannover: Hahnsche Buckhandlung, 1988.

———. *Past and Present in Medieval Spain.* London: Variorum, 1992.

Lourie, Elena. "A Society Organized for War: Medieval Spain." *Past & Present* 35 (1966): 54–76.

Lucas, H. S. "The Great European Famine of 1315–17." *Speculum* 5 (1930): 343–77.

MacKay, Angus. *Spain in the Middle Ages: From Frontier to Empire, 1000–1500.* London: MacMillan Ltd., 1977.

———. "Ciudad y campo en la Europa medieval." *Studia histórica* 2, no. 2 (1984): 27–53.

Maravall, José Antonio. *El concepto de España en la edad media,* 2d. ed. Madrid: Instituto de estudios políticos, 1964.

Martín, José L. *Economía y sociedad en los reinos hispánicos de la baja edad media*. 2 vols. Barcelona: El Albir, 1983.

Martínez Cea, Juan Carlos. *El campesinado castellano de la cuenca del Duero: Aproximaciones a su estudio durante los siglos XIII al XV*. Valladolid: Concejo general de Castilla y León, 1983.

Martínez Díez, Gonzalo. *Álava medieval*. 2 vols. Vitoria: Diputación foral de Álava, 1974.

———. *Las comunidades de villa y tierra de la extremadura castellana*. Madrid: Editora nacional, 1983.

Martínez García, Luis. "La concentración de la propiedad urbana burgalesa mediante la concesión de 'pasadas de tierra,' (1150–1250)." *La ciudad de Burgos: Actas del congreso de historia de Burgos*. Madrid: Junta de Castilla y León, 1985.

———. *El Hospital del Rey de Burgos: Un señorío medieval en la expansión y en la crisis (siglos XIII y XIV)*. Burgos: Ediciones J. M. Garrido Garrido, 1986.

Martínez Moro, Jesús. *La tierra en la comunidad de Segovia: Un proyecto señorial urbano (1088–1500)*. Valladolid: Universidad de Valladolid, 1985.

Martínez Sopena, Pascual. *La tierra de Campos occidental: Poblamiento, poder y comunidad del siglo X al XIII*. Valladolid: Institución cultural Simancas de la diputación provincial de Valladolid, 1985.

Mayoral Fernández, José. *El municipio de Ávila (estudio histórico)*. Ávila: Diputación provincial de Ávila, 1958.

Menéndez Pidal, Gonzalo. *Los caminos en la historia de España*. Madrid: Ediciones cultura hispánica, 1951.

Merchán Fernández, Carlos. *Sobre los orígenes del régimen señorial en Castilla: El abadengo de Aguilar de Campóo (1020–1369)*. Málaga: Universidad de Málaga, 1982.

Merino Álvarez, Abelardo. *La sociedad abulense durante el siglo XVI: La nobleza*. Madrid: Imprenta del patronato de huérfanos, 1926.

Molénat, Jean Pierre. "Chemins et ponts du nord de la Castille au temps des rois catholiques." *Melanges de la Casa Velázquez* 7 (1971): 115–62.

Monsalvo Antón, José María. *Teoria y evolución de un conflicto social: El antisemitismo en la corona de Castilla en la baja edad media*. Madrid: Siglo XXI, 1985.

———. *El sistema concejil: El ejemplo del señorío medieval de Alba de Tormes y su concejo de villa y tierra*. Salamanca: Universidad de Salamanca, 1988.

———. "La participación política de los pecheros en los municipios castellanos de la baja edad media: Aspectos organizativos." *Studia histórica* 7 (1989): 37–93.

Moreta Velayos, Salustiano. *El monasterio de San Pedro de Cardeña: Historia de un dominio monástico castellano (902–1338)*. Salamanca: Universidad de Salamanca, 1971.

———. *Rentas monásticas en Castilla: Problemas de método*. Salamanca: Universidad de Salamanca, 1974.

Moxó, Salvador de. "De la nobleza vieja a la nobleza nueva: La transformación nobiliaria castellana en la baja edad media." *Cuadernos de historia: Anexos de Hispania* 3 (1969): 1–210.

———. "Los señoríos: En torno a una problemática para el estudio del régimen señorial." *Hispania* 94 (1974): 185–236.

———. "Los señoríos: Estudio metodológico." In *Actas de las I jornadas de la metodología aplicada de las ciencias históricas*. II. Santiago de Compostela: Universidad de Santiago de Compostela, 1975.

———. "Los judíos castellanos en el reinado de Alfonso XI." *Sefarad* 35 (1975): 131–50; 36 (1976): 37–120.

———. "Campesinos hacendados leoneses en el siglo XIV." In *León medieval: Doce estudios*. León: Instituto de estudios leoneses, 1978.

———. *Repoblación y sociedad en la España cristiana medieval*. Madrid: Rialp, 1979.

Nieto Soria, José M. *Las relaciones monarquía-episcopado castellano*. 2 vols. Madrid: Universidad Complutense, 1983.

———. *Iglesia y poder real en Castilla*. Madrid: Universidad Complutense, 1988.

O'Callaghan, Joseph F. "The Cortes and Royal Taxation during the Reign of Alfonso X of Castile." *Traditio* 27 (1971): 379–98.

———. *A History of Medieval Spain*. Ithaca, N.Y.: Cornell University Press, 1975.

———. *The Cortes of Castile-León, 1188–1350*. Philadelphia: University of Pennsylvania Press, 1989.

———. "Image and Reality: The King Creates His Kingdom." In *Emperor of Culture: Alfonso X the Learned of Castile and His Thirteenth-Century Renaissance*, edited by Robert I. Burns. Philadelphia: University of Pennsylvania Press, 1990.

Ortega Varcárcel, José. *La transformación de un espacio rural: Las montañas de Burgos, estudio de geografía regional*. Valladolid: Universidad de Valladolid, 1974.

Ortega y Rubio, C. *Historia de Valladolid*. 2 vols. Valladolid: Imprenta y librería nacional y extranjera de Hijos de Rodríguez, 1881.

Pastor, Reyna. "La sal en Castilla y León: Un problema de la alimentación y del trabajo y una política fiscal (siglos X–XIII)." *Cuadernos de historia de España* 37–38 (1963): 42–87.

———. *Conflictos sociales y estancamiento económico en la España medieval*. Barcelona: Ariel, 1973.

———. *Resistencias y luchas campesinas en la época del crecimiento y consolidación de la formación feudal: Castilla y León, siglos X–XIII*. Madrid: Siglo XXI, 1980.

Pastor Díaz de Garayo, Ernesto. *Salvatierra y la llanada oriental alavesa (siglos XIII–XV)*. Vitoria: Diputación foral de Álava, 1986.

Pérez Bustamante, Rogelio. *Sociedad, economía, fiscalidad y gobierno en las Asturias de Santillana (s. XIII–XV)*. Santander: Estudio, 1979.

———. *Historia de la villa de Castro Urdiales*. Santander: Ayuntamiento de Santander, 1980.

Pérez de Urbel, Justo. *El condado de Castilla: Los 300 años en que se hizo Castilla*. 3 vols. Madrid: Editorial siglo ilustrado, 1969–70.

Pérez-Embid, Javier. *El Cister en Castilla y León: Monacato y dominios rurales (s. XII–XV)*. Valladolid: Junta de Castilla y León, 1986.

Pescador, Carmela. "La caballería popular en León y Castilla." *Cuadernos de historia de España* 33–34 (1961): 101–238; 35–36 (1962): 156–201; 37–38 (1963): 88–198; 39–40 (1964): 169–260.

Phillips, Carla Rahn "Spanish Merchants and the Wool Trade in the Sixteenth Century." *Sixteenth Century Journal* 14 (1983): 259–82.

Powers, James F. *A Society Organized for War: The Iberian Municipal Militias in the Central Middle Ages, 1000–1284.* Berkeley: University of California Press, 1988.

Proctor, Evelyn S. "The Interpretation of Clause 3 of the Decrees of Leon." *English Historical Review* 85 (1970): 45–53.

Raftis, J. Ambrose. *Tenure and Mobility: Studies in the Social History of the Medieval English Village.* Toronto: Pontifical Institute of Mediaeval Studies, 1964.

———. *Warboys: Two Hundred Years in the Life of a Medieval English Village.* Toronto: Pontifical Institute of Mediaeval Studies, 1974.

———, ed. *Pathways to Medieval Peasants.* Toronto: Pontifical Institute of Mediaeval Studies, 1981.

Razi, Zvi. *Life, Death and Marriage in a Medieval Parish: Economy, Society and Demography in Halesowen, 1270–1400.* Cambridge: Cambridge University Press, 1980.

Represa Rodríguez, Armando. "Notas para el estudio de la ciudad de Segovia en los siglos XII–XIV." *Estudios segovianos* 2, no. 3 (1949): 273–319.

———. "La tierra medieval de Segovia." *Estudios segovianos* 21 (1969): 227–44.

———. "Origen y desarrollo urbano del Valladolid medieval (siglos X–XIII)." In *Historia de Valladolid II: Valladolid medieval,* edited by José M. Ruiz Asencio et al. Valladolid: Ateneo de Valladolid, 1980.

Ringrose, David. *Transportation and Economic Stagnation in Spain, 1750–1850.* Durham, N.C.: Duke University Press, 1970.

Rucquoi, Adeline. "Molinos et aceñas au coeur de la Castille septentrionale (XIe–XVe siècles)." In *Les Espagnes médiévales. Aspects économiques et sociaux.* Nice: Faculté des lettres et sciences humaines de Nice, 1983.

———. *Valladolid en la edad media: La villa del Esgueva.* Valladolid: Ayuntamiento de Valladolid, 1983.

———. *Valladolid en la edad media.* 2 vols. Valladolid: Junta de Castilla y León, 1987.

Ruiz, Teofilo F. "The Transformation of the Castilian Municipalities: The Case of Burgos, 1248–1350." *Past & Present* 77 (1977): 3–33. (Most of my essays are collected in *The City and the Realm: Burgos and Castile, 1080–1492.* London: Variorum, 1992.)

———. "Expansion et changement: la conquête de Séville et la société castillane (1248–1350)." *Annales E.S.C.* 3 (mai–juin 1979): 548–65.

———. *Sociedad y poder real en Castilla (Burgos en la baja edad media).* Barcelona: Ariel, 1981.

———. "Una nota sobre la estructura y relaciones fiscales del Burgos bajo medieval." In *En la España medieval: Estudios en memoria del Profesor D. Salvador de Moxó.* vol. 2. Madrid: Universidad Complutense, 1982.

———. "Une note sur la vie rurale dans la région d'Aguilar de Campóo." In *Les Espagnes médiévales: Aspects économiques et sociaux.* Nice: Faculté des lettres et sciences humaines de Nice, 1983.

———. "Notas para el estudio de la mujer en el área del Burgos medieval." In *El pasado histórico de Castilla y León.* 3 vols. Burgos: Junta de Castilla y León, 1983.

———. "La formazione del mercato della terra nella Castiglia del basso medioevo." *Quaderni storici* 65 (1987): 423–52.

————. "Festivités, couleurs et symboles du pouvoir en Castille au XVe siècle: Les célébrations de mai 1428." *Annales E.S.C.* 3 (1991): 521–46.

Ruiz Gómez, Francisco. *Las formas del poblamiento rural en la Bureba en la baja edad media: La villa de Oña.* 2 vols. Madrid: Universidad Complutense, 1988.

————. *Las aldeas castellanas en la edad media: Oña en los siglos XIV y XV.* Madrid: Consejo Superior de Investigaciones Científicas, 1990.

Sáinz Díaz, Valentín. *Notas históricas sobre la villa de San Vicente de la Barquera.* Santander: Institución cultural de Cantabria, 1973.

Salomon, Noël. *La vida rural castellana en tiempos de Felipe II.* Barcelona: Editorial planeta, 1973.

Sánchez Albornoz, Claudio. "Las behetrías: La encomendación en Asturias, León y Castilla." In *Anuario de historia del derecho español* 1 (1924): 158–336.

————. "Muchas páginas mas sobre las behetrías." In *Anuario de historia del derecho español* 4 (1928): 5–141. (Both articles are reproduced in his *Estudios sobre las instituciones medievales españolas.* Mexico: Universidad nacional autónoma de México, 1965: 9–316.)

————. *Despoblación y repoblación del valle del Duero.* Buenos Aires: Instituto de historia, 1966.

Sangrador Vitores, Matías. *Historia de la muy noble y leal ciudada de Valladolid desde su mas remota antiguedad hasta la muerte de Fernando VII.* 2 vols. Valladolid: Imprenta de D. M. Aparicio, 1851–54.

Sinues Ruiz, Atanasio. *El merino.* Zaragoza: Consejo Superior de Investigaciones Científicas, 1954.

Slicher van Bath, Bernard H. *The Agrarian History of Western Europe, AD 500–1850.* London: Arnold, 1963.

Sobrequés i Callicó, Jaume. "La peste negra en la península ibérica." *Anuario de estudios medievales* 7 (1970–71): 67–102.

La sociedad vasca rural y urbana en el marco de la crisis de los siglos XIV y XV. Bilbao: Excelentísima diputación provincial de Vizcaya, 1975.

Ubieto Arteta, Agustín. *Notas sobre el patrimonio calceatense, siglos XII y XIII.* Logroño: Instituto de estudios riojanos, 1978.

Vaca Lorenzo, Ángel. "La estructura socioeconómica de la Tierra de Campos a mediados del siglo XIV." *Publicaciones de la Institución Tello Téllez de Meneses* 39 (1977): 229–399; 42 (1979): 203–387.

Valdeón Baruque, Julio. "Aspectos de la crisis castellana en la primera mitad del siglo XIV." *Hispania* 111 (1969): 5–24.

————. "La crisis del siglo XIV en Castilla: Revisión del problema." *Revista de la universidad de Madrid* 79 (1972): 161–84.

————. *Los conflictos sociales en el reino de Castilla en los siglos XIV y XV.* Madrid: Siglo XXI, 1975.

Vassberg, David. *Land and Society in Golden Age Castile.* Cambridge: Cambridge University Press, 1984.

Vázquez de Parga, Luis, J. Ma. Lacarra, and J. Uría Riu. *Peregrinaciones a Santiago de Compostela.* 3 vols. Madrid: Consejo Superior de Investigaciones Científicas, 1949.

Vergara y Martín, Gabriel M. *Estudio histórico de Ávila y su territorio desde su repoblación hasta la muerte de Santa Teresa de Jesús.* Madrid: Hernández, 1896.

Verlinden, Charles. "Draps des Pays-Bas et du nord de la France en Espagne au XIVe siècle." *Le Moyen Âge* 8 (1937): 21–36.

———. "La grande peste de 1348 en Espagne: Contribution a l'étude de ses conséquences économiques et sociales." *Revue belge de philologie et d'histoire* 17 (1938): 103–46.

———. *El comercio de paños flamencos y brabanzones en España durante los siglos XIII y XIV*. Madrid: Cátedra de la fundación del Excelentísimo Señor Conde de Cartagena, 1952.

Vicens Vives, Jaume. Director. *Historia de España y America social y ecónomica, II: Baja edad media*. Barcelona: Editoria Vicens Vives, 1974.

Villar y Macías, Matías. *Historia de Salamanca*. 3 vols. Salamanca: Imprenta de Francisco Núñez Izquierdo, 1971.

Villegas, Luis R. *Sobre el urbanismo de Ciudad Real en la edad media*. Ciudad Real: Excelentísimo ayuntamiento de Ciudad Real, 1984.

Villuga, Pero Juan. *Repertorio de todos los caminos de España*. Medina del Campo, 1546. Reprint. New York: Hispanic Society of New York, 1902.

Vitoria en la edad media: Actas del Ier congreso de estudios históricos. Vitoria: Ayuntamiento de Vitoria, 1982.

Way, Ruth. *A Geography of Spain and Portugal*. London: Methuen, 1962.

Index

Names of individuals before 1500 are indexed by first name. Whenever possible, individuals are identified by their place in the social order and/or occupation: peasants (p); nobles (n); merchants and/or artisans and/or bourgeois (m); royal and municipal officials (r/o and m/o); ecclesiastics (e).

University of Pennsylvania Press
MIDDLE AGES SERIES
Edward Peters, General Editor

F. R. P. Akehurst, trans. *The* Coutumes de Beauvaisis *of Philippe de Beaumanoir.* 1992

Peter L. Allen. *The Art of Love: Amatory Fiction from Ovid to the* Romance of the Rose. 1992

David Anderson. *Before the Knight's Tale: Imitation of Classical Epic in Boccaccio's* Teseida. 1988

Benjamin Arnold. *Count and Bishop in Medieval Germany: A Study of Regional Power, 1100–1350.* 1991

Mark C. Bartusis. *The Late Byzantine Army: Arms and Society, 1204–1453.* 1992

J. M. W. Bean. *From Lord to Patron: Lordship in Late Medieval England.* 1990

Uta-Renate Blumenthal. *The Investiture Controversy: Church and Monarchy from the Ninth to the Twelfth Century.* 1988

Daniel Bornstein, trans. *Dino Compagni's* Chronicle of Florence. 1986

Maureen Boulton. *The Song in the Story: Lyric Insertions in French Narrative Fiction, 1200–1400.* 1993.

Betsy Bowden. *Chaucer Aloud: The Varieties of Textual Interpretation.* 1987

James William Brodman. *Ransoming Captives in Crusader Spain: The Order of Merced on the Christian-Islamic Frontier.* 1986

Kevin Brownlee and Sylvia Huot. *Rethinking the* Romance of the Rose: *Text, Image, Reception.* 1992

Matilda Tomaryn Bruckner. *Shaping Romance: Interpretation, Truth, and Closure in Twelfth-Century French Fictions.* 1993

Otto Brunner (Howard Kaminsky and James Van Horn Melton, eds. and trans.). *Land and Lordship: Structures of Governance in Medieval Austria.* 1992

Robert I. Burns, S.J., ed. *Emperor of Culture: Alfonso X the Learned of Castile and His Thirteenth-Century Renaissance.* 1990

David Burr. *Olivi and Franciscan Poverty: The Origins of the Usus Pauper Controversy.* 1989

David Burr. *Peaceable Kingdom: A Reading of Olivi's Apocalypse Commentary.* 1993

Thomas Cable. *The English Alliterative Tradition.* 1991

Anthony K. Cassell and Victoria Kirkham, eds. and trans. *Diana's Hunt/Caccia di Diana: Boccaccio's First Fiction.* 1991

John C. Cavadini. *The Last Christology of the West: Adoptionism in Spain and Gaul, 785–820.* 1993

Brigitte Cazelles. *The Lady as Saint: A Collection of French Hagiographic Romances of the Thirteenth Century.* 1991

Karen Cherewatuk and Ulrike Wiethaus, eds. *Dear Sister: Medieval Women and the Epistolary Genre.* 1993

Anne L. Clark. *Elisabeth of Schönau: A Twelfth-Century Visionary*. 1992

Willene B. Clark and Meradith T. McMunn, eds. *Beasts and Birds of the Middle Ages: The Bestiary and Its Legacy*. 1989

Richard C. Dales. *The Scientific Achievement of the Middle Ages*. 1973

Charles T. Davis. *Dante's Italy and Other Essays*. 1984

Katherine Fischer Drew, trans. *The Burgundian Code*. 1972

Katherine Fischer Drew, trans. *The Laws of the Salian Franks*. 1991

Katherine Fischer Drew, trans. *The Lombard Laws*. 1973

Nancy Edwards. *The Archaeology of Early Medieval Ireland*. 1990

Margaret J. Ehrhart. *The Judgment of the Trojan Prince Paris in Medieval Literature*. 1987

Richard K. Emmerson and Ronald B. Herzman. *The Apocalyptic Imagination in Medieval Literature*. 1992

Theodore Evergates. *Feudal Society in Medieval France: Documents from the County of Champagne*. 1993

Felipe Fernández-Armesto. *Before Columbus: Exploration and Colonization from the Mediterranean to the Atlantic, 1229–1492*. 1987

R. D. Fulk. *A History of Old English Meter*. 1992

Patrick J. Geary. *Aristocracy in Provence: The Rhône Basin at the Dawn of the Carolingian Age*. 1985

Peter Heath. *Allegory and Philosophy in Avicenna (Ibn Sînâ)*. 1992

J. N. Hillgarth, ed. *Christianity and Paganism, 350–750: The Conversion of Western Europe*. 1986

Richard C. Hoffmann. *Land, Liberties, and Lordship in a Late Medieval Countryside: Agrarian Structures and Change in the Duchy of Wroclaw*. 1990

Robert Hollander. *Boccaccio's Last Fiction: Il Corbaccio*. 1988

Edward B. Irving, Jr. *Rereading* Beowulf. 1989

C. Stephen Jaeger. *The Origins of Courtliness: Civilizing Trends and the Formation of Courtly Ideals, 939–1210*. 1985

William Chester Jordan. *The French Monarchy and the Jews: From Philip Augustus to the Last Capetians*. 1989

William Chester Jordan. *From Servitude to Freedom: Manumission in the Sénonais in the Thirteenth Century*. 1986

Richard Kay. *Dante's Christian Astrology*. 1994

Ellen E. Kittell. *From Ad Hoc to Routine: A Case Study in Medieval Bureaucracy*. 1991

Alan C. Kors and Edward Peters, eds. *Witchcraft in Europe, 1100–1700: A Documentary History*. 1972

Barbara M. Kreutz. *Before the Normans: Southern Italy in the Ninth and Tenth Centuries*. 1992

E. Ann Matter. *The Voice of My Beloved: The Song of Songs in Western Medieval Christianity*. 1990

María Rosa Menocal. *The Arabic Role in Medieval Literary History: A Forgotten Heritage*. 1987

A. J. Minnis. *Medieval Theory of Authorship*. 1988

Lawrence Nees. *A Tainted Mantle: Hercules and the Classical Tradition at the Carolingian Court*. 1991

Lynn H. Nelson, trans. *The Chronicle of San Juan de la Peña: A Fourteenth-Century Official History of the Crown of Aragon*. 1991

Charlotte A. Newman. *The Anglo-Norman Nobility in the Reign of Henry I: The Second Generation*. 1988

Joseph F. O'Callaghan. *The Cortes of Castile-León, 1188–1350*. 1989

Joseph F. O'Callaghan. *The Learned King: The Reign of Alfonso X of Castile*. 1993

David M. Olster. *Roman Defeat, Christian Response, and the Literary Construction of the Jew*. 1994

William D. Paden, ed. *The Voice of the Trobairitz: Perspectives on the Women Troubadours*. 1989

Edward Peters. *The Magician, the Witch, and the Law*. 1982

Edward Peters, ed. *Christian Society and the Crusades, 1198–1229:* Sources in Translation, including The Capture of Damietta by Oliver of Paderborn. 1971

Edward Peters, ed. *The First Crusade:* The Chronicle of Fulcher of Chartres *and Other Source Materials*. 1971

Edward Peters, ed. *Heresy and Authority in Medieval Europe*. 1980

James M. Powell. *Albertanus of Brescia: The Pursuit of Happiness in the Early Thirteenth Century*. 1992

James M. Powell. *Anatomy of a Crusade, 1213–1221*. 1986

Jean Renart (Patricia Terry and Nancy Vine Durling, trans.). *The Romance of the Rose or Guillaume de Dole*. 1993

Michael Resler, trans. Erec *by Hartmann von Aue*. 1987

Pierre Riché (Michael Idomir Allen, trans.). *The Carolingians: A Family Who Forged Europe*. 1993

Pierre Riché (Jo Ann McNamara, trans.). *Daily Life in the World of Charlemagne*. 1978

Jonathan Riley-Smith. *The First Crusade and the Idea of Crusading*. 1986

Joel T. Rosenthal. *Patriarchy and Families of Privilege in Fifteenth-Century England*. 1991

Teofilo F. Ruiz. *Crisis and Continuity: Land and Town in Late Medieval Castile*. 1994

Steven D. Sargent, ed. and trans. *On the Threshold of Exact Science: Selected Writings of Anneliese Maier on Late Medieval Natural Philosophy*. 1982

Robin Chapman Stacey. *The Road to Judgment: From Custom to Court in Medieval Ireland and Wales*. 1994

Sarah Stanbury. *Seeing the* Gawain-Poet: *Description and the Act of Perception*. 1992

Thomas C. Stillinger. *The Song of Troilus: Lyric Authority in the Medieval Book*. 1992

Susan Mosher Stuard. *A State of Deference: Ragusa/Dubrovnik in the Medieval Centuries*. 1992

Susan Mosher Stuard, ed. *Women in Medieval History and Historiography*. 1987

Susan Mosher Stuard, ed. *Women in Medieval Society*. 1976

Jonathan Sumption. *The Hundred Years War: Trial by Battle*. 1992

Ronald E. Surtz. *The Guitar of God: Gender, Power, and Authority in the Visionary World of Mother Juana de la Cruz (1481–1534)*. 1990

William H. TeBrake. *A Plague of Insurrection: Popular Politics and Peasant Revolt in Flanders, 1323–1328*. 1993

Patricia Terry, trans. *Poems of the Elder Edda.* 1990

Hugh M. Thomas. *Vassals, Heiresses, Crusaders, and Thugs: The Gentry of Angevin Yorkshire, 1154–1216.* 1993

Frank Tobin. *Meister Eckhart: Thought and Language.* 1986

Ralph V. Turner. *Men Raised from the Dust: Administrative Service and Upward Mobility in Angevin England.* 1988

Harry Turtledove, trans. *The* Chronicle *of Theophanes: An English Translation of* Anni Mundi *6095–6305 (A.D. 602–813).* 1982

Mary F. Wack. Lovesickness in the Middle Ages: The Viaticum *and Its Commentaries.* 1990

Benedicta Ward. *Miracles and the Medieval Mind: Theory, Record, and Event, 1000–1215.* 1982

Suzanne Fonay Wemple. *Women in Frankish Society: Marriage and the Cloister, 500–900.* 1981

Jan M. Ziolkowski. *Talking Animals: Medieval Latin Beast Poetry, A.D. 750–1150.* 1993

This book has been set in Linotron Galliard. Galliard was designed for Mergenthaler in 1978 by Matthew Carter. Galliard retains many of the features of a sixteenth-century typeface cut by Robert Granjon but has some modifications that give it a more contemporary look.

Printed on acid-free paper.